SOULS IN TRANSITION

SOULS IN TRANSITION

The Religious and Spiritual
Lives of Emerging Adults

CHRISTIAN SMITH

with Patricia Snell

OXFORD
UNIVERSITY PRESS
2009

OXFORD
UNIVERSITY PRESS

Oxford University Press, Inc., publishes works that further
Oxford University's objective of excellence
in research, scholarship, and education.

Oxford   New York
Auckland   Cape Town   Dar es Salaam   Hong Kong   Karachi
Kuala Lumpur   Madrid   Melbourne   Mexico City   Nairobi
New Delhi   Shanghai   Taipei   Toronto

With offices in
Argentina   Austria   Brazil   Chile   Czech Republic   France   Greece
Guatemala   Hungary   Italy   Japan   Poland   Portugal   Singapore
South Korea   Switzerland   Thailand   Turkey   Ukraine   Vietnam

Published by Oxford University Press, Inc.
198 Madison Avenue, New York, NY 10016
www.oup.com

Library of Congress Cataloging-in-Publication Data
Smith, Christian, 1960–
Souls in transition : the religious and spiritual lives of emerging adults /
Christian Smith ; with Patricia Snell.
p.   cm.
Includes bibliographical references and index.
ISBN 978-0-19-537179-6
1. Young adults—Religious life—United States.
2. Spiritual life.
I. Snell, Patricia, 1978–
II. Title.
BV4529.2.S64 2009
200.84'20973—dc22   2009004850

1 3 5 7 9 8 6 4 2

Printed in the United States of America
on acid-free paper

Acknowledgments

THIS PROJECT IS THE result of effort and support by many wonderful people, to whom we owe our sincere gratitude. First, we owe many thanks to Chris Coble of Lilly Endowment Inc. for funding this project. The University of Notre Dame College of Arts and Letters and the John Templeton Foundation also provided funding to make our data collection possible. Special thanks to Mark Roche, Dan Myers, Jack Templeton, Kimon Sargeant, and Chris Stawski for their support. Terri Clark has been a fantastic NSYR Project Manager over two waves of data collection, providing excellent organization, direction, and insight for our developing work. Kyle Longest and Jon Hill both did excellent jobs of survey data analysis, for which we are immensely grateful. Kari Christoffersen and Katie Spencer also contributed importantly to the analysis of survey data for this book—many thanks. Others to whom we are thankful for their significant parts in the success of the NSYR third wave survey are Lisa Pearce, Melinda Lundquist Denton, Thu-Mai Christian, Michelle Temple, Teresa Edwards, and Peter Leousis. Peter Mundey, Carlos Tavares, Brandon Vaidyanathan, Steve Vaisey, Richard Flory, Ryan Lincoln, Terri Clark, Ria van Ryn, and Younoki Lee did a terrific job helping to conduct in-person interviews around the country. We are also grateful to Rae Hoffman, Alyssa Kane, Jillian Bohinc, Hilary Davidson, Amanda Bradley, Claire Peterson, Tracy Wickham, Sarah Walter, Nick Trapp, Kat Herzog, Sonja Grisle, April Hutchinson, Jarrett McGinnis, Chris Penland, Laura Hoseley, and Natalie Shaw for their transcribing and other valuable contributions to this project. Steve Vaisey was an extremely helpful critical reader of the manuscript, to whom we owe many thanks. Very many thanks we also offer to Cynthia Read, Joellyn Ausanka, and Brian Hughes at Oxford for being great pleasures with whom to work.

Thank you also to our family and friends who supported us in many ways throughout the course of this project. We appreciate your love, friendship, and guidance as we traveled for interviews, talked through our findings, and spent hours typing into our computers. Finally, very many thanks to all of the emerging adult survey respondents, to their family and friends who helped the researchers to track them down, and to the in-person interview respondents for being willing to meet with us for many hours to share the depths of their lives, thoughts, beliefs, troubles, hopes, and dreams. You have taught us more than a book can tell.

Contents

SOULS IN TRANSITION

Introduction

WHAT HAPPENS in the religious and spiritual lives of American teenagers when they start to grow up, end high school, and begin to leave home to launch their own new adult lives? What do the religious and spiritual lives of American 18- to 23-year-olds look like and why? What are the social influences that shape people's lives of during this phase? And how do people change or not change religiously and spiritually as they exit their teenage years and head into their twenties? These are the questions this book seeks to answer.

TRACKING TEENAGERS AS THEY BECOME EMERGING ADULTS

In this book, we[1] analyze and interpret data collected in the third wave of the National Study of Youth and Religion (NSYR) in order to better understand the religious and spiritual lives of what we will here call "emerging adults."[2] With our colleagues on the project, we have been studying the sample of young people on whom this study is based since they were 13–17 years old, when the survey started out—with a nationally representative telephone survey of 3,290 of them followed by personal interviews with 267 of them in 45 states around the country.[3] *Soul Searching: The Religious and Spiritual Lives of American Teenagers* was published in 2005, based on what was learned from that first wave of data collected.[4] In 2005, a second telephone survey was conducted with most of the same subjects, and 122 of the same respondents were reinterviewed.[5] Throughout these years, the researchers continued to systematically stay in touch with and track as many of the study respondents as was humanly

3

possible, and in 2007 and 2008 a third wave of survey (N = 2,458) and interviews (N = 230) data collection was conducted with them.[6] The respondents in this third wave were 18 to 23 years old. They had passed beyond the high school era and were entering into emerging adulthood. This book examines them at the third measured point of their ongoing life trajectories, which makes it possible to study them at that moment but also to look backward and see how their life conditions in previous years have shaped their current lives as emerging adults. They have transitioned to a new phase of life, are striking out on their own, and are encountering many new challenges and experiences. The research seeks to discover what happens, in the midst of those transitions, to their religious faith, practices, beliefs, associations, and commitments. How much do they change and why? Answering such questions well is the central purpose of this book.[7]

Better understanding the religious and spiritual lives of emerging adults will yield many valuable things. It will first of all improve general knowledge about the fairly recently developed stage of the life course called "emerging adulthood." What is it like to be an 18- to 29-year-old in America? What are the major strengths and problems of emerging adults today? How are they faring in their journey to full adulthood? Understanding the religious and spiritual lives of emerging adults better will also provide important insight into the nature of basic life course changes, both religious and otherwise, as youth transition out of their teenage years into adulthood.[8] What does it mean to shift from one life phase to the other? How are people changed by undergoing that process? What implications does that transition have for the different way people's lives turn out? How do different features of American culture and society facilitate or complicate the transition to adulthood?[9] Furthermore, the present study promises to broaden and deepen understanding of American religion itself. How important is religion for young people today? Are there generational changes afoot that seem to be strengthening or weakening religious faith and practice in the United States? What factors present in people's lives at younger ages appear to form religious and spiritual outcomes later in life? Why and how do some young people abandon or grow in their faith, or perhaps convert to new religions? What are the major social and cultural forces influencing the contours and texture of American religion today? Finally, this study provides what we hope will be an illuminating window on the character of contemporary American culture and institutions broadly. One of the best ways to understand the nature and quality of any society, we believe, is to look closely at how it views and treats its youth. Studying the lives of young people in social context is a great way to enrich adults' perspective on their own adult society and lives. By examining the world of contemporary emerging adults, we think we hold up a mirror that reflects back to adults a telling picture of the larger adult world— their own world—into which emerging adults are moving.[10]

ON "EMERGING ADULTHOOD"

We said earlier that we will in this book be calling the young people this study examines "emerging adults," and we want to explain here why.[11] In the last several decades, a number of macro social changes have combined to create a new phase in the American life course. Four have been particularly important. First is the dramatic growth of higher education. The GI Bill, changes in the American economy, and government subsidizing of community colleges and state universities led, in the second half of the last century, to a dramatic rise in the number of high school graduates going on to college and university. More recently, many feel pressured—in pursuit of the American dream—to add years of graduate school education on top of their bachelor's degrees. As a result, a huge proportion of American youth are no longer stopping school and beginning stable careers at age 18 but are extend their formal schooling well into their twenties. And those who are aiming to join America's professional and knowledge classes—those who most powerfully shape our culture and society—are continuing in graduate and professional school programs often up until their thirties. A second and related social change crucial to the rise of emerging adulthood is the delay of marriage by American youth over the last decades. Between 1950 and 2006, the median age of first marriage for women rose from 20.3 to 25.9. For men during that same time the media age rose from 22.8 to 27.5. The sharpest increase for both took place after 1970.[12] Half a century ago, many young people were anxious to get out of high school, marry, settle down, have children, and start a long-term career. But many youth today face almost a decade between high school graduation and marriage to spend exploring life's many options as singles, in unprecedented freedom.[13]

A third major social transformation contributing to the rise of emerging adulthood as a distinct life phase concerns changes in the American and global economy that undermine stable, lifelong careers and replace them instead with careers with lower security, more frequent job changes, and an ongoing need for new training and education. Most young people today know they need to approach their careers with a variety of skills, maximal flexibility, and readiness to retool as needed. That itself pushes youth toward extended schooling, delay of marriage, and, arguably, a general psychological orientation of maximizing options and postponing commitments. Far from being happy to graduate from high school and take the factory job their father or uncle has arranged for them—a job that actually does not likely exist anymore—many youth today spend 5 to 10 years experimenting with different job and career options before finally deciding on a long-term career direction. Fourth, and partly as a response to all of the foregoing, parents of today's youth, aware of the resources it often takes to succeed, seem increasingly willing to extend financial and other support to their children, well into their twenties and perhaps early thirties. According to best estimates, American parents spend on their children an average of $38,340 per child in total material assistance (cash, housing, educational expenses, food, etc.) over the 17-year period between ages 18 and 34.[14] These resources help to subsidize the freedom that emerging adults enjoy to take a good, long time before settling down into full adulthood, culturally defined as the end of schooling, a stable career job, financial independence, and new family formation.

These four social transformations together have helped dramatically to alter the experience of American life between the ages of 18 and 30. Studies agree that the transition to adulthood today is more complex, disjointed, and confusing than in past decades. The steps through and to schooling, the first real job, marriage, and parenthood are simply less well organized and coherent today than they were in generations past. At the same time, these years are marked by a historically unparalleled freedom to roam, experiment, learn, move on, and try again. What has emerged from this new situation has been variously labeled "extended adolescence," "youthhood," "adultolescence," "the twixter years," "young adulthood," the "twenty-somethings," and "emerging adulthood." We find persuasive the psychologist Jeffrey Arnett's argument that of all of these labels, "emerging adulthood" is the most appropriate.[15] That is because, rather than viewing these years as simply the last hurrah of adolescence or an early stage of real adulthood, it recognizes the very unique characteristics of this new and particular phase of life. The features marking this stage are intense identity exploration, instability, a focus on self, feeling in limbo or in transition or in between, and a sense of possibilities, opportunities, and unparalleled hope. These, of course, are also often accompanied—as we will show—by large doses of transience, confusion, anxiety, self-obsession, melodrama, conflict, disappointment, and sometimes emotional devastation. Many popular television shows of the last few decades—*Beverly Hills 90210*, *Dawson's Creek*, *Seinfeld*, and *Friends*—reflect through Hollywood's lens the character and challenges of this recently developing, in-between stage of life. We think it all signifies something big and serious.

To grasp the significance of emerging adulthood, it is necessary to realize that life stages are not naturally given as immutable phases of existence. Rather, they are cultural constructions that interact with biology and material production, and are profoundly shaped by the social and institutional conditions that generate and sustain them. So "teenager" and "adolescence" as representing a distinct stage of life were very much twentieth-century inventions, brought into being by changes in mass education, child labor laws, urbanization and suburbanization, mass consumerism, and the media. Similarly, a new, distinct, and important stage in life, emerging adulthood, situated between the teenage years and full-fledged adulthood, has emerged in American culture in recent decades—reshaping the meaning of self, youth, relationships, and life commitments as well as a variety of behaviors and dispositions among the young. As a result, life for many today between ages 18 and 30 years old, roughly, has morphed into a different experience from that of previous generations. The purpose of this book is to investigate what happens, as youth enter and begin to move through emerging adulthood, to their religious and spiritual lives in particular.

A related note on terminology. In the scholarly literature, "emerging adulthood" refers to 18- to 29-year-olds. The sample of Americans this book investigates and reports on, however, represents only the first half of emerging adulthood, ages 18 to 23. As a consequence, this book's cases, findings, and interpretations do not actually speak for or about all emerging adults in the

United States today but rather those emerging adults in the beginning portion of this stage. However, rather than consistently recognizing this qualification by adding another adjective to the front of every mention of emerging adult—such as "*new* emerging adult," with perhaps the clumsy acronym NEA for short—we will instead simply use the term "emerging adult." Readers should keep in mind throughout, however, that this is shorthand for convenience's sake to represent only the first half of emerging adulthood. Americans 24 to 29 years old may prove to look and sound quite different, though only more research will tell.[16]

WHAT FOLLOWS

The story of American emerging adult religion and spirituality unfolds in the following chapters in a particular sequence that moves from the very specific to the more general and then back to the more specific. The chapters also move back and forth between a primary reliance on qualitative interview data and on quantitative survey evidence. Chapter 1 begins with very specific instances, telling the stories of three particular case studies, drawn from interviews, of individual emerging adults whose experiences illustrate some of this book's major themes. These case studies are not in some way meant to be representative of all emerging adults in the United States. That would be impossible to do with a limited number of cases. Rather, these stories are meant simply to begin to convey some of the character of emerging adult life, to demonstrate the range of possible emerging adult experiences concerning religious and spiritual matters particularly, and to sketch out some concrete cases that will furnish specific examples to illustrate concepts discussed later.

Chapter 2 describes the main contours of contemporary emerging adult culture in the United States, in order to establish a broader context for this book's central focus on religion and spirituality. Drawing on personal interview data, we paint with a broad brush on a large canvas the most prominent cultural themes and features that characterize the assumptions, outlooks, experiences, beliefs, and goals of the majority of American emerging adults. Throughout this chapter, we highlight some varying alternative counterperspectives that some smaller groups of emerging adults expressed in interviews. Having thus described significant elements of mainstream and countervailing emerging adult culture, we then examine some of the more important possible implications of the prominent cultural themes and features we have identified for explaining emerging adults' religious and spiritual lives in particular.

Chapter 3 steps back to examine—with the help of data from the General Social Survey (GSS), one of the best national surveys of residents in the United States—the religiousness of contemporary emerging adults in both historical and life course perspective. Most of this book focuses on what can be known about 18- to 23-year-olds in the United States today. But we will be able to make much better sense in that examination if we begin by providing a sense early on of how contemporary emerging adults compare both to older adults today and to their young adult counterparts in prior decades. Answering those questions will provide a helpful perspective on the larger question we pursue in subsequent chapters.

Chapter 4 delves into findings from the NSYR survey data in much greater depth. This is the chapter that contains the most nationally representative data on emerging adult religion. Our purpose here is to map out the terrain of the religious and spiritual lives of contemporary emerging adults at a big-picture level. This chapter contains many statistics—mostly percentage differences across groups. However, the numbers are well worth studying in order to understand how religious they are and the ways that has changed—or not—since they were teenagers.

Having explored a mass of statistical evidence concerning emerging adults' religious and spiritual lives, we return in chapter 5 to analyzing NSYR interview data in order to identify key themes in American emerging adult religious culture. What are the cultural assumptions, beliefs, expectations, and concerns of emerging adults when it comes to religious faith and practice? In this chapter, we elaborate and illustrate a number of illuminating emerging adult cultural structures concerning religion and spirituality that help to explain the character and bearings of emerging adults' religious and spiritual lives.

Chapter 6 lays out a typology of emerging adult religious approaches into which most American emerging adults seem to fit. Typologies always oversimplify, but they can also help to bring useful clarity to masses of data. Our purpose in this chapter is to identify a limited number of religious types—defined by their religious commitment, knowledge, consistency, and interests—that describe well certain key underlying commonalities shared by different religious sets of emerging adults today. The religious and cultural themes described in chapters 2 and 5 will explain, in part, the features of these types. The typology itself should help to illuminate the multidimensional complexity of religious life among contemporary emerging adults.

Chapter 7 returns to many of the case studies originally presented in *Soul Searching* to see where their subjects' lives have taken them over the subsequent five years. Following these developments reveals yet another aspect of the shape and dynamics of the religious and spiritual lives of emerging adults in the United States.

Chapter 8 takes the analysis to a new level, exploring in greater depth a variety of factors that were measured when the survey's respondents were 13 to 17 years old that appear to influence religion and spirituality during the emerging adult years. Which among a host of possible factors appear to shape how religious emerging adults are five years later? The more complicated statistical techniques of multivariate regression and qualitative comparative analysis (QCA) are employed to ferret out the answers.

Chapter 9 explores possible differences in the life outcomes of emerging adults that appear to result from their different religious backgrounds, beliefs, commitments, and practices. Various studies of different populations have found that religion often makes a significant difference in a variety of life outcomes, from happiness to risk behaviors to mortality. *Soul Searching* found the same kinds of differences among 13- to 17-year-olds. Do these differences continue to hold up among 18- to 23-year-olds? Or do the religion-outcomes connections begin to break down during emerging adulthood? Chapter 9 sets out to answer those questions.

Chapter 10 is a step back and an attempt to make sense of all of the findings of the prior chapters. What, this chapter asks, has been revealed? What does it all mean? What do the implications seem to be? While this chapter is a conclusion to the book, it is also more than that: an attempt to interpret all of the pieces in terms of a larger, coherent framework that summarizes what the book has shown and makes clear its meaning and significance.

As a whole, this book offers readers a large quantity of statistical data and life narratives, as well as analysis, interpretation, and explanation of that evidence. To assimilate and make sense of it all may require some digesting and reflection. Overall, this book intends to provide the most comprehensive and reliable understanding and explanation of the lives of emerging adults in the United States today, particularly their religious and spiritual lives.

1

Brad, June, and Amanda

THIS CHAPTER OPENS UP our investigation of the religious and spiritual lives of emerging adults by telling the stories of three very different young people who were interviewed for this research project in the summer of 2008. Our purpose is to begin to convey some of the character of emerging adult life and culture generally, as well as some of the variety in emerging adults' religious and spiritual lives specifically. The three cases whose stories we narrate in this chapter will also serve as illustrative references for numerous more general points and themes that we develop throughout this book. Emerging adult life is of course far too varied and complicated—by race, sex, religion, social class, educational experience, family background, approaches to risk behaviors, and many other features—to be represented in a mere three case studies. The lives of Brad, June, and Amanda as we recount them here are not meant to be comprehensively typical of their generation or age cohort in any way. No three specific cases could ever be that. We have chosen them rather as real-life cases—to help open up this book by conveying some of the range and character of emerging adult life experiences, religious orientations, and cultural outlooks. Later chapters will introduce still other cases of other emerging adults to fill in some of the gaps in representative types left by this chapter. For now it will be enough to get to know three particular emerging adults whose lives reveal some things, but not everything, about who emerging adults are, how different their lives can be, what social forces influence their experiences, and how they think and talk about religion and spirituality.

BRAD

I meet Brad for breakfast at a Denny's on a Saturday morning not far from his house in a middle-class suburb of a Rocky Mountain state capital city. Brad shows up early, nicely dressed, clean cut, and cordial. A young man of 21—with dark features, fashionable glasses, and a businesslike demeanor that stands out against his somewhat still-boyish-looking face—Brad describes his history and life with an economy of words. He graduated from the local high school three years earlier, worked his way up from the mailroom to become a sales agent at an area branch of a national agricultural and construction machinery company, is taking online classes in business management part-time through an Internet-based university, and is in the throes of making last-minute arrangements with Amy, his fiancée, for their wedding, which is to be held in three weeks. Brad met Amy in high school, dated her for the last five years, and lived with her for the last two years, first in a rented apartment and then in a house he purchased. The time has arrived in their relationship, he explains, to "make it official." Both Brad's and Amy's parents live in the same suburb as they do, and everyone is happy about their relationship and impending marriage. Brad's parents both work clerical jobs in corporations. Brad has labored hard since middle school— first in his own lawn mowing company, then as a busboy in restaurants, and now in his "real" sales job—to save money for his own financial needs. In high school he bought his own car. Recently he bought the modest house in which he and Amy are living. Brad strikes me as responsible, very much in charge of his own life, not too dependent on or beholden to anyone else for anything. He says he gets along fine with his parents but is not too close to them. He has a lot of friends but feels no pressure to do anything with them that does not interest him. He reports rarely feeling sad or depressed. "I don't really talk to a lot of people about anything," he says. "I kind of like to do things on my own, feel I have made the right decisions on my own. I feel better and safer coming to conclusions on my own as opposed to asking other people's opinions."

Brad says that he liked high school and was not rebellious as a teenager; "Nothing major. I mean, there's always stuff that every teenager does, you know, staying out too late, sneaking around, getting your first car, like that, but I never really got into trouble for anything big." He did drink a lot of alcohol, but that never proved to be a problem, he says. Before meeting Amy, he dated one other girl in high school, for eight months, with whom he had sex for the first time. "I guess it just sort of happened. It worked out. Nothing bad ever happened." Brad has also "hooked up" with at least one other girl, although he did not elaborate on what exactly that meant and did not seem to want to discuss it. After graduating from high school, Brad lived with friends in a shared apartment. They drank a lot of alcohol together, which he says was fun. But after six months, he and Amy decided to move in together, so they got their own apartment. Now he is transitioning to a fully responsible adult lifestyle and is quite pleased with himself and his life.

As to religion, Brad definitely considers himself a Christian, just like his parents. He and his family together attend a very large, evangelical, somewhat seeker-oriented Bible church in the area that has quasi-denominational ties to its mother church in Southern California. I am surprised to learn that he attends an evangelical church, as he has been living with his girlfriend for two years, and most such churches condemn sex before marriage. Although he attends church somewhat regularly, overall, he seems fairly neutral and ho-hum about religion. Speaking of himself and his parents, he observes, "We're not strong, firm believers—we have the same religious ideas and concepts but we don't go to church every weekend, there will be times when it's weekly and then other times where we don't go for months. It's hit and miss, here and there. We don't go for the sort of hardcore Christian type." Brad has nothing in particular against his own church, other than his feeling that it is too large for his taste. "I enjoy a good sermon, a good speaker, I enjoy drinking the coffee," he says, chuckling. So why doesn't he attend more often?

> Kind of how busy the schedule is, depends on our lifestyles. We do lots of camping and stuff with Amy's family, go to the zoo, to the cabin, stuff life that. And working Monday through Friday, solid days, it's kind of our weekends to do our stuff. But if we get a free Sunday, we'll go with our parents or go ourselves once in a while.

Brad's parents used to attend church more frequently, he reports, but decreased their attendance when his mother started working a paid job five years earlier. Amy is also a nondenominational evangelical Christian, like Brad, although he doesn't know much about her religiously beyond that. Still, he notes, going to church "makes Amy happy, she's more inclined to go [than I am]. I think she likes the idea of us going." So he is amenable to attending church when they can.

Brad reports that overall he has gotten less religious in recent years. He was involved in his church's youth group during middle school—he especially enjoyed the bowling, he recalls—and used to attend church weekly. "I still have the same *ideas* now, I just don't go to church like I used to do every Sunday. Everyone's kind of got busier lifestyles, maybe higher priorities." He does not pray very often and does not read the Bible, though he makes a point of saying that he owns one. He also does not put money into the church offering plate and reports not really feeling much sense of belonging in his church. Family and friends are much more important in that way. At the same time, he says he suffers from no religious doubts, has absolutely no interest in any other religions, and thinks he will always remain a Christian.

So what does Brad actually believe religiously? "Go to heaven," he replies, "I believe that. I believe in the Rapture. I'm not sure what else. I believe there is a God and if we're saved by him, that sort of stuff." Seeming dissatisfied with his answer, he quickly adds:

> I mean I have my beliefs in my head. But I don't enjoy the whole religious scene. I'm not really into it like some people are. I have my

beliefs, I believe that's the way it is, and the way it should be, and I go to church every once in a while. But it's kind of low-key.

I questioned Brad about salvation and heaven and hell, in which he says he believes. "If you believe in Jesus and ask him to be in your life, it's a belief thing," he answers. So why, I continue, would anyone need to be saved or maybe would end up in hell? "Well, if they don't believe those things, believe that Jesus is real or—I don't know how to describe it, kind of if you're a bad person or committed sins that can't be forgiven, stuff like that, then you go to hell." What if someone is a good, nice person but has never heard of Jesus? I inquire. They go to heaven, Brad thinks, though he's not sure. Doesn't Brad's church teach against sex before marriage and cohabitation? I probe. "Yeah, I think they do, right. But I think it's all based on your situation, if that's what you want to believe at that kind of church, sure, that's great, if that's what they want to do. It's all relative." So then he believes sex before marriage is not wrong for Christians? "I think it's kind of, I don't really think that idea [no sex before marriage] is part of this time, this age." Brad and Amy are not getting married in church but in an outdoor public park in the city.

Behind many of Brad's answers is the apparent view that an individual's choice of beliefs—influenced by his or her family socialization, of course—is mostly what makes those beliefs true, at least for that person. When talking about the possible validity of non-Christian religions, for example, Brad says, "I think my beliefs, my religion is the right religion. If others believe different, then that's fine, I don't really know for sure, I just think that's what I believe. I don't know why or what, that's what I was raised to think and that's what comes to mind as what's right, so that's what's right." And when discussing what different people do and do not get out of church, Brad concludes, "I think in my head it's all personal opinion, whether you're going to believe it or choose to like it and listen or not." At the same time, and perhaps partly as a result, Brad seems somewhat lost on larger questions about morality. He says he believes in objective moral right and wrong, reporting: "I think I always do the right thing. I have never had any issues." But he's also not sure what morality itself is based on. "I'm sure it has to do with religion, maybe that plays a role in it. I don't know if I could go so far as to say it's a God thing, I don't know, I'm not sure what really decides that." At times, Brad says that morality is about "kind of everyone's perception of right and wrong, a group consensus or idea, kind of just a majority." At other times Brad emphasizes subjective moral intuitions. "I think everyone knows, for the most part, has a sense of right and wrong, and it's just part of who you are, feeling that something is wrong." When talking about how he would decide what to do in a morally ambiguous situation, Brad reports, "I'm leaning toward taking care of number one, what would make me happy, help me get ahead. You've got to do what's right for you. I'm always for myself, on a larger scale I'm always worried about myself first, I kind of need to go off my own ideas." What, I query, about the role of God or the Bible? "I think I always kind of lean toward the Bible, what God says is right, but I don't really rely on it." At bottom, Brad seems to summarize his situation by confessing, "I would say I'm kind of confused on the question, I guess. I think there is a straight path and objective right but I'm not sure what it is, where it comes from."

Socially and politically, Brad thinks he is probably a conservative. For him that means: "I kind of like things the way they've always been and keeping things natural, kind of the good old way it used to be." He values America's freedoms and rights. In our discussions, he strongly emphasizes individual choice and responsibility. He says he looks down on "crazy, drugged low-lifes, as I call them." Alcoholics and drug users have no one to blame for their irresponsible decisions but themselves. By contrast, Brad likes "outgoing, responsible, smart, family-oriented types of people." Brad believes in the death penalty and is antiabortion and firmly against gay marriage. "That's wrong, not the way God intended it to be. The Bible says it's a sin." Brad is also unhappy about illegal immigration and health-care rights for undocumented aliens. At the same time, Brad is not particularly interested in politics or global issues: "I'd say I watch the stock market more than I do world events." He does not expect to vote in the next election because none of the candidates appeal to him. Brad believes volunteer work is good to do, at least in theory, but he does not volunteer because he has "higher priorities" now. He advocates fiscal responsibility and is against people going into debt to buy consumer items. But he also believes in the absolute right to private property and freedom of consumer choice. "If people can afford whatever, fine. If they progress that far, they can have it, they can go buy eight boats if they want, if they can afford it."

What does Brad look for in life in the years to come? "I'd like to be successful, well-off, provide for my family. Along the way maybe travel a bit, play golf, go camping, visit places, stay at home, hang out with family, go to the park, stuff like that." What kind of material lifestyle would Brad like to have? "Materially, a nice house, reliable vehicles, nice cars to rely on to get you places, and maybe recreational activities on the weekends or whatever, a four-wheeler or something like that." Brad wants to have two children and expects that Amy will stay at home with them as a full-time mother after the first is born. Finally, what does Brad imagine he will be like religiously when he is 30 years old? "I don't know, it's hard to tell," he says. "I can only say the same as I am right now. With kids, probably we'll go to Sunday school."

I leave the interview with a lot of questions. What actually does it mean to "believe in Jesus and ask him to be in your life" in Brad's kind of faith? Why is Brad so sure that gay marriage is morally, even biblically wrong when he is so ready to disregard traditional church teachings against premarital heterosexual sex and living for "number one?" Does the leadership of Brad's evangelical church realize how relatively uncommitted and indifferent he is when it comes to his religious faith and practice? Is American Christianity really about personally enjoying sermons on occasion, "going to heaven," and meanwhile enjoying private family and recreational worlds of financial comfort and mass consumption while disregarding the common good, public life, and one's needy neighbors? Left with many more questions than answers,

I pack up my stuff and head on to the next interview, in the hope that in due time the research will begin to reveal some big-picture insights.

JUNE

I meet June for lunch at a Mexican restaurant in the modest-sized southern Appalachian mountain town in which she lives. I originally proposed to June that we meet for our interview at the Bob Evans restaurant in the same shopping center, but June said no because her ex-husband works there. She recommended the Mexican restaurant instead. June shows up late. But that gives me plenty of time to find a quiet, out-of-the-way table at which to conduct our interview and to get my recording equipment and paperwork ready. When June arrives, all of the restaurant staff recognizes her with "Hola! ¿Que Pasa?" Nobody in NSYR has ever interviewed June before—this is her first interview with our project. I have chosen to meet her because in her survey she has identified herself as a "Satanist." June turns out to be a friendly 19-year-old with plain features who is wearing a somewhat low-cut blouse and very short shorts. It also seems to me that she has, after the initial smiles are over, a somewhat sad disposition. We order our meals and start in on chips and salsa. The television in the far corner is playing the quarter-final European Cup match between Spain and Italy, totally engrossing the waiters, who are happy to leave us alone for the three hours of our interview.

There prove to be good reasons for June to seem sad. Not yet even into her twenties, June not only is already divorced but was badly physically abused by her ex-husband. Their divorce is recent. She is also the mother of a toddler son, Ben, who has been removed from her through court order by the state's child protection services. Ben is living with a temporary foster family somewhere else in the state, and June sees him only one hour a week. June is also unemployed, in trouble over past drug abuse, and only recently a fully recovered drug addict. It turns out that June's entire life these days—her nearly every thought and action—revolves around getting her son, Ben, back. That is why she has quit drugs—she failed an early drug test, and the state told her she would never get her son back if she did not clean up. That is also why she has divorced her husband—the state made her divorcing him a condition of the possibility of her gaining custody of Ben again. Even so, it turns out, June has still not entirely learned to make all of the right choices needed to get Ben back.

June describes life in her town as "pretty boring, not a lot to do at all. The biggest thing when I was younger was to go out and party. That was the big thing around here, to go out drinking, just out in the middle of nowhere, building a fire, going fishing, drinking." Partying also seems to involve risky sex:

> There's a lot of people having babies, and there's not a lot of jobs around. If you don't go to school for something, you're not going to get anything over minimum wage around here. Everybody's having babies. All kinds of teenagers, all of my friends, and a bunch of kids younger

than me. Everybody's getting pregnant at 16 or 17. I was one of them,
I can't lie. I was one of them too.

June got pregnant at age 17, before she was married. She was taking the Pill
for birth control, but it did not work. She says she thinks a lot of girls in her
area get pregnant "just to trap the guys they're with. I know a couple guys that
the girls told them they were on birth control, and they supposedly weren't,
and they got pregnant, and the guys felt obligated to stay with them." Drugs
are another issue:

> Drugs. There's a lot of drugs around here. There's a lot of meth
> [methamphetamines], and that's just a terrible drug. I've lost so many
> addicted friends because they just turn into liars. They don't care what
> they steal. They'll come to your house and steal your light bulbs. They
> don't care. They'll come steal all your tools, your stereo out of your car
> just 'cause they know it's in there, bust your windshield out and steal
> your stereo. They'll steal your whole car. I mean, that's a bad drug.

A lot of people in June's community also suffer from diseases, she says. She
says that in a larger city not too far away, "there's big chemical plants down
there and sometimes that has a lot to do with it because, I don't know if you
saw the stuff rolling out of the big towers down there, but I'm sure that that's
not good for anyone. There was this mysterious blue haze one night, on the
day of my grandpa's funeral, actually, and they talked about it all over the
news, and it was a blue haze, and they thought it was from one of the chemical
plants or some ridiculous thing."

Life was more fun and innocent when June was younger. She played vol-
leyball and softball in middle school. She and her mother used to show horses
competitively. And they sometimes traveled to Disneyland and various amuse-
ment parks, where they both enjoyed riding roller coasters. Then everything
changed. "On my first day of seventh grade, my mom had a stroke due to a
brain aneurism. I was 12." June's mother barely escaped death, suffered brain
damage, and has been in poor health since, enduring regular dizzy and faint-
ing spells. Since the stroke, June says she has been an occasional caregiver to
her mother, and more recently to some extent for her grandmother as well,
with whom they live. That responsibility is partly because her parents (and
grandparents) divorced when she was very young and her father now lives
in Texas. Until recently she had no relationship with him at all. "I never had
talked to my father till the night I delivered my baby." The sibling relations
are also a bit complicated: "I have an older and a younger half-sister, an older
step-sister, and a younger half-brother"—all but one now live in Texas, and
the one nearby is checked out. June explains:

> I feel like I should stay for my mom and my grandma because my
> mom's just been getting sicker and sicker. My cousins, they all left for
> the military, so they're in Iraq, and my sister, she moved in with her
> husband, and she's going to school full-time, working full-time, and
> they never see her. When I stay there with my mom, I try to help her

out. I go to the grocery store for her and my grandma. I take their trash out.

But June and her mother do not get on well. "She drives me crazy, all the time, accusing me of doing stuff that I'm not doing. She is always set on drama. My family is crazy. There's a lot of tension between us. She'll slam a door when she walks out, give me evil looks, just make these frustrated noises." June's mother has recently announced that if June does not get Ben back, then she will have to leave the house and live on her own. "She pretty much just told me if I don't get him back, then I have to get out. I'm not allowed to live there anymore." June's mother does help her with the complicated medical and legal chores of the process of resecuring custody of Ben, but they still do not get along. "I don't feel very close with her. I feel a lot closer to my dad now, and he's thousands of miles away. I can be completely honest with my dad on the phone now when we talk, but I can't be honest with my mom because she's very judgmental."

June recounts that she first smoked marijuana at age 11, when she came across it in her 21-year-old sister's bedroom. "I found it in her room, and I was like, hmm, I'm going to try this out." From then on, she smoked irregularly until age 14, at which point smoking weed became a routine. June paid for her pot by "bumming money at school, like, 'Can I have 50 cents? Can I get a dollar?'" Her uncle—her mother's brother—was her supplier. So why did June smoke? "Self-medication. Stress, anxiety. I have a lot of social anxiety, and depression. I used to have depression anyway. [I see now that] I never really knew depression till I lost my son, but *now* I know depression." June started smoking cigarettes when she was 13 or 14. "I was stupid. I don't know, at the time, I had a boyfriend who was 19. I got kicked out of my mom's house for a month, 'cause she was acting crazy, and we got a pack of cigarettes. I decided I was just going to smoke one of those cigarettes, and I got real bad nicotine buzz off of it." At age 19, June smokes a pack a day. She had it down to three cigarettes a day after Ben was born, but when he was taken away she started back up again, smoking a lot.

June drank her first alcohol at age 12, when the same sister gave her a mixed drink. "She told me that she would rather me drink with her than go out and do it with my friends, 'cause she saw where I was going with my friends anyhow. She knew I was turning rebellious." June started drinking heavily at age 16 or 17. "Then I went on a couple three-month binges, I was just drunk constantly. It was pretty stupid. That's when I met my ex-husband, was during the three month binge, and that's when I got pregnant, I was drunk at the time." It took a long time for June to realize that she was pregnant, she says, because when she would wake up with morning sickness she assumed that she was merely hungover from drinking. Only after missing her period for a couple of months did she start to suspect she was pregnant. Then she quit drinking. But on the day Ben was taken away, June got drunk again. Since then she has drunk excessively about 10 times, she guesses, both to have fun and to drown her sorrows. "But drinking doesn't fix your problems at all,"

June observes, "not for me. It makes it much worse. I get very emotional when I drink, so I tend to stay away from alcohol. Plus, it kills my stomach."

What about harder drugs, I inquired? "Where do you want me to start?" she asks. "I've tried coke, morphine, heroin, Lortem, Xanax, Klonopin, crack, meth. When I was 15 I did it for the first time. When I was 16, I did meth for a couple months, and then I never have done it again since." She stopped, she says, because she visited a lab where methamphetamine was made, and it revolted her. "I saw what they were putting into it, how they were making it, and I was like, oh, my God, I've been doing this for the last two months, how am I not dead? It turned my stomach enough to just be like, I'm going to go to jail or die." So why did June ever do hard drugs? "'cause I like the feeling, I mean I like getting messed up." Becoming a mother, however, altered her view:

> When I had my kid that changed the way I looked at things, changed everything. It wasn't about me any more. I couldn't be selfish, it's about my son. Since then I didn't do hard drugs. I would smoke pot, you know, every once in a while, but that's not really that hard of a drug— that doesn't comatose you so you lay there and can't move or function, like other drugs.

Does she ever worry about returning to drugs? "I feel pretty vulnerable with things like that now because it would be easy for me to go and just do some kind of drug, just try to make myself not hurt. But I'm not going to put myself in that situation." Thinking of Ben helps June resist her temptations to go back to drugs. "The thought's crossed my mind, but once it goes through my mind, it's gone, because he's my son. I made him inside my body, nobody else did it, that's mine, and I will get what's mine. I'm very determined about that."

June dropped out of high school in tenth grade—"That happens a lot around here, we have a very high rate of dropouts"—but later regretted not finishing school. Recently she earned her GED. In fact, she scored so high on her GED exams that she won a $3,000 scholarship to any college or school of her choice. She pulled her official scores out of her purse and showed me— indeed, she made the ninetieth-level percentiles on all subjects but math. But, as far as going to school, it is clear that June cannot focus on anything now except getting Ben back. Almost everything else seems to have been put on hold. For a while recently, June worked in the drive-through at Dairy Queen, but she left because her ex-husband's girlfriend was working there. "I just can't stand being around her. I was just like, I can't do this." The little money she makes now she earns from driving friends to destinations to which they need rides. "I haven't really looked for a job. I just give my friends rides and they give me money to give them a ride five miles, and I'm okay." As for possible future work, June says some of the best jobs in the area are in nursing, but she does not want to become a nurse. "I just can't stand nursing homes," she says. "I can't deal with sick people. It breaks my heart."

What a life, I keep thinking to myself. The more June tells of her story, the more world-weary I realize she looks. Later in my notes I will write that in her appearance she seemed "tired, depressed, used."

June, it turns out, was raised with extremely little religion in her life. She identifies herself as not religious, "because I don't know a lot about religion, so if you don't know something, then you can't really declare yourself in that category." June thinks she does believe in some kind of "higher being," but says, however, "That's just a comfort zone, I'd like to believe that. It's a security blanket for me." June prays, but mostly to ask whoever—she doesn't know—to give her Ben back. "I would do anything. Like, I've even bought this necklace from a witchcraft store in town, a 'When-in-Court Necklace,' I'd even be willing to do that. I will try anything at this point, I'm desperate."

I ask June about her mother's religion. She replies, "I don't really know, she confuses me. One day it'll be God, and the next day it'll be aliens or something. She's just being crazy." June's mother does not go to church. June thinks she has read the Bible some, but she does not know if she ever prays. June knows nothing about her father religiously, other than that once recently he said that he believes in God. June was taken to church only twice in her life, by her grandmother when she was a little girl. She does not know of any religious youth groups that were in her high school, although she suspects that there must be some religious groups around that she could be part of if she were interested. She also does not really know any people who are religious—nearly all of her friends are nonreligious. She does know people who claim that their house is haunted with ghosts, but she herself has never had a religious, supernatural, or paranormal experience. All in all, religion is simply not a part of June's life. So what, generally, does June think about religion? "Who cares, really?" she replies. "Not relevant. I never pay attention to churches really at all." In theory, June professes to be open to giving her life to God, if it would bring Ben back, but she does not know how to do that. "I wouldn't really know who to talk to. Actually, one of my friends, his grandfather is a preacher. That's probably where I would start." I am guessing to myself, though, that that is unlikely to happen.

I ask June about the "Satanist" answer she gave in her survey. It turns out to mean very little. Earlier in the year an "antisocial" friend "who doesn't like to drive" paid June $50 to drive him to a Pagan Maypole ceremony up in the mountains, where a woman friend of his was belly dancing. It was held at night, in the woods of a state forest. I asked what the ceremony was about. "I'm not too sure, it seems like it was a lot about women power, women's self-esteem and stuff, not to take any crap from men. I don't know what pagans believe, I'm not sure if they're like devil worshipers, or the earth worshipers, or what they are. I don't really know." What happened there? "Dancing and a lot of music—there was some singing and drums and stuff. They passed out drums. I was sitting there playing the drums." So who was there? "It was women that ran around the Maypole, mostly all women. There were more people there than I expected, a lot, must be more popular than I realized. Also there were a lot of gay guys, some I knew and some had their fingernails painted, that says gay to me." June recalled, "It was amusing, it kept me interested, kept my attention, which is hard to do. It was fun, I might go again next year, just for the heck of it." After the belly dancing and Maypole activities,

June and her friend left. "There were still people arriving," she remembered. "They had masks and devil horns on their heads and stuff. It was starting to get dark, and I was like, 'Man, I bet the pagans get crazy at night, and I'm glad we're getting out of here.'"

Throughout our conversation, June's cell phone keeps vibrating. She continually glances at it, and then puts it back in her purse. Something is happening with her friends, but she stays focused on our interview.

I change the topic to questions about morality. June assures me, "I think I have a pretty good sense of what's right or wrong. I don't know, probably it's just something inside of me. I think I just picked it up along the way more than anything." Is it easy or hard to know right and wrong in life? "Pretty easy." What are examples of wrong things? "It's wrong to rob people, or damage property, or just be mean to people in general." Okay, then what about *doing* the right thing, not just knowing it—is doing right easy or hard? "It's easy. I don't like to do wrong because I believe in karma." Karma? "I just think if I do wrong, then it's going to come back on me. Something bad's going to happen, whether it'd be I'm driving down the interstate and my car breaks down, or something. I've always believed in karma, because I can remember times when I've done the wrong thing and lots of bad things have happened to me." Where does karma come from? What makes it operate? "There is, I believe, there is a God. Maybe God, I don't really know. I can't really answer any of that because I don't know."

But what, I press, is it that makes anything right or wrong? "I guess it's all in my head, whatever I happen to justify, that makes it right or wrong, I suppose. And probably if it is illegal, probably somewhere along the way that makes it right or wrong too—anything that's illegal is probably wrong. Obviously, it wouldn't be illegal if it wasn't wrong." Is it always morally wrong to break the law, even to drive over the speed limit? "It depends on how you look at it, really. Everything, every situation has its right or wrong, really, every situation is different." So what if somebody else really thought it was just fine to hurt other people, would they be wrong? "No, I would probably think in my head that they were wrong, but I wouldn't voice my opinion because I'm not anyone to be able to judge anyone. I don't really have any say." So why is it a problem to judge others? "I don't know, because I just don't think that's right. I don't think it's anyone's place to judge anyone else." Are there universal rights and wrongs, I ask, or is morality ultimately relative? "I don't know. I'm so confused, I don't know really. I think that religion is probably something to study up on more just because I don't know a whole lot about it. I may just study up on all different religions and see what everyone has to think and maybe come up with one of my own." How, I ask, does June decide about right and wrong when she is unsure? "Probably do what would make me feel happy. Whatever situation I'd be in, whatever decision that would make me happy, that's what I would go for." Do people have a moral responsibility to help others? "Myself, yes, I think so," June says. "Other people may not. It depends on how they feel about it." Why, I press, do you think you are responsible to help others?

"Because I feel like if I'm good to other people and do good things, then good things will come to me." June then confesses that she looks down on "slutty" women, "girls who are all over whatever penis that is around, all over it, trying to make out with everything coming and going, including me. I just cannot stand to be around of those types of girls, they just degrade themselves so much, like strippers."

June has never volunteered or given money away—"People give *me* money now," she jokes—though she thinks giving and volunteering would be good to do because of karma. She is concerned about poverty, the war, government debt, crime, and abortion in the United States. But she also has no interest or concern with politics and has never been politically involved. She does not know enough about political positions or ideology generally to even know where she would stand. What *is* a liberal or a conservative, anyway? She doesn't know. June is definitely antiabortion, though:

> Would it be right for me to kill that guy right there? No. Then I don't believe it's right to kill an infant, even if it's unborn. It's still alive, its heart is beating. That decision was laid out for me, either having a baby or having an abortion, and I thought about it and I was like, "I can't have an abortion." If somebody wants to kill their kid, they can go have that baby and give it to me. I don't care. Somebody else will always take a baby.

I then ask about romantic relationships and sex. Altogether, June has dated eight men, six of whom she has lived with. She started dating guys and having sex with them when she was 13 or 14 years old—she can't remember precisely. Her first boyfriend was six years older than she was. "I met him at the movie video store, we exchanged phone numbers, and it just went from there." Within the year, however, he—"my first love," she calls him—was killed in an automobile accident, which was her first real encounter with death. She says this was very hard on her at the time. Between her first boyfriend and her later marriage, she dated and had sex with numerous other men. She says the men rarely used condoms but she simply was not concerned about sexually transmitted diseases. "Didn't care at the time. I look back and feel real lucky now. I knew the risk. I was just risking it." June says that a lot of people in her area do have sexually transmitted diseases, including AIDS, although the way she talks implies that she does not have one.

June first met her ex-husband, Nick, when she was 17, at a Pizza Hut. After running into him at a convenience store a week later, she "hooked up"[1] with him. They continued together after that. Nick gradually moved in with June in her mother's house—"He was already hanging around so much"— which her mother did not like but also did not refuse. In due time, June got pregnant, and she and Nick got married. They moved back and forth regularly between their parents' houses. Then Nick started abusing her. He occasionally smacked her, pulled her hair, or twisted her ear, but mostly he choked her, in front of their child, until she passed out. This happened more than two or three time a week, whenever Nick got mad at June. She left him a number of times but always returned. "I knew I needed to get away, I knew that. Deep down, I knew that, but I didn't leave."

Then the state agency found out about Nick, through a counselor June saw who reported his abuse to the state, which intervened and took Ben. June filed a restraining order against Nick, forcing him to stay away from her. June had to see a psychiatrist on state orders to determine whether she was fit to be Ben's mother. She started a drug rehab program because she failed a drug test. In the midst of sorting out Ben's legal custody, allegations were raised about child pornography on June's family's computer. June still does not know who made those charges, but she strongly suspects that it was Nick. That sealed Ben's fate for being put into the foster care system. After four months of analyses of the computer hard drive, June says, it was declared clean. In the midst of the drama, it also came out that Nick claimed that as a boy he had been sexually abused by cousins, so he began mandatory preventative sex abuse counseling. Despite all of this, June is not through with Nick:

> At first we didn't talk for a long time, and then we tried getting back together there for a couple weeks, and I realized it wasn't going to work because he already got abusive with me again, and I was like, just forget it, it's not going to work. But now we talk to each other on a regular basis, and we tell each other we love each other, because we do. There will always be feelings. We're going to have to be part of each other's lives, whether we like it or not. I think so anyway.

Since her divorce, June has lived with a guy named Frankie, who she met when she picked him up as a hitchhiker. "I gave him my phone number, and we just started hanging out. I don't know, we really liked each other." She soon moved in with Frankie, a roofer by trade. June's mother said nothing about it. June and Frankie lived together for two months and then, June says, "I just got tired of being around him all the time. Staying in a tight space with someone for long enough, you get annoyed and irritated with each other." She moved out. "We're not technically together, but we have feelings for one another." June and Frankie remain sexually involved, but she explains that they have a pact about nonmonogamy: "We have an agreement. If he does anything with anybody else, he'll tell me. If I do anything with anybody else, I'll tell him. And then we won't do anything with each other." Later June explains that Frankie is actually one of her current best friends, along with Frankie's brother, James, with whom Frankie is "always together, they're pretty much inseparable." She explains:

> A lot of times we just drive around. They drink a lot. But, we like to rent movies, and just go and chill out and watch movies. They like to drink a lot, like I said. I'm their designated driver. I'd rather me be out driving them around, than them hitchhiking or getting hit by a car.

So why, I ask, stepping back, did so many of June's intimate relationships end as they did? Her answer:

Me being a bitch. I'm a hard person to get along with. I've tried to change, but I'm just very moody. It doesn't take a lot to get on my nerves, and if you get on my nerves, I'm not shy to tell you. Usually I would get sick of the guys and tell them to leave, 'cause they were usually living with me.

June also explains that her troubled marriage has made her cautious about marrying again. "Oh yeah, I don't trust very well. I have issues with trust, I know, I do." She is not sure if she ever wants to marry again. In any case, June reports,

> I definitely am not going to marry somebody without living with them first. It's going to take a good, at least a year of me living with them, not just be dating. You don't know what's going to irritate you the most about them until you live with them for a while. They could be abusive, or an alcoholic and you don't know it. It's going to take a lot for me to marry somebody next time.

I ask: does June have any regrets about her relationships with other men, particularly getting involved with them sexually? "No, I don't have any regrets, because I don't believe that anyone should have any regrets."

Next topic: where or with whom, I ask, does June feel her greatest sense of belonging? "More with rebels than the Christian-y, churchgoing type. I'm more comfortable around the rebels." Why them? "Because I'm smarter than them, and I always like to surround myself with people that I'm smarter than, for some reason. I have more morals, and listen to right and wrong more than they do, and I'm like, 'No, you're not going to do that'—I do help them out, keep them out of jail." I ask her to tell me more. "Well, I look at life as a game too, it's just a big game of chess, and I can sit there and move all the pieces right exactly where I want them. Just keeping people in their place more than anything." June describes herself as "very stubborn," saying, "If I argue about something, I have to have the last word. If somebody tries to walk away from me when they're arguing with me, I try to stop them and get in their way." I ask her to elaborate on the life-as-a-game idea:

> Like I said, I can always get what I want and it's all about what I say to people and how I say it, and I can get what I want from about anyone. I think I manipulate people a lot. But, again that goes with life as being a game. I manipulate a lot of people. It's just a personality thing. I just enjoy it.

At about this place in the interview, a strange twist enters into the conversation. June mentions that she was here in this restaurant the night before, drinking margaritas. Who, I ask, was she with? "My ex-husband and two people he works with," she says matter-of-factly, to my only-somewhat-concealed astonishment. But wasn't that a violation of the restraining order? I ask. Couldn't she lose every chance of getting Ben back if anyone saw them drinking together? "Yes it was a violation," she answers. "But we come in at separate times, leave at separate times, try to sit back in the corner where nobody will see us, I put my hood on. I sit against the wall, and he's much bigger than me, so he towers over me." So, I realize, that is why the restaurant staff are on friendly terms with June—she's a regular, it seems. I repress my bewilderment about how someone who by every sign is so genuinely obsessed with getting her son back can jeopardize everything by having drinks in public with her ex-husband who not long ago regularly choked her into unconsciousness. Isn't alcohol something she is avoiding these days, I inquire? "I sipped it three times. I don't really drink. I don't know, it messes me up, makes me sick." Wow, I think, I don't know if June is 19 going on 39 or 19 going on 12. Seems like both.

During the last half hour of our interview, I notice that June's body language is becoming increasingly withdrawn, like she is pulling away, almost into a bit of a fetal position. She is also no longer speaking directly to me but instead out into the air of the open room. "My life is going nowhere fast," June says, "I hate my situation in life. I hate it." She says she has been having sleeping troubles. "A lot of times, I sleep all day and stay up all night. I didn't sleep at all last night. I've always had a problem with that. I won't sleep for two days and then I'll sleep for three days in a row. It has nothing to do with drugs, although my mom accuses me of drugs." June thinks the cause of her patchy insomnia is stress. In general, June says, she feels pretty disoriented and lost. "I am very depressed, but I try not to be, because if I walk around moping all the time then it just makes it worse." Does she have any way of dealing with her depression, I ask, any counseling or medications? No, she says,

> I just deal with it day to day. I don't have any suicide or homicidal thoughts. I have something to live for, I have my son. That's all I care about. That's all I want back, and it just depresses me that I'm not with him. But, I will be with him. Still, if I did something stupid like that [suicide or homicide] I'd never be with him.

June reports that her grandfather, with whom she was pretty close, died five months previously. She is sad and confused about that, but says, "I don't think I've ever really dealt with it, really. I think that I'm going to get to it when I can deal with it. I just don't think that right now I can deal with that too on top of everything else." June says her mom is grieved about the death of her father. Does June talk about it with her mom? I ask. "She just says 'I don't want to talk about it,' and she starts crying and stomps off into another room." About her life generally, June says,

> I feel like I've got the short end of the stick. It's just there. That's just how it is. That's the way I look at it, they can't do anything to change, there's no point to cry over spilled milk. What's there is there.

June's mother clearly seems to be a problem for her. In fact, June says that she never really enjoyed any good parenting in her life, that she increasingly realizes that she never had any parent who took care of her and taught her well. She says, for example, that she never learned manners from anybody.

"I had never been taught any kind of manners, like 'Please' or 'Thank you' or 'You're welcome' or anything like that. I never used to apologize if I did something wrong to somebody. I've lately gotten a lot better. Have started working on all of that, and I think I've gotten a lot better. Now I actually apologize for way too much stuff; I barely make somebody mad and I'm like, 'I'm sorry.'" She says she is also working more generally on a more positive attitude. "My mom's attitude made me a very negative person, and as of recently, I've been trying to be more positive about life, even though everything's been very negative recently. I've been trying to make it positive, and trying to make it a good thing." She elaborates:

> I try to be, like, grateful. I try to be positive, to wake up and think at least I'm alive today. I can still walk. I'm not blind. There's nothing too physically wrong with me. And I try to be thankful for those sorts of things. My son's in good health, even though he not with me. Try to look at the positive outlooks instead of all the bad things, that's what I'm doing.

I believe June's assertion that she is working hard to be positive and turn things around. That seems genuine. But it is also clear that June has not made a total break from some of her old life patterns. She has a lot to overcome.

What, I finally ask, does June ultimately want to get out of life? What would a good ending look like? "To be healthy, happy, to have a home, have my baby Ben, and for him to be healthy and happy. Have all my body parts, not be in a wheelchair, not be blind, or get any serious illnesses, anything like that. Pretty much I just want to be healthy and happy, that's really all I want to accomplish."

The interview ends. June's cell phone buzzes again. This time she answers. It's Frankie, wanting to know when she will be ready to leave. They are driving to somewhere in Ohio this evening to be part of some kind of weekend-long skateboard festival, which she says is going to be a "major big party." In fact, she needs the incentive money I am paying her for doing the interview to help afford the trip. We say goodbye, we shake hands, and off June goes.

Before heading back to the highway to drive home, I swing out on the business route through June's town to have a look around. I partly want to see if I can find the witchcraft store she mentioned. I can't. I also want to absorb a bit more of the social context of June's life. There are the usual gas stations, middle school, post office, aluminum-sided houses, and convenience stores. I pull over here and there to soak it all in. On the way out, right on the town's main drag, I notice an enormous red brick Baptist church. The parking lot is empty. But the big sign out by the road announces in large black plastic letters an upcoming performance by a gospel quartet, the Something or Other Brothers, who will be singing old-time gospel favorites. I look at the church building and imagine a partly filled sanctuary of nice, middle-aged and senior church members enjoying the gospel music in their pews on a Sunday evening. But I can't imagine June being any part of it. Her life was on a different track.

AMANDA

Amanda and I meet in a tourist town on the West Coast for lunch. We sit and talk at an outdoor table on a sunny deck overlooking the water, enjoying our salads, pizza, and conversation. Amanda is working that summer as a counselor at a religious overnight camp nearby and has agreed to devote her few hours off this week to our interview. She shows up just a little late, wearing funky clothes and a bright smile. She describes herself to me as "sweet and quiet, hard working, and considerate of others' feelings, though I wish I were more patient with other people and myself." She reports early on in the interview that she feels very blessed in life and has a wonderful family. The biggest challenges of people her age, Amanda reports, are "deciding who we are, the growing up process of separating from our parents and deciding for ourselves what we want to be and do, deciding a career, and relationships, and a lot of big decisions." Amanda is a history major in college, where she also takes voice lessons, sings in the chamber choir, belongs to a writer's club, and plays intramural sports. She says she has lost touch with most of her friends from high school, though she keeps in contact with a few by phone and MySpace.

It turns out that Amanda is quite involved in a small, very conservative evangelical denomination that encapsulates her life. Her father works on the staff of a high school academy run by her denomination, on whose grounds Amanda grew up and in which she herself was enrolled. Amanda is attending one of her denomination's colleges. She has recently traveled to Germany with one of her denomination's study abroad programs. And the summer camp at which she is currently working is owned and run by her denomination. All of her family are involved in her church, and her friends are also all members of this denomination. Amanda is quite aware that she had lived a pretty sheltered and parochial life. "A pretty small world," she admits.

At the same time, Amanda has recently struggled with a number of life transitions and difficulties. She has transferred colleges, programs, and living arrangements a few times. She suffered a devastating breakup with a boyfriend last year. And she is struggling with strained relationships with her father and brother. After graduating from high school, Amanda started at a denominational college on the East Coast, mostly to get away from all of her high school classmates who were planning to attend the denominational college closer to home. She enjoyed that, but then the next summer met a nice guy at her camp, one and a half years her junior, with whom she fell in love. They carried on a long-distance romantic relationship over her sophomore year, talking a lot on the phone. That spring, Amanda decided to transfer to the denominational college closer to home, where her boyfriend was enrolled, in order to be close to him. That involved a lot of moving around, but Amanda thought it would be worth it. Her boyfriend told her that he loved her, they talked about marriage, and, as she says, she gave him her heart. That summer they both worked at the same summer camp again, and their relationship grew increasingly physical. At that same time, Amanda observes in retrospect, he seemed to be becoming more emotionally distant. They talked less and less and "made out heavily" more and more. They mostly kept their clothes on, Amanda says, but there was "touching" that she now regrets. At the beginning of the fall semester, he dropped "the break-up bomb." She didn't know why. He tried to explain about "not having things in common and being incompatible," but Amanda didn't believe anything he said. "He was just making up excuses," she explains. "I think all of a sudden he just saw in college that there were a lot more girls and worlds out there that interested him." Amanda was devastated. "It was crushing, really disappointing, I was brokenhearted. For the first week, I couldn't eat anything, I was a mess. Really traumatic."

During the prior year, Amanda's father had told her that he thought she and her boyfriend were getting too serious, that "it was too much, too fast, and he didn't approve of the way we were interacting." Amanda was furious about that and stopped talking to him for a long while. Then when Amanda's boyfriend dumped her, she felt "humiliated," realizing her father was probably right. But then she did not want to talk to him because of that. In the midst of all of this, Amanda's brother—with whom Amanda used to be very close—married a woman from the same denomination, who is more conservative than anyone else in Amanda's family, pulling her brother toward an extremely strict outlook. Amanda, by contrast, says that she is something of a "liberal" relative to her denominational standards— she wears some jewelry and drinks coffee, which is officially proscribed by her faith, and skips church some weekends when she is exhausted, which is frowned on. "I tweak religious values my own special way," she explains. "I have a slightly different lifestyle because I'm single and young and living in a different time than older people like my parents were." As a result, she and her brother have drifted apart, which makes Amanda sad. "I think I have withdrawn from him some, because his lifestyle has changed so much. There are things in life that I like and enjoy, so we're so different it's hard to talk anymore. I still want to be able to be myself, but I don't want to make him uncomfortable, and I feel sometimes he judges me." In these and other ways, Amanda has been working through some difficult experiences and feelings in recent years.

When it comes to religious faith and practice generally, however, Amanda strikes me as anything but liberal. Most of her beliefs are quite conservative and central to her life. She tries to go to church regularly, whether at home, college, or camp. Sometimes at college she also goes to vespers on Friday nights. In Germany, Amanda went to a Bible study every Wednesday. Amanda has done missions trips overseas, which have included leading teams of students and being a public speaker. She has volunteered in college, for religious motives, to teach English to immigrants. She is adamant about no sex before marriage and has stuck to that in situations where many teens would not have. She reports that her most debilitating sin is losing her temper, which she knows "is wrong." Amanda prays daily and reads her Bible a few times a week. She has experienced God's providence guiding her life, and in some instances has heard God speaking to her. When I ask Amanda what she believes religiously, she, unlike many her age, lays it all out:

First and foremost, I believe that there is a God who is all-powerful and all-knowing, who created the whole universe. I believe what the Bible says about him. I believe that he is three, that there are three persons in God, not really sure how to explain that, but the whole Trinity concept. And that God sent his Son to die for us, every person, so that we could live forever. People who believe in Jesus and accept him as their Savior will be saved. When people die, they go to sleep but their bodies decay. When Jesus comes again the second time, to bring justice to the universe, there will be a judgment. Everyone will be raised back from the dead. God will recreate the bodies of the saved and will destroy those who do not believe, extinguish totally. He will cleanse the earth.

I ask Amanda why Jesus had to die on the cross, why he could not simply teach and die a natural death. "He had to come to die in order for us to be saved. He's taking the punishment of our sin, there has to be justice, so instead of us dying, Christ died, a real concrete expression of love and justice at the same time. He had to prove that what God does is out of love." So how, I ask, does all of this influence her life, if in any way? "I would definitely say it's a big influence in the way I live my life," Amanda replies, "the purpose I have in it, my attitude toward other people and why I'm here. I think it would really be hard for me to be happy and have a decent life, have something to look forward to, without faith." Amanda's religious beliefs come out strongly again when we discuss the basis of human morality:

For me, morality is generally guided by religion. I look at most things for a moral I should know, read the Bible, figure it out. Everything for me is based off of "Love God, love other people." If anything is a contradiction to that, then it's bad. The big stuff, most of it is stated right in the Bible. God created the universe and it is governed by his character and therefore his character is good and love and mercy and all that. Then everything outside of that is bad. That's my explanation, and the Bible has a lot more specific examples that I can look [up] for reference.

For these reasons, Amanda feels she is different from most people her age. "I'm definitely not the norm because I live by my faith instead of, I feel most people don't when they're 21, in college, maybe partying a lot and living for themselves. I don't do any of that stuff." She admits that she feels "abnormal," but insists, "I know mine's a good lifestyle 'cause I think I'm happier where I'm at." When it comes to the idea of trying drugs, for example, Amanda declares, "I've smelled enough pot that I don't need to try it—overseas, big crowds of people blowing smoke in my face. It's gross, unhealthy, gives people bad breath, and they do things they don't control—it doesn't sound fun to me."

At the same time, Amanda's religious outlook is not rigidly ideological. Besides the "liberal" practice of wearing jewelry and drinking coffee, for instance, Amanda has enjoyed a few alcoholic drinks without qualms when traveling outside the United States—another breach of denominational teachings. Asked about this, Amanda explains that her general approach to specific denominational prohibitions is "I try to research and find out, if the Bible does not necessarily state it and it doesn't go against my 'love of God, love your neighbor,' then it's okay." She notes that in one passage the Bible says that women should not braid their hair, yet women in her church do braid their hair, which makes her skeptical of biblical literalism. More generally, Amanda observes,

> My denomination tends to have a "we're right and everyone else is wrong" attitude. I don't think that's necessarily true, because, just from history, tons of different religious of people have had that attitude, and it's turned out they've been wrong. They've done terrible things. I think everyone probably has a piece of the truth and we're trying to make God a lot smaller than he is, trying to dictate every aspect of everything as either right or wrong. It's harder than that. If you take a commandment too hard, it becomes an idol.

Amanda also wants to build into her outlook an appreciation of human diversity. "There are different people, everything's different, and we all have different personalities and ways of worshiping. For me specifically, I'm really touched by words, I love poetry and writing, so reading the Psalms is just wonderful. But different genres in the Bible touch people in different ways, so differences in the Bible touch more people." So what about non-Christians, I ask?

> The best answer to that question is in C. S. Lewis's *The Last Battle*. Even if people do not have the gospel explained to them in words, there are still choices they make. How do you live your life? Are you going to live for yourself or others? Other religions, they don't necessarily have to call it God, but they can worship the Christian God. It's hard for me because I know the Bible says you have to worship Jesus. But if you don't know who Jesus is, how are you supposed to make that choice? Maybe God embraces everyone who really lives for him, whether they know it or not.

Amanda says she prefers the word "spiritual" to "religious," since " 'religion' carries connotations of organized church, so the term to me is so cold and logical." Amanda also tells me that she believes abortion is morally wrong but also that she knows that her mother has had an abortion. "So that's personal to me, and she had really good reasons. So it's a situation by situation thing." And on the question of her moral views of gays and lesbians, although Amanda believes same-sex sexual relations "violates what we are created for," she also says that "people are probably born with tendencies that aren't necessarily meant to be, but I don't think they're going to hell because of it."

So, how, I ask, has Amanda changed religiously and spiritually since her teenage years? "I think that now I'm a lot more willing to figure out on my own what I believe and not feel like I have to believe what somebody tells me is right. I feel like God is trying to get me to do that." She says she attends church about as often, reads the Bible a little less, and prays a lot more. "Being older, you can pray in different ways, more personal ways to talk to God." Amanda says that although her faith tradition is pretty strict, her parents have encouraged her to "go out and discover on my own what I think is right. They didn't force me." In recent years, Amanda has in fact developed her own views about church and the Sabbath:

> For me, personally I choose not to go to church sometimes because I need the sleep, because the Sabbath was created for refreshment and rejuvenation and spiritual fulfillment. I think a lot of times that happens in organized churches—you have a support group there, can share, and all help each other kind of thing. There's a certain amount of value in hearing the pastor speak, too, who's gone to school and studied the Bible and had that wisdom and knowledge that he can share. So I think there's definitely a balance there. But I think a lot of times what I need the most is just some quiet time with God, and walking and taking a hike with some friends and playing guitar up a mountain. To me that's church. I believe that, but a lot of other people in my church don't.

Still, she says, in general, "even though I'm now on my own, most of the core beliefs I have grown up with are still true, as far as I stand."

What about Amanda's own possible religious doubts? I ask. "I haven't had doubts about my relationship to God, I've gotten stronger in my faith. But my faith in my own denomination has gotten weaker." Amanda explains that her beliefs have been strengthened by personal experiences of God's care. For example, while traveling in Europe she once somehow got herself into a bad situation—alone, late at night, in a big city, by herself, wearing bright clothes, without knowing the language, and unclear where to go. She felt frightened about being assaulted, which, judging by what she has said, seems to have been a real possibility. "I just prayed to God and walked in the middle of the street. And I felt such a strong presence of God, it was just the kind of thing you cannot explain away." She got to where she needed to go safely. Amanda also recounts other experiences of confusion and danger overseas when helpful people showed up in highly unlikely ways, seemingly from nowhere, and took care of her. "I've seen things that have happened that I believe providence did. I don't know if I'd go so far as to say that was an angel, just God's spirit." On occasion, Amanda believes God has even spoken to her: "It was so clear and distinct from my own voice, it was like he talked to me, though that doesn't happen a lot."

I ask Amanda to reflect on her view of the relevance of mainstream religion for young people in America today. She answers:

> Religion is not made for young people. Look at the entertainment aspect: even education, the average elementary school all the way through college, it's so oriented around movies, video games, entertainment, fun books. Why on earth would young people go to church if it doesn't offer anything personal as a reward, especially when church

just tells them what they're doing wrong? Why would we go? To youth, it's boring. I myself didn't like going to church when I was younger, and sometimes still don't when I feel lectured at. I listen to lectures all week long, so that's not fun. It really doesn't give comfort when kids are doing all these things wrong in their lives. That's how a lot of youth view it.

Amanda also expresses her share of criticism of U.S. culture and politics. If she could change one thing about the world, for example, she said it would be for America to become "less consumer-driven. Like buying stuff and living the life you want is not important, compared to conserving the environment and helping people who are less advantaged. We in America lead our lives trying to collect all these things and we don't have time to enjoy them, I wish that would change." Amanda observes that many Europeans are more laid-back, which she likes. So she worries about America's "consumer-driven economy":

If you don't need something, well, like girls, for instance, will go out and shop, like, for therapy, buy stuff they don't need in order to "make over" their closet and get rid of all their other stuff. It just seems like such a waste. The raw materials it takes to make all this stuff, aside from just clothes, it's a waste. Common sense says, first of all, our environment, all the stuff we do, the plastics, the gas [is too much]. To have all that money, all you need, why not give it to someone else who isn't quite as fortunate?

Amanda also expresses concern about the United States' military endeavors overseas. "I don't really appreciate our whole policing-the-world attitude. The Iraq and Afghanistan wars are a mess." At the same time, Amanda does not trust any American politicians, does not expect to vote in the next presidential election—"I don't feel like my vote would count"—and is not politically involved in any other way.

Still, when it comes to more interpersonal relations and behaviors, Amanda is clear about what she thinks. She believes, for example, that everyone has a moral responsibility to help others in need, because "it's kind and compassionate, and that's what God would do. Everybody's deserving. That's what God *did* do when he was here—not to do so is very selfish, just sad." In discussing her own work volunteering to teach English as a second language, she notes, "That was exciting, to me, that's the way to live out my faith. I find a lot more fulfillment in helping someone else. It wasn't religious, just teaching English, but still cool." When she gets older, Amanda says she plans to tithe fully 10 percent of her income to the church, though she gives away very little money now because she says she has so little to spare.

As the end of our interview approaches, Amanda reports that she intends to teach high school history when she graduates from college. In the long run, she wants to earn her doctorate. "I've always wanted to be a doctor." About other future goals, she says, "I want to publish something. I want to go on some more missions trips, finish college, learn how to do stuff like rock climbing and dancing, stuff like that. That's what I want most." Amanda also desires to get married some day, though not soon. "Right now I'm just getting over my past relationship, and I don't really want to think of having one, personally, so I'm just waiting." But, she says, when the time comes, "I want to love somebody for life and have them love me for life, to be that close to somebody. You're committed to each other and it's that safe." Meanwhile, Amanda's rule about physical involvements now is "Anything that I would be ashamed of other people seeing, I'd try and stay away from." So what then, I ask, about the many young people her age who "hook up" for sex? She answers, "It seems like that would be pretty causal and potentially devastating for a lot of people. You just use people for physical gratification as the end result, which is pretty callous. It's out of touch, it should be more meaningful, seems pretty pointless." Amanda's view of cohabiting before marriage to test out one's relational compatibility is also not very sympathetic: "I think it's a great excuse to get all the good stuff without having a commitment." Her reaction to relativistic approaches to morality in general is also similar: "That's really wishy-washy. Some stuff is obviously wrong in every culture. That's where I have to come back to my belief on everything right or wrong is based off of God's character."

We finish up, and I wonder if I've gotten burned after sitting three hours in the sun. Amanda bids me a gracious goodbye and heads back to camp. I hang out a bit longer, enjoying the beautiful setting. I sit, trying to puzzle out the many life patterns and social forces that seem to be at work in the lives of the various emerging adults I am interviewing. They all seem so different. The diversity and complexity is immense. Yet I am beginning to hear some common themes. I hope, as I pack up, that I can come to better understand all of these matters by the time the interviews are completed.

CONCLUSION

There is, as we have said, no way for three emerging adults to somehow represent their entire age cohort. Brad, June, and Amanda are simply three young Americans, whose lives are quite different, whose stories serve here to introduce some life experiences that many emerging adults encounter, and whose stories will illustrate some of the findings that will emerge in later chapters of this book. If nothing else, their interviews reveal how broad a range of experiences American emerging adults can have in life. In other ways, far from being characteristic, the foregoing accounts have some highly atypical themes. For instance, Amanda's conservative views about sex before marriage, critique of mass consumerism, and expressed regrets about her past romantic relationship are unusual among her peers, as we will show in the next chapter. Still, Brad, June, and Amanda provide a helpful starting point from which to move forward and to which to refer back.[2]

2

The Cultural Worlds
of Emerging Adults

I T IS CRUCIAL TO UNDERSTAND the religious and spiritual worlds of emerging adults within the broader context of the larger cultural worlds in which they live and which they use to construct their own lives. Emerging adults' religious and spiritual assumptions, experiences, outlooks, beliefs, and practices do not exist in compartmentalized isolation from their larger cultural worldviews and lived experiences but are often related to and powerfully shaped by them. Before launching into our analysis of emerging adults' religious and spiritual lives, therefore, we need to provide an orienting overview of these larger cultural worlds. We will describe a number of prevailing, mainstream themes that emerged from the 230 personal interviews. Interspersed among these main themes we mention some less commonly voiced ones that indicate differing cultural emphases among smaller numbers of emerging adults, providing a counterpoint to the most common ones.

It is impossible to convey in one summarizing chapter like this the full richness and complexity of contemporary emerging adult culture. We are talking about 46 million young people in the United States whose lives encompass personal outlooks and experiences as diverse as those seen in the previous chapter. Most of today's emerging adults do share many elements of a common culture, which we seek to describe here. But even within that common culture we find different emphases, experiences, and cultural expressions. This summary chapter therefore unavoidably over-simplifies the actual reality of emerging adult culture, even as it works to provide some balance and complexity in the process.

33

IMPORTANT TYPICAL AND ALTERNATIVE CULTURAL THEMES

Most American emerging adults today assume, encounter, and express the kind of viewpoints and experiences described in this chapter. Among them are also intermingled some less common cultural outlooks and experiences that reflect some of the complexities and differences existing among emerging adults.

Transitions, Transitions, Transitions

Perhaps the most pervasive, consistent theme in the lives of emerging adults is the fact of their frequent and varied major life transitions. To an extent matched by no other time in the life course, emerging adults enjoy and endure multiple, layered, big, and often unanticipated life transitions.[1] They move out, they move back, they plan to move out again. They go to college, they drop out, they transfer, they take a break for a semester to save money, some graduate, some don't. They want to study architecture, they hate architecture, they switch to criminal justice, a different career path. Their parents separate, make up, get divorced, remarry. They take a job, they quit, they find another, they get promoted, they move. They meet new friends, their old friends change, their friends don't get along, they meet more new people. They get new roommates, their roommates don't work out, they find a new apartment. They buy insurance, they wreck their car, they cancel their insurance, they borrow a car. They find their soulmate, they get involved, their soulmate dumps them, they are crushed. They believe in saving sex for meaningful relationships, they hook up, they get angry with themselves, they look for a meaningful relationship. They smoke, they want to quit smoking, they quit for some days, they start smoking again. In these and other ways, for emerging adults not a lot in life is stable or enduring. Some of what seemed to be proves unreliable or unpredictable. Other things they know from the start are going to change. Changes are incessant. A lot is up in the air. There is sometimes too much to manage. Handling the basics of life demands a lot of time, energy, and attention. Thus many emerging adults said things like "I live at home with my dad. I had moved out on my own, I got an apartment, and I stayed out for about a year and a half, but I had to quit my job and I went to move in back home"; "Yeah, big transition. I just graduated from college and I was in town there so I'm moving back home, or to the city and going to law school in the fall, so I'm trying to get prepared for that and an apartment and figure out the roommate situation. A lot of stuff going on right now."

Standing on One's Own

The central, fundamental, driving focus in life of nearly all emerging adults is getting themselves to the point where they can "stand on their own two feet."[2] Life's major challenge for them is transitioning from dependence to independence, from reliance on others to self-sufficiency, from being under others' authority and eye to living on their own. Emerging adults know that life is not easy, and many are learning that it is even harder than they expected. Most of those who have not already ruined their chances in life through poor decisions and bad luck are well aware that they could still fail. They know that if they do not do things right, they could end up dependent, needy, and lacking the qualifications, experience, or resources needed to live the self-supporting and comfortable lives to which (as we will show) they aspire. So successfully getting themselves standing up on their own two feet, without the ongoing help of parents and others, is the ever-present and overriding challenge of life. Some are doing pretty well at it; others are struggling. In any case, learning to stand on one's own is priority number one. Here is what that can sound like:

> About three years ago, I was 18 or 19, just out of high school, you know, had my parents' car that I was able to use, so I was running around doing anything and everything that I could do at that time. Now, I pretty much just go to school, come home, stay with my little girl all day and things like that. So yeah, my views have changed a lot. Now I know I have to look at things in the bigger picture. I have to consider getting my own house, getting my car and my truck and things like that.

And:

> My parents still cover the bills because when I was a student, I didn't work, so I didn't have an income, at all. But now that I'm going to be starting to get a job, I'm going to start paying for my own bills, and kind of just, chip in to the family. And then, gradually, when I have the money, move out.

So Much to Figure Out

Most emerging adults are close to being overwhelmed with all of the skills, tasks, responsibilities, systems, and procedures they are having to learn. Whether or not they liked high school, they now realize that at least it provided a highly predictable structure that governed their lives for many years and told them what to do, how to do it, and when to get it done. Most of that secure structure is now gone, and the list of new things to learn in an open-ended world is endless and sometimes almost crushing. How do you get your car fixed when you have to work all the time? How do you get reimbursement from health insurance for an injury? How do you defend yourself in court against ridiculous charges by an arrogant police officer? How do you get more serious in a romantic relationship without it getting too serious or stalling out? How do you get into graduate school? How do you get out of a two-year lease on an apartment you have to leave? How do you delay your army deployment when you just found out your mom has cancer? Some enjoy meeting these challenges and take it all in stride. Others fall apart in various ways, "hit the restart button," move back in with parents, and start to figure life out again from square one. In any case, figuring it all out tends to consume huge amounts of time, energy, and attention. One emerging adult, for instance, said: "Currently, I work full-time, go to school full-time, am very busy, I don't have a lot of time for a lot of things—very stressful, very stressful. And this is my first quarter doing both working and going to school so I'm kind of having issues adjusting." Another observed:

> I think we are expected to always be doing or moving forward toward something and we are always pushed. Knowing I am graduating, I need money for things, you have to get a job, you can't just live without health insurance. I am learning that stuff, so it is kind of like, I don't know, you are kind of forced to settle for maybe a job you wouldn't want because you need those things.

Don't Have Enough Money

Most emerging adults feel broke, whether they objectively actually are out of money or not. By their own accounts, they live from paycheck to paycheck, just scraping by, hardly getting the money to cover the basics and enjoy the various fun items they want besides. Ask them about the idea of voluntary financial giving to worthy organizations, for instance, and they almost uniformly say "I don't have any money to give." For some, this is literally true—they are barely making it. For others, the perception of not having any money seems to result from the relative deprivation of having their eyes set on the more self-sufficient, financially comfortable, materially equipped lifestyles they are aiming for. Most of the transitions, the figuring new things out, and the learning to stand on one's own has—as we will show—the long-run goal of enjoying materially comfortable lives. And by the standard of that imagined goal, emerging adults are poor. As part of that, many also tend to be working at jobs that are not the career positions they aspire to land and do not pay the kind of wages they think they will earn in the future. So current pay can seem meager; often it is. How rich or poor one is has an objective side, but perceptions about the matter are also significantly influenced by what one uses as a reference point. Emerging adults today for the most part view themselves as tight on money if not poor. They therefore commonly say things like "I'm not one of those people that have the money"; "I'm a broke college student"; "I'm trying to get enough money so I can be self-sufficient but at the moment it's not really succeeding"; "I don't have any money to give right now, if I did I'm sure I would, but I have a minimum wage job and I'm not even getting full-time, I get maybe 30 hours if I'm lucky, so I really don't have that much money." And "I give a dollar at church and if I have money for the bums, a coin or something. But as far as money goes, I'm about to go to college, so I'm broke."

Optimism for Their Personal Future

The 230 emerging adults who were interviewed are as a group some of the most optimistic people we have ever encountered or listened to—at least when it comes to their own personal lives and futures. For the most part, their eyes are firmly set on the future, and they look to it with great hope and confidence. Some are beset with trepidation or despondency about what awaits them in their lives. But these are not many. Rather, for most, their hopes run high, their expected prospects are bright, good things are anticipated. If "reality" at some point settles in as people come to terms with the hard facts of their own limitations, misfortunes, and failures, it has not settled in for most of America's 18- to 23-year-old emerging adults. Even many of those whose lives are in desperate straits, beset by the most unfortunate blunders or terrible circumstances, tend nevertheless to gird themselves up with hope and confidence that things will get better, that the future will be bright. Even many young men and women who are self-imprisoned by addictions or debilitated by severe depression insist that things can and will only get better, that they are on the road to good things, that life will turn out well. In short, *cynical, weary, jaded, despondent, defeated,* and the like are words that describe very few emerging adults in America—at least, normally, for more than a day or two. Rather, they talk like this: "This is my optimal path, what I've always wanted. You know, I really think where I'm going is exactly where I wanted to go in high school and the beginning of college." "Right now I'm headed into finding my first, real, year-round job, and that's very exciting to me. A lot of changes have happened, but they're positive changes." "I think I'm making a turn-around, like before I was going down, things that were going on in my life or whatever I was doing was wrong. But now I think I'm going in the right direction." "My son's made me the happiest I've ever been in my life. Everything's not where I want it to be, but I think with time, it will be where I want it to be, because like I said, I'm very determined, I'm absolutely sure of myself." Even a single mother who was homeless with her children said this: "I'm still lost, still lost, just taking it one day at a time and God's gonna show me which way he wants me to go, because right now I am lost. I need to change, I am so lost, I haven't found my purpose but that doesn't really affect me. I'm just like one day he gonna show me, one day he gonna show me, I just haven't found that one day, but he gonna show me."

A Less Typical Theme—Struggling to be Optimistic. A minority of emerging adults we interviewed have already been dragged down by various difficulties in life and express a far more complicated and sometimes bleak vision of the future than most. They try to be optimistic but in the end find it difficult. Wavering between hope and despondency, they sometimes view their futures as fairly hopeless, offering little worth fighting for. A few of these—often starting from disadvantaged positions—have made what they know are foolish choices that have compromised their life prospects. A more extreme subset of these are emerging adults who seem to be clinically depressed and do not know about or have access to resources that might help them deal with their debilitating depression. They struggle on a daily basis simply to keep going, not to throw in the towel. Life is more of a battle, and though they may feel determined to make things work out, it is not entirely clear how they will. They say things like this:

> There's a lot of people I avoid. Like, I just found out that one of my friends slept with my kid's dad when we were still together, so I just avoid everybody. I'm just so mad, she was a really good friend. I just

never talk to her anymore. I just gave up. I don't really talk to a whole lot of my friends any more. I usually just stay at home most of the time. I don't go nowhere.

And: "Nothing really excites me. I've been through everything that could possibly ever be exciting to me, and it's like a ride, if you're riding the biggest ride first, you won't like the smallest rides later, they're not as exciting if you ride the big one first, they're boring, I've just gotten bored by it all." Such cases do exist, although among all emerging adults they are far from the norm.

Smarting from Hard Lessons Learned

Widespread emerging adult optimism about the future does not mean, however, that they have not suffered hard knocks in the past. Many have. Already by age 18 to 23, many emerging adults have endured some of their own or others' alcoholism, drug addictions, sexual exploitations, divorces, unpleasant arrests, relational betrayals, frightening accidents, academic failures, job disappointments, parental abandonment, racism, deaths of friends, and more. Many have suffered a variety of other consequences of their various risky behaviors and self-described poor choices. Many are stinging with the hurts of living problemed lives in what seems a broken world and are still working on recovering. From some, this sounds like "God, I was so stupid and, man, did I pay a price for those idiotic decisions! Will never do that again." For others, the litany of problems and hurts seems endless and irresolvable. Of course, some have lived fairly simple and easy lives, and most are coping more or less well overall. But many have definitely suffered some of life's bruising, are beginning to accumulate scars, and now grimace and smart as they look back and try to make sense of the hurt and blunders. The following sample gives an idea of the range of hard experiences and feelings with which emerging adults are often dealing:

> A good friend of mine died about a year ago. He, uh, committed suicide, and it was really a, a surprise to me. We'd been friends since, like, middle school. He was someone that, you know, you wouldn't expect to do that. He didn't leave a note or anything. So, it's been hard for me because now I wonder, do I really know my friends? Are they happy? Sometimes I think about that, and it makes me sad.

> My sister was raped three years ago. It, I, none of us are anywhere nearly the same people we were before. I can't even imagine my family without that. It's like that drastic.

> I was a dumb little girl, dumb. If I could go back to when I was 14, I would never have lost my virginity that young 'cause that's awful, 14 is awful. I cannot tell you how many people I would have told "No," but [instead] I was like "Uh-huh, okay." Just stupid decisions I made.

> I wasn't in school for a year, and so I feel like I'm really behind. And I'm not working, so I'm in a lot of debt. I just feel like everything just kinda went wrong. Now I'm just starting to get in the right direction.

My friend died of a brain tumor four years ago. I always feel guilty about it because I wasn't there for her when she died, just wasn't a very good friend. Honestly, thinking back on it I was mad at her for having cancer. I know it's silly, but she was always the perfect friend—the cheerleader, blond, smart. Everyone loved her. Everything about her was perfect. Then all of a sudden she gets cancer, and it's like, "No, you can't do that." I was just mad that my perfect friend, who I looked up to my entire life, was all of a sudden helpless. She was a good, really strong person, could conquer anything. And then all of a sudden there's something that she couldn't do, like honestly helpless. She couldn't help dying. So, I mean, I feel guilty for being angry at her and not being there to support her, just because I was just, uck. I did not like the situation. My way of dealing with it was to ignore it, which was terrible. I just didn't know what to do, so, yeah, I think about that all the time. And I'm just like [makes a sound of frustration], "Why did I do that?!" I should've been there with her every step of the way. I kinda inched away. But I should've been there supporting her, talking to her all the time. I shouldn't have felt uncomfortable talking to her, and so I just feel bad about that.

My boyfriend, he slept with my best friend[3]—since I was 11 years old, I had known her my whole life—in the same room I was sleeping in. And I did not handle it at all, in any way, shape, or form. Right after it happened, the first week after it happened, I was so depressed. I didn't get out of bed. I just didn't go to class. I didn't do anything. Well, I'd go to my two choir classes in the morning, which I liked, and then leave school, and I would go to my friend's house. Her parents worked, so they weren't there. And I would sleep in her bed all day long. That's all I did for a week. I really struggled with it for a really long time, and I honestly would say am just recently getting totally just okay with the whole situation.

Watching my dad get arrested was really bad, and then having to be in the courtroom with my mom for sentencing and hearing all his stuff for the first time. We didn't know about it, like, "Did you know?" and Mom was like, "No idea." It all came out at once, what actually happened, 'cause the whole time he was like, "I didn't do this. I didn't do this. I didn't do this." And then he was "Okay, well I did it." That was like being hit by a truck. It was a lot to take in, 'cause it has been going on since I was in sixth grade, I guess, and then to hear about it now. I'm a junior in college, and it's a lot. It's just made me more cautious, and that's sad, because he's the only the dad I've ever had. But it's hard for me to trust what he says. I wanna be, like, "You're still the best dad that I've ever had" and all that, but in the end it's, like, he lied to us for this long just to make himself get ahead.

I was a victim of attempted rape by someone really close to my family, a really old man, and my family didn't help at all. I was told not to talk about it, literally told to not bring it up: "You are not going to talk about it." To hide it. But you can't hide something like that, and it really hurts. That went on for three or four years. I was alone for a long time, had to take care of myself and get out of a really bad situation on my own. And none of them really helped. I am not really sure why my family was like that, you know? They are not those kinds of people at all. I don't think they realized how bad it was, or to this day understand what happened. And maybe my parents feel guilt because they are not around a lot. I felt alone for a really long time. I finally went to counseling, which gave me strength to talk to my family about it, because they were still around this person, and it was awful. I mean, then they had to believe me. And then I actually saw him. It was so bad, I mean it was really bad. I actually saw him last fall. He was at one of my parents' parties, and my family for the first time actually took care of me and told him to leave me alone. But because of that experience I have become a really strong, independent person, which I don't necessarily like. I know this sounds really weird, but when you become too self-reliant, it is hard to let other people in. It sounds really crazy, because you hear all these women who say they are so strong and independent, but sometimes that can work against you. Sometimes I don't want to be too strong. I want to make sure I am balanced, but I do have a guard up a lot. I have a lot of fears, and, I mean, rightly so. When something like that happens to you, you are going to be scared. But sometimes it can hinder relationships.

The guy that murdered my uncle, he got off. Yeah, he killed my uncle two days after his birthday. And then my youngest sister recently got assaulted. A boy hit her and broke her jaw in two places. So now my little 15-year-old sister, mouth wired shut for six weeks. The boy was 18. When we went to his house to confront him, they called the police on us. But when the police came, they didn't take him or nothin'. They didn't arrest him for assault on a minor or sexual harassment or nothin'. They just left him, and now they can't find him. We sat there in front of the house. The police got there. We didn't touch him. Nobody had guns. We didn't do nothin' to nobody. He assaulted a minor. He's supposed to be in the car. They didn't take him, so now my momma [is] pressin' charges against the police officer too. And now this boy's on the run. Makes me angry 'cause that's another one of my biggest pet peeves. I don't like liars, and I don't like women-beaters. Makes me very upset. What's the point of even callin' the police when they're not gonna solve the problem! They didn't punish him. We could've solved it, could've came around with guns, coulda shot the house up. But we didn't do nothin' like that. We sat around there, waited for the police, didn't get into no violent altercations. So why didn't this boy go? That made me upset. I guess because it was a young black girl [victim] or somethin'. I don't know. But I know if I hit somebody they woulda took me away.

No Regrets

Despite often smarting from hard lessons learned, most of the emerging adults who were interviewed explicitly denied feeling any regrets about any of their past decisions, behaviors, or problems. Reinforcing their widespread feeling of optimism about the future, most of the survey respondents—including many of those with miserably depressing histories and current problems, as well as those who seem to take full responsibility for their own mistakes and stupidities—insisted that the past was the past, that they learned their lessons well, that they would not change a thing even if they could, that what's happened is part of who they have become, and that they have no regrets about anything at all. In fact, many emerging adults also appear, we think, to harbor regrets about the past even when they deny that they do. They clearly do not want to see themselves as having regrets, even though they also get angry with themselves about mistakes and continue sometimes to be haunted by problems from the past. Their thoughts and feelings on this matter are inconsistent. It is almost as if they feel that admitting having regrets would somehow be capitulating to a self-doubt or compromise or nascent despondency against which they are holding out at all costs through the power of positive thinking. Many of these emerging adults, it seems, are too young to name and own the unalterable disappointments with life that admitting regrets might entail. Instead, the stance of "no regrets" puts a good face on matters that are in fact problematic, frames the difficult past in an encouraging light, and keeps all of life's energies moving forward in an upbeat and constructive direction. It also helps to protect a sense of personal self—which seems *sacred* to emerging adults—against threats to the ultimate good of "being yourself" in a world in which the self is central, since actually having regrets implies that the self one has become embodies something that is wrong or undesirable. When life is centrally about being "who I am," one must negate the existence of truly regrettable decisions and experiences, since even the worst and hardest have gone into making one "who I am." Furthermore, the very idea of regrets presupposes a clear sense of good and bad, right and wrong by which to judge, which—as we will show—many emerging adults lack. Therefore, answering whether quitting drugs had an impact on his life, for example, one guy explained, "Yeah, absolutely, I'm so much more clear-minded. Now that I'm where I am, it kinda makes me see it was bringing me down, even though I don't regret it, I don't really regret it all. I think everything that you do makes you who you are, so I don't really regret it." Expressing unhappiness about her first sexual experience, one woman said, "I'm not happy about it. I wish I would have waited later and maybe got with a person that I knew better, because I thought I knew him really well but I ended up not. But I don't regret it because I learned from it." Another spoke of the same topic in this way: "I was 15. It just happened. I mean, we had been dating for a long time, but I don't regret it. Even though it just happened, I don't regret it." And, after a long explanation by one girl about how she invested so much into promoting her boyfriend's career goals that she herself could never finish more than one semester of college, she concluded, "I put aside my dreams to try and help him follow his, for him to become a cop, but I feel like if I was just a little more selfish, I could have advanced myself a little bit more. It's a lesson learned. I don't really regret it at all."

A Less Typical Theme—Overcoming Major Obstacles: Some of today's emerging adults have already overcome big obstacles to living healthy, happy lives. It is not merely that they have been hurt by bad environments, harmful experiences, and poor decisions and are nonetheless facing the future with optimism and no regrets. Some have actually confronted and succeeded in overcoming major problems and debilitating challenges that threatened to seriously damage and in some cases destroy their lives. Some have broken free from life-threatening addictions to alcohol and hard drugs. Others have prevailed through appalling family and school situations and are moving on with their own flourishing lives. Some, with no resources or support, have devoted themselves to educational achievements that have required immense determination, perseverance, and hard work. Yet others have overcome sickness and disease, terrible tragedies, and other incapacitating hardships and misfortunes. In such cases, we, the authors and our interview team, found ourselves admiring and inspired by these young people who had risen to meet challenges of major proportions and succeeded. The following longer excerpts from three emerging adult women's interviews give some sense of these stories of overcoming great obstacles.

> Having my daughter and placing her for adoption was just incredibly sad and painful. At the same time, it was also very happy, because I was able to give something to her new parents that money can't buy, that they couldn't get for themselves. And I was giving her a better life. But that's the hardest and saddest thing I've ever done in my entire life. It took a while for it to really sink in. I knew that it was the best thing, and I haven't ever had regrets. But that doesn't mean it wasn't still sad and doesn't still hurt, even if you have done the right thing. It made me a better person to do something so completely and totally selfless. I was selfish, but it was still selfless. It benefited me personally, but it was also overwhelmingly gratifying to know that I had done for these two people and for this child [something] that nobody else could do.

> My dad was hit on his motorcycle by a drunk driver, flew 40 feet, wasn't wearing a helmet. I actually passed his body on the road, didn't realize it was him, and I went home. When his motorcycle wasn't there, I drove back, ran across the street, and I recognized it was him on the road. He was smashed up against the curb with paramedics working on him. He was in really bad shape, in the ICU for three weeks. It's been a really long road, and there's a long road ahead for us, like a year in recovery. He still can't walk. That's been the most life-changing experience of my life. It's crazy, but after I passed my dad's body on the road, I felt, I knew

it wasn't me thinking. I felt the Holy Spirit say to me, "We take life so much for granted," and it just hit me, "We do." And then everything changed. I still think back on that and don't wanna take life for granted. I don't wanna give up on my family just because of our problems, to give up on my dad just because he wasn't trying, because he prioritizes other things above me. I was kind of at that point then, like "Whatever, that's the way it is, fine." I was always afraid that he wouldn't walk me down the aisle because he has all these problems with my mom. And now I think that he will. So I don't wanna give up.

My children's father left me five days after my son was born. I couldn't go to work for six weeks, had an eviction notice on my apartment, had to sleep in my car with my kids. It was the hardest thing a mother could ever have to do. We had to get out and find somewhere to wash up. No matter how sick I was, I had to just suck it up and go to work and beg for whatever hours I could get, had to find any day care that would take them, had to go to the government office and try to get help. That made me stronger, not depending on nobody but myself. You keep going, and it's gonna be bad but you don't have time to cry, you suck it up, get up, let's go. Still, I would say I feel like I've been blessed beyond belief, because you know, I'm here, I made it. I lost my house, was homeless, but now I have my own house and car. I'm working; I have my health; my children are healthy. I'm not gonna complain. I didn't get the short end of the stick; I got a blessing.

Relationships with Parents Improving

During their earlier adolescence, when they were surveyed and interviewed for prior waves of data collection, relatively few of the respondents had serious problems with their parents. With some notable exceptions, most teenagers and their parents seem to basically get along most of the time, if not positively enjoy each other. During the ages of 18 to 23, most of the participating emerging adults have reported that their relationships with their parents are improving even more, that they and their parents have become closer, more able to talk, less bothered by conflict, and stronger in their bonds of understanding and affection. The change is not usually dramatic, but it is often perceptible nonetheless. Little issues many of the respondents and their parents used to fight about just do not seem so important anymore. Parents have often loosened their grip of authority on their children, which they greatly appreciate. Most emerging adults have also lived and matured enough to be able to appreciate their parents in new ways and from new perspectives. They have broken out of many, though not all, of the old ruts. Many of them feel good about being able to relate to their parents on a somewhat more equal basis, almost as real adults. One respondent, for instance, said that relations with his parents had improved "drastically, because three years ago I was still in high school. We just get along a lot better now. We don't necessarily talk that much more, but when we do talk it's not arguing as much, it's changed a lot." Another said, "Oh, yeah. We've become a lot closer than we were when I was in high school. When you're away from home and you see the big picture, you're not young and naïve, and you kind of see at your parents' level more than you did when you were in high school. So I think we're kind of, we're more on the same level now." A third explained:

> I think now my dad's realized that, okay, I am an adult and am doing something with my life and, you know, back off a little bit. So the dynamic has changed where I'm allowed more freedom. And we're trying to get to this thing where we respect each other as adults, even though I'm, like, way low on the totem pole. But at least I'm on it, so that's cool.

A Less Typical Theme—Ongoing Problems: That many emerging adults are enjoying relative improvement in their relationships with their parents does not mean that all problems and conflicts have been resolved. The case of June in chapter 1 shows otherwise. Some emerging adults for whom parental relationships are improving still suffer from underlying struggles with or distance from their parents—the improvement is relative. Others simply have lousy relationships. One respondent, for example, said, "I'm not close to my mom, it's not so great, don't talk much. [Even though we fight] I've never used physical contact with her, but, not good, not really, just arguing and fighting all the time. Hasn't changed much, is really the same as before." These are not the majority, necessarily, but they exist and are important. Yet again, some have recently concluded or are in the process of concluding, sometimes bitterly, that they think relationships with parents that have been minimal or troubled in prior years are never going to improve. Many are resigning themselves to the fact that these relationships are beyond repair, perhaps dead. Often this giving up on a parent involves a semiestranged (usually) father who left home after a parental divorce years earlier and with whom the emerging adult had long held out hope for an improved or reconciled relationship. But time and events make it clear that the parent has repeatedly lied, will never change or deal with his or her child's problems, has no interest in knowing his or her child, is hopeless. The emerging adult then has to confront and accept the hurt of the loss of the hoped-for but apparently never-to-be-reconciled relationship. He or she in effect resolves to emotionally abandon the lost parent, to drop the previous hope of getting that parent back, of seeing the mother sober, say, or of having an active father who is proud of one's achievements. Many seem to have put such resolutions behind them and to be moving on—although it is not clear how much and for how many the emotional difficulty continues to haunt them as they move forward. The following statements from three different respondents (male and female) convey some of the pathos of these broken relationships:

> The past few years have made me realize that he will never change, no matter how bad I want him to. He is always out to hurt me. He just never believed in me, or [was supportive] whenever I was up against a hard time. Like tennis, I went to a really huge national tournament

and I was seeded second in the nation and had worked really, really hard and ended up losing the semifinals in a really close match. And my dad told me I should just quit. After that time I just stopped talking to him.

I don't want to hate my father. Just wish for him to come back around. [So, it's his decision that he's not in touch?] Mmm-hmm. Him and my mom just fought all the time, and he just left and didn't keep in contact with any of us. It's hard [starting to cry]. It's just hard. [You miss him?] Mmm-hmm [softly]. [Did you have a relationship to him when you were younger?] Yeah, all the time. I'm a daddy's girl bad [laughs]. [Have you tried to keep in touch with him?] Yeah, I tried. It just didn't work. He got a whole new relationship, and it's all about her and her kids.

We were never really close. I thought he was a very nice guy and that he was good for my mom. [But he wasn't.] There's not really anything I would change now. I mean I would change everything that has happened. I wish he could take it all back and be a different person, but since he has done this stuff, I would never, I could never forgive him for it, never now. His just not contacting me would probably be the only thing that would make me happy. Three years ago, he was in prison and I was happy. I never thought I would see him again because he was supposed to be in there for a long time. So yeah, I really would be happy if I never saw him again. I wish it was that easy. Honestly, now if something bad happened to him, and I was the only person able to help him, I don't think I would. That's how much hurt I felt and how much I don't want anything to do with him. It's just kind of weird, I guess, the way it works, someone who can bring you on this earth and, you know, not be connected.

Hard to See an Objective Reality Beyond the Self

The majority of emerging adults can express very well how people are shaped and bound by their personal subjective experiences. But most have great difficulty grasping the idea that a reality that is objective to their own awareness or construction of it may exist that could have a significant bearing on their lives. In philosophical terms, most emerging adults functionally (meaning how they actually think and act, regardless of the theories they hold) are soft ontological antirealists and epistemological skeptics and perspectivalists—although few have any conscious idea what those terms mean. They seem to presuppose that they are simply imprisoned in their own subjective selves, limited to their biased interpretations of their own sense perceptions, unable to know the real truth of anything beyond themselves. They are de facto doubtful that an identifiable, objective, shared reality might exist across and around all people that can serve as a reliable reference point for rational deliberation and argument. So, for example, when we interviewers tried to get respondents to talk about whether what they take to be substantive moral beliefs reflect some objective or universal quality or standard are simply relative human inventions, many—if not most—could not understand what we interviewers were trying to get at. They had difficulty seeing the possible distinction between, in this case, objective moral truth and relative human invention. This is not because they are dumb. It seems to be because they simply cannot, for whatever reason, believe in—or sometimes even conceive of—a given, objective truth, fact, reality, or nature of the world that is independent of their subjective self-experience and that in relation to which they and others might learn or be persuaded to change. Although none would put it in exactly this way, what emerging adults take to be reality ultimately seems to consist of a multitude of subjective but ultimately autonomous experiences. People are thus trying to communicate with each other in order to simply be able to get along and enjoy life as they see fit. Beyond that, anything truly objectively shared or common or real seems impossible to access.

Right and Wrong Are Easy

When asked how difficult or easy it is to know right and wrong in life today. nearly all respondents said it is easy. Many hardly had to even think about it. When then asked how hard it is to know right and wrong—regardless of how difficult it is to do what is morally right—again, nearly everyone said it is easy. Morality is like common sense; unless you are actively resisting it, it is not hard to know what to do or to do it. The vast majority are moral intuitionists—that is, they believe that they know what is right and wrong by attending to the subjective feelings or intuitions that they sense within themselves when they find themselves in various situations or facing ethical questions. Those subjective moral intuitions are themselves reported to be the product of right moral principles implanted deeply within their consciences when they were children by their parents, teachers, pastors, and other adult authorities. That early moral socialization, their implicit account goes, is ineradicable and reliable. Having been laid down early and deep, the moral principles cannot be removed or altered. All one has to do is pay some attention to what one feels or intuits in any situation and one will definitely know what is the morally right thing to do. In this way, emerging adults profess to be navigating the moral challenges of life with relative proficiency and ease. Some say that their deeply ingrained moral principles guide them to form their relationships and practices in such ways that they actually rarely even have to face a difficult moral problem or choice in the first place. Moral difficulties are simply precluded and averted by structuring life in ways that avoid them to begin with. The majority of emerging adults interviewed had difficulty thinking of even one example of a situation recently when they had some trouble deciding what was the morally right or wrong thing to do. Most of those who finally did come up with an example pointed to the moral and emotional difficulty they had in deciding whether or not to break up with a boyfriend or girlfriend. In short, thinking and living morally is quite effortless—you merely pay attention to your inner self, and it all comes fairly naturally. So in discussions about knowing right from wrong and doing the right thing, they almost uniformly offered the following kinds of replies. "I base a lot off instincts. I was brought up with a good idea of what was right and wrong, and if it was okay my head and heart tell me. I don't think it's very hard." "It's pretty easy, I just stay away from certain situations. That hasn't really changed, it's just easy for me." "Usually it's not hard, usually the wrong choice kinda glares at me like, 'No! Wrong!'" "Doing the right thing, it's pretty easy. I would feel bad if I knew it was wrong." "I've always been a really quick decision-maker. Making decisions has never been hard for me, so in terms of wrong and right, it kinda clicks in my head." "Intuition, sort of. I use judgment with everything like, it just kinda comes naturally. I can't think of anything that really actively influences me to decide what's right or wrong, or good or bad. Maybe it's just sort of how I've developed as a person that kinda helps things like that along." "I know in my heart if it's something that I'm just not comfortable doing, I would feel uncomfortable doing in my heart. I would say it's pretty easy to know. I have kind of a gut feeling with some things, so overall, it's pretty easy to trust my own instincts."

Not Hurting Others Is Self-Evident

One of the core principles emerging adults seem to presuppose in thinking about moral behavior is the imperative not to hurt others. "Others" here means anyone else. In this, they are essentially ethical consequentialists: if something would hurt another person, it is probably bad; if it does not and is not illegal, it's probably fine. Curiously, very few emerging adults—probably like many adults as well—are able to explain exactly why they think hurting others is morally wrong.[4] To them it is just obvious. As interviewers, we pointed out that more than a few people and tribes and cultures in history and around the world have not thought hurting others outside of their in-groups to be particularly bad. Some people positively enjoy hurting others. But that information did not change respondents' thinking, nor did it seem to prod them to try to better explain why hurting others is a categorical wrong. They did not appeal, for instance, to God's will, natural law, utilitarian principles, the Bible, or any other supposed source of universal moral truth to justify this belief. "Don't hurt others" functions instead as a kind of free-floating, unjustified supposition that informs intuitive moral feelings and opinions. Sometimes respondents might say that hurting another person would make them feel bad about themselves or that they would not want to live in a society in which everyone hurt everyone else. But why that itself should count in a moral argument they cannot say. In the end, they have difficulty explaining why the thinking of someone else who does not believes hurting others is wrong is in fact incorrect.

Karma Will Catch You

A surprising number of those interviewed—not a majority, but more than a few—spontaneously, explicitly referred to "karma" as a way to explain why it's best to act morally and why the universe is ultimately a just place. In evoking karma, they meant that good attitudes and behavior will be rewarded in this life and bad will be get what it deserves, too. "What goes around comes around," they explained. "Karma's a bitch," another said, making the point that you can't escape its merciless consequences. Talking about karma does not mean these emerging adults have any real interest in or knowledge about Hinduism, Sikhism, or Buddhism or believe in reincarnation. Nor was it merely a hip shorthand for describing societal social control or divine judgment. Many did not even seem aware of those possible connections. Rather, karma appears to have become a shared, pop culture way of explaining the fair operations of good and bad in the world—among emerging adults, at least. Karma functions as a reminder for emerging adults that they can't get away with bad stuff. It catches up to you. It pays off in the future to do the right thing. Bad people will get theirs. Almost everyone basically gets what he or she deserves. Karma helps keep some moral justice in the world. At the same time, karma does not require belief in a specific God or commitment to a particular religious tradition. Karma does not necessitate involvement in a religious congregation or the exercise of any particular spiritual or religious self-disciplines. Nor does karma specify any long-term—particularly afterlife—consequences for living different sorts of moral lives. Karma is much more palatable and individually manageable than, say, belief in a final judgment, divine rewards and punishments, and especially heaven and hell. In short, while nobody can escape karma, neither does karma displace the final authority of individuals over their own lives.

Everybody's Different

If people in the world represent complex combinations of similarities and differences, emerging adults in the United States today tend mostly to see the differences. Conversations with them clearly reveal their great sensitivity to the belief "Everybody's different," as they frequently say. Nearly any question asked of them about any norm, experience, rule of thumb, expectation, or belief in life is very likely to get an answer beginning with the phrase "Well, everybody's different, but for me…" Although nobody expresses the underlying viewpoint in so many words, it seems to be that humans share very little in common with each other, that you can't count on any common features or interests across people that binds them together or gives them a basis on which to work out disagreements. And the differences emphasized are not merely cross-cultural dissimilarities between, say, Americans and Chinese. As in well-known postmodernist theory, the differences actually drive down to individual personalities. Any given person has his or her own unique beliefs, tastes, feelings, thoughts, desires, and expectations. Nobody can presume to impose on or perhaps even fully understand those of another. Literally every individual is different. This, it seems, is not merely basic American individualism. It is individualism raised on heavy doses of multiculturalism and pumped up on the steroids of the postmodern insistence on disjuncture, *differance*, and differences "going all the way down." Few emerging adults have actually read Jacques Derrida or

Stanley Fish, but their effects seem to have trickled down in this way into popular prereflective consciousness among this population nonetheless. And so interviewers heard them saying thing like "I think the last few years have made me more aware of [how] what's right for me may be wrong for someone else or what's wrong for me may be okay for somebody else. I think it's made me more aware of other people's feelings about things." Concerning religious faith, one said, "You know, the Muslim religion is not right for me, but it doesn't make it wrong for them. I just think it's all subjective to each person. I really do think that everything is pretty much subjective." And to the question about how much material stuff people should buy and own or not own, another replied, "That's a personal choice. I don't know, I guess that's personal for everybody."

It's Up to the Individual

It is hardly surprising, in light of much of the foregoing, that according to emerging adults, the absolute authority for every person's beliefs or actions is his or her own sovereign self. Anybody can literally think or do whatever he or she wants. Of course, what a person chooses to think or do may have bad consequences for that person. But everything is ultimately up to each individual to decide for himself or herself. The most one should ever do toward influencing another person is to ask him or her to consider what one thinks. Nobody is bound to any course of action by virtue of belonging to a group or because of a common good. Individuals are autonomous agents who have to deal with each other, yes, but do so entirely as self-directing choosers. The words *duty*, *responsibility*, and *obligation* feel somehow vaguely coercive or puritanical. Saying that somebody "should" do something is about as far as many emerging adults are comfortable going. You can't make anybody do anything, so don't even try to influence them. Stick to what you think is right. Tell others what you think, if they ask you. But respect the fact that everything is finally the other's own call. Thus, one respondent explained, "I have no other way of knowing what to do morally but how I internally feel. That's where my decisions come from. From me, from inside of me." Another said about the source of her own moral beliefs: "I think mostly myself. Some from religion, I guess, some from parents. But, I think for me to actually pick my views, I mean, it has to come from me." When asked what it is that makes anything right or wrong, another replied, "I think it's your own personal belief system. I don't think it's anything like social norms or like that. I think it's just what you think, it's dependent on each person and their own beliefs and what they think is right or wrong." Thus, as applied to the issue of people having any responsibilities related to material wealth and possessions, for instance, another said, "If someone works for their three billion dollars that they own, it's rightfully their three billion dollars. They should be able to buy whatever they want. Yeah, I think they should at least help some people out, but it's their money, they can do what they want. If they want to go out and get 40 different cars, whatever, that is [fine]."

More Open-Minded

Emerging adults, when reflecting on how they have changed since high school, often say that they have "become more open-minded" or "accepting of different ideas or lifestyles." They seem to mean this in a variety of senses. Generally, they explain that when they were younger, they tended to embrace fairly rigidly the views they were raised to hold. Since high school, however, they report having been exposed to a greater variety of kinds of people and lifestyles and viewpoints, to which they have often tried to be open and work out accommodating responses. For some this means dropping old prejudices or fears. For others this means loosening up the boundaries of their moral views or beliefs about what is safe or wise. Some have become "more open-minded" by starting to drink alcohol when their parents raised them to be against drinking. Some mean that they used to think that something was wrong with gays and lesbians but they've since come to believe that they are perfectly normal, or at least that it is misguided to try to oppose them. Others have become much more sexually active since high school, which they view as becoming more liberal or open-minded. Often, shifts in these directions do not signify major lifestyle or value transformations but rather marginal or incremental shifts toward freedom and acceptance, compared to somewhat more restrictive beliefs held in high school or to parents' current views. One emerging adult, for example, said,

> I have quite transitioned. I went from a sweet little innocent kid that perhaps had some morals left, to a dirty hippy with none. I have morals, but yeah, so, it's been good. [So what's the transition been about?] Nothing in particular, just I guess getting older, going to college, just meeting new people, and I'm just, I don't know, not exactly a new outlook on life, just a new like, I'm a little more casual about everything now. So I don't, I'm not so, like, uptight about everything as I used to be.

All Cultures Are Relative

Related to the previous point, when it comes to culture, most emerging adults seem to be what sociologists call social constructionists, whether they know it or not. That is, they mostly unquestioningly presuppose that most things about the sociocultural world are not fixed or given facts of nature but rather human constructions invented through shared social definitions and practices that are historically contingent, changeable, and particular. It apparently has not required the taking of multiple anthropology, sociology, and postmodern humanities classes for most emerging adults to have arrived at this view. For many, it appears that the sheer impact of the simple realization of the particularity of the conditions in which they were raised drives them to assume this de facto social constructionism. When they were younger, as for everybody, their personally experienced reality was, for them, simply reality. Now that they have grown older, have met some different people, and maybe have seen some of the world, they seem keenly aware that they were raised in a very particular way that is different from the way others were raised. Sociology and anthropology show that human cultures are indeed significantly socially constructed and vary in certain ways across time and space. That awareness by most emerging adults presses them— for better or worse—to relativize their own perspectives. For instance, they repeatedly frame and qualify their views on life with statements such as "Well, at least for how I was raised I feel that..." and "For other people it's different, but for me I tend to think that..." For example, one respondent observed, "Being raised in a certain culture you have certain norms for what are moral. I guess for me there is certain way to act based on my culture. But if someone else is coming with a different perspective, they would maybe have a different outcome, based on what they believe." Often these are not intentionally expressed statements of feelings-replacing-thought or opinions-replacing-beliefs, but rather unconscious habits of speech reflecting larger cultural norms. To whatever degree it is intentional, however, the phrase "I feel that" has nearly ubiquitously replaced the phrases "I think that," "I believe that," and "I would argue that"—a shift in language use that expresses an essentially subjectivistic and emotivistic approach to moral reasoning and rational argument.[5] Consider, for instance, this emerging adult's use of "feel" 12 times in seven sentences:

> Morality is how I feel too, because in my heart, I could feel it. You could feel what's right or wrong in your heart as well as your mind. Most of the time, I always felt, I feel it in my heart, and it makes it easier for me to morally decide what's right and wrong. Because if I feel about doing something, I'm going to feel it in my heart. And if it feels good, then I'm going to do it. But if it doesn't feel good, I'm going to know. Because then I'm going to be nervous, and I'm going to be tensed, and it's not going to feel good. It's not going to feel right. So it's like I got that feeling as well as thinking.

One of the apparent effects of this culturally relativistic view and the continual self-relativizing to which it leads is speech in which claims are not staked, rational arguments are not developed, differences are not engaged, nature (as in the natural world, the reality beyond what humans make up) is not referenced, and universals are not recognized. Rather, differences in viewpoints and ways of life are mostly acknowledged, respected, and then set aside as incommensurate and off limits for evaluation.

Relative Morality Depends on the Case

Following from the previous two themes, most emerging adults view morality as ultimately a personal, relative affair: morally right and wrong beliefs depend entirely on the specifics of the case and the "opinions" of the people involved. Not many grasp a strong sense of a natural or universal moral standard or law that in any way transcends human invention. To be sure, most emerging adults seem to believe in moral right and wrong. But when they are pressed, it becomes clear that for them, the moral character of a matter is ultimately rooted in the beliefs, socialization, and feelings of the individuals involved. In philosophical language—in which few have any formal training—most emerging adults seem to be believers in simplified versions of G E. Moore's antinaturalistic moral emotivism and Richard Rorty's relativistic moral pragmatism.[6] Again, it is difficult for emerging adults—lacking access or appeal to any real moral reference point independent of their own subjective perceptions, socialization, and experience—to see how commonly binding moral judgments might be rationally justified or moral disagreements adjudicated. All that humans finally have, they assume, is each person's experience, and different people see things different ways, so the best that anyone can do is to obey civil laws and not hurt each other. (Exactly what moral principles deserve to be institutionalized in law and why is often an opaque matter beyond their ability to explain; but in true pragmatic fashion, figuring that out actually doesn't often matter as much, for many, as simply knowing what in fact is in the law and working with it.) In the end, few emerging adults are equipped to make and explain broadly applicable, reasoned moral judgments. What they do instead is either form their own strong "opinions" and keep them to themselves or dismiss such concerns as impossible and simply do their best to live up to the beliefs they learned as they were raised. Case in point: In the middle of explaining that for religious reasons she does not believe in cohabitation before marriage, a young evangelical woman, who is devoted to gospel missionary work overseas, interrupted herself with this observation: "I don't know. I think everyone is different so. I know it wouldn't work for me, but it could work for someone else."

A Less Typical Theme—Rights and Wrongs are Objectively Real. We said earlier that most emerging adults in the United States have difficulty conceiving of a reliable, objective reality beyond individual selves in relation to which one might make reasoned evaluations of the worth of the self's beliefs, feelings, and desires—whether one's own or others'. We also said that most of them embrace the kind of cultural and moral relativism produced by a vulgar social constructionism, and that morality and ethics are viewed in highly personal and situational terms. This is the mainstream view among emerging adults. But an alternative minority view runs counter to the majority. According to some, certain definite things are good and bad, right and wrong, just and unjust, and that human beings as such can and should know them and live accordingly. This minority is unconvinced by arguments about cultural difference and relativism. Everything is not relative. There are clear moral rights and wrongs, even if some people want to pretend otherwise. These emerging adults believe they know—whether through common sense, the nature of universal reality, or divine revelation—that truth and goodness exist and that people can learn these and be responsible for them. Like Amanda, when they hear of peers expressing relativistic ideas, they dismiss it as self-indulgent rationalizing of wrong choices and behaviors for which their peers do not want to be held responsible. They themselves seek to live morally, with more integrity according to what they know is good, true, and right. One respondent, for example, reasoned: "Are

we going to get to a point that culture's going to evolve so much that the principle of not murdering is obsolete? No! That's wrong, you know? Or maybe
there are certain circumstances that are very special, very narrow, very rare
sort of circumstances. But I don't care if it's a thousand years down the road,
how far we are from biblical times, murder is never going to be okay." Another
argued: "I think there are definitely some issues that I don't find those to be
gray areas. I think some issues are wrong and some issues are right."

Uncertain Purpose

Some emerging adults have settled on what seems to be a clear and strong
sense of purpose in life. But they are the minority. At ages 18 to 23, most are
still sorting out what their purpose in life might be, to what good they want
to devote themselves. Here we mean not mainly some philosophical "ultimate
purpose of life"—what the Germans call "God-and-the-world" questions—
but rather the more prosaic issue of what one as a person ought to be doing
with one's life. Nearly all emerging adults have a general vision, as we will
show, of what a "good life" looks like. But more specific questions about
careers and causes and life devotions are as yet unformed. Some are impatient
about spending time in this limbo; others are relaxed and patient, trying to
enjoy the freedoms and pleasures of young life while they last. But either way,
this position certainly and inescapably involves uncertainty—a general lack of
sureness, direction, and intention. It sounds like this: "I feel like I should have
more done with my life right now, but also, like people my age, don't have it
all figured out like they used to. So I'm not really sure what to think, I guess,
about my own goals, and I'll do what I can do." And this:

> I would say it's still a little unclear about my purpose. I don't know
> what I want to be when I grow up. I know it's a little late for that, but
> I still don't know what I want to be. I know that for right now what
> I'm going to do is just keep doing what I'm doing until it comes to me.
> I guess as far as the bigger picture purpose, I don't know what there is
> for me yet. But I'm not worried about it either.

And like this:

> I've noticed a lot of people really upset and stressed not knowing what
> they want to do with their life. I know so many people that just get,
> like, broken down because they just have no idea what they wanna do,
> where they wanna go. Some people are dropping out of school because
> they need to do some self-exploration before they're sure that they
> wanna go to this institution that costs so much. Some of my friends are
> dropping out of college just because it's so expensive, and they don't
> know what they wanna do anymore. So they don't feel it's worth it. For
> a lot of people it's really kind of earth-shattering because things that
> they thought they wanted to do their entire life, they suddenly realize
> they don't. So right now, the biggest challenge for most people my age,
> is the transition from being a kid, like, from high school when you're

like, "Yeah, future looks great," to starting to transition into the real world. I mean it's still college and a lot of people are like "best time of your life," sorta like a dream world, no responsibility. But everything's kinda looming on the horizon right now. That's a big challenge.

Education Is of Instrumental Value

Many, though not all, emerging adults believe in the importance of finishing high school and getting a college education. Large numbers want to go to university, do well in school, get a degree, and put it to use. But for most, the motivating reasons behind their valuing higher education seem to have almost entirely to do with the instrumental advantages it produces—as well as the fun one can have while in college. What matters is getting the credits, earning the diploma, and becoming certified as a college-educated person so that one can get a better job, earn more money, and become a good salary earner and supporter of a (materially) comfortable and secure life. Not very many emerging adults talk about the intrinsic value of an education, of the personal broadening and deepening of one's understanding and appreciation of life and the world that expansive learning affords. Few talk about the value of a broad education for shaping people into informed and responsible citizens in civic life, for producing leaders and members who can work together toward the common good of all in society. An articulation of an understanding of the enduring worth of a broad liberal arts education for the development of persons and the sustaining of humanistic societies is not often heard from this age group. For most, higher education is good instead because—besides the fun one can have while in college—it promises to help secure for individuals more rewarding jobs, higher income, and so greater personal prospects for material and psychological well-being and security. For some, that means really learning information and skills. For example, one respondent said, "Right now I'm studying marketing, but I think I am going to change it to finance and accounting, so anything in business really. Because business is a very solid thing, businesses are going to be around for a long time. There will always be jobs, and I like math, so, accounting." For others, higher education is just so many hoops to have to jump through, whether in classrooms or over the Internet. Another respondent, for instance, said:

> Once I did find a job [I realized] it would be so much easier to do well if I did have a degree, just because of the way access is given people. People just recognize you more if you have a degree. That's why I decided to go back to school. But, really my heart is in the work that I do. If I didn't need to be in school, I wouldn't.

Either way, those who can afford it are mostly happy to do it because of the instrumental goods it will deliver and fun that college life offers. As one respondent said, "So many people are out of jobs and losing their houses, it's really kinda bad around here, so that's a reason why I want to go to school so I can make sure I get at least a decent job."

Drugs Are Pervasive, but Maybe Getting Boring

In the worlds of emerging adults, drugs are readily available and, for many, often used by friends and acquaintances if not by themselves. These drugs include not only marijuana but also methamphetamines, cocaine, heroin, and other hard drugs. Many emerging adults avoid drugs altogether with a spirit of antagonism and revulsion. Some have friends and relatives whose lives have been ruined by drug abuse and are determined to steer clear of such a fate. Some, even as young as 18 to 23, are recovered or recovering drug addicts themselves. Yet others continue only to dabble in drugs, smoking pot from time to time and perhaps experimenting with harder drugs on occasion. A minority does drugs regularly—either heavily but without having become addicted, or already having developed into addicts caught in dependences on various illegal substances. No matter what the personal attitudes and practices concerning drugs, the larger reality is that drugs are a pervasive fact of life in emerging adults' world. Drugs are not an anomalous rarity limited to highly deviant subcultures and are never far away. Again, not everybody takes drugs, but drugs are readily available for the taking. Emerging adults know that, and usually know people who do take them. This fact is reflected not so much in specific interview statements but rather in the regularity with which the subject comes up in various ways throughout most interviews.

Another drug-related theme that surfaced in the interviews was that numerous emerging adults report having smoked marijuana more frequently when younger but since become bored and disinterested in it. Smoking pot seemed to be a more exciting activity in high school and was surrounded then by more peer pressure to participate. Many of those interviewed said that they had fairly recently realized that they no longer really cared for "weed," it made them drowsy or loopy or stupid, continuing to smoke it risked job security and promotion, and they had cut back dramatically or stopped altogether. Some conveyed a sense that this was a natural progression that many make in life while growing up. Others seemed to look back at their heavier pot-smoking days and wonder why they were ever really interested in the first place. Overall, compared to younger adolescents, emerging adults seem to show less interest in smoking marijuana specifically and doing drugs generally and to reflectively assess their value more negatively. One respondent, for example, explained:

> I went through that whole drug phase when I was younger, and it was like the cool thing to do. And now when I see people my age doing that I'm like, "Wow, that's really sad that you're stoned on a Wednesday night." And there's people that I do hang out with that still do stuff like that, but I feel like there's more than sitting around and eating Cheetos and watching TV all day. I have other things to do.

Another said, "I used to smoke pot frequently, actually, but I stopped about a year ago when I started EMT school. I knew how bad it was for you, but once I was in paramedic school I just found out the horrendous things that people do to themselves, so I stopped." Another explained why he stopped smoking weed this way: "Because you have to—they drug test you to get into my school program. But more, there was one instance when I went to work [stoned], picked up the phone, talked to a customer, and when I hung up I could not remember who I had talked to or what the conversation was about, so I said, 'That's it, I cannot have my memory going like this. I have a job, I have responsibilities.'" Some emerging adults also said similar things about drinking alcohol. One respondent, for example, commented, "You know, there was a point in time where I was drinking almost every day, and we all had to drop that because it was just so not healthy." Another said:

> I didn't really drink that much. I did binge drinking when I was younger. I went through the whole "Let's be partying and rebellious and go home totally trashed and throw up everywhere." That's not fun for me anymore. I'm not gonna have, like, the big twenty-first and be completely plastered on my birthday, because that's stupid. I don't want pictures on Facebook like, "Wow, she's throwing up on the sidewalk. That's cute." I mean, I've done that. I've been down that road. It's not fun. It's not fun to be, like, with my mom, "So what'd you do last night?" [Sarcastically] "I got totally hammered, mom, totally hammered." And she would be like, "I'm so proud of what you're accomplishing with your life. Congrats." I guess I kind of outgrew the fun party drinking.

But these, remember, were a minority of voices. The majority have not necessarily foresworn or outgrown drugs or drinking.

Settling Down Is for Later

Except for those who have already settled down, the majority of emerging adults are very clear that their lives are not settled. The seemingly endless succession of life transitions they undergo highlights that fact. Rather than being settled, most of them understand themselves to be in a phase of life that is free, fluid, tentative, experimental, and relatively unbound. They want to enjoy it while it lasts. Here a bit of a tension over life goals is expressed. They want to acquire independence and the ability to stand on their own two feet. But most of them also do not want full adulthood to come too quickly. They find the current phase of life between their adolescence and their full adulthood challenging and sometimes difficult. But they also want to relish it as the time to be young, have fun, and avoid major responsibilities. Nearly all want to settle down eventually, someday—but not now. Many want to spend a good chunk of their twenties enjoying their newfound freedom, having a good time, doing things they think they will never be able to do again—maybe traveling, maybe partying, having lots of different kinds of relationships, and so on. As one respondent said, "Before getting married I think you should get all your education out of the way, start your career, do any traveling that you want to do. If you want to join the Peace Corps, join that before anything that you even aspire to before marriage." Someday in the future, when they've got their youthful passions worked out of their systems, then they will settle down. That means settling into a long-term career, finding a good spouse, becoming monogamous, having two or three kids, buying a nice house, getting some nicer cars, maybe a boat, enjoying some nice family vacations—the whole bit. But that is years, perhaps many years off in the future. One respondent summarized the dilemma this approach creates around money: "So, like, how do you budget money? Because obviously you don't want to live with your parents for the rest of your life, and then you want to still have fun and live the life of a young person. So it's hard." Furthermore, when it comes to romantic relationships and sex, many—if not most—emerging adults see little connection between the lives they live now before settling down and the lives they will live later after having settled down. Now—at least as a matter of the acceptable norms of the "cultural ocean" in which they "swim," if not their actual personal beliefs and behaviors—they can party, hook up with strangers, and generally play at being wild. Later, when they settle down they'll be sober, faithful, and responsible adults. The assumption seems to be "Whatever happens in my early twenties stays in my early twenties," and the memories and behavioral consequences will never haunt them down the road. As one young man said, "I think people should have a career and good income before getting married. Maybe get a lot of stuff out of your system, like messing around with girls and stuff, or partying, get that out of your system. Get all that stuff out of your system before you get married. Once you get married, you won't be able to do all that stuff."

A Less Typical Theme—Babies Change Everything. Relatively few 18- to 23-year-olds have children (8.5 percent of the survey's sample), especially children for whose care they are directly responsible. For most of those who do, however, it is clear that bearing children has put them on the fast track to maturity. Even many older teenagers with serious problems can get sober and serious quickly when they have kids. Having babies seems to be one of the few ways emerging adults are ever forced out of their individualistic focuses on freedom, self, and fun. Becoming a parent for many is a wake-up call that it is time—as we will show in the case of Alano in chapter 9—to leave behind the "emergent" phase of adulthood and enter full adulthood, whatever the other circumstances may be. For unless the emerging adult has debilitating problems that they cannot or will not shake—as does Raymond in chapter 9, we will show—introducing a child into his or her life confronts him or her with the need for and challenge of real self-sacrifice, to which most appear able to rise in their own ways. The emerging adults interviewed who had babies, like this one, say it flat out: "I am a mom now and need to be more responsible, just can't go out and partying on Friday nights and stuff like that." Another observed, "right and wrong are harder now, probably because of having my son and trying to find not just what's best for me, I can't think about me anymore, but what's best for him, I gotta think about that first." One new father put it this way: "Before my daughter was born, I thought I was just another average Joe coming home to my drunken girlfriend and being drunk myself, but when I had my daughter it gave me a lot more to live for, you know? Now that I have a little daughter, I feel like I have a little bit more to live for." Some also said having children affects their commitments in relationships: "My mom and my dad stayed together until my youngest sister was already 18, before they decided to split. That is something that I would do too, to stick it out with my boyfriend right now until my daughter is older, and not split up because we had one little argument."

Relationships Are Often Amorphous

By all accounts, the categories and statuses of different kinds of relationships among emerging adults are more nebulous than in previous generations. Young people relate at diverse levels of intimacy, expectations, and obligations. But what exactly to call different types of relationships and when to know which kind one is in at any given time seems problematic. Old, clear-cut labels, like "just friends," dating, courting, and engaged, for instance, are too black-and-white for the way many emerging adults relate today. For example, one of the major activities one engages in with a person we here will call a romantic love interest is "hanging out"—sitting around someone's home, munching, shooting the breeze, perhaps drinking or smoking, and watching TV or movies. But hanging out is also a major activity emerging adults engage in with ordinary friends, roommates, and new acquaintances. And often meetings of romantic love interests do not take place alone but with other friends, roommates, and siblings present. So the nature of an emerging adult's relationship, whether casual friendship or powerfully amorous, gets little definition from the social activities associated with it. As a result, it seems that not infrequently many emerging adults do not really know where they stand or how they relate to a lot of the people they interact with. So, romantically, the lines between just met, just friends, something a bit more than friends, "talking," "going out," "dating," being boyfriend and girlfriend, sleeping over, semicohabiting, cohabiting, and relating like married people can seem like passing through a series of gradually darkening shades of grey. For instance, a young man who had dated 10 young women "not seriously" the previous year explained it this way: "Like, you're just kind of dating but you're not really even going out. Like if someone asked if I was her boyfriend, I would say no. But at the same time we see each other fairly often and we hang out, but there's no public display of affection." Another girl explained some of her past relationships as follows:

> Last year I was dating one guy. It didn't last long, like a week or two. He was somebody I was actually seeing in my class, and we just kinda like decided to make it official. But he was a year younger than me, a good guy. But he hung out with somebody who was a bad influence on him, made him uninterested in being with one person. So it's, like, forget that, I don't need that. But in the last couple of years, not really dating, I haven't had time. I've been talking to this person, the one that

almost killed me in the car. He and I have been kinda off and on for several years now, but nothing really, just kinda more like a companion like to hang out with, go to movies or dinner. But I haven't even seen him in a few months.

Another young woman, after running down a list of young men she had dated in the past, concluded, "I've had boyfriends my whole life. If you look back at all my stuff you'd be like, 'Wow, she's never not had a boyfriend,' 'cause I haven't. But I'm gonna try not dating for a little while, see how long that goes." In the midst of all of this, even the status of "living together" is often unclear, since cohabiting does not always take the "standard" form of two people deciding to move into a new apartment together—rather, some simply spend every weekend living together when one is away at college but otherwise live separate lives; and others basically move into the house where the boyfriend or girlfriend is still living with a parent or parents, simply sleeping in the friend's bedroom, hanging out, and coming and going as they please. One woman who temporarily moved out from her boyfriend/sort-of fiancé's home when he decided he was unsure whether he really wanted to marry her, said:

> I packed up the bare essentials, and we were separated for about two weeks. I mean, we weren't seeing other people or anything. We just, we weren't together, but we weren't separate. It was kinda weird. I mean, he still expected me to call him, and he still called me all the time. But we didn't check in with each other. He went off and partied, and I hung out with my friends and did whatever I wanted to do.

Such tendencies toward nebulous relations has generated the need for what some young people call "the DTR talk," that is, an explicit discussion whose purpose is "defining the relationship." But that does not seem to happen often or effectively. Finally, it appears that emerging adult females have somewhat more investment than their male peers in getting clear on the nature of their relationships. But they also do not seem to feel empowered to demand that or to be up for challenging the larger amorphous-relationships culture. Mostly they seem to simply go along and try their best to figure out what's going on.

Hooking Up Is Common

One commonly named category of relationship distinct from friendships and dating that has become common in the last decade or two is "hooking up."[7] Most emerging adults have heard of hooking up and have friends who routinely hook up, and many do hook up themselves, although nearly all profess that they are not sure exactly what "hooking up" actually means. The ambiguity and vagueness of the term seems itself to help define the nature of the relational and physical encounters to which it refers. For some emerging adults, hooking up means hanging out and drinking at a party with a new acquaintance. Particularly for African American emerging adults, it seems, hooking up seems to mean simply being set up by a friend for a date with someone they do not know. For most, however, it also refers to time spent together that includes some kind of sexual activity with a person one has just met. For some, this may mean no more than heavy kissing and "messing around." For others, it also includes having sexual intercourse. The latter may happen once per unfamiliar person met or repeatedly over a length of time, but in any case the encounter happens between two people who are essentially strangers or "kinda friends." A lot of emerging adults suspect it means any and all of the foregoing, depending on what those hooking up want it to mean. Whatever hooking up is, it is not uncommon to the way of life of many emerging adults. It carries very little connotation of audacity, daring, or wildness. In most cases, even if a particular person has not hooked up, their friends have or do. It's not a huge deal. Some emerging adults hook up as much as they can for entertainment. Others do not believe in hooking up—the kind that involves sexual activity—but have found themselves doing it anyway, especially, it seems, when "on the rebound" after a romantic breakup—often with the consequence of feeling frustrated and angry with themselves, sometimes even feeling dirty. The following excerpts convey some of the ambiguity and familiarity of hooking up among emerging adults:

> Ah, you know just depends, anything from casual sex or just making out. It all just depends. I mean you can say, "Oh, I hooked up with her," that could mean from just making out to getting laid. Everyone has their own definition. I see dating that you're boyfriend and girlfriend—then you're dating. Hooking up I just see as hooking up, so we're not dating. There's no dating going on; we're just hooking up.

> "We had sex." That's hooked up for most, but not to me. Hooked up to me is like we made out for a while, for a long time, I guess. It usually doesn't lead to anything. Literally, like a random guy at the party will say, "Yeah, you're like pretty cute," and you start talking and the next thing you know you're making out. And then it's like, "All right, bye." I don't think you should do it while you're dating somebody else, for sure. That just leads to, just not fun. Hooking up is just for fun. It's like a recreational thing.

> Well, it's more physical. You just, you don't have to be dating them or going out with them. You just have a physical thing at a party or whatever.

> Making out with people, yeah. I used to drink too much, and I'd just kinda make out with my friends. So yeah, in terms of hooking up, if it was making out, then yeah. Some people, I don't know, I don't even know how to define it. Some people think hooking up is sleeping together. Some people think that it's just like making out or, I don't even know. I don't know what it means.

> Different occasions, different things. Hooking up can mean, yeah, I think for some people it means you have sex, and for others it means you've made out. To me, it just means making out. Something sexual happens, but it usually doesn't entail sex.

Just, you know, I don't know, like just hooking up. Not having [emotions], it's more of a physical thing, not an emotional thing. You don't have to worry about the emotions or the jealousy. But the only bad thing about that is that someone always ends up getting feelings [for the other], and then the other person [is caught in an uncomfortable situation]. It's not a good way to go, but you do it sometimes.

In my personal perspective, hooking up is completely different than getting into a relationship. If I'm just hooking up with a guy, I don't plan on dating them. It depends. It really depends on who you are as a person, on if you need that relationship to need to be okay. I personally think you need to be okay with yourself before you get into a relationship or it just doesn't work out. I'm okay with myself. I like who I am. So hooking up is fine with me. I don't need that commitment. I don't need that relationship. I don't need that love from somebody else. I'm fine with myself. Entertainment, thrill, all of it. Just for fun.

The main point here is that whether or not any particular emerging adult hooks up, hooking up as a phenomenon is an ordinary part of the worlds in which emerging adults live. Eyebrows are not raised. It generally passes as routine, as reflected in this one's musing about motivations for hooking up: "There are all sorts of reasons people hook up—I've had some who I really had strong feelings for and sometimes you're just glad that it happens, you just feel like it. You're like, 'Yeah, well we're here, I guess just go for it.' I don't know."

Devastating Breakups Happen

A significant number of emerging adults, it seems, have suffered devastating breakups involving romantic partners with whom they thought they were very seriously involved, probably on the path to marriage. Usually, but not always, the most damaged party is the woman involved, not the man. We interviewers were taken aback, actually, by the number of traumatic breakups we heard described, since we had embarked on the interviews with the belief that emerging adults generally want to hold off on seriously committed relationships. But the fact is that while most emerging adults do want to hold off, they—again, especially women, it seems—also yearn for the kind of intimacy, loyalty, and security that only highly committed relationships can deliver. So in the nebulous world of romantic relationships that they inhabit, some emerging adults, thinking they have found "the right" partners who feel the same way they do, jump in with heart, soul, and mind; often only to discover, later, when they are betrayed or dumped, that the partners did not share their understandings or expectations, or perhaps were experiencing a gradual change in their feelings or desires but did not communicate this along the way. These splits are not your run-of-the-mill middle school and high school breakups that sweep the local rumor mill, create lots of drama, and leave somebody crying for a few days. The breakups that many emerging adults recounted instead sounded much more serious. They often happened in the context of couples living together or semicohabiting and, in any case, being sexually involved. They often resulted in serious emotional and physical distress—dumped partners told tales of days spent sleeping and crying or lying in bed debilitated with depression, of anguish suffered at being cheated on or otherwise betrayed, of profound struggles with self-doubt, self-criticism, and hopelessness lasting for months, of uncertainty about being able to trust another man or woman whom they might love in the future. Some worked hard in their interviews to keep themselves from weeping. A few broke down in tears while recounting their stories. Their accounts suggested the experience of getting a hard divorce without ever even having gotten married. For many, the pain and fear linger even as they try to pick up the pieces and move on. Amanda in chapter 1 and Joy in chapter 9 are examples of this kind of case.

Cohabit to Avoid Divorce

We mentioned earlier that the paths into and forms of cohabitation in non-marital unions among emerging adults are multiple. But the vast majority of emerging adults nonetheless believe that cohabiting is a smart if not absolutely necessary experience and phase for moving toward an eventual successful and happy marriage. Generally, the only emerging adults who said they would not cohabit before marriage took that stand on the basis of religiously based scruples about sex and commitment. But the majority does not share those concerns. A good number of emerging adults separate their interest in cohabiting from the issue of marriage. For these, it is simply obvious that if you care for someone and want to spend time with them that you would do well to move in with them and live life together—marriage or no marriage. But a larger number maintained with complete assurance that one would be stupid to get married without first having lived together for six months to a year. The person who you thought you knew so well when living apart could prove in a 24/7 relationship to have problems or incompatibilities that would make you not want to marry them after all. By cohabiting for the good part of a year, one is able to "test drive" the relationship and confirm before it is too late that the marriage really will work. As one explained, "I lived with my fiancé because I thought it was good that we were able to see how we are on a more, you know, intimate level. You're with each other all the time, you see all the bad habits that person has, and I think that was good in regards to whether or not we wanted to be together for the long term. We were able to see if we could deal with those little things about each other." This approach is consistent with the general method of rational strategizing, managing, and risk reduction, which we discuss next, that emerging adults often carefully deploy in the challenge of learning to stand on their own in life. It also reflects the concerns of a generation of youth who have suffered the damaging effects of widespread divorce among their parents and who wish not to repeat it. Yet most emerging adults who adopt this approach strike us as having far too much confidence in cohabitation's ability to prevent divorce and ensure happiness. They simply believe it will work, that it will function as a fail-safe method for averting possible marital breakup. The examples some give for the kind of learning about one's fiancé that one might fortunately gain from cohabiting, which would be problematic enough to call off the impending wedding—that they squeeze the toothpaste in the middle, are a slob, get in grouchy moods, become sexually boring, and so on—hardly seem to reflect an awareness of the seriousness and complexity of issues and problems with which people in both successful and failed marriages often have to deal. Their accounts also do not reflect their having put a lot of thought into how to handle cases of significant but not terrible difficulties encountered in cohabiting situations. How bad or bothersome must a problem or difficulty be to justify canceling an engagement? What happens when only one person believes the impending marriage is risky but the other still wants to get married? And so on. Finally, none of the emerging adults who are enthusiastic about cohabiting as a means to prevent unsuccessful marriages seem aware that nearly all studies consistently show that couples who live together before they marry are more, not less, likely to later divorce than couples who did not live together before their weddings.[8] In fact, either something about living together before marriage itself or the very notion of approaching marriage with the mentality of hedging one's bets by shaking out the relationship with a provisional uncommitted marriage-like test, or both, significantly increases the probability of subsequently divorcing. But emergent adults are oblivious to these facts. And so most look forward to time spent cohabiting with their most serious partners, in order, they think, to help guarantee success and happiness in their eventual marriages.

Strategically Managing Risks

Emerging adults know full well that they live in a world of danger and risks— DUI accidents, addictions, pregnancy, sexually transmitted infections, overdoses, arrests, suspension or expulsion from college or work, date rape, police records, jacked-up auto insurance rates, and more. Some of them nevertheless live as if they were immune to those hazards of life—and often end up paying stiff prices. But most of them realize that one slip, one poor decision, one piece of bad luck could spell disaster. So they put some effort into managing their risks. Their challenge is to have a lot of fun without it coming back to hurt them. Some, we will show, do everything possible to avoid every danger they can think of. But only a few emerging adults are willing to adopt lifestyles that achieve absolute minimum risk at the expense of dramatically reducing fun. Most want to strike a balance between good times and danger. More than a few give some thought to the odds, increase their reliance on cautions and protections that entail the fewest constraints, and save their biggest gambles for their stupidest or most wildly fun moments. It can be a matter of learning how to live on the edge with as much safety as seems reasonable. One respondent, for instance, said:

> I'm on birth control. If you're not then how are you not going to get pregnant? Back in the 1800s they didn't have that stuff so if you had sex with somebody you could assume that you're going to get pregnant. But now they have all these different ways to protect yourself, and I think it's kind of a thing with all the STDs out there. If I was out

having sex with a bunch of different people, I would definitely want to be protecting myself, because it could ruin your life. It could kill you And I don't want to deal with that, because of a silly mistake I made one night.

In discussing whether people should be in relationships to have sex, another said, "Not necessarily. I mean for me, I prefer it, personally for myself. But if you really think that you want to do it with somebody that is just sort of a hook up, then just be safe about it and make good decisions, don't do anything dumb." The majority who take this approach know that they could get unlucky. The neighbors could call the police at the wrong moment, the condom could break, the nice guy could actually be a predator, one's partner might have been cheating with someone who has herpes or AIDS. But you can't live life in constant fear of disaster. So hope for the best, prepare for some of the worst, enjoy yourself, and deal with the fallout if and when you get unlucky.[9]

A Less Typical Theme—Risks are Best Avoided Altogether. Most emerging adults, as we have said, strategically manage their risks, gambling on avoiding some possible dangers in order to have enough fun and enjoyment in life. But some are more risk averse than that. They are not at all interested in courting disaster, no matter how small the probability of getting pregnant, getting arrested, getting a sexually transmitted infection, getting in a dumb accident, and the like. They make principled personal-policy decisions ahead of time simply to resolutely avoid choices, situations, and behaviors that run those kinds of risks. Whether or not to go out drinking or smoke weed or have sex is an option they completely take off of the table—it is simply not an open question for consideration or discussion. Some of these "abstainers" have moral scruples against the activities that entail the risks—they believe, for instance, in not having sex before marriage, even apart from the risks of pregnancy and diseases. For them, choosing as a matter of policy to avoid those temptations fits into a larger, coherent lifestyle package that makes moral and practical sense for them. Others are more purely pragmatic. In theory, they are not morally opposed to certain risky behaviors. They merely see too much at stake, too much of value to risk losing in order simply to have some fleeting fun. Some have learned the hard way their own limitations in making smart judgments after having one drink, after some heavy kissing, after hanging out for the day with friends who smoke dope. So they just avoid those situations altogether. Why jeopardize one's entire future career, some ask, over a drug bust? Why put oneself in the horrible position, others reason, of having to choose between becoming a young single mom with no economic future or aborting your own child? It's too stupid. Much better to be wise, play it safe, live with integrity, and be happier and healthier in the long run. Along these lines, people said things like:

I see everyone else drinking and smoking, and I've tried it before, but I think it's nasty and the side effects you get from it. It's a waste of money. You could do a whole lot better with $20 than drink nasty liquor and wake up sick the next day. It's not good for me, so. And my mom tried drugs once, marijuana when she was young. She told me all it did was make her sleepy. I've never tried it, and I don't really want to because I don't like the effect that I see on other people. And I don't really like something that I can't stop doing, an addictive thing, I don't want.

Another, who was "walking the talk," said, "I don't think people my age should be involved in sex at all, I don't believe in that stuff at all. So many people from my high school are getting pregnant and once you have a kid it just doesn't go back. I think everyone should just remain separate until you get married." Another said, "I don't do pot and drugs, they're so nasty. I hate the smell of them. They are just not good. And then drinking, my dad drinks wine every night, which kinda causes a problem because my dad has a little drinking problem. I come from a long line of alcoholics, so as far as I can stay away from it [I do]. It's fine if you drink around me; I just won't drink." Finally, another explained it this way:

> I just know, "No, I'm not going to do this. This is just isn't who I am." Sometimes it's hard because part of me doesn't want to let my friends down, but also part of me doesn't want to just do something outside of character just to prove myself to my friends, because I feel like I have nothing to prove. If they don't like me, they would have left me 10 years ago because I've known them forever. So something like "Wanna do drugs?" No, because they ruin your life. I know one guy I was friends with in elementary school and lives in my neighborhood. A couple months ago he was driving drunk and killed another drunk guy who ran into the middle of the street. So he's awaiting jail time from what he's told me. And he got suspended from high school the last two weeks of his senior year, didn't get to walk at graduation because he was busted for smoking pot. So that's just an easy thing for me. It's just stupid. Why would you want to mess up your brain like that? That's a type of person you wanna stay away from: drug addicts, alcoholics, people addicted to cigarettes, like that.

A Less Typical Theme—I've Got a Major Addiction. A second alternative theme to the strategic management of risks is the fact of major addictions. Most emerging adults appear, as we have said, to be in adequate control of their lives. Some walk a fine line between functionality and disaster. But even they generally seem to be managing. A minority, however, is beset with one or more addictions to alcohol, drugs, sex, pornography, and the like. The number of serious addicts in the emerging adult population does not seem to be large. But for those whose lives are bodily and emotionally dominated by substances and behaviors that they cannot or will not abandon, things get miserable. What is reasonable and good in their lives is pushed out by compulsiveness, senseless choices, violated relationships, self-destruction, and self-condemnation. The central challenge of emerging adult life, the end that nearly all of their peers are pursuing—learning to stand on one's own two feet—becomes sidetracked if not derailed by problems associated with the addictions. Some will get it together and turn their lives around. Others will not, but instead will disappear into homelessness, prison, mental hospitals, and early death. One example, recounted at length here from the story of Raymond (more fully told in chapter 9), conveys a strong sense of the problems:

> I didn't think AA [Alcoholics Anonymous] helped me. It might sound stupid to say it made me want to drink more, but it really did, as we sat there and talked. Like, "What's your favorite drink?" "Whiskey." "What's your favorite kind of whiskey?" "Jack Daniels." "How much can you drink?" I'm sitting there thinking, "Screw this, why don't we just go get a bottle, and I'll show you how much I can drink." You know? I did quit for a while, got 30 days. I did good, and I got the little AA keychain. And everybody shakes your hand and you feel so good about it. And you think, "Well, hell, I could go 60 days." I got 60 days, and got a different color keychain and everybody's like, "Oh my gosh, congratulations." Then I got to 63 days. And I don't know if this sounds stupid, but I'm sitting there and for no particular reason I just get that taste in my mouth. And your mouth starts watering, and it sounds like the best thing right now. And then, I don't know, I still had a bottle of Jack Daniels and it only had four shots out of it, one of the big 30- or 40-dollar bottles. I sure as hell wasn't going to throw that away, 40 dollars and [I] only got four shots out of it. So I thought, well maybe I will just save it, and maybe someone will give me twenty bucks for it. I didn't want to just give it to somebody else and give them a problem. For some reason I held onto it, and I got my 60-day thing. I was like, "Oh man, 60 days, maybe I'll just have a drink to celebrate because I made it." I just sat there and stared at the bottle for 20 minutes, 30 minutes, you know, I don't know, 30 minutes went by, and I cracked. I just threw the lid down and looked around, listened, made sure my mom wasn't coming down the stairs and, it was on the wood table in my room, and I slid the bottle across the table over to me [makes sound of drinking]. "Ahh," put the lid back up, hid it under my bed. I stopped for another few days, but I couldn't do it. Just having it there was my downfall, I think. If I wouldn't have had it, I would have gone a lot longer. I used to smoke pot, now I got a bigger problem, drinking, than smoking pot. I could pass up a joint before passing up a shot.

Consumerism Is Good Stuff

The interviews asked a set of questions probing emerging adults' attitudes about materialism and mass-consumerism. We, as the interview guide authors, worked hard to write questions that would not be leading in any way, out of concern that criticizing materialistic consumerism would generate—in today's environmentally conscious culture—social desirability effects, leading respondents to express distress about and condemnation of materialism and shallow consumerism that they really did not in fact feel or believe. As it turned out, that concern was entirely unfounded. Not only was there no danger of leading emerging adults into expressing false opposition to materialistic consumerism; interviewers could not, not matter how hard they pushed, get emerging adults to express any serious concerns about any aspect of mass-consumer materialism. As far as they were concerned—almost every single emerging adult interviewed—shopping falls on a spectrum of enjoyment between being simply uninteresting to being a major source of happiness, and there is little to no problem with the amount of material stuff everybody owns. As long as people can afford their purchases, they are fully entitled to buy and consume whatever they want. There should be no limits to what people might buy and own, and consuming products is often a great source of satisfaction that helps to define ultimate goals in life. Voices critical of mass consumerism, materialistic values, or the environmental or social costs of a consumer-driven economy were nearly nonexistent among emerging adults. Once the interviewers realized, after a number of interviews, that they were hardly in danger of leading their respondents into feigned concern about consumerism, the interviewers began to probe more persistently to see if there might not be any hot buttons or particular phrases that could tap into any kind of concern about materialistic consumerism. There were not. Very many of those interviewed simply could not even understand the issue the interviewers were asking them about. The idea of having any questions or doubts about the cycle of shopping, buying, consuming, accumulating, discarding, and shopping appeared to be unthinkable to them. To be sure, an atheist male who had studied world development in college and described himself as a socialist said he thought people were too obsessed with what they could purchase, and perhaps people should limit the material things they own. But other than him and one or two others, the consensus position of emerging adults was this: As long as people can afford it, they may buy and consume whatever they happen to want without limit. It is completely up to them as individuals. There is nothing at all problematic about America's consumer-driven socioeconomic system. Shopping and buying as a way of life is just fine, and owning some of the nicer things in life is a natural part of the purpose or goal of life.[10] Here is how it sounded in one conversation:

It feels good to be able to get things that you want, and you worked for the money. If you want something, you go get it. It makes your life become more comfortable, and I guess it just makes you feel good about yourself as well. You want to get something you work for it, and you can get it. [Do you have any particular feelings about all the consumption that Americans do?] I think it's a good thing if you work for it because then you gain that accomplishment and not like you were just given money. "I want to get this, you know, I'll buy that." It's like you actually work for it so you feel that you deserve it, you earned it. You earned that thing that you wanted. You weren't just given it. [Do you think there are limits to what people should possess or own?] I guess everybody has their own needs and wants.

Helping Others Is an Optional Personal Choice

When asked whether people generally have a responsibility or obligation to help other people or not, a minority of the emerging adults interviewed said yes, people do have a real responsibility to help others. A few said that this was what God taught in the Bible—"Love your neighbor." More evoked the idea sociologists call "generalized reciprocity"—that everyone benefits in a world in which each person helps specific others in need even when he or she will not be repaid directly by them, because somebody else will someday help that person when he or she is in need, so in the end everybody gets help from somebody. "Well," they asked, "if a person doesn't help other people, what are they going to do when they need help?" A few others said that people definitely have the responsibility to help others, but could not explain why. But these views were a minority. The majority of those interviewed stated the opposite—that nobody has any natural or general responsibility or obligation to help other people. In a reprise of the "It's Up to the Individual" theme described earlier, most of those interviewed said that it is nice if people help others, but that nobody has to. Taking care of other people in need is an individual's choice. If you want to do it, good. If you don't, that's up to you. You don't have to. Nobody can blame people who won't help others. They are innocent of any guilt, respondents said, if they ignore other people in need. Even when pressed—What about victims of natural disaster or political oppression? What about helpless people who are not responsible for their poverty or disabilities? What about famines and floods and tsunamis?—No, they replied. If someone wants to help, then good for that person. But nobody has to. Some simply declared, "That's not my problem." Others said, "I wish people would help others, but they really have no duty to do that at all. It's up to them, their opinion." Again, any notion of the responsibilities of a common humanity, a transcendent call to protect the life and dignity of one's neighbor, or a moral responsibility to seek the common good was almost entirely absent among the respondents. In the end, each individual does what he or she wants and nobody has any moral leverage to persuade or compel him or her to do otherwise.

A Less Typical Theme—We're Responsible for Each Other. Not all emerging adults are as just described. Some believe, as noted—even if they cannot say why—that people need to look out for and take care of each other, that people have mutual responsibilities to each other, that it is wrong for those who can help others not to do so. Some of this comes from currently embraced or formerly learned religious teachings, such as commands to care for the poor or the parable of the good Samaritan. Some of it comes from more general teachings at home and school that good people are kind and compassionate to those in need. And some of it comes from a strong distaste for what society would be like if everyone only took care of himself or herself, which generates for these emerging adults the moral rule that all should take care of one another. But, however they come to it, a sizeable minority of emerging adults have ended up convinced that people are not self-sufficient islands of independent choice but rather have moral obligations to take care of one another. One respondent put it this way:

> I think people have a responsibility to help each other, a duty to help others if we're in a position to help. I think if we can help someone, we should. That doesn't happen enough just because people get caught up in their own lives and don't want to feel obligated to another person. But I think it is part of our moral obligation, because if we have been blessed to have more than someone else, we should want to share that. Like if you're blessed financially, you can share that with other people who maybe aren't quite as blessed, you should feel a certain obligation—maybe not so much an obligation, but maybe a want to help others. We should want to be unselfish in that way.

The Middle-class Dream Alive and Well

Near the end of the interviews, we interviewers asked emerging adults what they wanted out of life, to describe their life goals and dreams. Nearly all of them replied with some version of the same essential answer: finish education, get a good job, marry, have children, buy a nice house with a yard, raise a family, become financially secure, drive reliable cars, enjoy family vacations, enjoy good relationships, maybe have a dog. In short, nearly all spoke sincerely as if they still believed in the American middle-class dream and greatly desired to achieve it. Typical was a woman who said, "I really want to have a family and a husband, just, I guess, have that 'American Dream' kind of thing. That's something I've always wanted to do, just after seeing my family and how close they are and how important a husband or a wife is." Respondents voiced very few alternative life dreams, like achieving major social reforms, living overseas, serving the poor, or pursuing any other alternative lifestyles. Not many emerging adults expressed a rabid ambition and materialism that would propel them to seek riches above all else. Many at the lower end of the socioeconomic hierarchy seemed content to achieve a modest version of the middle-class dream—a cozy house, a reasonable income, a decent car—just as long as they could enjoy a close, happy family with those things. Others had larger scale visions than that, describing higher-end lifestyles that they had in mind. But however modest or affluent the dream looked, nearly all described it as attaining material security and happy family life in a comfortable home. One respondent, for instance, said, "Just having a good job, being stable, not having to worry about things, bills and all that, or struggling, being able to pay for the bills, being able to go out once in a while, take a break, just being there with the good things that you want on your own time and just working, having a good job, being able to spend time with family—I think that'll be a good life." Emerging adults' replies to a question they were asked about what they would do with an unexpected inheritance of money, and why, reinforced their answers to the life dream questions. They were asked what they would do with $100,000 if a distant relative died and left it to them. They did not report—as teenagers may more typically say—that they would spend a good chunk of it on nice cars, clothes, travel, and other consumer items. Nearly all said they would invest most or all of it in the stock market, put it in the bank, pay off their credit card loans, finish paying college tuition, use it for the down payment on a house, and similar other, practical, get-a-real-adult-life-started kinds of uses. Some said that when they were younger they would have spent it on cars and fun activities, but now they realize that they have to make provisions for the future. Such fiscal practical-mindedness and investment prudence seems like a new concept to them, but one that is clearly motivated by their drive for financial and family independence and their desire to achieve the middle-class dream of security, comfort, and contentment—described by another as "kind of like the American dream, something you always see and hear about."

Still Believe in America's Freedoms

Interviewers also talked with emerging adults about their view of the United States—about what they see as American society's positive features and strengths, as well as its challenges and problems. They expressed different views on the problems side. But they spoke with near unanimity about America's positives. The best things about America, they said, are its freedoms—of speech, religion, assembly, private property, and so on. Some spoke about American freedom in well-informed and articulate terms, referencing the Bill of Rights, religious pluralism, and political and civil liberties. Others simply said, "Freedom. Anybody can do whatever they want." But the touchstone of nearly all answers, no matter how elaborate or civically minded, was freedom. America's emerging adults are not, as we will show, very politically interested or involved. But they definitely believe in and appreciate American freedoms, which they view as among the best in the world. Typical was this sentiment: "Of course America has its problems, but I think overall, we are blessed with a lot of freedoms, we have freedom of choice. We can speak our own opinions. Overall we may have our problems as all societies do, but I think it's a good society." Appreciating America's freedom seems closely connected to personal autonomy as a core value of emerging adults. At the same time, we will suggest in this book's conclusion, such a valorizing of personal freedom and autonomy can make it difficult for many emerging adults to "figure out who they really are" and know what a good life—to which it would be worth truly devoting oneself—might look like.

A Less Typical Theme—America Has Major Problems. Most of the respondents thought that America is not a perfect society but described it as one of the better ones on earth in which to live. They appreciated America's freedoms and valued its material prosperity. Often, but not always, they offered various ideas about what problems trouble the United States—such as self-centeredness, poverty, or intolerance. But for the most part, they expressed a benign view of their society and culture. A very small minority dissented from this viewpoint, however. Some said that America has major problems, without mentioning the positives of freedom. One, for instance, reported, "I feel confident that the United States is in decline from our status of comfort and false securities that we've had about ourselves. I think people are realizing the negative effects of capitalism and are trying to deal with that now and want reparations." Another observed, "It seems that gas prices are getting higher, costs are getting higher, and people are losing jobs, can't find jobs. Maybe it is because I am living on my own now so I see that now, but I see things getting worse."

Volunteering and Giving Someday, Maybe

The emerging adults studied in the interviews are not big on volunteering and voluntary financial giving, at least at this point in their lives. They are so focused on themselves, especially on learning to stand on their own two feet, that they seem incapable of thinking more broadly about community involvement, good citizenship, or even the most modest levels of charitable giving. It is not that they are apathetic—they do believe that helping others with time and money can be a good thing. They simply do not think that they have the resources to be concerned with such matters at this point in their lives. They think, we have already shown, they have no money to give to any good causes, even if they wanted to. Thus, they feel no responsibility for voluntary financial giving of even the most moderate sums, because they consider themselves broke. As one respondent said, "Somebody needs to give money to me!" They also view themselves as stretched thin when it comes to time, saying both that they have too many time commitments and obligations already to add anything else (especially that doesn't pay) and that their schedules are too unpredictable to responsibly commit to something like regular volunteering. As one respondent said, "I actually don't have the time for it. I feel like if I'm going to do something good for the community I might as well do something good that I get paid for too. I mean like, uh huh, but I don't have a lot of time." So they volunteer very little, if at all. They reflect only slight awareness that they may now even in small ways be establishing patterns and priorities concerning time and money that will carry through the rest of their lives. They also exhibit little appreciation for the fact that their time responsibilities and financial burdens will increase as their incomes and families grow, that the situation will not necessarily get much easier. Rather—as with their assumptions about the radical disconnect between the hooking-up and the settled-down phases of their romantic and sexual lives—nearly all assume that volunteering and financial giving are simply unrelated to their current existences, but perhaps will become more important at some future time in life. Someday, when they have a lot more time and money than they do now, they may begin to volunteer and give money to good causes—that is, if as individuals they then so choose. Meanwhile, financial giving is something that excessively rich people, such as Bill Gates, should be doing. Again, any sense of, say, their dependence on a larger social infrastructure or on shared institutional goods, which cannot be taken for granted but must be actively sustained, and to which they are thus obliged to contribute, if only in small ways, is nonexistent. Their view is essentially that they have grown up, have (more or less) played by the rules, and are now in the processes of learning to become fully independent.

Whether they in due time—because they are "good people"—choose to volunteer or give money are matters to be determined in the future.

Don't Expect to Change the World

Most emerging adults in America have extremely modest to no expectations for ways society or the world can be changed for the better. Very few are idealistic or activist when it comes to their making a mark on the world. Many are totally disconnected from politics, and countless others are only marginally aware of what today's pressing political issues might be. One of the respondents said about the possibility of getting involved in politics, "No. I try to stay out of the line of fire." Furthermore, few of them are bothered by these disconnections. Again, it is not that most are expressly apathetic or cynical, exactly—although, as one respondent suggested, there is a bit of that present: "Our Senator, when he first went into office, was talking about how he was gonna get us out of debt, this and that, and now we're twice in debt from then. The situation only got worse." Nor is it that emerging adults are generally vicious, "me first" social climbers and exploiters of selfish opportunities who do not care about others. They simply think of themselves as "realistic" about the likely influence they might have on the society and world around them. Helping to make good changes happen, when possible, would be a good thing. But getting all worked up with idealism is naïve, maybe even immature. "It's confusing," one respondent said.

> You have all these dreams when you are little. I am a big dreamer. Like if I wanted to sell lemonade, I thought I could sell a million of them. That is how I am. To save the world, you just start to realize that that stuff isn't necessarily possible. And it is just confusing because you have all the stuff you want to do, but how do you make it happen?

Why is it that so few emerging adults consider making change in the world a real possibility? For one thing, many of them feel nearly overwhelmed with the single challenge of standing on their own two feet—anything much beyond keeping money in the checking account, getting the GED or finishing up college, and keeping up with important relationships seems unmanageable. Furthermore, the political issue dominating the headlines during the five years prior to the 2008 round of interviewing was what the Bush administration called the "war against terror," especially as waged in Iraq and Afghanistan. The respondents were divided over the value of the war, but nearly all viewed it as well beyond their own influence or control. More generally, the world of politics and social activism similarly appear remote and ineffectual to most emerging adults. They seem to feel pretty powerless, in some cases hopeless, about influencing the larger public world in which they live. In many cases, a strong sense of fatalism creeps into their attitude about the larger social and political world. So while they are very optimistic about their own personal futures, they are hardly optimistic about the prospects of helping to make some aspect of the larger sociopolitical world a better place. At most, the "world around them" that they believe they stand a chance of influencing for the good is local: their families, careers, friends, and romantic interests.[11] The rest of the world will continue to have its good and bad sides. All you can do is live in it, such as it is, and make out the best you can.

A Less Typical Theme—We Can Change the World. While most respondents held very modest and sometimes no expectations about positive social or political changes that they could help to bring about, a small minority voiced a dissenting opinion. Some emerging adults believe that in fact they "can make a difference." They see opportunities for having an impact on society for the better and believe they are obliged to take on those challenges. They seek to enhance economic and educational opportunity, grassroots urban renewal, racial justice, the end of human trafficking, and other causes through creative communication, community organizing, and social movement activism. They view anything less as a selfish indifference that is morally intolerable. One respondent, for example, stated, "I think politics is good. I think people should be involved in their own world, rather than sitting back and complaining about issues, they should become more involved in politics. They should vote. If they're dissatisfied, they should run for an office. People should involve themselves in politics."

Submerge in Interpersonal Relationships

Emerging adults' evident lack of optimism, even fatalism at times, about their potential to influence the larger social and political world seems closely related, as indicated earlier, to the fact that most of them are withdrawn from the public square and instead submerged in interpersonal relationships in their private worlds. Few emerging adults are involved in community organizations or other social change–oriented groups or movements. Not many care to know much of substance about political issues and world events. Few are intellectually engaged in any of the major cultural and ethical debates and challenges facing U.S. society. Almost none have any vision of a common good. Citizenship is not a word to be found on their tongues. Some even said they were not planning on voting in the upcoming election. The extent of public disengagement among the vast majority of emerging adults is astonishing. On the other hand, they can be said to be extremely "socially engaged" in quite a different way: they are deeply invested in social life beyond their immediate selves primarily through their interpersonal relationships. And they pursue these private-sphere emotional and relational investments with fervent devotion. Much of their lives appears to be centered on creating and maintaining personal relationships. What makes emerging adults most happy are their good relationships with family, friends, and interesting other associates. By comparison, the larger public world, civic life, and the political realm seem to them alien and impenetrable. Few emerging adults are into hobbies, participate in community groups or other organized activities, or are even devoted to working long hours for the sake of careers—despite their also being concerned with being able to stand financially on their own two feet. Instead, they are absorbed with friends and family. Most emerging adults would rather spend large amounts of time merely "hanging out" with various intimates and acquaintances, for instance, than being part of clubs or interest groups, not to mention political parties or social movements. Thus the apparent move of Americans away from civic participation in public life and toward the enjoyment of "lifestyle enclaves"—previously noted by various cultural observers[12]—may for emerging adults be progressing yet further toward the nearly total submersion of self into fluidly constructed, private networks of technologically managed intimates and associates.

This strongly relational way of engaging their worlds clearly appears— as the phrase "technologically managed" suggests—closely connected to the technologies of communication that preoccupy their lives. Even during the interviews, many respondents repeatedly checked and sometimes answered their cell phones. Some text-messaged between interview questions. Others set their cell phones out on tables to be closely monitored. Yet others expressed real interest as a point of conversation in the latest cell phones and other communication devices that some of the interviewers owned. In short, emerging adults are keen on gadgets that facilitate their interpersonal communications. And managing personal relationships turns out for many to be not a distinct task reserved for routinely scheduled times of the day or week, but rather a ubiquitous, 24/7 life activity. Myriad friends and family members are always available at their fingertips, through cell phones, texting, IMing, blogging, and messaging. Many emerging adults routinely text-message friends while in class and on the job. They email from the bus. They blog late at night to share with peers every detail of their days' feelings and experiences. They check Facebook while doing homework, "just to check in with friends" and "to see what's going on with other people." The instant feedback and stimulation from friends and family about every choice and action and emotion they make and feel seems to be very satisfying to them, sometimes perhaps addictive. Yet all of these relationship-managing activities and private communications distractions seem to make it difficult for emerging adults to pursue tasks that require full concentration or patient dedication. These relationship-oriented activities also appear to fill up, however problematically, the void opened by their lack of civic participation in fostering the shared goods of public life.[13]

It's Too Easy to Fall Back into Old Ways

Emerging adults are in various stages of breaking away from their old high school lives. Some since leaving high school have made the total and clean break of moving on to completely different social circles and activities. Others remain highly involved in their old communities, social networks, and activities. Most, however, have only a few close ties to high school friends, numerous sporadic connections to old acquaintances, and various sets of different kinds of post-high-school good friends. Because most emerging adults live in limbo between high school days and full adulthood, however, many report occasional experiences of "regressing" to their old patterns of previous years. They think of themselves as currently older, wiser, and more mature. But when they return home on various occasions and get together with old friends from high school, they can find it difficult not to revert to old habits of speech and behavior in which they know their "real" selves no longer engage. They often then find that they are annoyed or embarrassed with themselves for acting like kids again. Similarly, when returning or visiting home for summers or holidays, those who have mostly lived on their own for a few years and think of themselves as generally grown up can find themselves asking permission to stay out late at night or arguing with their parents just like they did when they were 15 years old. They don't like it. It all reminds them of precisely that which they are trying to grow up out of—their former lives of childishness and dependence, in relation to which they have begun to taste the sweet freedom of escape and maturity.

IMPLICATIONS FOR EMERGING ADULT RELIGION

Different readers may encounter the various themes just discussed with gladness, indifference, or dismay, depending on their own perspectives and values. Our primary aim here is not to make value judgments, however, but rather to set a context for better understanding the religious and spiritual lives of emerging adults. The broad-brush picture we have just painted of the cultural worlds that most American emerging adults sustain and live in provides an expansive map of the larger sociocultural terrain within which we can locate and better understand their religious and spiritual lives more specifically. There are not always direct connections between the cultural structures just described—whether mainstream or alternative—and the contours of emerging adults' religion and spirituality. But there are at least some likely implications for faith and spiritual life that are worth observing here before moving on. We think the likely repercussions for religion and spiritual life of many of the cultural patterns we have just described include the following.

Disruptions

Religious faith and practice generally associate with settled lives and tend to be disrupted by social, institutional, and geographical transitions. This connection between religious and other kinds of disruptions is a broad sociological fact. Many life transitions and disturbances of diverse sorts—divorce, death of a family member, leaving home, job loss—have been shown by studies to correlate negatively with religious practices.[14] For example, people who move residences are significantly less likely to attend religious services than people who do not move.[15] That is so probably for multiple reasons. At a psychological level, restless and risk-taking personalities, for instance, who are more likely to move, may also be less religiously inclined than settled and cautious people and so may more easily drop out of religion.[16] For present purposes, important *causal mechanisms*[17] linking life transitions and disruptions with declining religious involvement likely include the following. Transitions by definition break patterns and routines, and establishing new ones that are very similar to the ones practiced earlier is more difficult than either simply continuing with the same ones or completely changing them. It is harder to find and get involved in a new religious congregation in a new community, for example, than to keep attending one from which you have not moved away. Transitions also tend to drain resources and attention, including those needed in the most basic areas of life—arranging transportation, setting up a new living situation, learning a new place and systems, and so on usually all consume time, energy, and money. It can be harder to think about visiting a church and praying or reading scripture regularly, for instance, when the new apartment sink does not drain, you have not figured out your favorite places to go shopping yet, and your new roommate is messier and louder than you imagined. Transitions also expose people to fresh contacts in new social networks, which increases the chances (relative to making no transition) that new and different relationships will pull those people in new directions, including potentially less religious directions. When a young man moves out of his parents' home into an apartment with his buddies and their friend, or a young woman moves from home into a big college dorm, they become exposed to new sets of people who likely have more different backgrounds and perspectives than the people their parents encouraged them to associate with during childhood and adolescence. Such an increased scope of diversity in social network ties (besides their newness per se)—especially those that prove to involve affective bonding of various kinds—is a structural alteration of life that increases the likelihood of reducing former religious practices, if not changing religious beliefs. Because of these and other causal mechanisms, we have good reason to believe that the sheer plentitude of life transitions that emerging adults experience themselves has the tendency to lessen the frequency and importance of religious practices and potentially undercut established religious beliefs. In face of these factors, emerging adults staying religiously active—assuming they even were active as younger adolescents—requires that the life of faith be made a high priority in life, one that can overcome countervailing forces.

Distractions

Besides the religion-undermining causal mechanisms set into motion by many significant life transitions, emerging adults engage in a number of other issues and activities that often distract them from possible religious and spiritual interests and involvements. To begin with, the central task of emerging adult life itself—learning to stand on one's own two feet—is in some sense one big, macro distraction from religious devotion. Emerging adults are primarily dedicated in this phase of their lives to achieving their own financial, identity, and household independence from their parents. Serious religious faith and practice do not necessarily directly conflict with that mission, but they are not crucial or intrinsic to it either. Learning to stand on one's own involves concerns that most view as this-worldly: finishing education, skills training, job experience, career development, paying bills, balancing bank accounts, setting up new households, buying cars, developing one's own social networks, and so on. Relating to God, going to religious services, reading scripture, getting involved in a religious community, praying regularly, growing in faith, and such concerns are rarely in American culture considered relevant to or important for achieving identity and financial independence. So investing wholeheartedly in the former can be thought of as having the effect of neglecting the latter.

At a more practical level, many emerging adults' lives involve concerns and activities that few people think of as connected to or supportive of religion or spirituality. One, for those who go to college, is school. Classes, homework, writing papers, and studying for exams are often demanding tasks that do not fit into nine-to-five work schedules and are often mentally pressing at all times. Most emerging adults, whether in school or out, also work at one or more jobs, which also consumes time, energy, and attention. Outside of work and possibly school, emerging adults spend a good amount of time attending to various errands associated with living on their own—searching for places to live, signing leases, buying household items, shopping for groceries, signing insurance papers, inquiring into new academic programs, getting the oil changed, and so on. More mature adults may feel little sympathy for emerging adults' struggling with these normal life demands. But from the perspective of emerging adults, youth who are newly trying to figure out adult life's many responsibilities, these errands and tasks can feel all-consuming. Emerging adults talk repeatedly about how busy they are. They would have a hard time imagining—if they thought about it—squeezing the demands of a committed religious life into their hectic and unpredictable schedules.

That is made worse by another factor: after school and work comes play. Fun-related distractions in many emerging adults' lives include going to parties, mixing with new people, watching movies, going camping or to the beach for the weekend, playing some golf, having a few drinks, playing paint ball, filming a movie, just hanging out for hours at a time, or any other number of recreational and social activities that take time, energy, and sometimes money and planning. On top of all that is time spent on gadgets like cell phones, iPods, and iPhones and online social networks like MySpace and Facebook. Plus there are the regular phone calls and visits home to parents that many emerging adults try not to neglect. Social life can be distracting and draining in other ways as well. Some friends, for instance, can be very high-maintenance—they need regular talking to or comforting, require a good amount of debriefing and gossip, may come home drunk or overdosed and so require an evening of caretaking, a ride to the courthouse or some other random destination, or any other variety of help and support that friends sometimes need. Crucial with regard to religious community and practice in all of this are Friday and Saturday nights, the emerging adults' key times for recreational and social life. Most of the week is consumed with work and maybe school. The fun emerging adults believe they are supposed to be having usually centers on the evenings and weekends, and especially weekend evenings. Even if one wanted to go to religious services, one has probably stayed up too late the night before to wake up, dress nicely, and head off to such a service in the morning. More generally, there is simply too much else going on at the time to go to church, synagogue, temple, or mosque. And even if one does manage to get to a religious service on occasion, the shape and demands of one's life tend to prevent that from becoming a regular occurrence, so no pattern gets established. Again, some religiously committed emerging adults manage to practice their religious faith regularly and, from their perspective, without much difficulty. But doing so requires that religion be a very high priority—or at least a consistent habit—that trumps the demands of the rest of life, a commitment around which the competing needs of school, work, and play are adjusted, rather than vice versa.

Differentiation

Part of emerging adults' central life task of standing on their own is establishing identity differentiation. Many people assume that this task is taken on mostly during the teenage years, those supposedly rebellious years when adolescents figure out who they are apart from being the children of their parents. Of course, identity differentiation begins during the teen years, but a great deal of it today is accomplished during the twenties, in emerging adulthood. Very few emerging adults want to drastically break their ties with parents. If anything, they actually want to improve their relationships with their parents, toward feeling closer and more friendly. But they want that on a renegotiated basis, such that their identity is independent. When emerging adults think about "Who am I and what is my life all about?" they do not want the answer to be defined much by their parents anymore. They want space, autonomy, differentiation. But they only have so many ways to achieve that. Many of them are still at least somewhat financially dependent on their parents. Some still live at home. Some go to college at a parent's alma mater. Many remain tied to friends of the family. Religion, particularly public religious practice, is one arena that effectively offers emerging adults an opportunity to achieve clear identity differentiation. For most of them, to attend religious services with their families of origin on a regular basis—holidays and special visits are exempt here—feels like being the old dependent child again, a role they feel they have outgrown. For some, even to attend services in another place at a religious congregation that is something like their parents' can feel the same way. Furthermore, in most households, parents think they have already done their job in religious training; many directly tell their emerging adult children that their religious beliefs and practices are now their individual choices, that they stand on their own. Religion also seems to many to be of less consequence than matters of education, finances, love interests, childbearing, and other more pressing areas, as a possible place to slack off, drop out, or otherwise become quite different from one's parents. So religion makes a good area in which one can demonstrate that one is different and independent from one's parents and perhaps younger siblings. On the one hand, religion is a department that concerns very basic life matters; on the other hand, departing from parents on religious matters, especially religious practices, seems to risk few costs. So identity differentiation around religion can be gained with little expense or loss. Not that this differentiation process is typically pursued in a conscious, rational, calculated, deliberate manner—often, none of the parties involved recognize what is happening in this identity differentiation. But we think that that process is nevertheless often at work. Typically, emerging adults do not seek identity differentiation by rejecting their parents' religious beliefs, whatever they are, outright. Usually, emerging adults retain many of their religious beliefs—even if they are compartmentalized or moved further into the background than they were in earlier years. What changes most, instead, are public religious practices, particularly religious service attendance but also involvement in youth groups, Bible studies, service teams, and other religiously based groups. With this social-psychological causal mechanism of identity differentiation in play, therefore, emerging adults who continue to regularly practice the religious faith of their parents might be expected to compensate for this "loss" of identity differentiation on religious grounds by some other means—marrying "young," for instance, or moving to a faraway city and starting a new career.[18]

Postponed Family Formation and Childbearing

This social causal mechanism that tends to reduce the religious faith and practice of emerging adults is easy to understand. Marriage, children, and religion tend to go together, at least in the United States. So the more marriage and children are delayed, the more religious involvement is postponed and perhaps never reengaged (if ever engaged in the first place). One of the strongest factors that brings young adult Americans back to religion after a probable hiatus during emerging adulthood is their formation of new families and especially having children.[19] For many of them, being involved in a religious community seems an appropriate part of a fully achieved adult life. And many young parents want their children to become religiously socialized, even if they themselves are not deeply committed to faith. In the causally reverse direction, being more religious also makes people more likely to marry at all, to marry earlier, to have children at all, and to bear them at a younger age[20]— thus, the strong family/religion connection in the United States is mutually reinforcing, even synergistic. All else being equal, then, we can say that the younger Americans are when they marry and bear children, the more religious they are likely to be. Here enters emerging adulthood, in that it is a relatively new life course phase that, as described earlier, is caused by, entails, and promotes an increasing delay of marriage and childbearing among American youth. This has the effect of increasing the number of years in the American life course during which young (often unmarried and childless) people feel much less need to be religiously involved. And that in turn decreases the number of years—formative ones at that—during which American young people are being actively shaped by public participation in religious traditions. So the postponement of "settling down" that is associated with emerging adulthood unintentionally produces, as a causal mechanism, the tendency for Americans to reduce religious involvements during this phase of life.

Keeping Options Open

The basic orientation of the majority of emerging adults' lives is to make the most of current opportunities for developing future opportunities as fully as possible. Emerging adults are generally loath to close doors or burn bridges. Instead, they want to keep as many options open as possible. Numerous dimensions of the culture of emerging adulthood—uncertainty about purpose, delaying settling down, the individual as authority, amorphous relationships, strategic management of risk, the tentativeness of cohabitation, aversion to moral judgments, reluctance to commit to social and political involvements and investments—reflect and reinforce their interest in maintaining as many live and promising options as is feasible. By contrast, missing opportunities, losing control, getting locked in, compromising autonomy, overlooking potential, surrendering freedoms are all bads to avoid if at all possible. The consequences for religion are evident. Religious experience sometimes takes the form of journey, renewal, freedom, exploration, surprise, or unpredictability. But America's main religions' principal modes of experience and involvement, by contrast, normally take the forms of trust, commitment, investment, discipline, and learning from and worshiping something bigger and authoritative beyond the self. Consider, for instance, the words "devotion" and "faithfulness" and how they relate to the notions of autonomy, deferral of full responsibility, and keeping open all options. They do not fit together well. As a result, a significant part of the underlying thrust of emergent adults' lives embodies contradictions with the central associations and experiences of American religion. If religion means being sober, settled, and steadfast, and if emerging adulthood means postponing those things, then it means not being particularly concerned about religion. Religion is part of settling down, which belongs to the future. Framed as a social causal mechanism, emerging adults' interest in indefinitely maintaining all of their options tends to decrease their desire and ability to commit to the investments, routines, and disciplines of religious faith and practice. Sustaining strong religious belief, practices, and membership in a specific community of faith requires emerging adults to forego some options, close some doors, make some consequential decisions, and commit to something particular that will involve opportunity costs.

Honoring Diversity

Emerging adults generally outshine their elders in being open to and usually accepting of people and lifestyles that are different from them and theirs. For most of their lives, from preschool on, most emerging adults have been taught by multiple institutions to celebrate diversity, to be inclusive of difference, to overcome racial divides, to embrace multiculturalism, to avoid being narrowly judgmental toward others who are out of the ordinary. In many ways, it seems that most emerging adults have believed those messages on a more general level—or at least have realized that they are supposed to believe them and might pay a price if they reveal that they do not entirely. Emerging adults can exhibit a very impressive ease in associating and getting on with people of different races, ethnicities, appearances, and other attributes that more easily separated people of former generations. They believe "Every person is different," "Judging people is wrong," and "Nobody should hurt other people." Despite the value of such inclusiveness and acceptance generally—particularly as related to racism and related problems that have plagued U.S. culture—this general orientation when brought to questions of religious life tends to undermine the effectiveness of particularities of faith traditions and practices. Most emerging adults do not hold anything against anyone simply because they are of a different religion. Whatever anyone else wants to believe is fine with them. But this also means that none of what is distinctive about any given religious tradition, history, worldview, worship style, and so on matters all that much to emerging adults. They suspect that these particularities might separate people of different religions, might bring into question the equal value of different cultures, might imply implicit judgments against others who are different. Emerging adults can easily see a religious particularity as carrying an implicit claim to being not merely somebody's personal preference but the right way, by conviction, to think about and do things religiously. Such an implication does not seem inclusive but rather exclusive and judgmental and so does not sit well with the majority of emerging adults. Here appears an enigma of inclusiveness: that a moral system valuing diversity that begins by valuing everyone's particular differences somehow ends up devaluing any given particular difference. In any case, as a result, most emerging adults are happy with religion so long as it is general and accepting of diversity but are uncomfortable if it is anything else. And here appears a second enigma concerning inclusive religion: that among all American religious traditions, the one that would seem to best suit the values and interests of emerging adults, because of its emphasis on tolerance and inclusion, is theologically liberal mainline Protestantism—yet that is precisely the religious tradition that, we will soon show, is faring among the worst in retaining and recruiting emergent adults.

There seem to be some tensions and incongruities at work in emerging adulthood culture as it relates to religious faith. But to return to the central point of this paragraph: Understood as a social-psychological causal mechanism, the tendency among most emerging adults to want to honor diversity, to avoid judging whatever is different, and to be socially inclusive has the unintended consequence of minimizing the importance of religious particularities and so encouraging emerging adults to conceive of religions as being generically similar. This produces a vision of religion in general that also turns out, we will show, to be not very appealing to most emerging adults. Those among them who are highly religious must mentally and socially negotiate this tension—either by rejecting the common governing notions of inclusion and equal acceptance altogether or by developing a fairly sophisticated understanding of how the genuine acceptance of and love for others can fully coexist with discriminating judgments of truth and the rejection of believed falsehoods, what is in their view erroneous.

Self-confident Self-Sufficiency

Most of the emerging adults interviewed exuded a strong sense of confident self-reliance. They were optimistic about their own lives. They expressed no regrets about their past lives, however problematic. Most of them thought they were close to standing on their own two feet as autonomous individuals. Yes, many of them had made stupid mistakes and poor judgments in the past, which had hurt them. But they thought that they had learned from those and were now moving forward with assurance. They were (almost) not dependent on their parents anymore. Few of them were yet making decisions with a marriage partner. They were authorized as individuals to know and choose what is right, at least for themselves. It was difficult for them to imagine an objective reference point of any kind beyond their own individual selves by which to evaluate themselves, their lives, and those of others. They could decide what to believe about ultimate reality based on what feels right to them, whatever fits their personal experience. And they were well on their way—they hoped and expected—to full independence of career, household living, finances, and identity. This is what their lives are all about now. One might wonder, then, how religion does or could fit into such lives. Why would an emerging adult want or need religious faith, religious teachings, a religious community to which to belong and contribute? Why might emerging adults need God in their daily or weekly lives? What role could there be for a religious tradition, a people of faith, a believing community to teach them about ultimate reality or ethical living or discipleship or self-sacrificial love for others? Is there an obvious purpose, for emerging adults, of disciplined prayer, study of scripture, and service to others? The logical answers to these questions, given emerging adults' self-confident self-sufficiency, would seem to be no, not much. The ways emerging adult culture constructs the lives of most 18- to 29-year-olds simply seems to leave little room or felt need for God, faith, worship, prayer, community, or other forms of religious learning, practice, and service. In short—stated in terms of a causal mechanism—most emerging adults' perceptions of their own self-confident self-sufficiency, when played out in the realms of social relations and felt requirements of life, trigger social-psychological and network-relational processes that tend to have the effect of reducing the felt need for and interest in religious faith, practice, and belonging. For an emerging adult to remain deeply involved in religious life, he or she probably have to feel a greater sense of dependence and need, in relation to which religion makes sense, than most of his or her peers do.

Self-evident Morality

The vast majority of emerging adults thinks and feels that what is morally good and bad, right and wrong, true and untrue is self-evident to any reasonably interested person. It is their belief and experience that they themselves instinctively and easily know what is morally and ethically good and right and true, and that they can act on it without much difficulty. Somebody would have to be a really bad person, they think, the kind of person who willfully and continually does the wrong things—like a murderer, rapist, or armed robber—not to know easily what is morally right and wrong. Of course, emerging adults believe that a lot of what children learn about morality they get from religion when they are little. But then again, they assume, all religions teach the same basic moral principles. And most nonreligious people know what is morally right and wrong apart from religious faith, simply through common sense or by coming up in society. And in the end, although people make mistakes and have problems, most people are actually morally pretty good. This is how most emerging adults think about moral knowledge and behavior.

Given these assumptions and outlooks, what important role might religion play in their lives in this arena? Not a big one. They believe, we will show in chapter 5, that the main purpose of religion is to help people to be good. But they also believe, as already discussed, that no one religion has a monopoly on helping people to be good, as religions all teach the same basic morals, and that people can know without difficulty what is good and act morally apart from religion, as a lot of nonreligious people are good. Finally, they know that a person's being religious does not guarantee that person being good, that some religious people are not good—again, every person is different, and you can only decide things on a case-by-case basis. In the end, therefore, religion plays an optional role in morally good living. The single thing in which it specializes—helping people to be good—is actually not needed in order for people to achieve that outcome. Religion thus serves a nonobligatory, noncrucial function in life. It does not have a corner on anything unique. Nobody has to believe in or practice it to live morally. As a result, its status becomes that of a lifestyle accessory, like options one might choose to have in one's new car according to one's preference. If someone particularly needs or wants to have religion in his or her life, as a support for good, moral living, then that is good and fine for that person. Religious faith can be helpful and important to some individuals if they need it or so choose it. But if other individuals happen to not need or want religion, then that is fine, too. It depends on the individual, and only the individual can know or decide for himself or herself. Framed as a social causal mechanism: the believed self-evidence and generalization of moral knowledge, motivations, and behaviors that defines religion as an optional lifestyle choice around personal needs and preferences makes it easy for most emerging adults—possibly wishing for other reasons to distance themselves from religion—to elect not to include religious faith in their larger set of lifestyle accessories. An emerging adult who is firmly committed to religious faith and practice, therefore, either must believe that he or she as an individual personally needs or wants religion in order to be a good or better person or must have bucked the prevailing idea that morality is quite self-evident and easy and so want to learn as a dependent disciple the moral teachings and disciplines of his or her particular religious tradition.

Partying, Hooking Up, Having Sex, and Cohabiting

One of the other reasons why many, though not all, emerging adults may want to distance themselves from religion is that religion in their minds conflicts with certain other lifestyle options that are higher priorities. Most of them want to party, to hook up, to have sex in relationships, and to cohabit; or if they do not do these things now, many at least want to keep them as options for the future. Many want to drink, or at least be able to drink, if they want to. Some want to smoke weed or, again, to be able to if they want. Many

want to have sex with a boyfriend or girlfriend, or to at least be free to do
so if the occasion arises, and many want to be able to hook up with someone
they meet to whom they may feel attracted. Many also want to cohabit with
current or future serious partners or fiancés before getting married. And all of
this, emerging adults are aware, contradicts the teachings of most religions. So
they simply avoid religion and thereby resolve the conflict. The basic cognitive
logic, as processed through the minds and wants of many emerging adults,
runs simply like this:

> Major Premise: *Serious religion means no partying and no sex before
> marriage.*
> Minor Premise: *I do or may want to party and have sex before marriage.*
> Conclusion: *I am not legitimately part of or interested in serious religion.*

Framed as a social-psychological causal mechanism: most emerging adults
reduce a certain cognitive dissonance they feel—arising from the conflict of
religious teachings against partying and sex before marriage versus their wanting to engage in those behaviors—by mentally discounting the religious teachings and socially distancing themselves from the source of those teachings. In
this simple way, the role of sex, drinking, and sometimes drugs is often important in forming emerging adults' frequent lack of interest in religious faith and
practice. It also helps to explain why some emerging adults assume that they
will become more religious when they finally settle down someday—because
they will then no longer want to party so much or, being married, need to have
sex outside marriage. Therefore, emerging adults who are serious about their
religious faith and practice have to do one of three things: choose to reject
heavy partying and premarital sex; dramatically compartmentalize their lives
so that the their partying and sexual activities are firmly partitioned off from
their religious activities in a way that borders on denial; or be willing to live
with the cognitive dissonance of being committed to two important things
that are incompatible and mutually denying. Not very many emerging adults
can or will do any of these things, so most of them resolve the cognitive dissonance by simply distancing from religion.

Religion as a Resource for Stability and Recovery

Most of the dynamics of emerging adult culture and life in the United States
today seem to have a tendency to reduce the appeal and importance of religious faith and practice. In many ways, the development of emerging adult
culture in the American life course in the last four decades has entailed some
strong religion-undermining effects that are outcomes of the causal mechanisms we have outlined here. But emerging adulthood does not tend to be
religiously corrosive in all ways. At least some features of religious faith and
practice seem to pull 18- to 29-year-old Americans back to them. One that
jumped out in at least some of the interviews concerned the resources religion
provides to certain emerging adults, particularly those who have led troubled

and difficult lives thus far: stability, structure, support, and guidance. The story of Andrea in chapter 6 is a case in point. Other respondents who have struggled and suffered in life—usually due in part to their own (self-described) stupid and self-destructive choices—have already begun to turn the corner, are beginning to get their lives together, and, in some cases, have "met God" or stumbled onto religious ideas and communities along the way. In such cases, religious beliefs, relationships, and practices often offer these persons helpful resources for getting their lives back in order. In religion, such emerging adults who are recovering from whatever troubles or problems have plagued them often find local communities of people who genuinely care about and for them—something that some have never before encountered in their lives and that attracts them back for more. They also find belief systems that set firm boundaries about what is real and unreal, right and wrong, good and bad, healthy and unhealthy—something that, again, they may never have been taught. They also find friendships not associated with their formerly destructive lives, networks of accountability, role models for healthy living, perhaps skilled counseling, and much more.

Our point here is not that religion rescues people but that some of the intrinsic features of mainstream emerging adult life—the many transitions, autonomy, financial tightness, moral relativism, individualistic subjectivism, pervasive drugs, extensive partying, amorphous relationships, sexual license, and perhaps estrangement from parents—leads, for some of them, to broken and compromised lives. For some people these features deliver very hard knocks that are not so easily overcome with assertions of "a lesson learned" and determined optimism. These emerging adults, if they have even been able to pull out of their damaged and damaging lives at all—some have not—need serious help to stop their self-destructive behaviors and engage in the hard work of rebuilding themselves and their futures. It seemed unlikely that some of these emerging adults would be able to overcome their debilitations, and so their futures seem bleak. For some of them, it turns out, religion provides a crucial source of this help. In this way, emerging adulthood's dark side—which touches the lives of more than a few American 18- to 29-year-olds—itself can create a desperately felt need for what religion is well suited to provide.

Ongoing Relations with Parents

This causal social mechanism counters the more dominant one of differentiation, noted earlier, but is still important among some emerging adults. The idea here concerns the ongoing, and often improving, relationships that many emerging adults have with parents. In a different way, this mechanism can also involve the ongoing problematic relationships that some others have with their parents. Most emerging adults are on a mission to stand on their own, out from under the authority and support of their parents. At the same time, most of them value their family relationships, are enjoying improved relations with their parents, and are interested in maintaining contact and amity with them. In such cases, *when parents are seriously religious, want their children to be seriously religious, and have raised them to be so,* the emerging adults' desire to have a good connection with their parents tends to encourage them to continue to affirm and practice their religious faith, even if perhaps in a less intense way. In such cases, to reject the religious faith of one's seriously religious parents, particularly when one already has a good and close relationship with them, would be symbolically and substantively to damage that relationship. For most emerging adults, this is not in their interest. Of course, more than a few parents are not very invested in how religious their emerging adult children turn out to be—and then this mechanism operates less powerfully. But for those parents who are, who have invested a great deal of their own effort to create religious commitments in their children, these children's religious and spiritual choices as emerging adults matter a great deal to them and so have significant consequences for the ongoing relationship. For a minority of emerging adults in this situation, continuing religious faith and practice at some significant level makes sense. Thus, as we will show in Chapter 7, having highly religious parents during the teenage years is one of the most important social factors in producing the most highly religious emerging adults. Such emerging adults have been well socialized for many years to carry on in the faith of the family and have few incentives, in terms of maintaining family relationships that they value, to dramatically reduce or simply drop religious faith and practice out of their lives. It is true, as we said, that this causal mechanism often tends to contradict the mechanism of differentiation, described earlier. But the fact is that multiple causal mechanisms can and do operate simultaneously in people's lives, in ways that are potentially reinforcing, independent, synergistic, contradictory, and neutralizing. Thus, one aspect of emerging adult life may tend to reduce continued religious involvement while another at the same time may tend to increase it. That complexity is normal. What matters, then, for determining actual outcomes are the strengths of the different causal tendencies, the combinations of those operating in any case, and the contextual circumstances (such as relative seriousness of parental faith) conditioning them. Our point here, however, is simply that when parents are particularly serious about their religious faith and practice and hold high expectations for their children, that has consequences. For their emerging adult children, carrying on in the religious faith of the families in which they were raised—particularly when they genuinely value their relationships with parents—becomes a strong causal tendency at work in their lives. In this way, parental commitment, socialization, and expectations often continue to powerfully shape emerging adults.

In quite a different way, a countervailing causal tendency can also operate: when emerging adults have very troubled relationships with their parents— when parents have neglected, abandoned, hurt, disappointed, or betrayed them—they often define their own lives in contrast to these problematic parents. For instance, when disappointing parents are untrustworthy, emerging adults often define themselves as honest and reliable. When hurtful parents act unlawfully, emerging adults often shape themselves to be law abiding. When a parent is rampantly hurtful, an emerging adult will often become a sensitive and caring soul. Not always, of course—some simply follow their troubled parents' footsteps. But often, particularly when there is at least one other parent or other adult who can help an emerging adult deal with his or her negative emotions and envision and pursue a more constructive life, that emerging adult addresses his or her emotions about troubled parental relationships by being different. In many cases, the parents with whom emerging adults have problematic relationships are either not seriously religious or are religious in ways in relation to which their adult children are able to create a religious contrast. In such instances, the desire not to be like the problematic parent, to become a contrast, can cause the emerging adult to seek out and embrace religion and spiritual life, as a means to help establish an identity difference from the parent or parents. In this way, the dynamics of emerging adult life can work in a minority of cases to foster religious commitment.

CONCLUSION

This chapter has presented an overview of many of the themes that characterize the assumptions, beliefs, experiences, and perspectives that define emerging adult culture in the United States today. The reality is, of course, more complicated than any single book chapter can represent. But the preceding pages provide most of the crucial elements needed for placing this book's inquiry on emerging adult religion and spirituality into broader sociocultural context. In the chapters that follow, readers should remember that emerging adult culture comprises not just dominant viewpoints and practices but also alternative, resisting, and conflicting outlooks and lifestyles—many aspects of which have implications for the shape and texture of emerging adult religious faith and practice. Before moving on to a focused analysis of the latter, however, the next chapter first places the religion question in a larger context of historical and life-course comparisons. Doing so will enable us later to draw on the understandings that both this and the next chapter provide: not only of the broad cultural features of emerging adulthood but also of how today's emerging adults compare with both those of earlier generations and with today's older adults.

3

Emerging Adult Religion in Life Course and Historical Perspective

THE PURPOSE OF THIS CHAPTER is to place the religious and spiritual lives of contemporary emerging adults in the historical context of the last quarter century and to compare them, in the area of religion, to older adults in more recent years. How different are emerging adults, as regards religion, from older adults today? How different are they from their age counterparts in previous decades? And how might those differences vary by religious tradition? These are the questions of life course and historical context that this brief chapter addresses.

AGE DIFFERENCES IN RELIGIOUSNESS

If one knew all about the religion and spirituality of emerging adults in the United States but knew nothing about how they compared to older adult Americans, one would lack a crucial sense of the extent to which they are different from or similar to people in other age groups. This section compares the religiousness of U.S. adults of different ages to see how they differ or not. The GSS data[1] collected between 1990 and 2006 have been pooled and the answers to questions about religion separated out by age. What is revealed is that emerging adults in the United States differ from older American adults on certain religious measures but not others. Figure 3.1 shows the ways religiousness varies by age among Americans for 1990–2006: younger adult Americans are less religious than older adults on these measures. The 42 percent of young adults who say that they pray daily or more often, for instance, is much lower

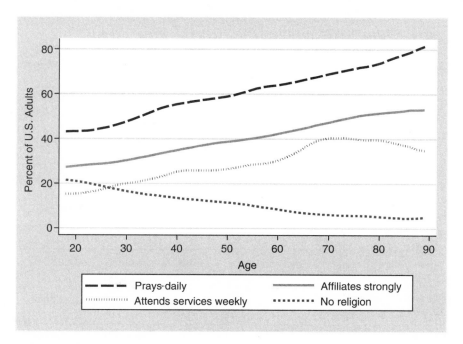

Figure 3.1. Changing Religious Indicators, by Age
Source: GSS 1990–2006.

than the 76 percent of those who are over 75 years old.[2] The percent who say they are "strong" adherents of their religion—as opposed to "somewhat strong," "not very strong," and "no religion"—steadily rises from a low of 27 percent among emerging adults to 53 percent among the oldest American adults. The percent of emerging adults who report attending religious services weekly or more often is 15 percent but rises to nearly 40 percent for older adults.[3] And the percentage of emerging adults who identify as not religious— as opposed to belonging to any religion—stands at a high near 20 percent and declines among older American adults to a low below 10 percent among the oldest. In short, when it comes to prayer, strong affiliation, religious service attendance, and religious identity among American adults, emerging ones are much less religious than older ones.

But emerging adults are not consistently less religious or spiritual on all measures. Figure 3.2 shows that the levels of religiousness of nearly all age groups in the United States are similar. Nearly all American adults say they believe in life after death—as opposed to not believing—about 80 percent in every age group. The percent of emerging adults who report believing that the Bible is the Word of God and is to be interpreted literally is no lower than that of most U.S. adults of working age, and the percentage among retirement age adults expressing that belief increases no more than about 10 percent.[4] Finally, the percentage of American adults who identify as religious liberals[5] is

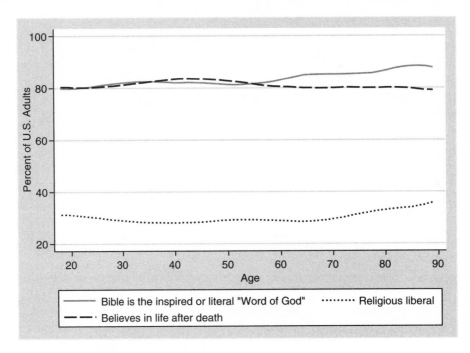

Figure 3.2. Stable Religious Indicators, by Age
Source: GSS 1990–2006.

fairly steady across all age groups. So emerging adults do not appear to have less belief than older adults in life after death or a literalistic view of the Bible. Nor do higher levels of religious liberalism appear among emerging adults. On these measures during these survey years (1990–2006), emerging adults looked similar to older adults. Whether emerging adults are less religious than older adults depends, therefore, on the religious measure in question.

The foregoing analyses of age differences focus on all Americans grouped together and then pulled apart by age. Interesting variations emerge, however, when Americans are disaggregated into different major religious groups. The survey sample does not contain enough members of minority religious groups—Jews, Mormons, Muslims, and the like—so the analysis here must focus on four major Christian groups: evangelical Protestant, mainline Protestant, black Protestant, and Catholic.[6] Figure 3.3, for instance, shows differences in daily prayer by age, separating out these four major groups into different sloping lines.[7] In daily prayer, roughly parallel upward trends appear moving from younger to older Americans. But the slopes and levels of the lines vary by religious tradition. The age differences in daily prayer among Catholics and mainline Protestants are much more dramatic than among evangelical Protestants and black Protestants. While the vast majority of the oldest Americans in all traditions tend to pray daily, only about 40 percent of Catholic and mainline Protestant emerging adults pray daily. Black Protestant

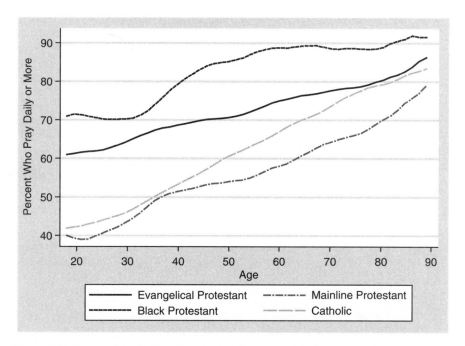

Figure 3.3. Percent Praying Daily or More, by Age and Religious Tradition
Source: GSS 1990–2006.

and evangelical Protestant emerging adults are much more likely to pray daily than their mainline and Catholic peers.

Figure 3.4 shows a similar pattern in "strong" affiliation with religious tradition. Among all four major faith traditions analyzed here, older members report stronger adherence than younger ones. But the gap in strength of affiliation between black Protestant and evangelical Protestant emerging adults, on the one hand, and Catholic and mainline Protestant emerging adults, on the other, is sizeable—roughly 20 percent. Whereas the oldest Catholics report stronger religious affiliations than the oldest evangelical Protestants, nearly 20 percent more emerging adult evangelical Protestants report "strong" affiliations than do emerging adult Catholics. Overall, American Catholics show the largest differences in strength of affiliation across age groups. (For similar figures showing similar results on age and faith tradition differences in religious service attendance, belief in life after death, and religious affiliation measures, see figs. A.1 and A.2.)

The findings reveal that American emerging adults[8] in recent years are on many measures of religion less religious than older adults. Emerging adults are less likely than older adults to pray daily and attend religious services weekly. They affiliate with their faiths less strongly and are more likely to identify themselves as not religious. They are not, however, less likely than older adults to believe in life after death or hold literalistic views of the Bible, and they

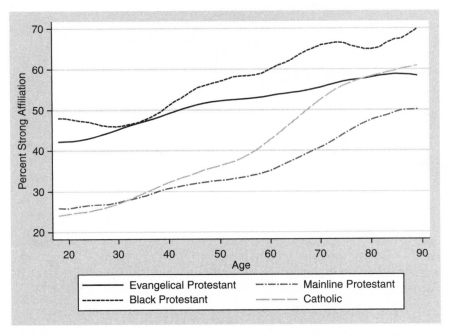

Figure 3.4. Percent Strongly Affiliating with Religious Tradition, by Age and Religious Tradition
Source: GSS 1990–2006.

are not more likely to be religiously liberal.[9] Those differences vary by religious type, however. In general, evangelical Protestants and black Protestants exhibit higher levels of religiousness across all age groups than do Catholics and mainline Protestants. And the differences across age among mainline Protestants and sometimes especially Catholics tend to be relatively greater. Stated differently, Catholic and mainline Protestant emerging adults tend to be separated from older adults in their own religious traditions on most religion measures by wider percentage differences than are evangelical Protestants and black Protestants. In the coming chapters, we will examine social causal mechanisms that will help to explain why emerging adults generally tend to be significantly less religious than older adults in the United States.

Meanwhile, we need to register an important caveat that provides some helpful perspective here. Emerging adults are not only less *religiously* committed and involved than older adults but also tend to be less involved in and committed toward a wide variety of other, nonreligious social and institutional connections, associations, and activities. Emerging adults, for instance, belong to fewer voluntary associations, give less money in charitable donations, volunteer less, and read newspapers less than do older adults.[10] Many of these age differences are represented in figures 3.5, 3.6, and 3.7. This information indicates that lower levels of religiousness among emerging adults in the United States do not entirely or even necessarily at all have to do with the

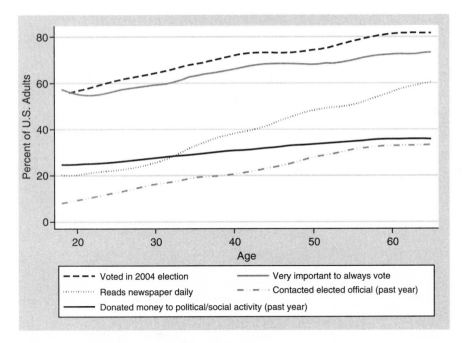

Figure 3.5. Political/Civic Activity by Age, Age 18–65
Source: GSS 1990–2006; GSS 2004; GSS 2006.

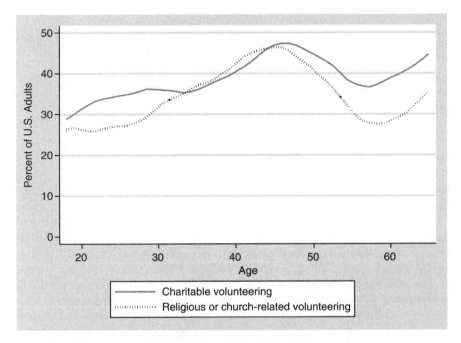

Figure 3.6. Volunteering Activity during Previous Year by Age, Age 18–65
Source: GSS 1998.

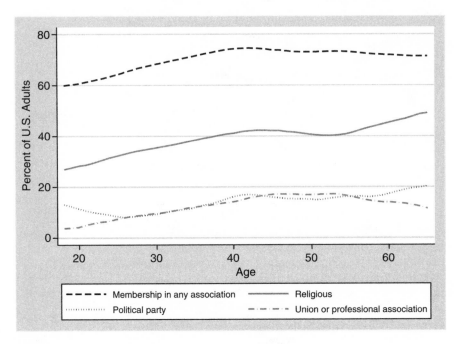

Figure 3.7. Active Association Membership by Age, Age 18–65
Source: GSS 2004.

religious nature of the beliefs and practices being investigated here. Emerging adults are not less interested and involved in religious matters only—they are relatively less interested and involved in a wide array of social associations and activities generally. Their relatively lower degrees of religiousness are only one part of a larger package of lower levels of social and institutional concerns and involvements generally.

HISTORICAL TRENDS IN RELIGIOUSNESS AMONG EMERGING ADULTS SINCE 1972

How religiously different, if at all, are American emerging adults today from their counterparts in previous decades? Have American emerging adults become more or less religious than those of prior generations? To answer these questions, we look next at 18–25 year old General Social Survey respondents, separated out by the year they completed the survey, from 1972 to 2006. Here again, some change and some stability appear. Figure 3.8 shows measures of religion on which emerging adults have changed some over the decades. A 12 percent *increase* appears, across 24 years, in the percentage of emerging adults who believe in life after death—growing from 72 percent in 1972–76 to 84 percent in 2004–6. Also apparent are a 12 percent growth in emerging adults identifying themselves religiously as liberal (from 23 percent in 1972–76 to 35 percent in 2004–6) and a 12 percent increase in the number of emerging adults

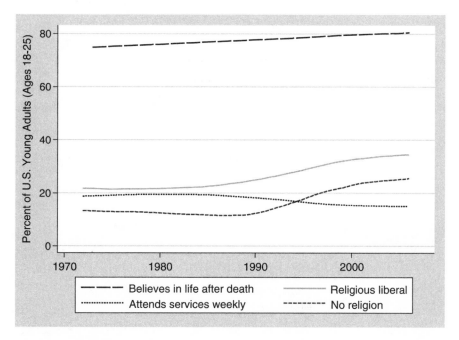

Figure 3.8. Changing Religious Indicators, by Year (Ages 18–25)
Source: GSS 1972–2006.

who say they have no religious affiliation (from 14 percent in 1972–76 to 26 percent in 2004–6). Finally, we note a slight decline in weekly or more frequent religious service attendance among emerging adults, dropping from 19 percent in 1972–76 to 15 percent in 2004–6. In these ways, emerging adults in the United States have become slightly less religious over the last quarter century.

As with the analysis across age groups in the prior section, however, emerging adults today appear no less religious than those of previous decades on at least some measures. Figure 3.9 shows that today's emerging adults are hardly different at all from those of prior decades when it comes to daily prayer, Bible beliefs, and strong religious affiliation.[11] Not much appears to have changed.

Next, as was done earlier, all emerging adults were disaggregated into the same four major Christian traditions, so as to study the religious differences across those groups for each year the survey was conducted. Pulling the religious groups apart this way reveals interesting differences between them in trends over time. Figure 3.10, for example, shows that changes in weekly or more frequent religious service attendance that appeared fairly stable across the decades for all groups combined (in figure 3.8) actually varied dramatically for emerging adults in different religious groups. Evangelical Protestant emerging adults in different years show a slight increase in regular church attendance between 1972 and 2006. Black Protestant emerging adults show a similar increase, though one starting from a lower baseline level. By contrast,

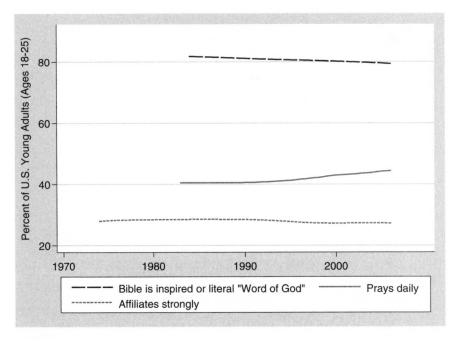

Figure 3.9. Stable Religious Indicators, by Year (Ages 18–25)
Source: GSS 1972–2006.

the percent of Catholic emerging adults attending church weekly or more often has declined by 10 percent over this 24-year period: from 25 percent in 1972–76 to just below 15 percent in 2004–6. The proportion of mainline Protestant emerging adults attend church weekly or more often has also declined, from nearly 15 percent in the early 1970s to below 10 percent by the year 2000. When all of these groups are merged together, as in figure 3.8, their differences cancel each other out, and their combined church attendance trend line remains stable. But when different religious groups are separated out, as here, real differences appear in the church attendance practices of their emerging adults over the decades.

Disaggregating emerging adults into different religious types reveals different trends for these persons over time on other religion measures. Figure 3.11, for instance, examines changes in emerging adults (ages 18 to 24) reporting a "strong" religious affiliation between 1972 and 2006. The percent of strongly affiliated black Protestant emerging adults increased by more than 10 percent during this time period, especially after 1995. The percent of "strong" evangelical Protestant emerging adults also increased, although not as much and starting from a slightly lower baseline. The percent of mainline Protestant emerging adults reporting a strong religious affiliation increased a few points during these years, although a 10–20 percent different remains between them and their black Protestant and evangelical Protestant counterparts. Catholic emerging adults reporting a strong Catholic affiliation, in contrast, decreased

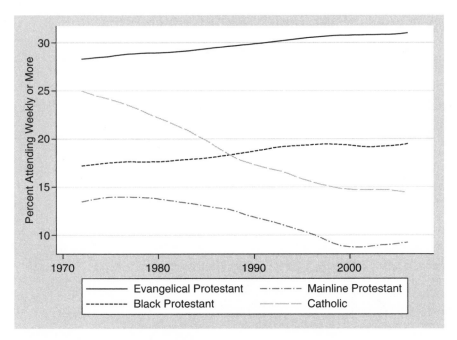

Figure 3.10. Percent of 18- to 25-year-olds Attending Religious Services Weekly or More, by Religious Tradition, 1972–2006

Source: GSS 1972–2006.

by a few percentage points. Again, it is evident that trends in the religious practices and identities of emerging adults over the last quarter century have varied significantly by religious tradition.

Two other religious belief measures viewed in historical perspective and disaggregated by religious tradition reveal interesting findings. First, with regard to emerging adults' beliefs about the Bible, we noted in figure 3.9 that over time they remained quite stable. But figure 3.12 shows that the levels of change in these views vary varies considerably with emerging adults' different religious traditions. The proportion of evangelical Protestant emerging adults who believe the Bible to be either the inspired or literal word of God increased about 5 percent between 1972 and 2006. Black Protestant emerging adults increased more dramatically during the same time period in this regard, gaining nearly 15 percent—such that they started well below the level of evangelicals in 1972 and ended up above evangelicals in 2006. By contrast, the percents of Catholic and mainline Protestant emerging adults who hold these beliefs remained stable between 1972 and 2006, ending up about 10 percent lower than the percents of evangelical Protestants and black Protestants.

Finally, figure 3.13 shows that the levels of change in emerging adults' belief in life after death vary in accordance with their different religious traditions. Evangelical Protestant and mainline Protestant emerging adults both show very slight but steady increases in belief in life after death at the high end

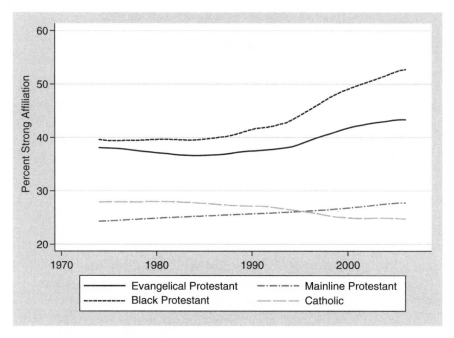

Figure 3.11. Percent of 18- to 25-year-olds Strongly Affiliating with Own Religious Tradition, by Religious Tradition, 1974–2006
Source: GSS 1974–2006.

of the mid-80 percents. Both Catholic and black Protestant emerging adults, by contrast, exhibit marked increases between 1972 and 2006 in their belief in life after death, each gaining significant percentages. (For a similar display of results for faith tradition differences in daily prayer by year of survey, see figure A.3.)

In addition, emerging adults were also disaggregatd by gender (male, female), educational experience (at least some college, no college), and annual income (less than $25,000, $25,000–$100,000, more than $100,000), to enable examine of religious changes over time across these groups. The results (not shown) were unexceptional. Emerging adult men and women, for example, track each other closely in changes in religion between 1972 and 2006. Women are always about 5–10 percent higher on religion measures than men, but any changes over time generally happen in tandem. When the percent of emerging adult men reporting no religious affiliation rises in the late 1980s, the same happens for women at the same time and in the same proportion. The only religion measure examined here for which changes over time do not parallel for men and women is belief in life after death. There the overall slight increase is greater for men than for women—so that men, who started off believing in life after death less than women in 1972, changed at a greater rate and ended up by 2006 more likely than women to believe in life after death. Even so, the differences in changes there are not dramatic. The same

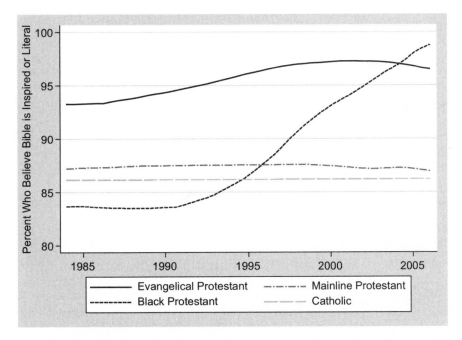

Figure 3.12. Percent of 18- to 25-year-olds Believing the Bible Is Inspired or Literal Word of God, by Religious Tradition, 1984–2006
Source: GSS 1984–2006.

general observation applies to differences in education and income. Emerging adults with some exposure to higher education score higher on all the religion measures except more traditional views of the Bible. But their trends in changes over time do not differ significantly from emerging adults not exposed to higher education. The same is true of trends among emerging adults in different income groups. When they differ, the lowest income group tends to be the least religious. But none of the income groups are dramatically different from the others in how they changed religiously between 1972 and 2006—any modest upward or downward trends tended to happen in all income groups similarly.[12]

This backward historical glance at the religiousness of emerging adults reveals that, on the whole, 18- to 24-year-old Americans have not since 1972 become dramatically less religious or more secular. When viewed as a single group, they have on most measures changed by only a few percentage points in either direction. On the one hand, the percent of emerging adults who pray at least daily and who believe in life after death has increased slightly. On the other hand, compared to prior decades, more emerging adults as a group today claim no religious affiliation, and somewhat fewer attend religious services weekly or more often. The percent of emerging adults who identify religiously as liberal has also grown since 1972. Yet emerging adults in America have not since 1972 significantly changed in their views on the Bible,

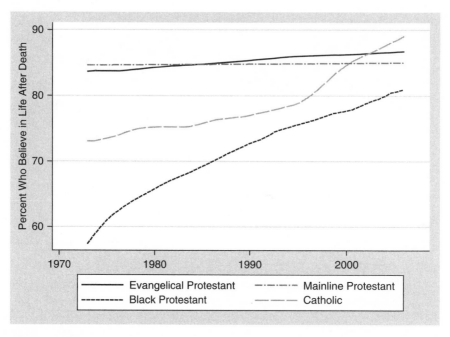

Figure 3.13. Percent of 18- to 25-year-olds Believing in Life after Death, by Religious Tradition, 1973–2006

Source: GSS 1973–2006.

or declined in the percent who report being strongly affiliated with a religion. Of course, the very cultural meanings of terms such as "liberal," "strong," and even "religious" could have changed over recent decades, undermining the reliability of the meaning of these measures over time. Survey measures can only tell so much about qualitative change in cultural meanings and practices over time. At the very least, however, we can confidently say that it is difficult, based on these data, to conclude that emerging adults in the United States have as a group become less religious or more secular in the last quarter century. If such a trend is indeed perceptible, it would seem to be weak and slight. And if such a trend is operating over a time frame extending further back into history than that examined here, as some studies suggest,[13] it is beyond our ability with these data to detect it.

What these data do show with greater certainty, however, is that varying levels of religious strength or vitality among emerging adults are evident in different major American religious traditions. Evangelical Protestant and black Protestant emerging adults generally reflect higher levels of religious commitment and practice and more allegiance to at least certain theological beliefs than do Catholics and mainline Protestants. In the last quarter century, the latter two groups, especially Catholics, have experienced significant declines in regular religious service attendance by emerging adults; have not kept pace with the increases among evangelical Protestants and black Protestants in percent identifying as strongly religious; and, unlike evangelical Protestants and black Protestants, have seen no increase in the percent holding more traditional views of the Bible. On the other hand, Catholic (and black Protestants) have significantly increased in the number of their emerging adults who believe in life after death, effectively matching by 2006 the evangelical Protestants' and mainline Protestants' levels. Overall, then, the preponderance of evidence here shows emerging adults ages 18 to 25 actually *remaining the same or growing more religious* between 1972 and 2006—with the notable exceptions of significantly declining regular church attendance among Catholics and mainline Protestants, a near doubling in the percent of nonreligious emerging adults, and significant growth in the percent of emerging adults identifying as religiously liberal.

One plausible—though certainly not definitive—interpretation of these results is that the larger cultural world has changed around emerging adults from the 1970s to the 2000s in certain ways that have heightened young people's openness to and comfort with religious and spiritual matters. Emerging adults in the 1970s were the first generation to carry out in middle class American life the cultural revolution of the 1960s.[14] The larger popular culture of that era was still oriented around the outlook of ideological modernity—most ordinary people still assumed or believed in universal rationality, liberal progress, scientific objectivity and enlightenment, and shared projects of human emancipation.[15] Part of that culture of modernity involved skepticism about, if not outright rejection of, religion. In such a cultural climate, emerging adults would have felt some pressures against taking religion very seriously. By the 1990s and 2000s, however, modernist ideology had been at least partly displaced, especially in certain spheres of social life,[16] by a "postmodern" culture that stressed difference over unity, relativity over universals, subjective experience over rational authorities, feeling over reason, situated perspectives over objectivity, the local over the national, audiences over authors, and a more general skepticism toward any "master narratives," not merely the specific narratives of religion, "superstition," and tradition. In this cultural climate, religion lost, at least in theory, any remaining principled, authoritative standing to make truth claims that it might have enjoyed in previous eras of history. Nevertheless, religion at least now enjoyed a somewhat more "level playing field" among all ideologies and movements, insofar as all perspectives were relativized by postmodernism and so were assumed ultimately to be equally valid or invalid. As a part of this cultural shift, spiritual characters and themes increasingly began to show up noticeably in mainstream mass media, representing an apparently growing acceptance of elements of spirituality and religion among both media producers and audiences.[17] In this kind of context, emerging adults would have felt less pressure, compared to an earlier era dominated by ideological modernity, to distrust or spurn religion—even if they would not have necessarily felt compelled to take religion very seriously either. Such a cultural shift may help to explain the evidence in this chapter for modest increases in religiosity among emerging adults in recent decades—increases that at least some other studies have also noted.[18]

CONCLUSION

On the basis of the findings in this chapter, one can be confident that what-ever the remaining chapters reveal about the religious and spiritual lives of contemporary emerging adults, these persons are not typical religiously of all adults of all age groups in the United States. Younger adults in America tend to be significantly less religious in a variety of ways than older adults. Whether today's emerging adults will become significantly more (or perhaps less) religious as they grow up is not yet known. Evidence not presented in this chapter suggests that most likely some of them will become more religious as they age, but also that this change is likely to be less widespread in the end than has been the case in previous generations.[19] To return to the evidence of the current chapter: Emerging adults are, on most sociological measures, the least religious adults in the United States today. Furthermore, Catholic and mainline Protestant emerging adults tend to be less religious than evangeli-cal Protestants and black Protestants, according to the sociological measures used here. This chapter has also shown that emerging adults in America since 1972 have generally not become less religious, at least as measured by the variety of sociological survey questions considered in this chapter. The signifi-cant exception here is weekly or frequent church attendance by Catholic and mainline Protestant emerging adults, which has dropped noticeably in past decades. Other than that, however, most emerging adults have since 1972 either remained stable in their measured levels of religiousness or have actu-ally increased somewhat. We see little evidence here of massive secularization among America's emerging adults in the last quarter century—the excep-tion being regular church attendance declines among Catholics and mainline Protestants—at least the kind that survey questions are able to detect. If there has been any form of increasing religious decline, weakening, or decay in the past quarter century, it has to have been of a more subtle, cultural, or inter-nal nature—for example, a growth in more social club–oriented motives and in less God- or religious convictions–oriented motives for attending church at the same frequency, a decline in the overall shared cultural standards for what counts as a "strong" religious faith, or an increase in the selfish and instrumental use of personal prayer. Those kinds of possible cultural religious transformations are much more difficult than frequency of church attendance and prayer to measure and track. This book contains little that can speak with authority to those kinds of questions. Our concern rather is to describe and explain the religious and spiritual lives of the present generation of emerging adults; we turn more directly to this task in the next chapter.

4

Religious Affiliations, Practices, Beliefs, Experiences, and More

THIS CHAPTER DRAWS ON NSYR survey data to provide nationally representative descriptive statistics about the religious and spiritual lives of American emerging adults ages 18 to 23. It also compares these statistics with those of the same youth sample surveyed five years earlier, when they were 13 to 17 years old. This enables us to examine the distributions and proportions in various religious measures among emerging adults in 2007 and 2008 and how they may have changed over the five-year period representing the transition from the teenage to the emerging adult years of life. In the following tables, the statistics representing 18- to 23-year-old emerging adults are presented first without parentheses. These statistics are then compared to statistics on the same survey measures taken five years earlier, presenting the percentage increase or decrease for each measure in parentheses. There are in this chapter a lot of numbers to digest, which takes focused concentration. But the numbers are revealing and important for telling a crucial aspect of this book's larger story, and so worth making the effort to grasp what they reveal.

RELIGIOUS AFFILIATIONS

Basic Religion

The first question addressed here concerns the religious affiliations of emerging adults. By this we mean stated membership, association, or identification with different major religious traditions and organizations. We begin this chapter by presenting differences in religious affiliations considered in different ways:

basic religion, broad religious traditions, and, for Protestants, specific denominations. Table 4.1 begins with a look at the distribution of emerging adults
across religions. Respondents were categorized into the religions listed in this
table simply on the basis of their stated religious self-identities—regardless
of where they might have attended religious services. In the column labeled
"U.S.," it appears that the largest number of all emerging adults considered
together—though not a majority—identify as some kind of Protestant, at 46
percent. The second largest group of emerging adults, when it comes to basic
religious identification, is the 27 percent who identify as not religious, shown
at the bottom of the table. Catholics are the second largest religious group and
the third largest group overall, representing 18 percent of emerging adults.
After those three major groupings, the remaining 9 percent fall into a variety of quite small religious groups. Almost 3 percent identify as Latter-Day
Saints[1] (LDS; Mormon), slightly more than 1 percent as Jewish, and about 0.5
percent as Jehovah's Witness. Buddhist, Orthodox, Pagan, Muslim, Hindu,
Unitarian Universalist, Native American, and other religions fall into groups
ranging from less than 0.5 percent down to 0.1 percent. About 1 percent
simply did not know their religion or refused to answer about their religious
identification. In short, somewhat less than one-half of emerging adults affiliate as Protestant, more than one-quarter as not religious, almost one in five as
Catholic, and the remainder as a mix of various minority religious types.

Table 4.1 also shows in parentheses the aggregate percent changes in religious identifications among emerging adults in the five years that transpired
since the same sample reported their religious identities as 13- to 17-year-olds
in 2002–3.[2] That column shows little change, with three important exceptions.

Table 4.1. Religious Affiliations of U.S. Emerging Adults, Ages 18–23 (Percents)

Respondent religious affiliation	U.S.	% change since age 13–17
Protestant	46.0	(–7.0)
Catholic	18.0	(–6.0)
LDS	2.8	(–0.3)
Jewish	1.1	(–0.4)
Jehovah's Witness	0.6	(+0.1)
Buddhist	0.4	(+0.1)
Eastern Orthodox	0.4	(0.0)
Pagan or Wiccan	0.3	(0.0)
Muslim	0.2	(–0.1)
Hindu	0.1	(0.0)
Unitarian Universalist	0.1	(0.0)
Native American	0.1	(–0.1)
Miscellaneous others	1.8	—[a]
Don't know/refused	1.1	—[a]
Not religious	27.0	(+13.0)

Source: National Survey of Youth and Religion, 2007–2008.
[a] Direct comparison across survey waves on these answers is not possible due to different skip-patterns
and categorization protocols in the two surveys; percentages may not add to 100 due to rounding.

First, the percent of emerging adults who identify as Protestant declined 7 percent since that group was 13 to 17 years old five years earlier. Second, the percent who identify at Catholic declined 6 percent. Third, the percent who identify as not religious increased by 13 percent. Other than that, LDS lost 0.033 percent of its self-identified teens, and the Jewish category lost 0.04 percent. The numbers in the other religious categories changed by only very small amounts. In sum, Protestantism and Catholicism together lost 13 percent of their youth adherents in the aggregate over these five years, while the nonreligious category gained 13 percent—an exactly offsetting amount. To be clear, however, this table does not show exactly which percent of which youth switched to which other categories. Seeing that will require another table, shown later. So we cannot conclude here that the 13 percent loss to Protestants and Catholics is the exact same 13 percent gain to the nonreligious. In fact, it is not. The changes shown in this table only reveal *aggregate* shifts—that is, the final outcomes in each category resulting after everyone who changed in any way makes whatever changes they do make. And that story on aggregate change is this: overall losses to Protestantism and Catholicism and gains to the nonreligious category.

How much real change do these numbers represent? By calculating the five-year change as a proportion of the original affiliation, one can see that the category Protestants lost about 13 percent of its baseline total (7 / [46 + 7]), Catholics lost 25 percent (6 / [18 + 6]), LDS lost about 10 percent of its total (0.3 / [2.8 + 0.3]), and Jewish lost almost 27 percent (0.4 / [1.1+0.4]). So it is apparent that even though the differences in the absolute percentage decreases across these four groups are large, the Jewish and Catholic categories lost the largest percentages as proportions of their original percent totals.[3] By comparison, the number of self-identified nonreligious emerging adults grew by nearly 93 percent of its original teenage years total (13 / [27 – 13])—nearly doubling in size. That is an important change. The first, simplest conclusion that one may draw from these findings, then, is that over the half decade between the teenage years of ages 13 to 17 and the emerging adult years of 18 to 23, there is a significant though not massive decline in religious identification—most of which in absolute numbers is drawn from the two main Christian traditions of Protestantism and Catholicism, but in relative numbers is taken especially from Judaism and Catholicism. And the only clear "winner" among all of the categories, in terms of numerical growth, nearly doubling in size, is nonreligious—a change of no minor significance.

Major Religious Traditions

Another common way in sociology to group major religious affiliations is to use the categories shown in table 4.2. This approach, based on state-of-the-art religion measurement research,[4] splits Protestants into three major types—conservative (primarily white) Protestants, mainline Protestants, and black Protestants—and groups all non-LDS and non-Jewish minority religions into one category: other religion. Respondents here are categorized into the religious types on the basis of additional information: first, on the kind of

Table 4.2. Religious Tradition of U.S. Emerging Adults,
Ages 18–23 (Percents)

	% age 18–23	% change since age 13–17
Conservative Protestant	27.6	(–3.0)
Mainline Protestant	10.8	(–0.5)
Black Protestant	7.2	(–3.1)
Catholic	19.5	(–7.1)
Jewish	1.1	(–0.6)
LDS	3.0	(–0.9)
Not religious	24.1	(+13.1)
Other religion	2.6	(+0.2)
Indeterminate	4.1	(+1.8)

Source: National Survey of Youth and Religion, 2007–2008.
Note: Percentages may not add to 100 due to rounding.

religious congregations where they attend religious services, for those who attend, and second, their stated religious self-identities. This different method of measurement and categorization leads to slightly different numbers in table 4.2 than in table 4.1—a fact of life in social science when different methodological approaches to religious categorization are employed. Using this categorization scheme, one sees that the 46 percent of all Protestants breaks out into nearly 28 percent conservative Protestant, 11 percent mainline Protestant, and about 7 percent black Protestant. Catholic persons here represent 19.5 percent of emerging adults, Jewish ones 1.1 percent, LDS ones 3 percent, and nonreligious ones 24.1 percent.[5] Other religions combined represent 2.6 percent, while the indeterminate religion category—most of which are likely nonreligious—stands at 4.1 percent.

Changes in religious affiliations shown in table 4.2 parallel those of table 4.1. The nonreligious category gained about 13 percent. Protestant lost almost 7 percent altogether, mostly from the conservative Protestant and black Protestant categories, and Catholic lost about 7 percent. Other religious traditions lost varying fractions of percents, except the combined Other Religion category, which gained a negligible amount. Again, overall and in the aggregate, during the time between the teenage and emerging adult years, religious affiliation through attendance and self-identity declined significantly but not precipitously, and the number of youth affiliating as nonreligious increased.

Protestant Denominations

Our last descriptive look at the distribution of emerging adult religious affiliations focuses on the specific denominational differences of the 46 percent who are Protestant, as seen in table 4.3. Baptist stands out by far as the largest single Protestant group, claiming 14 percent of all emerging adults. Almost 6 percent of all emerging adults belong to independent and nondenominational churches, more than 5 percent say they are "just Christian," nearly 4 percent belong to Methodist churches, and a bit more than 3 percent to

Table 4.3. Denominations of the Congregations Protestant Emerging Adults Attend, Protestant U.S. Emerging Adults, Ages 18–23 (Percents)

Denomination	% age 18–23	% change since age 13–17
Adventist	0.61	(+0.24)
Assemblies of God	0.64	(−0.12)
Baptist	14.00	(−3.20)
Bible Church	0.08	(−0.14)
Brethren	0.04	(−0.08)
Charismatic	0.59	(+0.59)
Christian and Missionary Alliance	0.25	(+0.22)
Church of Christ	1.15	(−0.10)
Church of God	0.62	(+0.31)
Congregationalist	0.09	(−0.16)
Disciples of Christ	0.15	(+0.06)
Episcopalian	0.80	(−0.20)
Evangelical, Independent	0.12	(−0.21)
Evangelical Covenant	0.02	(0.00)
Evangelical Free Church	0.14	(+0.05)
Four Square	0.15	(+0.07)
Friends/Quaker	0.03	(−0.05)
Holiness	0.32	(−0.02)
Independent/ Nondenominational	5.72	(+2.49)
Lutheran	3.14	(−0.49)
Mennonite	0.11	(−0.05)
Methodist	3.62	(−1.07)
Missionary Church	0.05	(+0.04)
Moravian	0.01	(+0.01)
Nazarene, Church of the	0.29	(−0.26)
Pentecostal	1.65	(−0.04)
Presbyterian/Reformed	1.46	(−0.59)
United Church of Christ	0.07	(−0.04)
Wesleyan Church	0.11	(−0.09)
Just Protestant	1.57	(+1.40)
Just Christian	5.29	(−7.28)
Don't know/refused	1.10	(−1.55)

Source: National Survey of Youth and Religion, 2007–2008.
Note: Percentages may not add to 100 due to rounding.

Lutheran churches. The rest of Protestant emerging adults are spread thinly among a variety of other kinds of Protestant denominations. As for changes over the five years between the first and third surveys of the NSYR, the absolute largest Protestant denominational tradition, Baptists, are also the largest losers, showing a decline of 3.2 percent.[6] Methodists also lost slightly more than 1 percent. The vast majority of denominations show very slight losses or gains. Only the independent and nondenominational category gains much at all: 2.49 percent between the teenage and emerging adult years. Overall, 18 different Protestant denominations suffered losses of some magnitude, compared to only 11 that enjoyed gains, however modest.[7] Stepping back, one larger lesson to be learned from table 4.3 seems to be that—with the possible exception of Baptists, who lost nearly 19 percent of their total baseline teenage affiliates (3.2 / [14 + 3.2])—no specific Protestant denomination is suffering major losses as youth transition from their teenage to emerging adult years—rather, the total Protestant losses seen in previous tables appear to be spread out across a variety of different denominations.

In sum, standing back from the tables examined thus far, a good deal of change in religious affiliations is evident. Most religious categories experience varying amounts of exiting and entering youth over this five-year period. When it all shakes out in the aggregate, some religious traditions and denominations gain or lose more than others. Catholic and Jewish teens are especially likely to drop those affiliations as they transition from the teenage to the emerging adult years. And the category of nonreligious gains the greatest number during the same time period. In short, while moving into emerging adulthood, many youth remain in the religious tradition of their teenage years, but many others shift to some other religious tradition or to becoming nonreligious altogether. A great deal of religious change happens. But that is also counterbalanced by a larger amount of religious continuity.

SWITCHING RELIGIOUS AFFILIATIONS

So far, when it comes to religious change, we have examined only aggregate change outcomes. Next we look more closely at how many teens from each religious tradition do and do not shift to which other religious traditions, in order to get a better sense of the total switching going on beneath the simple aggregate changes. Table 4.4 shows all of the percent changes and the weighted numbers between each religious affiliation from ages 13–17 to ages 18–23. Each tradition should be read down in the columns, which represent the religious affiliations of respondents when they were 13–17 years old. The rows represent the religious affiliations of the sample five years later, at ages 18–23. The numbers in bold show the percents in each column's religious affiliation that remained the same affiliation five years later—that is, each religion's "retention rate." The other numbers show the percents and weighted numbers that changed to other affiliations. Studying table 4.4, one sees, for example, that 64 percent (weighted N = 479) of 13- to 17-year-old conservative Protestants remained conservative Protestants as emerging adults five years later. Ten percent (weighted N = 78) switched to mainline Protestant churches, 2 percent switched to black Protestant churches, 3 percent became Catholic, 1 percent joined some other religion, and 15 percent affiliated as not religious five years later. Five percent of the original teenage conservative Protestants reported answers as emerging adults in the 2007–8 survey that were indeterminate affiliations—most of which, we believe, belong in the nonreligious category, further increasing the size of the nonreligious group switched to from conservative Protestant to up to as high as perhaps 20 percent.

Table 4.4. Current Religious Traditions of U.S. Emerging Adults, Ages 18–23, by Adolescent Religious Traditions at Ages 13–17 (Column Percents and Column Weighted Numbers)

Column Percents

Religious Tradition Age 18–23	Religious Tradition Age 13–17								
	CP	MP	BP	RC	J	LDS	OR	NR	IND
Conservative Protestant	64	20	21	6	~	3	3	11	29
Mainline Protestant	10	50	2	3	~	4	3	4	9
Black Protestant	2	1	55	~	~	3	1	3	4
Roman Catholic	2	2	3	66	~	~	1	7	3
Jewish	~	~	~	~	61	~	~	~	~
LDS	~	~	~	~	2	72	~	1	~
Other Religions	1	1	~	2	~	~	60	2	~
Nonreligious	15	24	11	20	37	17	30	68	46
Indeterminate	5	2	8	3	~	1	1	5	10
Total	100	100	100	100	100	100	100	100	100
N[a]	793	292	271	609	102	65	62	286	52

Weighted Numbers

Religious Tradition Age 18–23	Religious Tradition Age 13–17								
	CP	MP	BP	RC	J	LDS	OR	NR	IND
Conservative Protestant	479	54	54	40	~	3	2	28	16
Mainline Protestant	78	140	5	21	~	4	2	11	5
Black Protestant	17	3	140	3	~	3	1	9	2
Roman Catholic	19	4	7	429	~	~	1	17	1
Jewish	~	1	1	~	25	~	~	~	~
LDS	1	~	~	1	1	70	~	2	~
Other Religions	8	3	~	10	~	~	36	6	~
Nonreligious	109	66	27	132	15	16	17	182	25
Indeterminate	39	6	20	16	~	1	1	13	5
N[b]	750	277	253	652	41	96	60	269	55

Source: National Survey of Youth and Religion, 2002–2003; National Survey of Youth and Religion, 2007–2008.
Note: Percentages and numbers are rounded to the nearest whole number and may not add to 100; cells of <1 are reported as ~. [a]Unweighted Ns. [b]Weighted Ns; note particularly that the unweighted Jewish N (102) but is made to look smaller than it actually is through weighting.

Viewing the overall pattern in table 4.4, a variety of differences appear in religious changes across the religious groups. The LDS and the nonreligious have the highest retention rate, at 72 and 68 percent, respectively. Mainline Protestants exhibit the lowest retention rate, at 50 percent. Between those extremes range the remaining religious traditions. Table 4.4 also shows that American youth experience a good deal of religious shifting between these categories in only the five years between the NSYR teenage and emerging adult years surveys. Between 28 and 50 percent of teenage affiliates of U.S. religious traditions change to a different tradition or become nonreligious by their emerging adult years. In most cases, the largest movement from the teenage religious traditions is to the nonreligious category—especially when the indeterminate cases are added to that, as in most instances they probably should be. Nearly one-quarter of teenage mainline Protestants, one-fifth of teenage Catholics, more than one-third of teenage Jewish respondents, 17 percent of LDS teenagers, and 15 percent of conservative Protestants surveyed as teenagers affiliate as not religious by ages 18 to 23. If indeterminate religion were added to nonreligious, those percents would be higher in most cases. The other sector of major religious tradition switching entails the relatively "close" transitions between different types of Protestants. For example, 21 percent of teenage black Protestants and 20 percent of teenage mainline Protestants shifted to the conservative Protestant category as emerging adults. Comparatively, 10 percent of teenage survey conservative Protestants moved to mainline Protestant affiliations as emerging adults. In many—if not most—of these cases, there is little religious transformation or conversion going on; rather, youth with probably mostly the same beliefs and dispositions are merely switching Protestant congregations that shift them into a different category according to this analytical method.

Six other observations deserve mention. First, Jewish is the only religious category into which other teenagers did not switch—at least, in numbers totaling greater than 1 percent of their original tradition—as they grew into their emerging adult years. Judaism is generally not a conversion-seeking and proselytizing faith, the unsurprising results of which are evident here. Second, given its reputation for strong mission evangelism and overall growth, it may be somewhat surprising to some that few non-LDS teenagers switched into the LDS church as they grew into their emerging adult years—only a few out of the entire sample, in fact, converted to LDS from being Jewish and nonreligious. Overall growth of LDS, such as it is, must be due to other factors—such as higher fertility rates and conversions among other age groups—since it appears from these data that emerging adults are not disposed to LDS conversion. Third, nearly one-third of nonreligious teenagers change to a different religion (or an indeterminate status) by their emerging adulthood. More than 1 in 10 nonreligious teenagers becomes conservative Protestant by the age of 18 to 23, and 7 percent become Catholic. Altogether, one-quarter of all nonreligious teenagers become some kind of Christian by their emerging adult years.

Fourth, non-LDS minority religious groups have the highest chances of becoming nonreligious of all the examined religious categories. We have noted that 37 percent of Jewish teenagers affiliate as not religious by emerging adulthood. The next most likely religious group to disaffiliate into a nonreligious status is the combined other religions, at 30 percent. That is, 3 out of 10 "other religion" teenagers in the United States become nonreligious within five years. Fifth, mainline Protestants are not only the most likely among these groups not to stay the same religiously but are also the most likely to polarize in their religious changes. When mainline Protestants "defect" between their teenage and emerging adult years, they are most likely either to become more conservative or to become altogether not religious. One out of five mainline Protestant teenagers shifts to conservative Protestantism by emerging adulthood, and another nearly one in four becomes nonreligious. Sixth, we need to reconcile two apparently contradictory facts: the fact apparent in table 4.4 that fully one-half of teenage mainline Protestants "defect" to some other religious or nonreligious group by emerging adulthood and a fact apparent in table 4.2, that mainline Protestantism lost only 0.5 percent of its "market share" between the NSYR's waves of data collection.

How do those marked differences fit together? The answer is found in the absolute number of adherents switching in table 4.4. There it is apparent that although 20 percent of mainline Protestant teenagers switched to conservative Protestant congregations by emerging adulthood and only 10 percent of conservative Protestants switched to mainline Protestant congregations, the absolute number of conservative Protestant teenagers to start with was much larger than that of mainline Protestants. So the 79 conservative Protestant teenagers (10 percent of 793) who switched to mainline Protestantism as emerging adults outweighed the 58 teenagers (20 percent of 292) who switched in the opposite direction. That—along with the new emerging adults mainline Protestantism "picked up" between waves from the other categories—helped to sustain its overall "market share" of about 10 percent among youth, despite massive losses among the teenagers who appear to have been raised in that tradition. In other words, if this interpretation is correct, mainline Protestantism is relatively bad at retaining its *own* youth as they transition into emerging adulthood but is also relatively *good* at attracting new emerging adults who grew up in other religious traditions—good enough, in fact, to hold their own over these five years in terms of overall "market share." This is noteworthy because it counters so much of the "bad news" that has been continually reported over the last four decades about mainline Protestant decline.

In sum, again, in the five-year transition from the teenage to the emerging adult years, one-half or more of all youth every major religious tradition stay in their "baseline" tradition. Most, in other words, remain as emerging adults in the same religious tradition they occupied as teenagers. Even so, substantial minorities—and, in the case of mainline Protestantism, up to 50 percent—do switch to other religious traditions. Some, such as conservative Protestant and black Protestants, tend to shift to faith traditions that are sociologically "close by." Others, particularly mainline Protestants, tend to move far away if they move at all. Major portions of the Jewish, other religion, mainline Protestant, and Catholic groups of teenagers shift to being not religious by their emerging adulthood, which helps to explain the major substantial growth of the nonreligious category during this time period. At the same time, nearly one-third of nonreligious teenagers shift to some religious category or other within five years—and one out of three of those who switched ends up in the single category of conservative Protestant. Again, a great deal of change in religious affiliation is apparent, within a broader context of continuity.

RELIGIOUS IMPORTANCE AND PRACTICES
Major Practices and Beliefs

Religion, of course, has to do with much more than mere affiliation. This section examines the reported religious practices and professed importance of religious faith in the lives of emerging adults. Table 4.5 begins with a simple look at three important variables. First is frequency of religious service attendance. According to NSYR survey data, at the high end, 13.5 percent of emerging adults attend religious services once a week, and another 6.8 percent attend more than once a week. If these are added together with the 10.6 percent who report attending religious services two to three times a month, and are called "regular," then one in three emerging adults (30.9 percent) reports attending religious services regularly. At the low end, 35.4 percent of—more than one-third—reports never attending religious services. The remaining one-third attends religious services at frequencies between a few times a year and once a month. If attending religious services only a few times a year or less is counted as "not attending," then well over half of all emerging adults (54.6 percent) are religious service nonattenders. Turning to the right-hand column, it is apparent that the five years between the two NSYR survey waves

Table 4.5. Religious Service Attendance, Importance of Faith, and Belief in God among Emerging Adults, Ages 18–23 (Percents)

	% age 18–23	% change since age 13–17
Religious service attendance		
More than once a week	6.8	(−11.0)
Once a week	13.5	(−11.4)
2–3 times a month	10.6	(−2.3)
Once a month	7.8	(+1.2)
Many times a year	6.5	(−1.1)
A few times a year	19.2	(+6.1)
Never	35.4	(+18.4)
Don't Know/Refused	0.1	(0.0)
Importance of faith in daily life		
Extremely Important	19.9	(−0.2)
Very Important	23.9	(−8.3)
Somewhat Important	29.4	(−1.0)
Not Very Important	14.0	(+3.3)
Not Important At All	12.8	(+6.1)
Don't Know/Refused	0.1	(+0.1)
Belief in God		
Yes	77.6	(−6.6)
No	6.0	(+3.3)
Don't Know/Unsure	16.1	(+3.2)
Refused	0.2	(+0.1)

Source: National Survey of Youth and Religion, 2007–2008.
Note: Percentages may not add to 100 due to rounding.

involve a significant decline in religious service attendance. Overall and in the aggregate, "regular" attendance, as defined earlier, decreased by 24.7 percent, while "not attending," also defined earlier, increased by 24.5 percent. That is a substantial decline in this social practice for such a relatively short period of time—a great deal of which is surely explained by numerous factors already described in the previous chapters.

The middle of table 4.5 examines the reported importance in emerging adults' daily lives of their religious faith. By this measure, emerging adults in the United States appear more religious than the religious service attendance numbers would suggest. About 44 percent say that religious faith is very or extremely important in their lives. That is much more than the 26.8 percent who say religious faith is not very important or not important at all. At the same time, the column on the right indicates a shift from very important toward less important. Thus, the transition from the teenage years to the emerging adult years is marked by an overall decline in professed importance of religious faith in life, but that decline is not major, nor does it approximate anything like the decline in religious service attendance. In other words, even though both religion measures are weakening, the subjective value of religious faith remains stronger for emerging adults than does their public participation in religious meetings.

Finally, table 4.5 shows emerging adult belief in God. More than three-quarters of emerging adults say that they believe in God. Only 6 percent does not. Another 16.1 percent is unsure. Like the entire U.S. population, then, American emerging adults continue to profess to be theists. Like professed importance of faith, however, theist beliefs decline slightly between the teenage and emerging adult years. Almost 7 percent fewer of the NSYR survey sample believe in God as emerging adults than did as teenagers. That loss represents a gain for disbelief and uncertainty.

Importance of Faith and Interest in Religion

Table 4.6 breaks out the professed importance of faith by American emerging adults into the major religious traditions in which they were found at age 13 to 17—presumably in which most were raised. The top row shows that the religious traditions of the emerging adults who are more likely than the national average (44 percent) to say that their faith is very or extremely important in shaping their daily lives are black Protestant (72 percent), LDS (59 percent), and conservative Protestant (57 percent). By contrast, the groups less likely to say that religious faith is very or extremely important than the national average are Jews (16 percent), nonreligious (17 percent), mainline Protestants (33 percent), and Catholics (34 percent). The numbers of emerging adults who report that religious faith is not very important or not important at all reflect the inverse. Jewish, nonreligious, and mainline Protestant emerging adults are the most likely and black and conservative Protestants and LDS the least likely to report low importance of faith. In sum, what can be seen here are sizeable overall shifts in the direction of reduced religiousness associated with the transition from the teenage to the emerging adult years.

Table 4.6. Importance of Faith of and Interested in Learning About Religion among U.S. Emerging Adults, Ages 18–23 (Percentages)

	U.S.	Religious Tradition Age 13–17						
		CP	MP	BP	RC	J	LDS	NR
Importance of religious faith shaping daily life								
Very or extremely important	44	57	33	72	34	16	59	17
	(−9)	(−13)	(−16)	(−1)	(−8)	(0)	(−10)	(+2)
Not very or not important at all	27	15	37	6	28	61	23	57
	(+9)	(+9)	(+20)	(+1)	(+13)	(+23)	(+9)	(−3)
Degree of interest in learning about religion								
Very Interested	32	40	25	50	21	22	62	22
	(−1)	(−5)	(−5)	(+3)	(−1)	(+3)	(+1)	(+12)
Not very or not at all interested	26	16	32	11	35	32	20	40
	(+3)	(+4)	(+9)	(−1)	(+7)	(−9)	(0)	(−15)

Source: National Survey of Youth and Religion, 2002–2003; National Survey of Youth and Religion, 2007–2008.
Note: Percentages are rounded to the nearest whole number; percent changes from the first survey wave (age 13–17) are reported in parentheses.

The numbers reported in the parentheses, below the percents, report the percentage increases or decreases for each category observed between the age groups 13–17 and 18–23. During that five-year transition from the teenage to the emerging adult years, the high end of importance of faith declined by 9 percent, and the low end increased by the same amount. Studying the numbers for the various religious traditions in which emerging adults were located as teenagers reveals interesting differences. Mainline Protestantism was the biggest overall loser in the shift from high to lower importance of faith, with a decrease of 16 percent on the high end and an increase of 20 percent on the low end. By comparison, black Protestants comprise not only the highest absolute number on the high end (72 percent very or extremely important) but also show very little overall decline in importance of faith over these five years. Jewish youth here decline none at all from their already relatively low number on the high end (holding 16 percent) yet increase by the comparatively largest percent (23) on the low end—most of that increase on the low end, therefore, has come from the "somewhat important" category in the middle (not shown). Conservative Protestant, LDS, and Catholic lost significant amounts on the high end, at 13, 10, and 8 percent each, respectively; the same religious traditions also gained notable numbers on the low end, at 9, 9, and 13 percent each, respectively. The only respondents who as a group moved in an opposite direction—that is, who as emerging adults report overall increases in importance of faith—were those who were nonreligious in their teenage years. A few of them, it seems, have become more religious. In sum, the absolute levels of professed importance of religious faith by emerging adults, and the overall modest decline in these levels between the teenage and emerging adult years, are distributed unevenly across different religious groups. In particular, in a pattern that is repeated in numerous tables that follow, conservative Protestant and black Protestant and LDS emerging adults report the highest levels of importance of faith; while Jewish, nonreligious, mainline Protestant, and Catholic emerging adults report levels lower than the national average.

Table 4.6 also presents findings on another measure of importance of faith: how interested emerging adults are in learning more about their religion. Emerging adults who as teenagers were LDS, black Protestant, and conservative Protestant exhibit numbers higher than the national average for being very interested, at 62, 50, and 40 percent each, respectively. Emerging adults who as teenagers were Catholic, nonreligious, Jewish, and mainline Protestant report numbers below the national average, ranging from only 21 to 25 percent being very interested in learning more about their faith. The absolute value of all of the numbers is also instructive. Among emerging adults, only for LDS do more than half state a very strong interest in learning more about their religion—in all other categories, half or less are very interested. Emerging adults who as teenagers were Catholic, Jewish, and mainline Protestant are in fact no more likely to be very interested in learning about religion than those who were nonreligious. This could of course be because they already know everything about their religion or because they simply are not very interested—though what is known about teenagers' knowledge of their own faiths strongly suggests the latter as likely.[8] It is also apparent that about one-third of emerging adults who as teenagers were Catholic and Jewish, one-fifth who as teenagers were LDS, and 4 out of 10 who as teenagers were not religious report that they are not very, or are not at all, interested in learning more about their religion. Those numbers are smaller for conservative Protestants and black Protestants. Studying the percent changes shown in the parentheses, less overall change in interest in learning more about one's religion than in importance of faith earlier is apparent. There a small increase in interest in learning about religion among emerging adults who as teenagers were black Protestant and Jewish. A significant increase appears among those who as teenagers were nonreligious, who appear to have since become religious. Among those who as teenagers were conservative Protestant and mainline Protestant, slight decreases in interest in learning about their religion are apparent. Overall, then, when it comes to interest in learning more about their religion, significant variance exists both across the religious traditions and within them, as well as—with the exception of the nonreligious—only modest aggregate change in interest between the teenage and emerging adult years.

Religious Practices

Table 4.7 examines a variety of religious practices—service attendance, prayer, scripture reading, and more—in greater depth. First, table 4.7 breaks out the religious service attendance percents shown for all emerging adults in table 4.5 by religious tradition, across which appears major variance. Sixty percent of emerging adults who as teenagers were LDS attend church services once a week or more. The same is true for only 12 percent of those who as teenagers

Table 4.7. Religious Practice of U.S. Emerging Adults, Ages 18–23 (Percentages)

	U.S.	Religious tradition age 13–17						
		CP	MP	BP	RC	J	LDS	NR
Religious service attendance								
Once a week or more	20	28	12	25	15	10	60	5
	(−22)	(−31)	(−31)	(−17)	(−26)	(−2)	(−13)	(+5)
Never	35	24	38	18	36	62	22	73
	(+18)	(+21)	(+28)	(+11)	(+25)	(+38)	(+18)	(−20)
Frequency of praying alone								
Daily or more	30	42	24	43	22	8	54	18
	(−8)	(−10)	(−7)	(−9)	(−11)	(−3)	(−3)	(+7)
Never	20	10	23	6	20	45	23	48
	(+6)	(+5)	(+12)	(+1)	(+9)	(+18)	(+9)	(−3)
Frequency of scripture reading alone								
Daily or more	6	10	5	7	2	5	23	4
	(−2)	(−6)	(−1)	(−4)	(−1)	(+2)	(+1)	(+2)
Never	50	31	59	30	66	87	24	68
	(+10)	(+13)	(+17)	(+9)	(+14)	(+14)	(−1)	(−10)
In prior year, respondent:								
Practiced religious or	16	13	24	7	14	29	30	17
spiritual meditation not	(+5)	(+6)	(+14)	(−2)	(+2)	(+20)	(+19)	(+3)
including prayer								
Tried to practice a weekly day	21	31	12	23	14	14	71	6
of rest or Sabbath	(−10)	(−10)	(−15)	(−12)	(−17)	(−8)	(+6)	(+3)
Fasted or denied self something	23	21	17	23	28	34	66	7
as spiritual discipline	(−2)	(−2)	(−8)	(+2)	(−3)	(−11)	(+1)	(+2)
Played or sang in a religious	17	23	15	34	9	4	44	4
music group or choir	(−12)	(−17)	(−21)	(−13)	(−11)	(−7)	(−4)	(+3)
Read a devotional, religious,	29	39	27	26	22	18	67	10
or spiritual book other than the	(−2)	(−9)	(−2)	(0)	(−1)	(−16)	(+2)	(+9)
scriptures								
Shared own religious faith with	40	51	42	40	36	11	65	18
someone not of faith	(−5)	(−8)	(−8)	(−1)	(−5)	(−45)	(−7)	(+14)
Attended a religious Sunday	11	15	6	15	4	2	44	4
school or religious education	(−16)	(−24)	(−21)	(−11)	(−16)	(−21)	(−18)	(+3)
class weekly or more often								
Never attended a religious	55	34	63	32	77	83	20	82
Sunday school or religious	(+27)	(+21)	(+44)	(+20)	(+38)	(+47)	(+10)	(+5)
education class								

Source: National Survey of Youth and Religion, 2002–2003; National Survey of Youth and Religion, 2007–2008.
Note: Percentages are rounded to the nearest whole number; percent changes from the first survey wave (age 13–17) are reported in parentheses.

were mainline Protestant and 10 percent who were Jewish. By comparison, 62 percent of emerging adults who as teens were Jewish, 38 percent who were mainline Protestant, and 36 percent who were Catholic never attend religious services. As shown for all emerging adults in table 4.5, the shifts away from high to low religious service attendance over the half decade from the teenage to emerging adult years is pronounced for most specific religious traditions. Emerging adults who as teenagers were conservative Protestants or mainline Protestants or Catholics show the largest decrease in weekly or more frequent religious service attendance, at 31, 31, and 26 percent, respectively. Those who as teenagers were Jewish, mainline Protestant, and Catholic reflect the greatest increase in never attending religious services, at 38, 28, and 25 percent, respectively. Only for emerging adults who as teenagers were not religious—but some of whom have apparently become more religious since— is there an aggregate increase in religious service attendance, evidenced by a 20 percent decline in never attending. In sum, there is apparent here an overall decline in religiousness, a decline that varies somewhat by religious tradition and measure of religious practice.

In the next block of numbers in the same table, differences across religious groups in frequency of personal prayer are apparent. Following an already established general pattern of religiousness across traditions, emerging adults who as teenagers were LDS and black Protestant and conservative Protestant are most likely to pray daily or more often, at 54, 43, and 42 percent, respectively. Those who as teenagers were Jewish, nonreligious, Catholic, or mainline Protestant were less likely than the national average to pray daily, at 8, 18, 22, and 24 percent, respectively. Those who as teenagers were nonreligious, Jewish, mainline Protestant, and LDS are also higher than the national average for never praying alone. And those who as teenagers were black Protestant and conservative Protestant are much less likely than the national average to never pray alone. The greatest loss over time in daily personal prayer was among those who as teenagers were Catholic and conservative Protestant, while the largest increase in never praying was among those who as teenagers were Jewish and mainline Protestant. Again, only those who as teenagers were nonreligious increased in their overall frequency of personal prayer. Thus, overall, frequency of praying alone also generally declines during this same time period.

The numbers in table 4.7 on frequency of reading scripture alone show overall lower levels. Twenty-three percent of emerging adults who as teenagers were LDS read scripture daily or more often, and 10 percent who as teenagers were conservative Protestant do the same. For the other groups, the numbers are lower. More than one-half of emerging adults who as teenagers were Jewish, Catholic, and mainline Protestant (87, 66, and 59 percent, respectively) and nearly one-third of them who as teenagers were conservative Protestant and black Protestant (31 and 30 percent, respectively) never read scripture alone. Overall, all groups show slight declines in the percents reading scripture daily, and notable increases in the percent never reading scripture— the two exceptions to the latter trend being emerging adults who as teenagers were nonreligious or LDS.

Finally, table 4.7 displays percents and percent changes for emerging adults engaging in seven other different religious practices. Readers can study these statistics in detail according to their interests; we will provide here only some general observations. The first is that emerging adults who as teenagers were LDS engage in all of these religious practices at the highest level, usually significantly higher than all other groups. They also appear to have increased the most (for positive change) or, conversely, decreased the slightest (for negative change) when change over time is evident in these practices. Second, with the exception of the LDS group, in all but one case—conservative Protestants sharing faith, at 51 percent—only minorities of emerging adults in any category engage in any of these religious practices. On the whole, the majority of emerging adults from whatever religious background (except LDS) are not participating in these religious practices. Third, in general, emerging adults who as teenagers were Catholic engage in all but one of these religious practices— fasting or self-denial as a spiritual discipline, such as giving up, say, chocolate during Lent—less than the national average. Being a Catholic teenager does not portend solid engagement in religious practices in the emerging adult years. Fourth, those who as teenagers were conservative Protestant and black Protestant tend to engage most, though not all, of these practices at levels higher than the national average. Otherwise, differences vary by the specific religious practice. For example, emerging adults who as teenagers were Jewish engage in spiritual meditation and fasting at rates higher than the national average. The same is true for those who as teenagers were mainline Protestant on spiritual meditation and sharing religious faith. In some cases, this reflects the fact that different religions emphasize different spiritual practices. Sixth, patterns of change over time are notable. Every group but black Protestant increased in the practice of spiritual meditation. For most groups, significant decreases are apparent in practicing a weekly day of rest or Sabbath, playing or singing in a music group or choir, and regularly attending Sunday school or religious education classes. The largest changes are evident around Sunday school and religious education classes. Only small minorities of emerging adults attend Sunday school or religious education classes weekly, while substantial minorities, and in some cases substantial majorities (mainline Protestant, Catholic, and Jewish), never attend Sunday school or religious education classes. Some of the numbers here are very large: the percent increases of emerging adults who never attend Sunday school or religious education classes are 47 percent for those who as teenagers were Jewish, 44 percent who were mainline Protestant, and 38 percent who were Catholic.

What then might we say in summary about the findings presented in the tables in this section? The overall story is clearly one of general religious decline among youth transitioning from the teenage years into the emerging adulthood. That decline varies by measure and religious group, and there are some notable exceptions. But the dominant trend is one of decline.

RELIGIOUS BELIEFS

Beliefs about and Closeness to God

What do emerging adults believe religiously and how may their beliefs have changed since the teenage years? Table 4.8 begins with a look at belief in God. It appears that 78 percent of emerging adults profess belief in God, 16 percent are not sure, and 6 percent do not believe in God. Over the five years from when the respondents were first surveyed as 13- to 17-year-olds,

Table 4.8. Beliefs of U.S. Young Emerging about God, Ages 18–23 (Percents)

	U.S.	Religious Tradition Age 13–17						
		CP	MP	BP	RC	J	LDS	NR
Belief in God								
Believes in God	78	87	68	97	80	50	83	47
	(−7)	(−8)	(−17)	(0)	(−6)	(−17)	(+1)	(+2)
Is unsure in belief about God	16	11	25	3	14	31	13	35
	(+3)	(+7)	(+12)	(0)	(+1)	(+3)	(−2)	(−3)
Does not believe in God	6	2	7	0	5	19	4	17
	(+3)	(+1)	(+5)	(0)	(+5)	(+14)	(+4)	(0)
Views of God								
A personal being involved in	63	74	57	78	62	32	78	36
the lives of people today	(−4)	(−5)	(−15)	(+3)	(−5)	(−7)	(+4)	(+5)
Created the world, but is not	10	9	9	9	13	11	5	9
involved in world today	(−2)	(+1)	(−2)	(−4)	(−2)	(−1)	(−4)	(−4)
Not personal, something like a	17	11	24	9	17	32	14	34
cosmic life force	(+4)	(+4)	(+12)	(+1)	(+4)	(−5)	(+5)	(+2)
How close respondent feels to God								
Extremely or very close	29	35	22	45	23	7	55	12
	(−8)	(−13)	(−18)	(−4)	(−9)	(−2)	(+13)	(+2)
Extremely or very distant	12	8	17	6	10	17	10	23
	(+4)	(+4)	(+11)	(+2)	(+6)	(−2)	(+5)	(−3)
Does not believe in God	6	2	7	0	5	19	4	17
	(+3)	(+1)	(+5)	(0)	(+5)	(+14)	(+4)	(0)

Source: National Survey of Youth and Religion, 2002–2003; National Survey of Youth and Religion, 2007–2008.
Note: Percentages are rounded to the nearest whole number; percent changes from the first survey wave (age 13–17) are reported in parentheses.

in the aggregate, definite belief in God declined by 7 percent, and uncertainty about God and disbelief in God each gained 3 percent. Belief in God, as with most measures examined in this chapter, vary by religious tradition. Emerging adults who as teenagers were black Protestant, conservative Protestant, LDS, and Catholic report that they definitely believe in God at rates higher than the national average—at 97, 87, 83, and 80 percent, respectively. Two-thirds of those who as teenagers were mainline Protestant report definitely believing in God (10 percent below the national average), while around one-half of those who were Jewish and nonreligious as teenagers definitely believe in God. The largest declines between the teenage and emerging adult years in the definite belief in God category occurred in the mainline Protestant and Jewish groups, with 17 percent decrease each. Most of that loss for the mainline Protestant cases shifted to the "unsure about belief in God" category, while most of the Jewish loss moved to the disbelief category. In sum, most religious traditions experience declines in the number of their youth who definitely believe in God as they grow out of their teenage years and into emerging adulthood, although those decreases vary widely by religious tradition, with mainline Protestant and Jewish youth undergoing the largest declines.

The uncertainty-about-belief-in-God numbers are interesting. One may not be surprised that 35 percent of emerging adults who were not religious as teenagers are not sure whether they believe in God. Perhaps less expected is that uncertainty about belief in God among emerging adults who as teenagers were conservative Protestants increased by 7 percent so that more than 1 in 10 of them are now unsure whether they believe in God. More noticeably, 12 percent of emerging adults who were mainline Protestant in their teenage years have shifted from definitely believing in God to being unsure, so that one in four of them stands uncertain about God in their early emerging adult years. By comparison, very few emerging adults who were black Protestants as teenagers are uncertain about God. Finally, as to definitely not believing in God, emerging adults who were Jewish and nonreligious as teenagers stand out, at 19 and 17 percent, respectively. And in addition to the one-quarter of emerging adults who were mainline Protestant as teenagers being unsure about belief in God, another one in every fourteen of them (7 percent, an increase of 5 percent) definitely does not believe in God. Furthermore, over the course of five years from the teenage era to emerging adulthood, the percent of the Catholic and LDS groups not believing in God increased by 5 and 4 percent, respectively. In sum, the majority of emerging adults profess to believe in God, although that number is smaller than it was for the same respondents five years earlier. The "attrition" in belief in God is particularly evident among those raised as mainline Protestants and Jews, and the latter are more likely to not believe in God than emerging adults who as teenagers were not religious. Relatively few emerging adults—other than those who were Jewish as teenagers—definitely do not believe in God. But sizeable and growing proportions of them are unsure if they do believe in God.

The middle section of table 4.8 examines the kind of God or higher being in which emerging adults who do or may believe in God think they believe. Not quite two-thirds of emerging adults (63 percent) believe in God as a personal being involved in the lives of people today. One in ten believes God created the world but is not involved in it today. And 17 percent believes that what people call "God" is not personal but something like a cosmic life force. Belief by emerging adults in a personal, involved God declined by 4 percent since when they were teenagers; belief in an impersonal life force increased by the same amount over the same time period. The majority of religious types of emerging adults believes in a personal God; those in the Jewish and nonreligious groups are the exception. A fairly even proportion of emerging adults in the different groups—about one in ten—is unsure about God, with the LDS group the one exception at the lower end, at only 5 percent, and the Catholic group slightly more on the higher end, at 13 percent. About one-third of emerging adults who as teenagers were nonreligious and Jewish and about one-quarter of those who were mainline Protestant believe not in a personal God but in an impersonal, cosmic life force. The largest five-year growth in that category (a 12 percent increase) is evident in the mainline Protestant group.

Finally, table 4.8 examines how close emerging adults who do or may believe in God feel toward God. About 3 in 10 report feeling very or extremely close to God, while 12 percent report feeling very or extremely distant from God (the remainder either does not believe in God or feels only somewhat close or distant). Emerging adults who as teenagers were LDS and black Protestant and conservative Protestant are most likely to feel very or extremely close to God, with LDS youth standing out among those three groups in both absolute amount and growth over time in closeness to God. Meanwhile, the Jewish, nonreligious, mainline Protestant, and Catholic groups are less likely than the national average to feel very or extremely close to God. The largest five-year declines in the very and extremely close category are in the mainline and conservative Protestant groups, at 18 and 13 percent decreases, respectively. The largest gain is in the LDS group, at 13 percent. Emerging adults who are most likely to feel very or extremely distant from God are those who as teenagers were nonreligious, Jewish, and mainline Protestants, at 23, 17, and 17 percent, respectively. Still, the percentage of the Jewish group that reported feeling very or extremely distant from God declined by 2 percent during the five years between the first NSYR survey of 13- to 17-year-olds and the subsequent survey of 18- to 23-year-olds. On the other hand, the largest gain in the very and extremely distant categories was the mainline Protestant group, with an 11 percent increase. In sum, minorities of most religious types of emerging adults feel quite close to God, and even smaller minorities feel quite distant from God. Significant chunks of emerging adults state that they feel only somewhat close or distant from God (not reported in the table). But the overall trend over the half decade between the teenage and emerging adult years is clearly away from feeling close to God and toward either feeling distant from God or not believing in God at all.

Jesus Christ, Creation, and Heaven

As for more specific theological beliefs about Jesus Christ, the origins of the world, and who goes to heaven, none of these specific issues were addressed in previous waves of the NSYR survey, so we are not able to report changes over time. But the simple, cross-sectional, descriptive statistics reported here, in table 4.9, are themselves revealing. About two out of three emerging adults (68 percent) claim to believe that Jesus was the son of God who was raised from the dead. Eleven percent says Jesus was an important human teacher but not the son of God. And 1 percent says Jesus never existed. Not surprisingly, these beliefs are distributed unevenly across different religious traditions. Emerging adults who as teenagers were black Protestant (90 percent), conservative Protestant (83 percent), and LDS (78 percent) are the most likely to affirm that Jesus was divine and resurrected, while those in the Jewish (5 percent) and not religious (35 percent) groups are the least likely to affirm that. Those in the Jewish, nonreligious, and mainline Protestant groups are significantly more likely than the average to believe that Jesus was an important but not divine human teacher, at 45, 24, and 20 percent, respectively. Not many in any

Table 4.9. Beliefs about Jesus, Origins of the World,
and Going to Heaven, Ages 18–23

| | U.S. | Religious tradition age 13–17 | | | | | | |
		CP	MP	BP	RC	J	LDS	NR
Which of the following comes closest to your beliefs about Jesus Christ?								
Jesus was the son of God who was raised from the dead	68	83	59	90	67	5	78	35
Jesus was an important human teacher, but not the son of God	11	5	20	1	9	45	9	24
Jesus never really existed	1	1	1	0	2	4	2	3
Which of the following comes closest to your beliefs about the origins of the world?								
God created the world and did not use evolution	24	41	15	34	13	10	28	7
God created the world and may have used evolution	42	41	41	52	48	18	53	25
The world is a product of purely natural forces	28	13	39	3	34	62	16	58
Which of the following comes closest to your beliefs about who goes to heaven?								
There is no heaven	16	8	21	4	13	30	19	38
All people go to heaven	8	5	12	9	11	14	12	5
Only good people go to heaven	11	7	11	8	21	24	4	7
Only people whose sins are forgiven through faith in Jesus Christ	43	64	33	65	29	3	36	25

Source: National Survey of Youth and Religion, 2007–2008.
Note: Percentages are rounded to the nearest whole number.

category believe that Jesus never existed. (The balances for each group adding to 100 percent consist of "something else" and "unsure" responses.)

The middle of table 4.9 focuses on beliefs about the world's origins. At issue is belief in some kind of divine creation versus belief in the world's origins in purely natural forces. About one-quarter of emerging adults believe in divine creation through nonevolutionary means. Nearly 30 percent believe in the world's origins through purely natural forces. The largest group, at 42 percent, believes in the divine creation of the world perhaps, but not necessarily, using evolutionary means. The conservative Protestant and black Protestant groups are especially likely to believe the first answer: nonevolutionary, divine creation. The LDS, black Protestant, and Catholic groups are particularly likely to endorse the second answer: divine creation perhaps through evolution. And the Jewish, nonreligious, and mainline Protestant groups are most likely to believe the third answer: purely natural causes.

Finally, table 4.9 shows emerging adult answers to the question about belief in heaven and, for those who believe, who goes to heaven. Nationally, 16 percent of emerging adults do not believe in heaven. Eight percent are universalists, believing that all people go to heaven. Eleven percent think only good people go to heaven. And 43 percent believe that only people whose sins are forgiven through faith in Jesus Christ go to heaven. Disbelief in heaven is highest among emerging adults who as teenagers were nonreligious, Jewish, and mainline Protestant. Perhaps surprisingly, given the overall pattern of statistics, 19 percent of LDS cases—3 percent more than the national average—say they do not believe in heaven. Black Protestant cases are the most likely to believe in heaven, at 96 percent. Emerging adults who were Jewish, mainline Protestant, and LDS as teenagers tend to be slightly higher than the national average on all people going to heaven. Catholic and Jewish types are significantly higher on good people going to heaven. And conservative Protestants and black Protestants are very high on forgiveness of sins through Jesus Christ as the way to heaven. Some of the absolute percentages are worth noting. More than 1 in 13 cases of conservative Protestant and 1 in 8 cases of Catholic teenagers do not believe in heaven by the early emerging adult years. More than one-third of conservative Protestant cases do not believe that heaven is for those whose sins have been forgiven by Jesus Christ. Less than 30 percent of Catholic cases believe the forgiveness of sins in Jesus Christ is the way to heaven, and not many more mainline Protestant cases believe that. Overall, emerging adults exhibit significant variance in their views of heaven and who goes there.

In summary concerning table 4.9, substantial minorities of emerging adults in most, thought not all, religious traditions profess a traditional Christian teaching about Jesus and a belief in heaven. Most emerging adults in all but the Jewish and nonreligious categories believe that God created the world, whether through evolution or not. With regard to the question of who goes to heaven, emerging adults are divided—many believe that this happens through the forgiveness of sins by Jesus Christ, while others take approaches more based on human goodness or universalism. In brief, emerging adults are spread around the map on theological questions, though significant groups tend to affirm traditional beliefs.

Other Religious Beliefs and Doubts

The NSYR asked about a number of other religious, spiritual, and metaphysical questions, the answers to which are reported in table 4.10. There it appears that almost two-thirds of emerging adults believe in a judgment day on which God will reward and punish people. More than one-half believe in the existence of angels; slightly fewer than one-half believe in demons or evil spirits. Sixty-two percent believes in miracles from God, and exactly half believe in life after death. Sixteen percent—a little less than one in six—believes in reincarnation and 11 percent—about one in ten—believes in astrology. Only 5 percent of emerging adults say they have many doubts about religious beliefs in the prior year; more than half say they have no doubts at all. At the national level, table 4.10 shows little change between the teenage and emerging adult years—aside from 7 percent declines in both belief in a divine judgment day and in angels, as well as an 8 percent increase in not believing at all in astrology, the data reveal only slight changes across time regarding these beliefs.

Emerging adults coming from different religious traditions show significant variance in their likelihood of believing in the items listed in table 4.10. The general pattern on the traditional "biblical" beliefs—in a divine judgment

Table 4.10. Religious Beliefs and Doubts of U.S. Emerging Adults,
Ages 18–23 (Percents)

	U.S.	Religious tradition age 13–17						
		CP	MP	BP	RC	J	LDS	NR
Believes in a judgment day when God will reward some and punish others								
Yes	63	81	47	87	56	15	85	36
	(−7)	(−7)	(−15)	(−4)	(−11)	(−8)	(+1)	(+6)
No	29	16	43	13	38	66	11	45
	(+7)	(+6)	(+12)	(+6)	(+10)	(−2)	(+6)	(+1)
Believes in the existence of angels								
Definitely	56	70	40	75	51	16	72	34
	(−7)	(−10)	(−21)	(−2)	(−5)	(−9)	(−6)	(+1)
Not at all	11	5	14	2	10	33	11	26
	(+3)	(+2)	(+9)	(−1)	(+4)	(+11)	(+10)	(+2)
Believes in existence of demons or evil spirits								
Definitely	47	63	32	60	38	10	73	25
	(+5)	(+3)	(−4)	(+12)	(+11)	(−2)	(+3)	(+3)
Not at all	24	14	28	19	26	54	19	42
	(−1)	(−2)	(+4)	(−7)	(−2)	(+11)	(+8)	(+2)
Believes in divine miracles from God								
Definitely	62	74	53	81	57	20	75	37
	(0)	(−5)	(−5)	(+5)	(+2)	(−6)	(+4)	(+12)
Not at all	14	5	19	5	13	40	9	32
	(+5)	(+3)	(+11)	(+1)	(+7)	(+19)	(+5)	(+2)
Believes there is life after death								
Definitely	50	67	44	58	44	28	73	24
	(−1)	(+2)	(−8)	(+7)	(−1)	(+6)	(−4)	(−1)
Not at all	9	8	6	8	8	14	6	19
	(−3)	(−4)	(−4)	(−10)	(−3)	(+1)	(+4)	(+3)
Believes in reincarnation								
Definitely	16	9	9	25	19	15	11	21
	(+3)	(+3)	(−2)	(+16)	(+6)	(−7)	(+1)	(−1)
Not at all	55	71	54	44	47	36	78	40
	(+4)	(+2)	(−2)	(0)	(+6)	(−5)	(+6)	(+11)
Believes in astrology								
Definitely	11	8	11	9	14	6	7	15
	(+2)	(+3)	(+5)	(−4)	(+2)	(+3)	(+7)	(+4)
Not at all	68	75	66	67	64	66	78	61
	(+8)	(+6)	(+2)	(+11)	(+12)	(+15)	(−7)	(+7)
Believers' doubts about religious beliefs in prior year								
Many doubts	5	4	6	3	6	8	7	—
	(+1)	(+2)	(+2)	(−3)	(+2)	(+8)	(+3)	—
No doubts	53	54	48	66	48	40	64	—
	(+2)	(+1)	(−3)	(+8)	(+3)	(−15)	(+12)	—

Source: National Survey of Youth and Religion, 2002–2003; National Survey of Youth and Religion, 2007–2008.
Note: Percentages are rounded to the nearest whole number; percent changes from the first survey wave (age 13–17) are reported in parentheses.

day, angels, demons, miracles, and life after death—is that emerging adults who were conservative Protestant and black Protestant or LDS as teenagers are more likely to believe in them and those who were mainline Protestant, Catholic, Jewish, and not religious are less likely. Black Protestant, Catholic, and nonreligious cases are more likely than the national average to believe in reincarnation, and Catholic and nonreligious cases are more likely than the average to believe in astrology. No group is especially likely to have had many doubts about religious beliefs in the previous year, although black Protestant and LDS cases are somewhat more likely than the national average to have had no doubts and Jewish cases somewhat less likely to have had no doubts. Examining the five-year change in what we have called traditional "biblical" beliefs, a clear pattern emerges: the group with the greatest shift from belief to unbelief are emerging adults who were mainline Protestant as teenagers. Their belief in a divine judgment day, in angels, and in life after death, for instance, declined by 15, 21, and 8 percent, respectively. Jewish cases not believing in angels and divine miracles picked up 11 and 19 percentage points. Nonreligious teenagers who by their early emerging adult years definitely believe in divine miracles increased 12 percent to a total of nearly four in ten. For some reason, black Protestant cases who definitely believe in reincarnation increased by 16 percent over five years, and the percent of LDS cases believing in astrology increased from 0 to 7 percent in the same time frame. Overall, in sum, a modest majority of American emerging adults believes in traditional "biblical" beliefs, which are especially concentrated among the conservative Protestant and black Protestant and LDS cases. Only modest minorities of emerging adults believe in reincarnation and astrology, with those beliefs spread fairly evenly across the religious types examined here. Finally, change in these beliefs between the teenage and emerging adult years is slight but perceptible, particularly among those from certain traditions.

In short, when it comes to religious beliefs, the previous three tables show considerable diversity of theological commitments among emerging adults. Many gravitate toward more traditional biblical or Christian beliefs. But substantial numbers, especially in some religious traditions, profess different views—such as that God is an impersonal, cosmic life force, that Jesus was not the son of God, that God did not create the world, and that heaven does not exist. For those measures for which change over time can be tracked, also evident are general shifts away from certainty about God, felt closeness to God, and definite belief in other traditional, "biblical" teachings. These shifts are often especially pronounced among Catholics and mainline Protestants.

RELIGIOUS EXPERIENCES

An important aspect of religious and spiritual life, other than associations, identities, salience, practices, and beliefs, are religious and spiritual experiences. Table 4.11 reports on emerging adults' responses concerning numerous religious experiences. The NSYR asked respondents, for instance, whether in the previous two years they had become more religious, less religious, or stayed

Table 4.11. Religious Experiences and Activities of U.S. Emerging Adults over Past Two Years, Ages 18–23 (Percents)

	U.S.	Religious Tradition Age 13–17						
		CP	MP	BP	RC	J	LDS	NR
In the past two years have you...								
Become more religious, less religious, or stayed about the same?								
Became more religious	24	27	16	37	16	15	51	20
Stayed about the same	59	53	60	49	66	66	33	73
Became less religious	17	20	23	13	17	19	13	7
Experienced a definite answer to prayer or specific guidance from God?								
Yes	48	63	38	71	38	13	66	23
Witnessed or experienced what you believe was a miracle from God?								
Yes	41	53	31	66	29	19	60	26
Made a personal commitment to live your life for God?								
Yes	37	47	32	63	28	12	64	14
Attended a religious retreat or conference?								
Yes	24	33	21	30	18	14	53	9
Gone on a religious missions team or religious service project?								
Yes	15	22	17	16	10	7	35	4
Been invited to attend religious services with someone?[a]								
Yes	69	79	71	79	61	66	75	66
Regularly prayed to give thanks before or after mealtimes?								
Yes	43	55	31	76	33	12	63	20

Source: National Survey of Youth and Religion, 2007–2008.
Note: Percentages are rounded to the nearest whole number; [a]Only asked of those who do not attend religious services more than once or twice a year.

about the same. The majority (59 percent) reported that they had stayed about the same. Of those who changed, however, more (24 percent) said they had become more religious than those (17 percent) who reported having become less religious. This may strike one as odd, considering that many of the statistics discussed earlier seem to suggest a modest overall decline in the religious affiliations, importance, practices, and beliefs of emerging adults. But this question asks emerging adults for an overall self-assessment of their religiousness and—taking all things into consideration—this is what they reported. It could be that what some or many emerging adults count as important in being "religious" is not adequately tapped by the standard sociological measures displayed here. In any case, from their own perspectives, most new emerging adults had not changed much religiously in the previous two years, and more reported becoming more religious than less religious. Emerging adults who were LDS or conservative Protestant or black Protestant as teenagers were the most likely to have become more religious. Mainline Protestant cases were the most likely to have become less religious. Nonreligious cases were the most likely to have stayed the same.

Almost one-half of emerging adults say that they have experienced a definite answer to prayer or specific guidance from God in the previous two years—a report particularly made by LDS and conservative Protestant and black Protestant cases. Four out of ten report having witnessed or experienced a divine miracle in the prior two years—an experience reported at higher rates by the same three groups again. More than one-third of American emerging adults (37 percent) say that they had made a personal commitment to live their lives for God during the prior two years. Again, the LDS, conservative Protestant, and black Protestant groups are highest on this measure. Note, too, that 14 percent of emerging adults who as teenagers identified as not religious answered yes to this religious commitment question; 35 percent of them became conservative Protestant as emerging adults, 10 percent became Catholic, 7 percent became black Protestant and mainline Protestant each, and 24 percent remained not religious as emerging adults.[9] Nearly one-quarter of emerging adults report having attended a religious retreat or conference in the previous two years, with the LDS and conservative Protestant and black Protestant groups again being more likely do have done so. More than one in seven emerging adults (15 percent) say they went on a religious missions team or service project in the prior two years, an activity particularly engaged in by LDS and conservative Protestant cases. Nearly 7 in 10 emerging adults who do not attend religious services more than once or twice a year have been during the previous two years invited by someone else to attend religious services. The numbers are somewhat higher for the LDS and conservative Protestant and black Protestant groups but are fairly even across all groups, including 66 percent of the nonreligious group. Finally, 43 percent of emerging adults report regularly praying to give thanks before or after meals—again, with the LDS and conservative Protestant and black Protestant groups doing this the most. Previous survey data are not available for any of these measures, unfortunately, so we are unable to compare to measure changes over time.

What, in sum, does table 4.11 demonstrate? It appears that sizeable numbers of the 18- to 23-year-olds encountered significant religious experiences during the two years before the latest survey. About one in four says they became more religious over two years, nearly one-half experienced divine guidance or prayers answered, and 40 percent witnessed or experienced a divine miracle. More than one-third committed their lives to God, one-quarter attended a religious retreat or conference, and nearly one-half regularly pray before or after mealtimes to give thanks. We do not know, of course, the actual extent or impact of many of these experiences. But at the very least we can say that this does not seem to be a particularly secularized generation that lacks religious engagements and encounters. Sizeable minorities of American emerging adults appear to have various religious and spiritual experiences. In fact, fully 46.4 percent of all emerging adults have experienced at least two out of these five religious experiences: an answer to prayer or divine guidance, witnessing of a miracle, making a personal commitment to God, attending a retreat or conference, or going on a missions trip or social service project. That is a fact that needs to be fitted into the overall picture developed in this book.

RELIGION AND SOCIAL RELATIONSHIPS
Religion and Parents

Another important aspect of religious life is how it intersects with social relationships in families, among friends, and in organized groups. What does that look like among emerging adults today? Table 4.12 shows emerging adults' perceived similarity to their parents when it comes to religious beliefs. It is apparent that about two-thirds view themselves as similar to their mothers and fathers. Most of the percent differences across the religious groups are not huge. Emerging adults who as teenagers were conservative Protestant and black Protestant and LDS report they are more similar to their parents than the national average reports when it comes to religious beliefs. Furthermore, the reported levels of similarity to and difference from mothers and fathers compared to each other correlate highly—that is, the emerging adults reports tend to vary similarly for both mothers and fathers.[10] Emerging adults who as teenagers were nonreligious stand out as particularly less similar to both their parents—with more than one-half being somewhat or very different from their mothers and fathers when it comes to religious beliefs. As for changes over time, 8 percent fewer emerging adults are similar to their mothers on religious beliefs, and 6 percent fewer are similar to their fathers since their teenage years. Emerging adults who were mainline Protestant as

Table 4.12. Religion and Relationships with Parents of U.S. Emerging Adults, Ages 18–23 (Percents

	U.S.	Religious Tradition Age 13–17						
		CP	MP	BP	RC	J	LDS	NR
How similar are your religious beliefs / beliefs about religion to your mother's?								
Very or somewhat similar	66	74	61	76	65	61	75	48
	(−8)	(−8)	(−16)	(−2)	(−9)	(−8)	(−7)	(−8)
Very or somewhat different	34	26	39	24	35	39	25	52
	(+8)	(+8)	(+16)	(+2)	(+9)	(+8)	(+7)	(+8)
How similar are your religious beliefs / beliefs about religion to your father's?								
Very or somewhat similar	64	72	61	76	58	50	75	49
	(−6)	(−7)	(−6)	(+8)	(−13)	(+2)	(−5)	(+3)
Very or somewhat different	36	28	39	24	42	50	25	51
	(+6)	(+7)	(+6)	(−8)	(+13)	(−2)	(+5)	(−3)

Source: National Survey of Youth and Religion, 2007–2008.
Note: Percentages are rounded to the nearest whole number.

teenagers are most likely to have changed away from their mothers' faith (by a decline of 16 percent similarity, twice the national average) and those who were black Protestant the least likely (by only a 2 percent decline). The largest decrease in similarity to one's father's beliefs is seen among emerging adults who as teenagers were Catholic (13 percent). By contrast, 8 percent of the black Protestant group and 2 percent of the Jewish group reported increasing religious similarity to their fathers as emerging adults compared to when they were teenagers. Since this analysis does not specify the religion of the parents, we do not know in exactly what ways emerging adults are similar to and different from them. What is revealed here, however, is that most emerging adults see themselves as similar to their parents religiously, although the transition from the teenage to the emerging adult years brings a modest decrease in similarity to both parents, particularly among certain religious groups.

Religion and Friendships

Table 4.13 examines the religious character of respondents' friendship networks. In the survey, respondents were asked to nominate up to five of their closest friends. Respondents were then asked a series of questions about these five friends regarding religion. It appears, for starters, that 53 percent of all emerging adults' close friends are religious. That number varies by their religious traditions during the teenage years: In the cases of emerging adults who were black Protestants as teenagers, 67 percent of their close friends are religious; for those who were conservative Protestant and LDS, that figure is 60 percent, and for those who were Catholic and mainline Protestant, 50 percent.

Table 4.13. Religion and Close Relationships with Friends of U.S. Emerging Adults, Ages 18–23 (Percents)

	U.S.	Religious Tradition Age 13–17						
		CP	MP	BP	RC	J	LDS	NR
Average (mean) percent of close friends who are religious	53	60	49	67	50	33	60	37
Average (mean) percent of close friends who are not religious at all	32	29	34	19	31	43	29	51
Average (mean) percent of close friends whose beliefs about religion are similar to respondent's beliefs	63	65	57	72	61	46	68	63
Average (mean) percent of close friends who are involved in the same religious group as the respondent	17	22	11	21	13	16	48	6
Average (mean) percent of close friends who the respondent talks with about matters of religious belief and experience	49	56	48	58	40	52	68	38

Source: National Survey of Youth and Religion, 2007–2008.
Note: Percentages are rounded to the nearest whole number.

For those who were Jewish, this number is only one-third—4 percent less than the percent for those who as teenagers were nonreligious. Religious background is thus associated with different levels of subsequent relationships with religious friends. It is also associated with different amounts of close friends who are not at all religious. Emerging adults who as teenagers were black Protestant and conservative Protestant and LDS have the fewest number of close friends who are not religious, at 19, 29, and 29 percent, respectively. And those who as teenagers were nonreligious, Jewish, and mainline Protestant have the highest number of friends who are not religious, at 51, 43, and 34 percent, respectively.

Except in the cases of those who were Jewish as teenagers, the majority of emerging adults' close friends hold beliefs about religion that are similar to their own, ranging from 57 percent for mainline Protestant to 72 percent for black Protestant. In short, emerging adults tend to gravitate in close friendships to those who are like them in terms of religious outlook. Even the 43 percent of close friends holding similar beliefs about religion among those who were Jewish at teenagers is impressive, considering that Judaism is numerically a small, minority faith in the United States, as are the numbers on religious similarity for the LDS, as they, too, are a minority faith. The same is true for the minority of emerging adults who were nonreligious as teenagers, the majority of whom, as table 4.4 showed, remain nonreligious as emerging adults: 63 percent of their friends share their presumably mostly nonreligious, beliefs about religion. Thus, again, for every group under consideration, the close friendship networks of emerging adults appear to be relatively homogenous with regard to beliefs about religion. The numbers dwindle, however, when it comes to close friends involved in the same religious group. Nationally, only 17 percent of emerging adults' close friends is involved in the same religious group. Comparing traditions, it appears that those who as teenagers were LDS and conservative Protestant and black Protestant have more than the national average number of close friends in their own religious group (48, 22, and 21 percent, respectively), while the other have fewer than the national average. Finally, about one-half of emerging adults have close friends with whom they talk about religious belief and experience. The percents are slightly higher for those who as teenagers were LDS (68 percent), black Protestant (58 percent), and conservative Protestant (56 percent), and Jewish (52 percent), and only particularly lower for those who were Catholic (40 percent) and nonreligious (38 percent).

In sum, since most emerging adults tend to be religious to some extent, most friends of emerging adults, who are largely their own peers, are also religious to some extent. And this shows up in their descriptions of their close friends. Half of emerging adults' close friends are reported to be religious and to talk with them about religious beliefs and experiences. Nearly two-thirds are thought to be similar in their beliefs about religion. More than one in six of the friends of the typical emerging adult is involved in the same religious group as he or she is. Only about one-third of emerging adults' close friends— roughly the proportion of nonreligious emerging adults—is not religious at all. In general, emerging adults who as teenagers were LDS and conservative

Protestant and black Protestant tend to surround themselves more than those of other groups with close friends who are more religious and more religiously similar to them. This greater attraction to religious sameness—what sociologists call "homophily"—is very likely both a cause and a consequence of the relatively stronger and higher levels of religiousness, at least as sociology is able to capture it, that is evident in these three groups.

Group Involvements

Another approach to exploring the religious social relationships of American emerging adults is to look at their participation in the meetings of organized religious groups other than those of regular worship services. Table 4.14 shows findings on this point. Only 15 percent of all emerging adults participate in such religious groups as Bible studies, prayer groups, or other similar religious meetings. The percents are somewhat, though not dramatically, higher for those who were LDS and conservative Protestant and black Protestant during their teenage years; and lower for the other categories. The Catholic group is notably only a few points higher than even the nonreligious. Of that minority that is involved in some other religious group that is different from their regular worship service, 33 percent is involved in two or more such groups. Among the 15 percent of emerging adults who participate in such groups, the majority, especially among the conservative Protestant

Table 4.14. Religious Group Involvements of U.S. Emerging Adults, Ages 18–23 (Percents)

	U.S.	Religious Tradition Age 13–17						
		CP	MP	BP	RC	J	LDS	NR
Is involved in any organized religious groups such as Bible study, prayer group, or religious group, not including regular worship service attendance?	15	22	15	22	8	10	37	5
Involved in two or more groups[a]	33	35	37	43	26	—[b]	26	—[b]
About how often respondent attends the group's meetings and events[a]								
Once a week or more	66	81	60	50	52	—[b]	56	—[b]
Once a month or less	16	9	26	9	29	—[b]	22	—[b]
This group is a part of the religious congregation respondent attends[a]	68	58	47	79	75	56	96	—[b]
Is now or ever has been involved in any college-based religious groups (of respondents who ever attended college)	25	40	26	28	15	20	46	5
Percent of all emerging adults who ever attended college and who are or ever have been involved in a college-based religious group (row percents)[c]	100	46	15	9	18	2	7	1

Source: National Survey of Youth and Religion, 2007–2008.
Note: Percentages are rounded to the nearest whole number; [a]Only asked of those who attend an organized religious group; [b]Cell sizes too small to report meaningful numbers; [c]Two percent, not reported in the table, were from other religion or an indeterminate religion.

group (81 percent) attends them once a week or more often. Somewhat larger percentages of the Catholic and mainline Protestant groups (29 and 26 percent, respectively) attend their groups only once a month or less often. For the majority of most religious types—68 percent for the whole—most of these other groups are a part of the religious congregations that respondents attend. The 37 percent of emerging adults who as teenagers were LDS mark the highest end, at 96 percent of their other religious groups being part of their regular congregations. Still, viewed from the opposite direction, among the non-LDS traditions, between 21 and 53 percent participate in other religious groups that are not part of their regular religious congregations. That is, sizeable minorities of emerging adults in most religious traditions are involved in other religious groups that are organized either by different religious congregations or by parachurch or other noncongregational religious organizations.

The second-to-last row shows that among NSYR emerging adult respondents who have ever been to college, one in four has been or is involved in a college-based religious group. Those who as teenagers were LDS or conservative Protestant mark the high end with 46 and 40 percent, respectively. Those who as teenagers were nonreligious (5 percent), Catholic (15 percent), and Jewish (20 percent) have been involved in a college-based religious group in the smallest proportions. By dividing these numbers by the percent of the ever-attended-college population represented by each religious tradition, one can calculate a ratio of the number of different kinds of emerging adults who have ever been involved in a campus-based religious group in relation to what would be expected on the basis of their numbers for ever attending college. If everyone was involved in a campus religious group in the exact same proportion to their representation in college, everyone's ratio would be one to one. As it is, the ratios for LDS and conservative Protestant background emerging adults ever in college are 1.84 and 1.6 to one, respectively, on the high end. At the low end are the ratios for those who were as teenagers not religious, Catholic, and Jewish, at 0.13, 0.58, and 0.71 to one, respectively. In sum, there are nearly twice (1.84) the number of LDS types in campus religious groups than one would expect on the basis of the number of them who have ever attended college, while the number for Catholics is nearly half (0.58) of what one would expect and for those with nonreligious backgrounds almost one-tenth of what one would expect.

The last row in table 4.14 shows the distribution (in row percents) of all emerging adults who have ever attended college and have been involved in a college-based religious group by their religious tradition measured during their teenage years. It appears that 46 percent of such participants come from conservative Protestant, 15 percent from mainline Protestant, and 18 percent from Catholic teenage backgrounds. Only 1 percent comes from nonreligious backgrounds. In other words, perhaps unsurprisingly, the vast majority those who populate college-based religious groups come from religious backgrounds; such groups appear to have little success drawing in college students who were not already religious as teenagers.

ATTITUDE ABOUT MAINSTREAM RELIGION

More can be learned from another angle by examining the attitudes of emerging adults about mainstream or organized religion in the United States. Table 4.15 presents their responses to a number of questions on this subject (because these questions were not asked on prior surveys, however, change cannot be tracked over time). A large majority (79 percent) say that they have a lot of respect for organized religion in America. Those who as teenagers were LDS, black Protestant, conservative Protestant, and Catholic are more likely to respect organized religion, and those who were mainline Protestant, Jewish, and nonreligious are less likely. Even so, majorities of every religious group report that they respect organized religion in the United States. Again, with the second question, which reverses the direction of respect to affirm the negative, only a minority of emerging adults (29 percent) saying that organized religion is a big turnoff for them. Seven out of ten do not agree with that statement. Again, emerging adults who as teenagers were mainline Protestant, Jewish,

Table 4.15. Views of Mainstream Religion in the U.S. among U.S. Emerging Adults over Past Two Years, Ages 18–23 (Percents)

	U.S.	Religious tradition age 13–17						
		CP	MP	BP	RC	J	LDS	NR
I have a lot of respect for organized religion in this country.								
Strongly agree/agree	79	84	73	89	81	58	91	60
Strongly disagree/disagree	21	16	27	11	19	42	9	40
Organized religion is usually a big turnoff for me.								
Strongly agree/agree	29	23	36	14	26	52	21	51
Strongly disagree/disagree	70	76	63	85	72	48	79	49
Generally, how positive or negative do you feel about religion in this country?								
Very or somewhat positive	55	61	50	66	55	22	75	34
Very or somewhat negative	19	14	28	13	17	37	16	30
Too many religious people in this country these days are negative, angry, and judgmental.								
Strongly agree/agree	68	71	71	66	66	67	56	68
Strongly disagree/disagree	32	29	29	34	32	33	44	32
Most mainstream religion is irrelevant to the needs and concerns of most people my age.								
Strongly agree/agree	42	38	40	43	42	55	28	48
Strongly disagree/disagree	56	60	59	54	55	42	72	50
I have very positive feelings about the religious tradition in which I was raised								
Strongly agree/agree	80	84	76	90	77	76	84	—
Strongly disagree/disagree	19	15	23	9	22	19	16	—

Source: National Survey of Youth and Religion, 2007–2008.
Note: Percentages are rounded to the nearest whole number.

and nonreligious are the most likely to see organized religion as a turnoff, but at most a slight majority of them do. The numbers begin to shift somewhat on the question of how positively or negatively respondents feel about religion personally. That seems to be because this question introduced a "neither" answer category (not shown in the table) that attracted nearly one-quarter of respondents. Well more than twice the number feel positive than feel negative. In keeping with the established pattern, those who as teens were LDS, conservative Protestant, and black Protestant are the most positive. Those who were mainline Protestant are almost as negative as those who were nonreligious.

The perspective of emerging adults shifts dramatically, however, when a question is asked about whether too many religious people in the United States are negative, angry, and judgmental. More than two-thirds agree with that statement. And the percentages of nearly every religious group (the LDS being the minor exception) tend to agree at similar levels. In fact, those who as teenagers were conservative Protestant share the high end (with mainline Protestants) in thinking that religious people are too negative, angry, and judgmental—higher than even the nonreligious—perhaps because they feel themselves socially closest to such attitudes in their own religious traditions. In any case, a majority of emerging adults across all religious faiths clearly think that too many religious believers in the United States have condemnatory and off-putting attitudes. How relevant or irrelevant do emerging adults think religion is to most people their age? Here they are more evenly split. A slight majority does not believe religion is irrelevant, though 42 percent agree that it is irrelevant. Again, emerging adults across all but two traditions tend toward the national average here. The LDS cases tend more to affirm religion's relevance and the Jewish ones are more likely to affirm its irrelevance. Those who as teenagers were not religious are nearly evenly split. Finally, do emerging adults have positive feelings about the religious traditions in which they were raised? Fully four out of five (80 percent) say yes, they do. Those who were raised as black Protestant, conservative Protestant, and LDS are somewhat more likely to have positive feelings. Catholics and mainline Protestants are the least likely to express positive feelings, but not by large margins. But overall, the vast majority of emerging adults feel positively about the faith traditions in which they were raised.

RELIGIOUS PARTICULARITY AND SYNCRETISM
Religious Exclusivity, Particularity, and Institutions

Table 4.16 shows results for various questions about religious particularity and syncretism. The first question concerns the truth of one, many, or no religions. Most emerging adults (57 percent) believe that many religions may be true. Nearly 30 percent believes one religion is true, and 12 percent believes there is very little truth in any religion. Those in the LDS and black Protestant and conservative Protestant groups are most likely to affirm that one religion is true. Emerging adults in the Catholic, mainline Protestant, and nonreligious groups especially say that many religions may be true. And the Jewish and nonreligious stand out in saying there is very little truth in any religion. Nationally, little

Table 4.16. Beliefs of U.S Emerging Adults about Religious Exclusivity, Spirituality, and Institutions, Ages 18–23 (Percents)

	U.S.	Religious tradition age 13–17						
		CP	MP	BP	RC	J	LDS	NR
Beliefs about religion's truth								
Only one religion is true	29	45	22	38	15	11	60	11
	(–2)	(–4)	(–4)	(+4)	(–4)	(+4)	(–5)	(+5)
Many religions may be true	57	45	66	49	71	53	32	66
	(–2)	(0)	(–1)	(–11)	(–1)	(–24)	(+9)	(+2)
There is very little truth in	12	7	12	8	13	36	8	22
any religion	(+4)	(+4)	(+7)	(+4)	(+5)	(+21)	(+1)	(–4)
Okay to pick and choose religious beliefs without having to accept teachings of faith as a whole								
Agree	52	40	61	37	61	69	37	67
	(+7)	(+8)	(+8)	(+2)	(+8)	(–11)	(+8)	(+6)
Disagree	47	58	38	61	38	31	63	32
	(–6)	(–7)	(–8)	(–2)	(–8)	(+11)	(–8)	(–4)
For believers to be truly religious and spiritual, they need to be involved in a religious congregation								
Agree	25	34	16	31	21	16	49	7
	(–8)	(–2)	(–12)	(–13)	(–12)	(–2)	(–9)	(–4)
Disagree	75	65	84	68	79	84	51	92
	(+8)	(+1)	(+13)	(+13)	(+12)	(+2)	(+9)	(+5)
Respondent considers self "spiritual but not religious"								
Very true	15	15	17	20	11	20	13	17
	(+8)	(+8)	(+11)	(+8)	(+6)	(+20)	(+7)	(+4)
Not true at all	40	43	42	36	35	38	62	36
	(–5)	(–8)	(–6)	(–1)	(–9)	(+8)	(+9)	(+1)
Beliefs about religious conversion attempts								
Okay for religious people to try	49	66	43	60	36	19	84	31
to convert others	(–7)	(–7)	(–16)	(+4)	(–10)	(+4)	(+3)	(–1)
Everyone should leave everyone	48	31	53	36	62	79	16	66
else alone	(+6)	(+6)	(+16)	(–5)	(+10)	(+3)	(–1)	(+1)
Beliefs about religious particularity								
People should practice only	41	56	31	58	33	14	56	20
one faith	(–5)	(–6)	(–7)	(0)	(–7)	(–10)	(–2)	(–4)
It is okay to practice religions	56	40	66	36	65	86	44	77
besides own	(+5)	(+7)	(+6)	(–5)	(+7)	(+11)	(+7)	(+4)

Source: National Survey of Youth and Religion, 2002–2003; National Survey of Youth and Religion, 2007–2008.
Note: Percentages are rounded to the nearest whole number; percent changes from the first survey wave (age 13–17) are reported in parentheses.

aggregate change on this question appears, with a slight shift toward perceiving very little truth in any religion. Among specific religious traditions, the only major shifts are that fewer teenage Jewish and black Protestant respondents say that many religions may be true and that more teenage Jewish respondents say that there is very little truth in any religion. Is it okay to pick and choose religious beliefs without having to accept the teachings of faith as a whole? Emerging adults as a whole are nearly evenly split, though there are noticeable differences across religious traditions. Those who as teenagers were Jewish, nonreligious, Catholic, and mainline Protestant are more likely to agree that it is okay to pick and choose; those who were LDS, black Protestant, and conservative Protestant are more likely to disagree. Even so, 4 out of 10 conservative Protestants, for instance, agree that it is okay to pick and choose. We do not find overwhelming evidence here of groups affirming the need to accept the teachings of a faith as a whole. Across all but one group (the Jewish), a growth in the view that it is okay to pick and choose religious beliefs is apparent. Results are similar on the question of whether religious believers need to be involved in a religious congregation to be truly religious and spiritual. Three-quarters disagree with that idea, as does the majority of every single religious tradition. Furthermore, an increase is apparent across all religious traditions in disagreeing about the need to be in a religious congregation, especially among the mainline Protestant, black Protestant, and Catholic groups. Clearly, personal involvement in actual religious communities is not for most of the emerging adults of any tradition examined here a necessary part of a life of faith.

Do emerging adults consider themselves "spiritual but not religious?" *Soul Searching* reports that very few teenagers viewed themselves in this way. What about when the same youth move into emerging adulthood? It is apparent in table 4.16 that only a minority of emerging adults (15 percent, ranging between 11 and 20 percent across religious traditions) say that it is "very true" that they are spiritual but not religious. Forty percent say it is not true at all. The balance report that it is somewhat true (not shown in the table). The numbers in the parentheses, however, show change over time. There, for each religious group an increase is apparent in the percent saying that spiritual but not religious is very true—ranging from 4 to 20 percent). Evidently, the move from the teenage to the emerging adult years is accompanied by a modest growth in youth seeing themselves as spiritual but not religious. Even so, the percent for whom this is very true is a fairly small minority. A modest decrease is also apparent in the belief that it is okay for religious people to try to convert others. Emerging adults who were Catholic and mainline Protestant as teenagers are especially likely to stop believing that attempting to convert others to a different religion are okay. Even so, 84, 66, and 60 percent of the LDS, conservative Protestant, and black Protestant groups, respectively, still believe it is okay to try to convert others. The majority of the other groups disagree. Finally, what do emerging adults believe about the need to practice only one faith versus the possibility of practicing multiple religions? Only a large minority (41 percent) believe people should practice only one faith. The black Protestant and conservative Protestant and LDS groups are more likely to believe that, each with a majority. But majorities of the other groups—particularly the Jewish—believe it is okay to practice multiple religions. And every group reveals a shift between the survey waves away from religious exclusivism and toward the acceptability of practicing multiple religions. Perhaps surprisingly, 40 and 44 percent of emerging adults who as teenagers were conservative Protestants and LDS, respectively, say that it is okay to practice more than one religious faith.

Syncretistic Spiritual Practices

Finally, what about actual religiously syncretistic practices? Table 4.17 reports findings about emerging adults concerning their own possible spirituality practices from religious faiths not their own. Eight percent of them report integrating practices from Buddhism, Hinduism, Zen, or another Asian religion—an increase of 4 percent since they were 13–17 years old. Most likely to show an increase in this category are those who as teenagers were Jewish, LDS, and mainline Protestant, at plus 17, 11, and 9 percent, respectively. The number practicing Wicca, witchcraft, or another pagan religion is only 2 percent—down by 1 percent since the teenage years. Four percent of all emerging adults (minus those who were Jewish in the first survey) report including Jewish religious practices in their spirituality—a growth of 2 percent. Two percent say the same about Islamic practices, with the relatively largest comparative increase coming among those who as teenagers were black Protestant. Of the types of religious practice included by those of other religions, the largest percent is Christian, at 20 percent. However—unlike the percent of the other religious practices represented, which is growing—that number dropped by 14 percent since the first survey: far fewer cases who were non-Christians as teenagers include practices from Christianity in their spirituality as emerging adults. That effect seems especially pronounced among the nonreligious group. The outreaching influence of

Table 4.17. Syncretistic Spiritual Practices of U.S. Emerging Adults, Ages 18–23 (Percentages)

	U.S.	Religious tradition age 13–17						
		CP	MP	BP	RC	J	LDS	NR
Includes in own spirituality any practices from (not asked of own religion)								
Buddhism, Hinduism, Zen, or other Asian religion	8 (+4)	4 (+3)	14 (+9)	4 (+1)	8 (+2)	23 (+17)	11 (+11)	10 (+6)
Wicca, witchcraft, or other pagan religion	2 (−1)	1 (−1)	2 (−1)	1 (−1)	1 (−1)	5 (+4)	2 (−1)	2 (−1)
Judaism	4 (+2)	4 (+1)	5 (+2)	0 (−1)	5 (+3)	—	6 (+6)	3 (+1)
Islam	2 (+1)	1 (0)	2 (+1)	4 (+3)	2 (+1)	0 (−1)	0 (0)	2 (+2)
Christianity	20 (−14)	—	—	—	—	11 (0)	—	22 (−21)

Source: National Survey of Youth and Religion, 2002–2003; National Survey of Youth and Religion, 2007–2008.

Note: Percentages are rounded to the nearest whole number; percent changes from the first survey wave (age 13–17) are reported in parentheses.

the dominant religion, therefore, appears to be receding some among youth transitioning from the teenage to the emerging adult years.

RELIGION AND SCIENCE

Another way to get an understanding of the place of religion in the lives of emerging adults is to examine their views about the relationship between religion and science. This relationship reemerged as a hot topic in the United States in the late twentieth century. During many midcentury decades, science was considered an almost sacred authority, whose voice was assumed to provide the final word on any dispute.[11] Religion was mostly reduced to a private-sphere interest or opinion. At best, science explained what was really real and how it really worked, and religion, for its part, was thought to perhaps explain the meaning and purpose of reality and perhaps fill in some areas of cultural life—such as "values" and morality—that science ignored. Even in that culturally constructed peaceful coexistence, however, science typically held the upper hand as the ultimate cultural authority. In the last decades of the twentieth century, things changed somewhat. Religion reasserted itself as a visible countercultural authority that claimed it deserved a hearing on matters as diverse as creationism and evolution, medical ethics, sex education, science teaching in public schools, "intelligent design," euthanasia, abortion, and the morality of bioengineering. At times, rival authorities in these debates worked out amicable solutions. At other times, they generated intense conflicts. Today's emerging adults grew up in the midst of these public disputes over religion and science; those disputes have been a part of most of their entire lives. What sense do they as 18- to 23-year-olds now make of religion-and-science conflicts? And what does their sense-making reveal about the kind of authority that religion does and does not hold in their lives?

Table 4.18 begins the analysis by focusing on the possible clash or compatibility of religion and science, asked about from two different angles. A strong majority, 70 percent, of emerging adults believes that the teachings of religion and science ultimately conflict with each other. With the exception of LDS, nearly the same proportion of emerging adults in every religious group believe the same. The LDS are more likely to think that religion and science do not conflict with each other. Nearly the same is evident on the question whether the findings of science and teachings of religion are entirely compatible. Two-thirds disagree that science and religion are compatible, with few major differences across the religious traditions. On the question whether some of the discoveries of science have strengthened emerging adults' views about religion, respondents are more evenly divided. Still, the majority in most cases—with LDS the only exception—disagrees that science has strengthened some of their religious beliefs. The next question addresses whether science should be able to conduct even controversial research with full autonomy from religious influences and concerns. Emerging adults nationally are evenly split on the matter. Jewish and nonreligious ones are especially likely to support full autonomy, with LDS and conservative Protestants more likely to oppose it. Emerging adults who as teenagers were black Protestant and Catholic more closely reflect

Table 4.18. Views of Religion, Science, and Public Life among U.S.
Emerging Adults, Ages 18–23 (Percents)

	U.S.	Religious Tradition Age 13–17						
		CP	MP	BP	RC	J	LDS	NR
The teachings of science and religion often ultimately conflict with each other.								
Strongly Agree / Agree	70	70	74	69	72	65	46	72
Strongly Disagree / Disagree	28	29	26	28	26	35	54	27
The findings of science and teachings of religion are entirely compatible with each other.								
Strongly Agree / Agree	32	33	28	35	34	27	39	22
Strongly Disagree / Disagree	67	66	69	62	66	70	60	76
My own views about religion / religious faith have been strengthened by some of the discoveries of science.								
Strongly Agree / Agree	41	45	41	36	37	36	60	39
Strongly Disagree / Disagree	57	54	58	60	62	64	37	61
Scientists should be free to do any research, even on controversial subjects like human cloning, without any interference from religious morals or teachings.								
Strongly Agree / Agree	51	39	59	47	55	79	35	66
Strongly Disagree / Disagree	48	60	41	51	43	17	65	33
Religion is a private matter that should be kept out of public debates about social and political issues.								
Strongly Agree / Agree	59	44	64	39	71	87	55	76
Strongly Disagree / Disagree	40	55	36	60	29	13	42	23

Source: National Survey of Youth and Religion, 2007–2008.
Note: Percentages are rounded to the nearest whole number.

the national average. The final, more general statement measures attitudes about the full privatization of religion when it comes to social and political debates. A modest majority of all emerging adults agrees that religion needs to be privatized, though that view is concentrated especially among Jewish (87 percent), nonreligious (76 percent), Catholic (71 percent), and mainline Protestant (64 percent) cases. Conservative Protestants and black Protestants alone tend to disagree with the privatization of religion. Because these questions were not asked on prior surveys, changes within groups over time cannot be measured. In sum, emerging adults are divided about the authority of religion and science and their possible clash. The majority believes they are not compatible but in conflict, and that science does not support religious claims. Slight majorities also believe in scientific autonomy from religion even in controversial research, and that religion is best privatized so as to be kept out of public debates. Across different religious types of emerging adults, however, it is LDS, conservative Protestant, and black Protestant ones who tend to resist reducing the scope of religion's authority when it comes to science.

EXPECTATIONS FOR THE FUTURE

Finally, when emerging adults think about their own personal futures, how does religion seem to fit in? Table 4.19 presents findings on two future-oriented religion questions. The first is whether emerging adults expect to be attending religious services when they are 30 years old. Fifty-three percent of all emerging adults say yes, they expect to be attending religious services when they are 30. That number is slightly higher than the reported percent of emerging adults currently attending religious services many times a year or more often, as seen in table 4.5. Looking across the different religious traditions, it is apparent that emerging adults who as teenagers were black Protestants are the most likely (at 72 percent) to expect to be attending church in the future, followed by the conservative Protestant and LDS groups (67 percent each), and then the Catholic and mainline Protestant groups (49 and 48 percent, respectively). At the lower end, 38 percent of those with Jewish backgrounds and 22 percent with nonreligious backgrounds expect to be attending religious services at age 30. Of course, there is no way of knowing now whether these expectations will prove correct. What these numbers do reveal is that more than half of emerging adults today anticipate being involved in a religious congregation when they enter into the age that typically marks full adulthood status.

Another indicator of the significance of religion in emerging adults' lives is the importance they place on marrying someone of the same religion. Most emerging adults hope to marry someday. How much emphasis do they place on marrying someone of the same faith—or lack of faith, for nonreligious respondents? One-quarter of emerging adults say that it is very or extremely important to them to marry someone from their own religion. By contrast, more than one-half said that that it is not very important or not important at all. (Almost one-quarter said that it is only somewhat important [those results not reported here].) Once again, the LDS, conservative Protestant, and black Protestant cases rank highest on wanting to marry within their religious faith. Even so—except for the LDS group, which, at 54 percent, barely breaks into

Table 4.19. Religion in the Future for U.S. Emerging Adults, Ages 18–23 (Percents)

	U.S.	Religious tradition age 13–17						
		CP	MP	BP	RC	J	LDS	NR
Expects when 30 years old to be attending religious services	53	67	48	72	49	38	67	22
How important is it to marry someone who is of your own religion (or not religious if respondent is not religious)?								
Extremely or very important	25	39	20	30	14	12	54	9
Not very or not at all important	52	39	55	43	60	60	25	74

Source: National Survey of Youth and Religion, 2007–2008.
Note: Percentages are rounded to the nearest whole number.

a majority—most emerging adults across the religious groups do not appear to place particular value on marrying within their own faith. Again, there is no way to know if this is how they will actually behave as they choose their mates in coming years. But to the extent that a desire for religious solidarity within a marriage can be taken as a meaningful measure of commitment to their own religious faiths, then these findings indicate that the majority of emerging adults does not seem especially invested in its faith—at least enough to warrant marrying someone with whom they will share the same faith.

CONCLUSION

What have these nationally representative statistics revealed? First, the majority of American emerging adults—more than 60 percent—identify as religious, of one religion or another. The vast majority of these continues to identify as Christians, either Protestant or Catholic. Among Protestant emerging adults, conservative Protestants—sometimes also called evangelicals—hold the largest share of adherents. As for specific denominations, however, emerging adults are fragmented among a great many, none of which dominates. In all of this, there is a general trend toward considerable disaffiliation from religious traditions and a significant growth in the proportion of American emerging adults who identify as not religious. The aggregate changes seen in Tables 4.1–3, however, mask greater religious shifting taking place between the teenage and early emerging adult years. Between 28 and 50 percent of youth in various religious traditions had during the five years between being teenagers and emerging adults switched from one to another religious category. Sometimes the switch was to a tradition that is theologically similar to the original one. For many emerging adults, however, the religious shift at the end of the teenage years is toward becoming outright nonreligious—11–37 percent of adherents of the original religious traditions measured during the teenage years, and more if one counts the indeterminates as nonreligious.

Most sociological measures of religious practice, salience, and belief also decline over these years. More objective and public religious practices, such as religious service attendance, decrease in a particularly conspicuous way. Subjective aspects of religiosity, such as belief in God and importance of faith, decline somewhat less dramatically. At ages 18–23, fewer than 1 out of 10 emerging adults is attending weekly or more frequently an organized religious group or meeting other than a worship service. Only one in four thinks it is important to marry someone of his or her own religious faith.

At the same time, most emerging adults themselves report little change in how religious they have been in the previous five years. And those who do report change are more likely to say they have become more, not less, religious. The majority of emerging adults also still are theists, believe that God rather than purely natural forces created the world, and identify with a more traditional view of the nature of God, Jesus Christ, divine judgment, angels, evil spirits, miracles, and life after death. Furthermore, most emerging adults seem positive about organized or mainstream religion in the United States. Most have respect for, are positive about, and are not personally turned off by it. The vast majority also have positive feelings about the religious tradition in which they were personally raised.

Emerging adults are somewhat more divided on the issue of heaven and who might go there. Significant minorities of them engage in various religious practices, have had sometimes dramatic religious experiences in recent years, and say they feel very close to God. In their personal relationships, emerging adults tend to report that they are quite like their parents and somewhat like their close friends when it comes to religion. At the same time, most think that too many religious people are negative, angry, and judgmental, and nearly half say that mainstream religion is irrelevant to people their age. In and through all of this, emerging adults are friendly to an individualistic and pluralistic view of religion, thinking many religions may be true, that it is okay to pick and choose what one believes, that they do not need to be part of a religious congregation, and that people can practice more than one religion. Still, only 15 percent say they are clearly spiritual but not religious. Most practice only their own one faith. Finally, about half of them expect to be attending religious services when they are 30.

In sum, the importance and practice of religion generally declines between the age periods of 13–17 and 18–23. Some or even many American youth go into something of a religious slump during these years. But that decline or slump does not seem to be cataclysmic for their religious lives—at least as far as statistics can reveal. Most of them do not appear to abandon their faith, decide that it is entirely unimportant, or radically alter their beliefs. Most appear to retain and perhaps soften the subjective aspects of their religions and simply further background and downplay their faith as a salient and publicly practiced part of their lives during these years. Chapter 2 and this chapter have offered a variety of reasons why this may happen.

In all of this, there also continues to be a lot of variance among emerging adults when it comes to religion and spirituality. A minority—particularly, though not exclusively, those with LDS, conservative Protestant, and black Protestant backgrounds—remains quite highly religiously involved and even reflects some growth in religion. The majority of emerging adults is then distributed across a spectrum from being somewhat regularly involved to being sporadically involved to being hardly religiously involved at all. A sizeable and growing minority locates itself at the hardly-religiously-involved end of the spectrum. Chapter 6, attempting to give the religious and spiritual differences among emerging adults more clarity and meaning, will suggest that most emerging adults fall into one of six distinct religious categories. First, however, in the next chapter we will explain and illustrate the dominant cultural structures that shape emerging adults' assumptions, beliefs, attitudes, and practices regarding religion.

5

The Cultural Structures in Emerging Adult Religion

EMERGING ADULTS COMPRISE TREMENDOUS DIVERSITY when it comes to religion and spirituality. They fall along broad spectrums of various kinds and dimensions of religious, spiritual, and nonreligious experience and belief. Still, the majority of emerging adults gives voice to certain thematic perspectives when speaking about religion and spirituality. These reflect prevailing cultural structures governing their assumptions, categories, outlooks, habits, and thought. The prevailing themes described in this chapter reflect the presuppositions, ideas, and beliefs of the majority of emerging adults today when it comes to religion. But these are not the only views out there. Various smaller groups of emerging adults hold different perspectives, some of which we describe as less common voices. What follows, then, is a description of a number of mainstream and counterpoint themes that emerged from the survey's 230 personal interviews. In all of this, what we wrote in chapter 2 is also true of this chapter: it is impossible to convey in one summary chapter the richness and complexity of contemporary culture when it comes to emergent adult religion and spirituality. Most of today's emerging adults do share many elements of a common culture about religion, which we describe here. But even within that majority we find some different emphases and experiences. This summary chapter somewhat oversimplifies the actual reality of emerging adult religious culture, even as it attempts to provide some balance and complexity in the process. We believe, however, that overall it nonetheless accurately represents the main contours and textures of emerging adult religion and spirituality.

PREVAILING AND LESS COMMONLY VOICED
RELIGIOUS CULTURAL THEMES

Not a Very Threatening Topic

According to conventional wisdom, religion, like politics, is a notoriously controversial topic, best to be avoided. Not so for many emerging adults. They generally seem happy to talk about religion, if it happens to come up. Some emerging adults got a bit uncomfortable when talking about religion with us as interviewers, though usually that did not seem to have as much to do with the contentious nature of the topic as this particular group feeling a bit guilty for not practicing religion as devotedly as they think they are supposed to—something like feeling a bit guilty about knowing one is not eating as many fruits and vegetables as one knows one should. In the ordinary lives of many emerging adults, religion actually doesn't come up often as a topic of conversation, but that is not because most are actively avoiding it. It is simply not a big deal, not something of central importance that most would expect to recurrently come up in discussions. So it is also not particularly threatening or controversial. Talking about religious matters might be interesting. Or it might not. It can be fun to speculate and hear about different people's views. Then again, there are many more important things to think and talk about. In any case, for most it's just not a big issue, not a problem, nothing to get worked up over. For this reason, the nonproblematic nature of talking about religion makes it difficult even to identify illustrative excerpts from interview transcripts, since the matter itself is not something emerging adults talk about overtly. It simply is.

A Less Typical Theme—I Have No Idea. A fairly small subset of nonreligious emerging adults are so disconnected from anything religious that they simply have no opinions or beliefs about religion. It is not that they are antagonistic about or dismissive of religion, or are being lazy in their answers to interviewers' questions. They simply have lived lives involving such little first-hand experience of religion or spirituality that they literally do not know or think much at all about it or hold any particular views about God, faith, church, or anything else related. When asked, they simply do not have much to say. They are not so much indifferent as uninformed and therefore neutral. They simply do not know about religion and do not mind saying so. It sounds like this, for one person:

> I don't know enough about it to fully...Not that...I believe in it, of what I know, but I just, I don't know enough about it to really truly be that religious, I guess. I probably should know something to fully believe in it, and I don't know enough about it to. I do believe in it, I just don't know it enough to be fully religious, you know, more religious.

Another said: "I just don't...I guess it's being raised not...I mean my grandparents went to church and stuff, but my parents never did, and it just never was a part of my life. So now to look back on what I believe or what I don't believe is, I don't know, it's like I never really thought of it, never had a sense of it."

Indifferent

Religion is fine. But for most emerging adults, it just doesn't matter that much. It is not that there is anything bad about religion, in most cases. If it isn't causing violence or getting too extreme in its beliefs, then religion is probably a pretty good thing. But for very many emerging adults, religion is mostly a matter of indifference. Once one has gotten belief in God figured out, they think, and perhaps feels confident about going to heaven—if there is a heaven—there is really not that much more to think about or pay attention to. In this way, religion has a status on the relevance structures or priority lists of most emerging adults that is similar to, say, the oil refinery industry. Of course, people know it is there, and it is important in some removed or distant way. Most people are glad someone is out there taking care of that business. But you really don't have to think much about it or personally get involved in it, unless it happens to be an individual interest. Religion for the most part is just something in the background. Asked how his religious faith shapes his life, one replied, "Very little. Just a couple of days a year, I do some stuff." As for whether she thinks much about religion, another said, "I guess I used to, but not now. I'm too involved with school and everything like that. I'm not really involved with all that type of thinking right now. I'm really involved in my life and where I'm heading right now." Another observed more generally, "I feel like the majority of kids my age are apathetic about religion and just don't care. They don't take the time either way to find out one way or the other and there's always going to be your extremists. I'm part of that mainstream in that I'm agnostic and just don't really care that much, like other kids." One simply said, "My faith's not that strong, so it just tends to be kinda flexible. Not much to break."

The Shared Central Principles of Religions Are Good

Different religions claim to be unique and do in fact emphasize distinctive ideas and rituals. But ultimately, most emerging adults say, all religions actually share the same core principles, at least those that are important. All religions teach belief in God and the need to be a good person. These things are what *really* matters. At heart, in this way all religions are essentially the same, the majority of emerging adults claim, because all religions share the same basic beliefs and values. Therefore, anybody who follows any particular religion is ultimately just like any other religious person following any other religion. People can choose different faiths for themselves, but underneath the different faiths are about the same things. They only differ in their outward appearances and emphases. So common is this view that it is hard to choose among the host of statements that illustrate it. One respondent said, "I think religions all go to the same path, you know I think it's all religions are a way of how to live your life and they all kinda lead to the same goal—that's how I believe in it." Another observed, "I believe that if you do right, then you will have good consequences, you know what's right and wrong. It's the same in all the religions." Yet another explained, "The line of thought that I follow is that it doesn't matter what you practice. Faith is important to everybody, and it does the same thing for everybody, no matter what your religion is." For some, this "shared principles" approach is a way to avoid exclusivism, as with one who said, "I find it really hard to believe that one religion is exactly true. I would say that if anything's right, it would be probably something common in most religions." Another emphasized the common object of religious belief in this way:

> God is symbolic of, pretty much I think every people in every culture and religion, even polytheistic people, have had that father god figure. I guess it doesn't have to be male but just that one head honcho guy, and that is God. So there's one God for Christians and one for Jewish people, even Hindus and Buddhists, they have that Buddha and that's the big figure. I think that the Christian God is just a coalition of all those gods, like all those figures come together.

Some suggest that this approach helps to avoid religious conflict, as was implicit in this observation: "I think everything has the same basic principles, you know, obviously we differ in some points, that's why they are separate religions. But to have these fights and quarrels over religion, you know, [is wrong, since] everyone ultimately wants the same thing in life. I think ultimately the same basic beliefs are active in all these religions." Others emphasize the common "values" of religions that have related historical roots:

> All religions are true, all the classical ones, in the sense that they all have a common denominator. Which is certain values they portray, and that value is the same. They may be different stories, but a lot of the stories are the same too. They all come from two major, three major religions anyways. There're 12 classic religions but like three major religions. Each one has its branches so they have to be intertwined in some way.

Religious Particularities are Peripheral

It is fine if different religions want to emphasize specific customs or beliefs or ceremonies, if some people want to do that. But none of the particularities of any religion, emerging adults think, are really what is important or valuable about it. Those things are external and incidental. They help give each religion its own particular culture. But what really matters about religion are the core principles that are shared across all religions—belief in God and basic morals. So it is perfectly fine to adhere to the basic ideas and pretty much disregard the external particularities. One Protestant emerging adult—who equated Protestants with "Christians," versus Catholics who are presumably not Christian—used dismissal of "nit-picky details" as a way to affirm Christian unity: "I think like between Catholics and Christians, they both believe in God, in Jesus, and the Holy Spirit, that he was crucified and everything like that, so it's basically 'Believe and you shall be saved.' If you believe in that, it doesn't matter, you know, the other little, nitpicky details that you believe or not believe in." For others, the mystery of God obstructs a belief that any one tradition could understand God: "I think God is inexplicable, not understandable, that people can't really grasp. But I do think that parts of God are understandable, that everybody's connected through God even if God isn't like something that's privileged for, like, Greek Orthodox Christian people. Every religion has a concept that's pretty much the same." What insightful people need to do, this one said, is to brush aside the direct particularities of faith and focus on religion's "general logic":

> If you're an intelligent person you can kind of cut away the fat. These [scriptural] things are written to be beautiful, they're poetry, not necessarily to be, like, logically perfect. You know, like semantics, so you can't necessarily derive a direct meaning from it. When you take away the fat and you look at the meaning, you'll see like a general logic that's inherent in all religions.

Dissolving religious particularities has the added benefit of the promise of universalism in life after death:

> Who am I to sit here and say that Catholicism is right? That's the big joke, that Catholic is the correct religion and everyone else is just playing games. I truly believe that I don't care what you believe in, but you have to believe in something. [Okay, so are Muslims believing the correct things or?] I don't even know what the correct thing is. I wish I did know, but as long as they're believing in something, I guess that's something you're believing in. [So can a Muslim or Hindu end up in heaven?] I hope. I hope everyone can. I hope it's one big party up there.

Another emerging adult offered this variant on the "one big party" theme in which heaven consists of multiple parties in the same apartment complex:

> I don't want to think there is one heaven and one hell. I think that it's like an apartment building. There's like the Hindu heaven, is totally different than mine, but I'm not getting into that party. They're not coming to my heaven, and they're not going to the Catholic peoples' heaven. I think there's one for each. I don't think there's the one, like the Baptist heaven and hell and everyone who's not Baptist is going straight to hell. I don't think that at all. There should be one for everyone.

A Less Typical Theme—Actually, MY Religion Is True. Some emerging adults genuinely believe that their religious faith is true, that other beliefs and worldviews may have elements of truth but that their own religion expresses the best, most complete understanding of religious truth and reality. These tend to be evangelicals, Mormons, black Protestants, and a few Catholics and Jews. This minority of emerging adults opposes religious, cultural, and moral relativism. They are generally not obnoxious or pompous about it. They simply do not believe that all religions are the same, that all beliefs are equally true, or that it is impossible to judge between different varying religious claims. They are aware that this is a minority position not assumed or promoted by the larger culture, and they do their best to negotiate the tensions involved in those differences. But in the end it is not too difficult for them to affirm to themselves and sometimes to other people that they believe they have the truth and at least some others do not. One respondent, for instance, stated, "I think one religion is true. I think Christianity is the only way. Only one road goes to Heaven, not many roads, that's just what I personally believe." Another explained, "I was raised how our religion is based upon, that there's really one God and he had a Son. And if I begin to open to other religions I'm doubting my religion and not really fully believing it. That's just how I really perceive it." Finally, a third said, "I definitely think that Christianity, that my belief is the one that I think is correct. But if someone else has a different spiritual belief, that's their own, I'm not going to try to convert them or judge them, that's their belief."

Religion Is for Making Good People

The real point of religion, ultimately, in the eyes of most emerging adults, is to help people be good, to live good lives. Bad people are bad—emerging adults do not like or want to be bad people, at least not *really* bad people, like murderers and bank robbers and wife beaters. Religion is usually good because it gives people the basic training in morals that helps them be good, helps them learn to know instinctively what is right and wrong. Children especially need to be given the moral basics that religion teaches, emerging adults commonly say. Even as adults, a lot of people need that kind of reinforced moral compass, so for people with that need it's important that religion keep doing its job. One explained succinctly, "Religion keeps me on the straight and narrow, knowing that I'm going to account for things that I do. It keeps me making good decisions." Another spoke of faith more as a background influence reinforced by parents: "I really don't think my faith has anything to do with my daily decisions. I think it's just helped make the line between right and wrong a lot more clear. My parents have taught the Ten Commandments, and so it's given me a rough estimate of what is or is not a good idea, which has been reinforced by my parents." Even some emerging adults who deny the objective truth claims of religion still value faith for the moral behaviors it teaches:

> What do you mean by religious truth? Because all religions pretty much have a good message that people can follow. I would say that basic premise of the religions, like where they get their message from, is false, but the message itself is good, so. [So how do you know what's true and not true when it comes to religion?] Well, pretty much I think all religions and religious claims are false, so. [Okay, but you say the messages are also good?] Right, like it makes everybody a good person and stuff like that.

Religious Congregations Are Elementary Schools of Morals

It can be important to be part of a religious congregation for awhile, according to emerging adults, because that is where kids learn right and wrong—in Sunday school, from sermons, Bible school, that stuff. So it is a good idea for kids to get exposed to moral teachings when they're coming up, to lay down the basics. Thus, in reply to a question about the relevance of religion for young Americans, one respondent said, "I think people can find their answers in religion, and I think for some that religion is the best way to go to help them develop a sense of right and wrong or things like that." Another explained in this way what her youth group was trying to teach its teens: "To keep kids on the right track, going the right direction in life so they don't fall off track with partying with friends, stuff like that." Another talked about what she learned from church growing up like this: "I've just been given a certain sense of what I should do and, I don't know how to say this, basically right and wrong is the biggest thing and I definitely think that religion shapes that in a large part." Of course, they believe, by the time a kid becomes a teenager or young adult, that person has pretty much learned his or her morals and so can effectively "graduate" and stop attending services at the congregation. What is the point, after all, of staying in school after you have been taught everything it has to teach? You don't need it anymore. You've learned it. When someone goes on to have kids someday, they probably should think about taking their kids to a religious congregation, too, so they can learn right and wrong—just like they did when they were young. But eventually there is no need for anyone to stay in school after they've learned what is taught and graduated—any more than one needs to keep going to driver education classes after one has learned how to drive. Consider, for instance, this exchange an interviewer had with an emerging adult who never attends church now:

> I: Would you say these religious beliefs shape your life in any way?
> R: I guess.
> I: Foreground or background?
> R: I guess they, yeah, they've kind of taught me what's right or wrong kind of thing.
> I: So if you wouldn't have been taught these things, you would live differently?
> R: Yeah, probably.
> I: Like what would happen?
> R: I don't know, because some of my friends aren't religious at all, never have been, and they think differently about some things than I do.
> I: How do they think differently?
> R: Like things that they believe are right or do, rather than what I do, they know it's not a good thing, but they don't really care kind of thing, like cheating on a boyfriend or a girlfriend, or having an abortion or something like that.

I: So because of your religious background, even though it's not in the forefront of your mind, it's given you some kind of belief system or structure?
R: Like a box that I know what's right, and every once in a while I step out of the box and do bad things, but for the most part the box is always there.

Family's Faith Is Associated with Dependence

The main job of emerging adults is to learn to stand on their own two feet, to become independent. The religion in which emerging adults were raised is connected with an earlier phase in their lives when they were dependent on their parents. Independent persons do not keep doing all the things that belong to their earlier dependence. Therefore—not that emerging adults normally consciously think about it in these terms—learning to stand on one's own two feet means, among other things, getting some distance from one's family's faith and religious congregation. Emerging adults aren't asking their parents for a weekly allowance anymore, so why should they keep going to their church or keep practicing their faith in the same old way? That might feel too much like hanging onto parental oversight and dependence. One has to make a break. Although that does not necessarily involve altering one's basic religious beliefs, it usually does mean making changes to one's involvement in one's family's religious habits and activities and associations. At best, an emerging adult might keep going to church with parents as a sign of respect for them, but for the most part parents realize that their emerging adult sons and daughters would rather not do that anymore. The following three accounts portray the kind of subtle break from parents' faith that we are describing here:

My mother is like, "We should go to church on Sunday, you should dress up at church," just be who the African American community says is a Christian. I'm more along the lines that it's 2008. Times are changing, and those things are not working anymore. So I told her not too long ago that I'm not a Christian, not religious. I just can't understand some things, so I don't really feel like I am a Christian. [And does that cause conflict or is she okay with that?] No, she's not okay with that. But I tell her all the time, if I didn't have my own opinion, then you failed me as a parent. A parent is supposed to raise up the child so they can stand back and make their own decisions, you know, not what the parents wants, but make their own decisions. I think a good parent does that, but she doesn't really understand. [Would you say she's happy or not with where you are in your faith?] I think she's torn. Happy I am able to make my own decision and when I say something I mean it and stand behind it. But at the same time she kind of wishes I was more like her in her thinking.

Another emerging adult said this:

My parents and I are pretty close on religion. The only thing that's different is my parents go to church every week. They try to make me go every week, but sometimes I don't. I'm more like around two times a month. [Why do you attend less than them?] I don't know, usually it's like I spend the night out at a friend's house on Saturday night, and I just don't feel like getting up in the morning to go to church. [So, do you agree or disagree with them about religion?] I think our beliefs are the same.

And another reported:

Religious issues come up occasionally at home, but I try to stay out of that conversation because there's usually some kind of disagreement. My mom's much more hard-nose or old-school on religion, and I'm not that way. My parents, they're happy with me, there are small things, but looking at it in terms of the big picture... [Your mom doesn't want you to be more "old school?"] Well it's more like small things, she wants me to go to church when I'm not with the family, like at school. She's upset about that.

A Less Typical Theme—"My Faith" Is Really Important to Me. A certain set of emerging adults are more serious about and committed to their religion than most, in a particular way that they persistently describe as "my faith"—as in, "My faith is this, my faith is that, I'm really into my faith." More serious young adult Catholics perhaps especially use this kind of "my faith" language. "My faith is what's best for me," one said, for example. "I believe in my faith, it's what I've learned, it's what I've grown up with, and it's a personal decision that I've made to be a Christian, so I don't see myself needing to look elsewhere for answers." Another said, "My faith shaped the person that I am today. It's given me the morals that I have, it's taught me, just made me the person that I am." And another explained, "People ask me why I make moral decisions. It's always something that I answer with 'Because of my faith.' It's definitely the foundation of how I live." For some such people, "my faith" seems to have the quality of a solidified entity that is a key component of their personal identity, like an ascribed (born into) status that shares a central space in their clothes closet or is the picture most proudly hung on their bedroom wall. "My faith" expresses a more personal embrace of a religious way of life than simply "my religion." Yet it can seem to lack the subtlety or complexity of religious expression conveyed in talk about personal religious beliefs, relations to God, spiritual journeys, personal growth, personally meaningful practices, and so on. "My faith"—for those who use this term in the way we mean here—almost seems to represent a neatly constructed package tied up with a bow that settles religious matters, a shorthand that not only represents greater spiritual depth but perhaps comes to serve as a substitute for it. Even so, "my faith" believers are distinctly more invested in religion than the majority who express most of the aforementioned prevailing themes.

Not a Place of Real Belonging

If an emerging adult wants to go to religious services somewhere that they like or to join in with some religious group, that's fine. But that is not likely their place of real social belonging. They belong when they hang out with friends, at college, at a job they like, maybe visiting family. But do emerging adults feel a strong sense of belonging in any religious congregation— if they even have one—or in some other religious group? Nah, not really, actually not very much at all. They're usually not uncomfortable in religious services—they often describe their religious congregations, when they have one, as "friendly"—but they really don't feel much actual belonging or sense of being at home. At best, they go to religious meetings, probably enjoy them well enough, are friendly with the people there, and then leave, heading off to more important things. One Catholic, for instance, said, "No, not a sense of belonging at mass. I do feel a childhood, I feel happy thoughts and I feel safe, like memories. But not belonging." A Protestant reported, "I wouldn't say belonging in the church I'm in now. I mean they're Southern Baptist, but it's run basically by really old people, basically conservative, wear a dress, wear a suit to church every Sunday kinda thing." Another felt put off from belonging in church because of the many perceived "petty differences" there:

> I guess this might be a time in my life when it's going to change over time. I'm not uncomfortable [in church], but I would prefer to keep a certain distance because I feel like there are so many petty differences that, I don't really think it's the best atmosphere to be attached to or just be able to act yourself, be yourself. So many different religious groups are really the same, they just have minor things that keep them apart and they harp on them to make themselves look more distant from other religious groups.

Many emerging adults spoke of finding belonging and community in a variety of nonreligious groups and activities. One, for example, described baseball, football, and rugby teams as the place where he found his strongest sense of belonging: "The team, everybody's going after the same goal, and it brings people together. At the same time there's always a game going on, something that's distracting, so I don't have to carry a conversation, just anything that you thought of could go. I could have said anything, and it wouldn't be weird while I was just watching or playing the game." Did this person feel any sense of belonging in any religious group? "Never really participated in any—hmm, I guess I pretty much would go to religious services, but I would make friends when I was skipping them, I dunno. Not paying attention to them or anything, so, I don't think that was a big influence on me." Another described his college fraternity as the source of his sense of social belonging:

> Now that I live with my fraternity, I have a sense of direction with everything, everyone being around me. We have a cultural view and identity, and it really groups us together in a tight-knit bond. We're very tight brothers. And I think that even though I've just met them, that

these guys are going be there for the rest of my life. [Are there any other places where you feel a sense of belonging?] Out with my friends. I only act like who I am, I'm always myself, I'm always true, I'm never fake. [Any other religious groups besides your fraternity?] No, not really.

Friends Hardly Talk about Religion

Although religion is not a particularly divisive topic of conversation, it is not something most emerging adults talk about with their friends or romantic partners.[1] Whatever subjects friends do talk about, religious beliefs and interests are simply not among them—beyond perhaps finding out that someone else is, say, Catholic or Jewish. For most emerging adults, that is because religion is simply not important or relevant enough to everyday life to warrant any real discussion. In that, religion is like favorite family recipes: people often have them and may even love them, but they don't necessarily want to discuss them. For many emerging adults, their friends appear to be similar to them religiously, so they do not see anything particular to talk about regarding this taken-for-granted matter—birds of a feather flocking together, after all, do not typically talk about their feathers, since feathers are not what the flocks are centrally about. For some, not talking about it is because religion is a private matter not to be bandied about in group conversation. For others, the absence of religion as a subject of discussion with friends may reflect a personal uneasiness about discrepancies between who or what they think they should be religiously, spiritually, or morally and the shape and direction of their actual lives—in which case it is easier to push religion out of their minds. Whatever the cause, in the end many, if not most, emerging adults do not even know the religious backgrounds or basic beliefs and commitments of their friends. If they do, it is fairly superficial knowledge, like knowing that a friend does or does not believe in God or was raised Christian or something else. One quite conservative evangelical guy reported about his close friends, for instance: "We don't talk a whole lot about religion. We talk about it sometimes, but it's just not really a hot topic. I don't know, but I think a lot of my friends, I'd like to think that most of them are Christians or are on the same level I am." In answer to a question about the religious faith of his friends, another emerging adult said, "Um, I don't know, I can't really speak for them. Um, I would hope that you know it has some kind of impact on their life, but I mean I really don't know." When asked how different she feels from other people her age, one emerging adult replied:

> I don't know. I don't really have that question come up a lot. It's not one of the things. You don't really want to push people away by making them feel like you're pushing your religion on them, and you don't want them to feel like ostracized for what they believe. So it's just kind of one of those things I try to like stay clear of. If they bring it up, I'm fine with talking about it, but I'm not gonna be like, "So what do you think about...?" They'll be like, "Wait, are we having fun here? What are we doing?"

Religious Beliefs Are Cognitive Assents, Not Life Drivers

Most emerging adults have religious beliefs. They believe in God. They probably believe in an afterlife. They may even believe in Jesus. But those religious ideas are for the most part abstract agreements that have been mentally checked off and filed away. They are not what emerging adults organize their lives around. They do not particularly drive the majority's priorities, commitments, values, or goals. These have much more to do with jobs, friends, fun, and financial security. Yes, basic religious beliefs indirectly help people to be good. But that comes out of deeply socialized instincts and feelings, not anything you have to really consciously think about or actively commit to. In this way, most emerging adults maintain various religious beliefs that actually do not seem to matter much. On his religious faith, one observed, "I don't think it's the basis of how I live, it's just, I guess I'm just learning about my religion and my beliefs. But I still kinda retain my own decisions or at least a lot of it on situations I've had, and experiences. But I think the core values have been built in with religion." Another who said she holds various religious beliefs explained about the frequency of church attendance:

> Not that often. A couple times a semester, really. And my friends would say the same thing. But it's funny how we're all just crazy, and they just party a lot, but we're all actually pretty religious. We try to be. We just need to get back into church.

More generally, it was clear in many interviews that emerging adults felt entirely comfortable describing various religious beliefs that they affirmed but that appeared to have no connection whatsoever to the living of their lives.

EXCURSUS: WHAT'S HAPPENED TO MORALISTIC THERAPEUTIC DEISM?

It is time to step aside for a moment and address a pertinent question. *Soul Searching* argued that the real, tacit, de facto religion of the majority of American teenagers is not any of the many historic religious faiths one usually think of when one thinks of religion but is a new, de facto religion: moralistic therapeutic deism (MTD). *Soul Searching* presented five key beliefs held by followers of MTD. First, a God exists who created and orders the world and watches over human life on earth. Second, God wants people to be good, nice, and fair to each other, as taught in the Bible and by most world religions. Third, the central goal of life is to be happy and to feel good about oneself. Fourth, God does not need to be particularly involved in one's life except when God is needed to resolve a problem. Fifth, good people go to heaven when they die. That was the dominant religious worldview the earlier survey found was held by most American teenagers, ages 13–17. The question for present purposes in the context of this chapter is what has become of MTD five years later, now that those teens have become emerging adults?

The latest wave of research reveals that MTD is still alive and well among 18- to 23-year-old American youth—as many themes and quotations in this chapter suggest. Not simply a religion embraced during the teenage years, MTD continues to be the faith of very many emerging adults. Often what emerging adults said in interviews—some of which we will recount here— expressed an MTD very close to the one they had articulated five years earlier. At the same time, the variety of religious viewpoints they expressed was somewhat greater than when they were teenagers. Language and outlooks were somewhat more varied. Some emerging adults—the irreligious, for instance—were more explicit than most teenagers were about their disbelief in and disrespect and hostility toward religion. Others—some of the spiritually open—expressed more of a genuine interest than the teenagers had in the possibility of life-engaging spiritual realities. Still others—particularly among the committed traditionalists—were more clear and definite about their faith convictions as emerging adults than the more religiously involved teenagers were. So any discussions about religion among the emerging adults definitely exhibit somewhat more variety and originality than did those among the teenagers. In this regard, the concentration of MTD talk among emerging adults has been somewhat diluted, but that is not to say that MTD has disintegrated as a de facto believed and practiced faith. It has not. It simply is set within a wider range of alternative ways that emerging adults think and talk about and practice religious faith.

Why might this shift toward diluting the concentration of MTD among emerging adults be occurring across these years? The first and most obvious answer is that emerging adults have a lot more personal, real-life experience than teenagers do. And as the teenage faith of MTD has had to confront and address life's realities during the transition to emerging adulthood—the five years studied here—MTD itself has been put to the test. For some, MTD seems to have sufficed for managing life. For others, it seems MTD has simply proved too thin or weak to deal with life's challenges. Confronted with real existential or material difficulties, some emerging adults appear to have backed away from the simple verities of MTD or perhaps have moved forward into somewhat more complex, grounded, or traditional versions of religious faith. In short, there seem to be certain tests in life through which some youth find that MTD proves an unrealistic account or an unhelpful way to respond. Another factor at work diluting the concentration of MTD in emerging adulthood seems to be the partial decoupling from parents' religiously. Both *Soul Searching* and this book have emphasized parents' centrality in shaping their children's religious lives. That is true. But compared to teenagers, most emerging adults have lost some of the close proximity to parents that was reflected in their religious speech during their teenage years. *Soul Searching* suggested that teenagers learned their MTD primarily from their parents. If that was right, then it is not surprising that youth who were still closely tied to their parents' lives would express MTD so consistently. But now that most emerging adults have put some distance between themselves and their parents, the capacity for parents to "channel" their own MTD through the voices of their teenage children, so to speak, has been reduced. To some degree—despite the fact that parents remain important influences in most emerging adults' lives—emerging adults speak, as a matter of expression, more clearly with their own voices as informed by their own developing experiences. Many of those experiences do in fact reinforce MTD. But for some, at least, the consistency and coherence of MTD seems to be breaking down into either less or more assurance about faith in general, and into either looser or tighter connections to more traditional religious faiths specifically. Where all of this is heading in coming years, however, one cannot yet say. Meanwhile, we will return to this chapter's examination of the mosaic of themes and counterthemes comprising emerging adult religious culture.

"What Seems Right to Me" Is Authority

What or who gets to determine what is true or good or right in or about religion for most emerging adults is each person for himself or herself. Religion doesn't have any authority per se, any more than shopping malls have authority over their customers. Religion offers ways to be helpful in life, ways to make good decisions. Each individual knows best for himself or herself what ideas or help he or she might need. What decides for emerging adults, then, about what to believe or practice in religion—what "opinions" they want to hold—is the subjective personal sense of "what seems right" to them, what fits their experience, what makes sense to them given their viewpoint. Thus, one stated, "I think that what you believe in depends on you. I don't think I could say that Hinduism is wrong or Catholicism is wrong or being Episcopalian is wrong—I think it just depends on what you believe and what you've been brought up to believe. I don't think that there's a right and wrong." To think otherwise, for many emerging adults, feels like coercion and not free choice, as is evident in this one's explanation of the basis of his religious beliefs: "Myself—it really comes down to that. I mean, how could there be authority to what you believe? Somebody could force you and say you need to believe this, but you really can't force yourself to believe in anything. Force is not a choice." Thus, when asked how she decided which of many interpretations of scripture is correct, one interviewee answered simply, "My own." When asked to explain how he evaluated different religious claims, another replied, "It's pretty much just my authority." Yet another expressed the epistemological approach as, bluntly, "I believe that if you believe it's true, then it's true. I don't believe in any of that [religious] stuff myself, but if you think it's true, you can think it's true." Such views also worked their way into understandings of spirituality:

> Being spiritual seems almost like a more individual thing to me. You can be spiritual and be religious, be spiritual through religion, or you can just be spiritual on your own, or you could be religious and not be spiritual, like you go to church every week but you could really care less—you're just doing it to go through the motions. So I guess that's what I think about it.

Take or Leave What You Want

Religion exists to support individuals, according to emerging adults, to provide useful beliefs and morals that help people live better lives. People should take and use what is helpful in it, what makes sense to them, what fits their experience— and they can leave the rest. There's no need for religion to have to all hang together in a single, coherent package of beliefs and lifestyle. Believing and doing most things—not to mention every last thing—a religion teaches is too much, that's for people who are way too into it, maybe even extremists. Ultimately, religions consist of a lot of accumulated beliefs and rituals that different people have made up for different reasons, which may or may not be relevant for today. At least some parts of religions are "outdated." Emerging adults are the authorities for themselves on what in religion is good or useful or relevant for them. They pick and choose what works. Everything else can just be left out and not worried about. No big deal. Thus, one explained: "Instead of fighting various religions, I just kinda combined religious ideas that were similar or sounded good and just made, again like I said, excluding some beliefs, and I took them in [as what I decided to believe]." Explaining that over recent years religion has become less the basis of how he lives his life, one respondent said, "Saturday nights I go out and hang out, and I don't have to necessarily worry about getting up to go to church in the morning. It's just a lot easier, I think, to leave certain things out." One respondent said he liked religious tradition and history but did not accept certain views of sin, priestly celibacy, and positions on abortion:

> I've always enjoyed the tradition, lots of tradition, lots of history things like that. But there are some things I don't agree with, like ideas about sins. Some of the traditions I just think are outrageous. But I still think it's rich in history, and they are important. But I don't know. I don't agree with having priests not become married, so things such as that. I don't necessarily agree on abortion. I used to think that taking an unborn child's life, or whatever, was wrong, and personally I don't think I would ever do that, but I don't think we as individuals have rights to tell someone else whether or not they should do it or not.

Another expressed a similar authority to determine what religious teaching she would and would not accept:

> I agree with church every Sunday, with a lot of the beliefs, well, basic ones like the Ten Commandments, all that, going to church on holy days. All that I would say I agree with. Disagree? There's a few things that I think they feel too strongly on. Most religions that I know of do not agree with sex before marriage, but then, like, the Catholic religion thinks even if you're married, you're not supposed to use birth control. I kind of think maybe that's a little too out there. I'm not 100 percent sure on their views of abortion, but some of them tell me like they don't even agree with abortion if someone was raped, and that, I think, is definitely wrong. So there's certain things I can disagree with.

Evidence and Proof Trump "Blind Faith"

It can be pretty hard for some emerging adults to believe religious teachings sometimes because there's no "proof" for them. Science, experiments, research, and people's own personal observations provide solid evidence, most emerging adults think, that certain things in reality are proven, are positive and reliable. Everyone should believe those things. But religion is not like that. It requires what some emerging adults call "blind faith." People ultimately either just believe it or don't. For some emerging adults, that's fine. Religion does valuable things that science cannot, and so it is okay to trust blind faith. What else does anyone have to rely on when it comes to certain kinds of matters in life? Besides, that is how they were raised, and no other rival belief system is particularly appealing anyway. But for other emerging adults, blind faith just isn't good enough. For them, if you don't have real evidence for religion, then it's far-fetched, there's no good reason to believe it. Thus, explaining why so many people view religion and science as conflicting, one respondent observed, "I mean there is proven fact and then there is what's written in the Bible—and they don't match up. So it's kind of whatever you wanna believe: there's fact and there's a book, and some people just don't wanna believe the truth." One atheist explained his disbelief in God on this basis: "I would just say [I believe in] more like a scientific approach, and that's all the evidence I would believe." Another skeptical respondent said, "I'm pretty sure there's no afterlife. I can't be completely sure, but modern neuroscience and philosophical arguments have made me very skeptical about any sort of afterlife." Yet another related this story:

> One of my religious friends said derogatorily to me, "It sounds like science has become your god." And I'm like, well, yeah I guess. Because I just don't think the way they do. Religion, like Noah's Ark, there's absolutely zero evidence, and there's no plausibility that it could ever happen. And they're like, "Well, it just was a miracle." I just can't accept that because some book says that there was going to be massive floods.

Those who are more friendly to religion also put a lot of stock in empirical evidence and proof. "Sometimes I just want to believe what I want to believe, what I want to believe, and not question," one said. "But at the same time, there's scientific proof for certain things, and you have to be open-minded about that, too." According to another, "You have to take the Bible as symbolic sometimes. If you take it as literal there's definitely a problem. There's scientific proof [that contradicts it]. So you have to take it piece by piece and choose what you want to believe." The trust in empirical evidence and proof sometimes works on behalf of religious faith. One respondent, for instance, explained that he resolved some religious doubts through the balance of scientific evidence: "If you don't know about Jesus, did he exist? Is there archaeological evidence? But I feel like there's enough evidence to support his existence I guess, that was a big wrestling I had with my faith." For others, the authority of science, as they understand it, makes them vulnerable. Thus, one answered a question about what could possibly cause her to lose her faith in this way: "Maybe science. If there was some science that could even get that far, I think that might be the only way to sway me really, to be able to prove that there isn't a God." Thus, in the minds of many emerging adults, religion can only stand up to empirical proof by accommodating its teachings to science, as this person explained:

> Science relies on evidence, whereas the majority of religion relies on some kind of faith, of belief in something that can't be justified or something that can't be measured. I think religion can modify, that's what happens usually. Religion eventually stepped down and says, "Well maybe science is right," that biblical passages can be dismissed or interpreted as metaphorical. In the end, it's religion that always has to morph into something new, to be compatible with science if it morphs enough. But I don't see it as anything recognizable [as traditional religion] anymore.

A Less Typical Theme—I'm Open to Some Kind of Higher Power. A small number of emerging adults, sometimes with little personal background in religion, are quite open to matters of faith, God, church, spirituality, or at least some kind of spiritual force or higher power. Some are passively interested in such matters; others are more actively seeking. In either case, they are neither indifferent to nor dismissive of religion. They find it interesting to think and talk about spiritual or divine realities that they are uncertain about. They may experiment a bit with praying to see what happens. Some even have started visiting or attending religious services or groups that they find intriguing. They are aware that they may end up believing religious things that they do not now believe, but they do not yet know what those beliefs might be. But they are open. They reflect less of a consumerist and instrumental mentality about religion. They are a bit more amenable to the idea that some things beyond their particular lives really may be true and, if so, would be worth learning about and changing their lives to get in tune with. The following excerpts convey this stance well:

> I'm not an atheist. I guess maybe that there's something—maybe there's God. I don't know. I haven't decided or fully thought about everything, haven't come to that junction in my life. I guess there very well could be someone, something out there. Spiritually, I guess I believe in God. As far as maybe there's something out there that is a higher being, or something like that. But I don't have any direct, religious reason to believe in God.

> I'm spiritual, yes, which is now starting to sound like a cliché. I feel weird saying I'm spiritual. I guess what I think it means is, I don't know, whether it's God or what it is, that you just believe that there's something better, something bigger than you, and that you're trying to reach for it, whether it's just a goal that you set for yourself, or it's a

God that you're after or it's an afterlife. It's just something progressive that you're trying to reach for I guess.

I don't know about God, that's something I'm still trying to discover. I believe that there is something that is God. I don't know if it's a he or a she, I don't really, you know, I guess like, you know. I've had some traumatic experiences in my life, but, like, I haven't really…I do believe in Judaism, and I believe in its teachings. But like I said, I just, I don't know enough about the religion where I could say I believe in this, this, and this. I do believe in it, and you know, I think I'll study it more, learn about it more, figure it out before too long.

I wouldn't call what I do praying. More like sometimes I kinda reach out for help. I don't know, it's not like I'm asking for like a divine favor, it's just like, "Universe, please work with me." It's like sometimes I just kinda like I make wishes, not to God, it's just, "Universe, world, karma, somebody let this come true." So it's sorta that kinda thing. Usually it's more sort of talking to myself, but yeah, I don't really pray. [So do you believe in God?] Not, maybe like, not exactly a god, just maybe some sort of a presence. I don't know if I'd even call it a deity or divine being, just some sort of a presence, like supernatural, superhuman sort of a thing. Just kinda there, like a life force. Almost like karma in a way, just something that's kinda there sort of inching things along. But I'm not really sure how to explain it, it's kinda tough.

Mainstream Religion Is Fine, Probably

Most religions can be pretty good. Of course, in any case, all persons can think and do whatever they want, especially with something so personal as religion. Most emerging adults, it turns out, don't know too much about the specifics of most religions out there, but for the most part think the majority of religions are probably just fine. What about, they were asked, conventional religion for people their age? Is mainstream religion in America generally relevant or irrelevant to young people or not? Most said that it is not necessarily irrelevant, for some maybe, but for others not. It depends on the religion and the person. Are prominent religious leaders too angry and judgmental? Emerging adults say they don't know—it depends on the individual, they guess, some are, some aren't. Do emerging adults feel alienated from "mainstream religion?" Their interview answers suggest that, no, they do not particularly, not really—whatever mainstream is, anyway. It's just what it is. It's up to each person to decide.[2] When asked their opinion about mainstream religion in this way, emerging adults said: "I really don't have an opinion over it. They can do whatever they want, really, I mean it's their thing that's what they do and it's not affecting me in any way"; "I think everything can be carried too far, but currently I think the majority of people aren't too far. The majority of people are within an acceptable range"; "It gives them something to believe in, and if they're willing to believe it, that's great." Others answered: "I think it's a good idea, but

I don't necessarily think that people need to go to church or should think bad about other people because they don't necessarily go to church"; "I don't have a problem with it. You know, people believe what they want to believe, I'm not going to be sitting here telling them what to believe in."

A Less Typical Theme—Mainstream Religion Is a Problem. A minority of emerging adults voiced a great deal more skepticism and disappointment about "organized religion" than most did. Some dismissed religious congregations as mere social clubs: "I'm less interested in what happens at church because, like I said, it's a society thing—like the uppity class goes to this church and others to black churches and you have the normal middle-class churches, and it's become more of a seen-and-be-seen kind of place." Others suspect that religious adherents actually do not know or believe what they claim to believe:

> Everybody's just kind of being like in high school, the cool click, and everybody just goes with it and tell themselves it's what they believe. I don't know if they all believe it, whether if you had a room with a hundred people and you said, "You all really believe this?" and then start like listing off the things, I think some people would be like, "We believe that? What?!" I don't think everybody believes it, they just say that they do.

Some critique the hypocrisy of their religious peers: "I've seen through experience that it's kinda hypocritical. Some of them preach the word and try to act like they are all high and mighty with God, and then they go out and do the same things I do, do drugs and go out and drink and party. But then you'll see 'em at church the next day." Others—such as this one describing what he learned from his former youth group—attack the hypocrisy of adults in church: "I learned that there's a lot of people that are really hypocritical. Some of the adults would be, 'You shouldn't drink ever in your life,' and then you'd see them out at dinner or tailgate parties, and they'd be totally plastered. I could never understand that." Another told a similar story:

> My mom worked in a synagogue for 12 years, so I saw behind the scenes a lot of corruption, things that just should not have been going on. People stealing money, having affairs, just not appropriate in places of worship, you would think, going on among the religious leaders themselves. I just saw that, and it turned me so off of organized religion. It's not like every synagogue's like that, not like every church or synagogue has this problem. The thing is, they start off well, but the bigger they get, the more they're influenced by other things. When I first went to this synagogue, it was really small and everyone knew each other, was really close, like a community. But by my senior year, it was seven hundred families, and that's just too much. It's become too big to the point where you don't have closeness. There's a disconnect.

Yet others are put off by clergy whose behaviors they do not like:

People are going to church to be like, "Cool, I feel good for a week, I went to church for an hour." Sitting through that hour is just kind of boring. I think you could do more on your own than you can with church. And the preacher they have now, he's all about telling you what's good and what's bad, like, "You all need to come to confession." I don't like that. Why do I need a confession booth and a priest for me to ask for forgiveness? So I'm kind of distant away from the whole organized, mainstream religion type thing.

Others simply think that religious organizations are no better than any other kind of screwed-up organization: "I'm skeptical of the existence of a higher power and of humans in general, because people are just so messed up and corrupt and have their own agendas. Do you know why Catholics eat fish on Fridays? Because there was this hoax back in the day and he [the pope] was buddy-buddy with a fish merchant who needed more sales, so he was, like, no more meat on Fridays—so we eat fish instead, changed everything."

A Less Typical Theme—Close to God. A few emerging adults place a high value on the experience of being "close" to God in a "personal relationship." Although this language of spirituality has definite evangelical subcultural roots in the United States, its expression today is not limited to conservative Christians. Talk about being close to God in a personal relationship can be heard among some emerging adult Muslims and Catholics. Having a personal relationship with God in this case does not mean faithfully adhering to the belief and practice requirements of a religious tradition. Rather, it means being present to God, mindful of God, praying a lot, listening for God's voice, attending to God's leading, being open and receptive to the life lessons God would teach. One described this in their life in this way: "He's forgiving, he doesn't judge you, he doesn't put you down. He's always there 24 hours a day, seven days a week. You can always call him, he's listening, right now he's probably wanting to, he's listening." This spirituality is highly personal. It seems utterly sincere, unaffected, or unpretentious, rolling out in stories told about God that appear entirely un-self-conscious. At the same time, emerging adults' experience of being close to God is not easily fully described, because it is for them so experiential, subjective, and personal. But to keep it in perspective, these cases are few and far between.

Personal—Not Social or Institutional

Religion is a personal choice to the vast majority of emerging adults, ultimately an individual, private matter. Nobody can tell anyone else what's right for him or her. If someone is religious, he or she has certain beliefs, follows certain morals, goes to services. It's up to that person. Religions and their congregations are merely groups of people who tend to think alike and want to be together. But when it comes to group matters, religions are not particularly social or corporate realities or collectivities. In any case, religious institutions are probably bad when they get too rigid, so it is probably best for religion not to get too formal like that (even so, if people want to, that's okay for them as long as they don't impose on others). Do emerging adults have ideas about what a "tradition" might be? They're not sure what a tradition is, it probably means something people have believed for a long time. Maybe some of it is good, but you have to make sure it keeps up with the times, too, that it is not irrelevant for today. Along these lines, one respondent said, "I believe in God, I trust that there is a God and Jesus and that kinda stuff. But I don't really feel any push to go to church, don't feel any need to. I have my faith, that's all I feel I need." Another likewise explained, "I think it's become more of a private thing. I don't need a church to go worship. I think it's my own thing." Others also emphasized this institutional-is-artificial theme:

> Church has become less important, I guess, because organized religion. I just see it as something to do. What people really think about when they're there, you get people's mind wandering, you see somebody maybe balancing their checkbook, playing. I think it's more a believing than doing, they just want to get in the habit of doing something. It's sort of like, I don't know, just, "We're about organized religion."

The strong tendency in such cases is for many of those who have an interest in religious faith to turn to the subjective and private, as explained here:

> I guess I am a religious person, but I'm not, like, dedicated. I don't go to church every Sunday, read my Bible every day. I think it's more an inner than an outer thing. I think a lot people go to church and to be seen, so people in society are like, "Oh they are good people. They go to church." And I don't want to be that person. I want to be a good person for me and for what I believe, so that I don't think I take part in all the avenues of religion.

There Is No Way to Finally Know What's True

According to most emerging adults, everybody believes whatever they believe, and that is fine. If anyone was raised a certain way, then it makes sense for them to basically believe that way. There are probably not a lot of reasons for them to doubt or reject it. People should just go with what seems right to them and not criticize others. But, in the end, most emerging adults think, there is really no way to know what is really true. Anybody could be right, or wrong, or some of both. Still, since most or all religions teach essentially the same thing, they are actually probably all basically correct. But there is no way to be certain. You just can't know. So it is best, most presume, if everyone sticks with whatever seems right by their experience and doesn't think too hard about impossible questions. Life is too short to get worked up about what you simply cannot know. Thus, one person asked:

> Who am I to say what's true and not true? Only God really knows if that's true or not. [So how do you have faith in your own religion?]

Oh, that's a tough one. I would probably say just because I was raised to be that religion. I mean, it could be the wrong religion, probably not, but I was raised to be Catholic so I would just stay Catholic. Plus, most Christian religions are similar. Maybe those could be untrue but who am I to say? For all I know I might die and I could be wrong, you know?

Likewise, in answering how she knows what to believe about religion, one admitted, "I don't. Not at all. Honestly, I have no idea. I just believe what I believe because I was raised that way, and a lot of it, like the morals, makes sense. But besides what is right and wrong, all these other things, heaven and hell, abortion, gay marriage, political, I just don't know at all." So for some, religious commitments feel like individual perspectives: "I think it's in the [eye of the] beholder, you know, what you make of it, I guess. What your viewpoints are because you could say one religion is true, but each person says their own religion is true for the most part. I think it's really what the person views and how they were raised, I guess, what their viewpoints are on it." It is not only emerging adults who are uninterested in religion who feel stuck about knowing what's really true about religion. The seriously committed, including this case, sometimes do as well:

I really don't know, but that's what I'm trying to get at right now. I don't know if what is in the Bible is actually true or how it is interpreted, because I've heard thousands of different sermons and they all have been different. I think I need to find the whole way that fits for me. [How do you plan on doing that?] I don't know. I think I'm gonna, I don't really know. I don't have a plan for that. Kinda bad. It's something I definitely want to work on, but it's not something where I know, "That's how I'm gonna do it." I don't know if asking questions works, because then you're gonna get the same problem that I'm in right now. I've got one question and seven different answers and I don't know how to sort through those to like, "This answer's right and this has it partly right." I don't know how to tell the difference.

In the end, many simply fall back on their personal upbringings: "I have no idea, I don't know what's true in mine. I don't know what's true in anyone else's, and I don't know if [Joseph Smith's] golden spectacles [translated the] found testaments. I mean, I don't know a lot of that. I don't know whether any of that is true. I just know what I was brought up on, and I believe it." But in this larger situation, only some can believe it simply because they were raised that way. Others hold on only tenuously, and yet others simply stop believing.

CONCLUSION

There is much to be said in commentary about the religious cultural structures of emerging adults. But we will refrain from engaging that reflection here.

Rather, we will press on into the analyses of the next chapters, waiting until chapter 10 to reflect on the bigger picture of all we will have examined by then, including on the meaning of the cultural outlooks of emerging adults about religion. In the next chapter, we complicate the findings of this chapter by sorting out some major different religious types of emerging adults who emphasize somewhat differently the various themes this chapter has developed.

6

Six Major Religious Types

SORTING THROUGH THE MANY VOICES, experiences, beliefs, and stories that emerging adults expressed about religion and spiritual issues in their lives, we who conducted interviews began to see a pattern of different major types into which most emerging adults seem to fall. Every typology is of course an oversimplification and needs to be used with caution. Not every last person falls neatly within one category or other. Some people seem to straddle types, and others are simply very unique. Nevertheless, empirically informed categories that represent major differences in groups of people can bring helpful analytical clarity to what would otherwise be a complex mass of data. We believe that most emerging adults in America today fall into one of six different types when it comes to religion and spirituality. Those types are as follows.

1. Committed Traditionalists embrace a strong religious faith, whose beliefs they can reasonably well articulate and which they actively practice. Personal commitment to faith is a significant part of their identities and moral reasoning, and they are at least somewhat regularly involved in some religious group. The religions to which they adhere tend to be grounded in established, mainstream faith traditions—typically conservative white Protestantism, black Protestantism, and Mormonism—rather than being customized personal spiritualities or unusual faiths. They also seem to focus more on inner piety and personal moral integrity than, say, social justice or political witness, and can keep their faith quite privatized in a way that does not violate American

society's broader "culture of civility" that requires tolerance and acceptance of difference.[1] The basic orientation of this group could be summarized by the statement "I am really committed." In size, Committed Traditionalists are a fairly small minority, probably no more than 15 percent of the total emerging adult population.[2]

2. Selective Adherents believe and perform certain aspects of their religious traditions but neglect and ignore others. They are less serious and consistent about their faith than Committed Traditionalists, but more grounded and convinced about what they believe, or at least know they should believe, than the Spiritually Open (the third type). Selective Adherents often have had fairly solid religious upbringings but as emerging adults are more discriminating than Committed Traditionalists about what they are willing to adopt of their religious tradition's beliefs and practices, some of which they think are "outdated." They often hold certain "different opinions" and desires from what their religion allows, so they pick and choose what they want to accept. Selective Adherents disagree, neglect, or ignore the official teachings of their faiths most often on the following religious issues: sex before marriage, the need for regular religious service attendance, belief in the existence of hell, drinking alcohol, taking drugs, and use of birth control (for Catholics); some Christians among them also doubt doctrines about the Trinity and the divinity or resurrection of Christ. Some feel genuinely torn and wrestle with guilt over not being entirely faithful, as they see it. Others—operating on more of a "cafeteria" believer style—do not pay so much attention to such conflicts and feel fine about personally customizing their faiths to fit the rest of their lives. In both cases, they compartmentalize their experiences more than Committed Traditionalists do, partitioning them into religious and various nonreligious segments that they tend to keep separated, whether with a bad conscience or not. They may have been raised in any religious tradition and often include "culturally" Jewish and Catholic emerging adults. Their outlook can be summarized as, with a shrug of the shoulders, "I do some of what I can." In size they are a significant minority, perhaps 30 percent of all emerging adults.

3. Spiritually Open emerging adults are not personally very committed to a religious faith but are nonetheless receptive to and at least mildly interested in some spiritual or religious matters. They may be skeptical or critical toward certain forms of religion or spirituality but are definitely open to others. They may be currently exploring specific religious ideas, groups, or relationships, yet they still lack a specific commitment. They probably believe in some kind of higher power but are not sure what that is or means. Typically, the Spiritually Open are heretofore nonreligious or are nominal or former believers in some faith in which they were raised but may have since abandoned, perhaps especially Catholicism and mainline Protestantism. The attitude of the Spiritually Open might be summarized as "There's probably something more out there." The number of Spiritually Open emerging adults is fairly small, most likely about 15 percent of the emerging adult population.

4. Religiously Indifferent emerging adults neither care to practice religion nor oppose it. They are simply not invested in religion either way; it really doesn't count for that much. They may profess to be religious or at least to appreciate religion. But the Indifferent are too distracted with and invested in other things in life and are sufficiently unconcerned with matters of faith to pay any real attention to religion. Religion may be fine, they are willing to talk politely about it if asked, but religion is simply not a particular interest, priority, or commitment in their lives. It is way in the background. Unlike some Selective Adherents, they feel no real guilt or remorse for their lack of religious interest and practice. Indifferent emerging adults can come from any religious tradition or from a nonreligious background. Their motto, to put it in a nutshell, would be, "It just doesn't matter much." Indifferent emerging adults appear to be one of the larger types, representing at least 25 percent of that population.

5. Religiously Disconnected emerging adults have little to no exposure or connection to religious people, ideas, or organizations. They are neither interested in nor opposed to religion. They cannot be either, because they have only the faintest relational and institutional ties to religion. Faith simply has not been a part of their lives in any significant way, and it does not seem that it will become so in the near future, if ever. The family backgrounds of the Religiously Disconnected and the structure of their social relationships simply happen to isolate them from most things religious. So the Religiously Disconnected have little content knowledge about or personal opinions on religion. They lack religious language competency—if you ask them anything about religion, they simply can't say; they just do not know. The Religiously Disconnected normally come from nonreligious backgrounds. Their position can be summarized as "I really don't know what you're talking about." Because most Americans with whom other Americans interact are at least nominally if not actively religious, the size of the Religiously Disconnected is inevitably small, no more than 5 percent of all emerging adults.

6. Irreligious emerging adults hold skeptical attitudes about and make critical arguments against religion generally, rejecting the idea of personal faith. They may concede that religion is functionally good for some people, but their general attitude is incredulous, derogatory, and antagonistic. Many Irreligious have paid some attention to intellectual and existential questions about religion and have already decided against religion and faith in favor of some version of secularism. Some are angry toward religion, others are simply mystified that anyone could believe or have any interest in things religious. Most were raised in nonreligious families or are ex-believers of some faith in which they were raised; emerging adults who identify as atheists or agnostics generally fall into this type. If they had an identifying motto, it would be "Religion just makes no sense." Irreligious emerging adults are small in number, comprising no more than 10 percent of the whole.

ILLUSTRATIVE CASES

Brad, June, and Amanda, presented in chapter 1, represent three of this chapter's different religious types. Brad was a case of a Selective Adherent, in that he was religious but acted as his own authority to pick and choose what of his religious tradition he did and did not want to believe and practice. June was an instance of a Religiously Disconnected emerging adult, since the contours of her life gave her little exposure to communities of religious faith, effectively cutting her off from possible religious relationships, knowledge, or involvements. Finally, Amanda was a Committed Traditionalist who knew what she believed and was committed to practicing it consistently and faithfully. The following three more cases exemplify the other three religious types.[3]

Spiritually Open Andrea

I meet Andrea in the Pacific Northwest during the summer of 2008; I have never interviewed her before. We eat salads off in the corner of a chain restaurant. Andrea is medium height, has brown hair and eyes, some complexion problems, and a winning smile, which, however, only appears on occasion. Andrea looks older than her 21 years, and it will emerge that she is more experienced than most her age in dealing with difficult life experiences. Andrea's biological parents were both alcoholics who divorced when she was young, after which Andrea was sent to live with her grandfather and stepgrandmother in New Mexico. Andrea's mother lives in Alaska, is still an alcoholic, "has mental problems," and moves in and out of treatment programs. The last time Andrea saw her mother in person, she was nine years old. She now occasionally talks to her on the phone but only "about the weather." Andrea's father was disabled in a DUI car wreck that he caused years ago and is unable to work. Andrea's grandparents lived far from any town or city when she was growing up and, she says, enforced very strict rules. They rarely went to church, however. Until age 14, Andrea grew up with their solid support and lived a fairly normal, rural life. At age 14, however, Andrea started drinking alcohol, got into trouble, and was sent to live with her father back in Oregon. Now, seven years later, Andrea attends college full-time at a local state university, works full-time managing a coffee shop to support herself, lives in an apartment with her boyfriend, whom she plans to marry in a few years, and enjoys good relationships with her large extended family, who also live in the area. She says she and her father are now very close. "My dad's pretty much my best friend." She has also recently become involved in a local Christian church that has a strong outreach mission, which she finds intriguing and attractive. Despite her very busy work and school schedule, Andrea attends three different meetings a week at church. To understand why and what that means, however, we need to return to age 14 and learn about Andrea's high school years.

Andrea's moving back to live with her father was the start of a rebellious, self-destructive existence that lasted for four years. Unlike her strict grandparents, Andrea's father knew nothing about parenting or discipline and enforced no rules. "I knew I could get whatever I wanted if I threw a fit enough," she recalls. Andrea was entirely free to do as she pleased. "If anything, it was like reversed roles: I had to take care of him with his disabilities." Furthermore, when Andrea's extended family tried, in her recollection, to "force me to go to Catholic church, which I hated," she also rebelled strongly against that. In retrospect, Andrea also realizes that she has a strong risk-seeking personality that did not serve her well. Andrea was new in town at age 14 and did not know anybody, but she started hanging out with a crowd that was much older than she was. They proved to be a bad influence. She was already drinking alcohol and increased her consumption. In addition, one of her father's 20-year-old female roommates soon introduced her to drugs. In short order, Andrea was heavily into pot, coke, meth, heroin, "everything," she says. Being a heroin addict was the worst, she recalls. To pay for her drugs, she also sold them as a dealer. For the next four years, Andrea was drugged out. She got in trouble for DUI infractions, had run-ins with the law, was subject to drug tests, was put into drug rehab programs, and worked her way through the drug court system. Sometimes her sister had to call her probation officer to turn her in for drug violations. Sometimes her father committed her to detention and treatment centers. She ended up moving around to different residential living situations five times. As a 14-year-old, Andrea also got an 18-year-old boyfriend, who she dated on and off for nearly four years. He also did drugs and drank too much. She quickly became sexually active, having sex with him and others in casual relationships "a lot." She recalls:

> At that age, I really didn't care. It was just something people did. I didn't even really care about it the first time. I didn't care or think about it too much. It was a bad age for me, sex was just random. Some people [who I had sex with] weren't anything, they didn't mean anything to me. What I did, I just didn't care. I was on drugs and alcohol and it was just, sex just happened.

Andrea says she wrecked most of her immediate family relationships and friendships during those years. Still, she says, "I hid it really well from a lot of other people. Like, I was high in every class I took in school, but if you asked my teachers they would say they never knew. I did my work and was in class, so they never knew." Andrea's extended family in the area knew she was struggling in life, but most had no idea how bad things were. Amazingly, despite her drug addictions and related problems, Andrea graduated from high school a year early and spent her senior year taking classes at a local community college. "School was always just pretty easy," she says.

Fortunately for Andrea, throughout all of this, she had a nearby aunt, "who acted like a mom to me," Andrea says, and who stuck with her and helped her deal with her problems. Between the ordeal of living a drug addict's life and the influence of her aunt and other caring family members, Andrea realized at age 18 that "my life wasn't going anywhere," that things had to change. In retrospect, she does not know why it took so long to see it, but she finally comprehended that "I needed to stop." She gave up her heavy drinking and quit taking drugs. Realizing that she also needed to break away from her drug-oriented social networks, she left town and went to live with a trustworthy male friend in Oklahoma for a year while she recovered. She did not say whether she entered any institutional rehabilitation programs. But whatever she did, it worked. A year later, she was clean and ready to start a new life. I express to her that breaking a heroin addiction must have been extremely hard. She gives me a look that says "You have no idea, you cannot possibly imagine." What she verbalizes is "Well, I am definitely grateful. I turned my life around. That came with really hard work and a lot of things that sucked. But I did get through it." On returning home from Oklahoma, Andrea had more work to do: "I had to go back and repair all of the messed-up relationships with all of my family members." Having gotten most of her life back in order, Andrea then landed a job and started college. Soon afterward, she met Bob. From there, most things began to go well.

So how, I ask, does going to church fit into all of this? It turns out that one of Andrea's girlfriends from work—who, she tells me, was recently devastated on finding out that her fiancé was cheating on her with her best girlfriend, and who often asks Andrea to go out to bars with her for fun—invited her a year ago to a religious meeting in her neighborhood of a group that calls itself The Quest. Andrea describes it as "kinda going for the people who don't really know what religion they are and don't really have a church established." She found The Quest appealing. Andrea now attends Sunday morning worship services there, weekly meetings of various two-month-long classes to learn about Christianity, and weekly meetings of an ongoing, small fellowship group called a Life Group. This group is a small assembly in which people of various ages discuss recent sermons, read the Bible, share what is going on in their lives, and pray together. Andrea says it "helps you get through your problems." Bob goes with Andrea to worship services but not the other weekly groups. When asked about her own religious or spiritual identity or beliefs, Andrea says, "I'm still kind of confused about it, but definitely intrigued, I want to know more." So what actually attracts Andrea to The Quest? "I like the people at my church and their beliefs. I'm learning something, and it gives me a sense of belonging somewhere else than family, where I feel secure, at church. So I feel an interest in going because I know I'll need people, and church is kind of a real close group of people."

Andrea says she believes in "God or some kind of higher power, because I don't honestly think I could have changed my life around all by myself. I think there was something else [at work], and my family says they were praying for me all the time." Andrea prays by herself sometimes. But she also says, "One of the things that's kinda holding me back from fully feeling religion is that I've been kinda antireligion for such a long time in my life." She also reads the Bible on her own about once a week. "I got this little card that tells spots to look around and read in. But a lot of it doesn't make sense, religion still confuses me a lot, there's a lot I don't understand." So does Andrea actually have any solid personal religious beliefs? "It's still pretty vague for me. I think there's some sort of higher power, but I don't know exactly what that is." Andrea says she "has no idea" where she is headed with this whole religion thing, but she is sure for now that she will continue to be involved in The Quest. "They're really welcoming and they reach out to people. I really like it." Is she interested in looking into other religions? "I have friends from different religions," she answers, "so I'm exposed, but they never really made sense to me. I think Christianity makes the most sense."

Looking back on her former life, Andrea expresses remorse. She wishes she had not so badly disrespected her father. She now finds herself wanting to avoid people she knew from high school. She remembers, when I ask, that there were school programs that tried to warn kids away from drugs, but, she says, "Some of them just made me more curious. My attitude when I was younger was I couldn't learn anything from other people's experiences, I was set on trying to learn on my own." She also confesses: "I'm ashamed of the sex in those years. But it's just something that happened that I can't change. I just get over it." Is there anything she wishes she had known earlier about sex? "I just wish that it had been pounded into my head when I was younger that sex is something that is special. I think that would have made a difference." She realizes, now that she has a committed relationship with Bob in which sex is really valuable and special, how pathetic her old life was. Andrea is also now disgusted with the whole dating scene. "It's not really worth wasting my time on. I just don't like the process of forcing yourself to get to know another person and then getting to the point where you want to break up with them." Looking around her now, Andrea observes: "A lot of people my age are kinda immature, not really focused on their futures. They're just all, let's float around, not too really concerned about school. They're simply different in view I guess than where I am in life and what's important to me now." That prompts Andrea to remark that she guesses she feels thankful that she got her rebellious stuff done with early on, so that now before she is too old she can focus on school, work, family, Bob, church, and a life worth living.

Even though Andrea has started to explore faith at The Quest, she has not converted to Christianity and is not well formed in that tradition's faith and morals. In a somewhat meandering discussion about the basis of morality, for example, she says that morals are "just kind of instinct," "what you think as a person," "what society and family taught you growing up," and each person's "own choice, what they think is right, depending on their circumstances." Eventually, though, Andrea also says that morality is "sort of located in religion, I think definitely some of it comes from a higher power that people believe in. And then your conscience tells you what is right and wrong." In that sense, she says she definitely thinks that morality is more than merely people's opinions. But Andrea voices a fair amount of moral subjectivism and relativism as well. People can do what they want, she says, "as long as they can live with that on their consciences. Hurting somebody, for example, I think is wrong, but not for everybody, I guess, then they can act how they want. I don't feel that's right, but people are still going to act how they're going to." Andrea herself emphasizes the importance of treating people well, being respectful, being nice. But exactly why should people be nice? I press.

"Karma," she answers, not missing a beat, "It will come back. I believe in karma." Okay, so what is karma? "What you give and how you act, it'll come back to you," she explains. "If you're a good person, then eventually you'll get that back, versus if you're hurting people, then others will hurt you—it's gonna come around." So what, I ask, makes karma work that way? Why or how does it operate as it does? "That is a good question. I have no idea," Andrea confesses.

Andrea has done a lot of community service, but it was required for probation, not voluntary. She does not care at all about politics and believes most politicians do not tell the truth. Although she is done with hard drugs, Andrea still smokes cigarettes, continues to drink some alcohol in moderation—"I pay attention to how much, though, I can drink responsibly"—and still smokes pot on occasion, especially when she's camping in the mountains with friends. She also tends to feel that sex outside of marriage is fine, "whenever people feel ready, it's a personal thing, that's their choice, I don't think it's necessarily right or wrong." She herself thinks that sex is best saved for marriage, "because it creates a lot of conflict in relationships when you've slept with a lot of people before and they've slept with someone you know. It's always hard to think about the person that you love and care about having been with someone else." Still, Andrea is a realist and knows that saving sex for marriage won't usually happen. "People just explore it and don't really put a lot of reason behind it." As for her extended family, however, Andrea is somewhat hiding from them the fact of living with Bob. "To the extent that they're Catholic, they wouldn't like it. I wouldn't lie if they asked but I'm not gonna tell them."

Andrea says she and Bob are "very serious." It is only a matter of time before they marry. Why, I ask, don't they just marry now? "Money," she replies. "Obviously for the rings and the wedding, that will require money." Andrea wants the whole church ceremony, white dress, large family in attendance, big reception, nice honeymoon—the works. That, she knows, will require a lot of cash. So they are waiting a year or two and saving up. Meanwhile, Andrea is focusing hard on school and work. She has three years of college left, after which she wants to become either a crime scene police investigator or a phlebotomist. She's most attracted to the first, but thinks the second would be a more stable job with better pay. Whatever her career turns out to be, Andrea is clear that she wants to "finish school, get a job, stay close to her family, have a husband, and have a family of my own." And what of religion when she is 30 years old? What does she imagine there? "I know," she replies, "that I'll be pretty involved in my church then, get things better figured out. I could see myself being a quite seriously committed Christian."

We finish up. Andrea has to rush off to work. I leave the interview with a powerful sense of admiration for Andrea, for her having kicked her drug addictions and for working hard to get her life back together. I cannot imagine the courage and effort that must have taken. Some teenagers and their parents do have their struggles, I think, but at least some of them as emerging adults are getting their acts together. And for some of them, like Andrea, spiritual seeking plays a significant role in that process.

Religiously Indifferent Andy

I have interviewed Andy on three separate occasions, at age 14, 16, and 19. Across those years, he has remained essentially the same person, friendly, polite, and interesting to talk with. Andy is not religious. "My mother is Jewish by ethnic background, and so that makes me essentially Jewish," he explains, "but we never practice High Holy Days, so religion has never been part of my life. I just have never paid much attention to it." Andy has friends who are religious, has visited an LDS church service, and knows who he would talk to if he were interested in religion. But now he does not have the time or energy to pay attention to religion.

Andy is tall, thin, somewhat handsome, has some scruffy facial hair and zits, and wears knitted wool hats. His parents divorced when he was young, still live in the same area, and have had a shared custody arrangement, so during school days he has lived with both for alternating blocks of time. A year before our interview, Andy graduated from high school. He is keenly interested in making films and is getting set to move to New York soon to begin film school. In high school, Andy had a talented video production teacher, and his class actually won a prestigious national prize for a group project, which paid for a trip to Los Angeles for an award ceremony. Since graduating, Andy has worked as a photographer at a local television news affiliate and gotten some real life experience in media production. With getting a real job, Andy has become able to afford living in a rented house with three male friends, some of whom are also interested in movie production and all of whom drink a lot. During the previous year, Andy has spent many thousands of dollars on digital video editing hardware and software and a large-screen television, which he now regrets, since he needs as much money as he can get to afford film school. Also during the previous year, Andy's mother has divorced his stepfather—his medical problems made him grouchy all the time, Andy said, and "it gets to the point where you get tired of living with someone"—but that has affected Andy little, he says, as he was already living out on his own.

Andy has an interesting, if not entirely coherent, view of morality. On the one hand, he believes that it is wrong to hurt other people and that an "underlying principle of decency" exists as common sense. Andy describes himself as a "liberal democrat" and has volunteered at the local food bank because "it helps the community, it fights against poverty, it's a good cause." He also says that charitable financial giving is good because "it's good to give toward causes. People need help, and you can help give them a better life by giving them money sometimes." When he was 10 years old, in fact, Andy gave $80 of his own savings money to a homeless man with no legs. "I knew he wasn't a scam, and it was around Christmastime. I was happy to do it, because I knew he needed the money." More recently, Andy has given some clothes and furniture to the Salvation Army. Working in the news industry has also made Andy aware of political issues and world events—unusual for his age—and Andy has actually on his own time participated in some political protests against the war in Iraq. At the same time, Andy has difficulty explaining the basis for such moral commitments. For himself, he believes his ideas are "just how I was raised, basic principles my parents taught me, so I just go with my gut instinct and feel like as long as I don't get sucked into anything too bad I will be okay." But what about other people? "Well, all individuals, everyone," he explains, "has their own different morals, every different person thinks different things, and I think what I think. But it's not my part to say if another is doing right or wrong, I can only speak for myself." As Andy explores his moral thinking, it turns out that morality is mostly about "pragmatically people needing to get along with each other" and that "you have to draw the line somewhere or you just end up with total anarchy." Therefore, "the government creates broad parameters and then individuals do what they want within them. Individuals can do and think what they want as long as they're not too extreme. But it's all on an individual basis, you can't tell someone else if they were raised differently." What, I ask, if someone was raised that it is okay to date-rape someone else, for example? That, he says, gets back to the "underlying principle of basic decency." But that doesn't seem to add up. As Andy is someone who early in life has actually done things to help others in need, I am surprised to hear him say "People do not have a moral responsibility to help others, there is no moral obligation for that. People may do it to feel better but not because they ought to or are supposed to help others. It's better if people help others, but I don't think it's a universal." But when I press Andy about why it is better or why anyone should help others if there is no moral obligation to do so, he can only speak vaguely about legal rules and civil liberties.

Andy is so focused on work and making films that he can hardly fit romantic relationships into his life. After his high school class won their national award for their video project, Andy says, he suddenly attracted attention from many girls in his school and ended up dating six of them during his senior year. "Girls were interested in me the way they weren't before, and I found myself attracted to them." With one of them he had sex, and with another he simply "messed around." But these liaisons did not last long. "I ended up spending more time working on video production than dating or spending time with girls, so all six of them broke up with me. They wanted more time out of me, but I didn't want to invest in them. Nothing hard, really, I'm still friends with them all." In theory, Andy thinks sex outside of relationships is fine, "if both want to," but he prefers sex in the context of relationships. Still, he does not know what to expect at film school. "College is supposed to be a time when people are experimenting and hooking up. A lot of that goes on, and I guess that's just the way it is. I guess I expect to have a girlfriend in New York. I would like to have those kinds of relationships when I'm away at college." Andy thinks he wants to get married in his late twenties or early thirties. "But first I want to establish myself as a filmmaker, make sure I have a well-established career and that marriage does not get in the way of becoming the kind of filmmaker I want to become."

I explore religious matters further with Andy. "I have no preference," he says. "I think I might drift toward religion someday but not now. I'm not really interested in that stuff. I'd say I'm an open agnostic, I just don't know what I believe, if I have any beliefs." Nobody in Andy's family attends religious services. Andy says he has prayed a few times, "not really knowing if it meant anything, just being hopeful if there were some higher power out there." Andy has religious friends, but "it's not something we talk about or are interested in. Most feel the same way I do, that we'd rather talk about more relatable things like movies we enjoy." He did read some religious history in an advanced placement English class in high school, which he thought was interesting. And since age 13, Andy says, he has "become more open" to religion. But the variety of world religions makes him skeptical whether any one is really true. Most of all, Andy reports, "I'm just too busy with other things." As for the future, "I'll probably be more into Judaism, my heritage, because Hollywood almost demands that you be Jewish to be successful there," he jokes. "So I'll probably be somewhat more serious about Judaism, but I'm not really thinking about that now."

Irreligious Ruth

I have also interviewed Ruth, like Andy, three times over five years. When we meet for our third interview, Ruth has recently turned 20 years old. She is pleasant, short, pudgy, has some acne, and is overall rather average looking. Both of her parents are self-employed and make little money. Ruth has always explicitly thought of herself as "very intelligent." In all of our interviews, in fact, she has given me the impression that she thinks herself superior to me and that her job is to help me understand life from an intellectually gifted point of view. Middle school and high school were "below" Ruth, so she dropped out after her freshman year, home-schooled herself instead, and began to take college courses at the local state university, she says, at age 14. She worked on the side as a library assistant, which fit with the bookworm identity she projected. In interviews, Ruth takes time to think about her replies before voicing them, usually in precisely enunciated, proper English. She has recently graduated from college with a joint degree in classics and cultural studies. After a road trip by herself to the Grand Canyon to celebrate graduation, Ruth returned home, rented a "shoebox apartment," and looked for a real job. It took her seven "horrible" months to find one—she does not say why—and she is fairly disappointed now with having only landed a clerical job at an insurance company. Besides working, her current activities seem to consist of hanging out with friends and with her boyfriend.

In earlier interviews, Ruth reported that she had no friends and needed no friends. She said she was "self-sufficient." At this interview, however, Ruth says she has developed some friendships, and she seems to be loosening up a bit. Most of her current friends, she says, are about five years older than her. "We all have a very quirky sense of humor that a lot of people don't get. We like to watch terrible movies and make snarky comments about them. We also all do lots of video games and are very into the Internet culture." Ruth says she got really drunk one time, at a friend's wedding after which a wild party was held. "But then I felt like I was going to die and so haven't done it since. I learned my lesson, so there you go." She does no drugs, and cigarettes, she says, are "gross."

Four months prior to our interview, Ruth decided to rent a house with her boyfriend so they could live together. He is her first boyfriend ever; she refers to him affectionately as "the boy," even though he is her age. She met the boy on a blind date, arranged by a friend. "I like the boy," she says, "The boy is a good thing. He's the boy, and he is very nice, and I like him. So we just keep doing this." Ruth and the boy split all of their expenses exactly in half, although she has recently learned that he is in debt, which has her stressed out. Cohabiting with the boy, I learn, however, does not mean that Ruth has had sex. She has not—not with the boy or anyone else. She and the boy sleep naked in the same bed, she relates, but have not engaged in intercourse. "The boy is not a religious person," she explains, "but it would be his preference to wait till marriage, so that is what we do. He has this notion of honor, like he feels that once he has been physically involved with someone, he has a responsibility to them." Later Ruth explains that the boy is also terrified of having children, that he hates them, in fact, and that this may have something to do with their current semiplatonic relationship. She also says that they work opposite job hours, so they hardly see each other during the week. They do in fact kiss, she clarifies, and engage in other activities that are "less than intercourse," but intercourse remains off limits. "It's just the actual, physical, oh-my-god sex act thing" that is a problem, she notes. Can they really exercise that kind of self-control? "Apparently," she comments. "A lot of people don't buy that, but it's true." Ruth and the boy are thinking about marriage, but only "so we could get into a better tax bracket, and maybe add an air of legitimacy for other people who care." But they are leaning against having children, because, aside from the boy hating children, Ruth says, "they're expensive and they take lots of time."

When it comes to religion, Ruth states, "My dad and I are hard-core atheists. I don't think I've ever talked to my mom about it." How long has Ruth been an atheist? "Pretty much as long as I can remember. I look at religion and religious people and I just don't understand. It is like a totally foreign thing to me. I don't get it. I do not understand how you could think that this exists, and you've never seen it." Ruth has never been religiously involved, never attends religious services, never prays, never reads any sacred scripture, does not believe in life after death, and has never had a religious experience. At times, she makes fun of religion. "My dad and I are diehard NPR fanatics," she tells, "so if we hear a religion story on the radio we might talk about it and be like, 'Ha, ha, aren't they silly.'" She also says with glee that at home she has a stuffed Flying Spaghetti Monster, which is the deity of Pastafarianism, a parody religion invented by Bobby Henderson, an Oregon State University physics graduate, in 2005 to protest the Kansas State Board of Education's decision to require the teaching of intelligent design as an alternative to evolution. Pastafarianism has its own creation account, which it demands be taught in public schools. It also "believes" that global warming is caused by the decline of piracy, since the two are historically correlated. Ruth tells me that I simply must read Pastafarianism's bible, *The Gospel of the Flying Spaghetti Monster*. All kidding aside, Ruth believes science is far superior to religion as a source of knowledge. "The thing about science is that you have these empirical facts which you can get over and over again. Observing things is very important. Science produces something you can hold in your hands that is concrete proof, and I do not see that anywhere in religion." For all of these reasons, Ruth expects that with regard to religion in the future she will "not be all that different than I am now."

Ruth says she does not believe in right and wrong but prefers to think about "morality" as "things that you would not like if they happened to you." She explains, "You would like people to be nice to you, to be forthright, because the world is a very unpleasant place when they do not. To do so in return seems only fair, I guess." Where "fair" comes from, however, Ruth cannot really say. There is no larger moral truth, she reasons, "because you can't have an independent arbiter of those kinds of things, and if there is literally nobody who can make that kind of decision, then it is not necessarily a decision to be made." In short, since God does not exist, neither does an objective morality. Ruth thinks it would be good if cultures could adjust their notions of what is good and bad downward, toward lower expectations, since fewer people would then have reason to feel hurt, offended, and upset. But she does not expect that to happen soon. Meanwhile, being consistent, she does not believe that anyone has a real moral obligation to help other people in need. At best, "It would be nice if someone did that." But, again, what differentiates nice from not nice in Ruth's world, or makes the former preferable to the latter, remains unclear. In general, however, Ruth seems to think that most people are decent and that her view of morality can sustain the kind of world in which she wishes to live. "I have not killed anyone lately, and do not feel like I personally know any mean or evil people. I have never met anybody that I have watched do something out of spite or evilness. Sometimes the world is a scary place, but I think there are enough sane people to hold it together."

CONCLUSION

It bears repeating that the three emerging adults presented here to illustrate the religious types to which they belong do not represent all of those types in every way. Ruth, for instance, is not in general a "typical" irreligious emerging adult, except on the specific point of her alienation from and antagonism toward religion. Many other Irreligious emerging adults are quite different from Ruth and from each other in various ways. The same is true about Andrea and Andy compared to other persons in of their religious type. The three cases recounted in this chapter serve simply to illustrate in particular detail what each of their religious types can sound and feel like in particular instances. They tell us stories that help make the typology come alive. More generally, they help to fill out this book's larger portrayal of the reality of contemporary emerging adult life and culture in the United States, which we thematically described in chapter 2. In this chapter's narratives, we clearly hear again some of the normalcy of multiple life transitions for emerging adults, the challenge of standing on one's own, the need to figure out a great many things at once, the tightness of money, the smarting from hard lessons learned, the optimism about personal futures, the need sometimes to overcome major obstacles, the improved relationships with parents, the widespread cultural and moral relativism, the frequent belief in karma, the emphasis on individual differences, the pervasive availability of alcohol and drugs, the amorphousness of intimate relationships, the normalcy of casual sex and difficult breakups, the readiness to cohabit, the common estrangement from politics and public life, and the widespread interest in achieving middle-class material success and family togetherness. Not every emerging adult displays all of these features, obviously. But these are themes that arose over and over again in the course of our interviews.

The cases presented in this chapter also help to extend our understanding of the various ways contemporary emerging adults relate to religion. Some with little religious background, like Andrea, are open to spiritual matters and may even be beginning tentatively to explore spirituality and religious faith. Others, like Andy, simply have no time or interest in matters religious and spiritual. Someday they may, but at the moment they are indifferent and preoccupied. Yet others, like Ruth, are positively incredulous about and antagonistic to religion. They simply cannot imagine how anyone could believe or practice such nonsense and tend to enjoy their own irreligiousness. Putting these types together with the three others portrayed in chapter 1—Brad the Selective Adherent, June the Religiously Disconnected, and Amanda the Committed Traditionalist—we see that emerging adults cannot be easily pigeonholed into just one or two types when it comes to religion and spirituality. Rather, they fall in differing proportions into at least six different categories that represent very different religious and spiritual outlooks and orientations. If one is to understand the religious and spiritual lives of emerging adults well, one needs to take this diversity seriously.

7

The Teenagers of *Soul Searching*
Five Years Later

SOUL SEARCHING, PUBLISHED IN 2005 using NSYR first wave data, portrayed a variety of case studies of American teenagers drawn from our sample of respondents who were interviewed in 2003 when they were between 13 and 17 years old. Most of them were reinterviewed in the second wave in the summer of 2005, and again a third time in the summer of 2008. One of the strengths of the NSYR is the longitudinal nature of its data, as it has tracked the same sample of youth for five years (so far) in order to follow and assess patterns in various developmental changes in their lives. This chapter, by providing an update on many of the teenagers portrayed in *Soul Searching*, capitalizes on what can be learned from qualitative case studies that are followed over time. Readers familiar with *Soul Searching* will gain the most from this chapter, although what follows should be informative for all readers. Here we present updates on these previously described teenagers five years later, in order of their presentation in the original book.[1] Readers need to remember that these cases are not nationally representative of all emerging adults in the United States today. They were originally presented in *Soul Searching* to make particular points in that context. What is of greatest value to learn here does not concern the typicality or representativeness of these specific cases but concerns, rather, how particular lives change over time and what social and relational forces influence these changes. One important theme that emerges from the following is that while some people's lives do change dramatically, the dominant tendency in developing lives is continuity. Most people simply continue being essentially the same people that their lives growing up have shaped them to be, including their way of relating to religion. There is room for variant experiences within the same overall trajectories on which people's lives are heading. But in most—though not all—trajectories, the forces of continuity tend to be much stronger than the forces of change. This we will show in many of this chapter's cases.

Chapter 1 of *Soul Searching* told the stories of two Baptist girls, Joy and Kristin. Here is where they were five years later, in 2008.

JOY

When I first met and interviewed Joy in the summer of 2003, she was 16 years old, working through a lot of pain, and looking at a pretty dismal future. Joy was seriously depressed, ridden with guilt over her broken relationship with her father, who had died unexpectedly, and she was doing drugs. She had troubled relationships with her mother and stepfather, was having suicidal feelings, and was drinking a lot of alcohol. Joy seemed to have few clear moral bearings, no positive relationships with mature and healthy adults, and was having sex with men much older than herself. She had been raised a Baptist but doubted whether God loved her and in any case said she did not care about religion. When I left Joy after our first interview, I had no idea in what condition she would be two or three years later if I came back for another interview.

Two years later, Joy was interested in another interview, so in the summer of 2005 we met at the same location. Her life situation had improved only marginally. Between our first and second interviews, Joy had graduated from high school and moved in with her boyfriend, Sony, who lived in another state a few hours' distance from her home. Sony worked at a mill. He and Joy smoked weed, drank a lot, and watched a lot of television. Joy believed that she and Sony were going to marry and, to help facilitate that, she stopped taking birth control, without Sony's knowledge, and became pregnant. During her pregnancy, however, Sony began to grow more distant and behaved abusively toward Joy more than once. She did not appear to consider this a reason to leave him. In her last trimester, Joy learned that Sony was cheating on her—sleeping with one of her friends. Sony and the girlfriend were pretty rude about the matter. Joy was crushed.

Some months after these events, before Joy was interviewed the second time, she delivered her baby, a girl she named Alice. At the time of the interview, Joy was once again living with her mother and stepfather, with whom she was still arguing a lot, and was sleeping with her baby in the living room on the foldout couch, since apparently no separate bedroom was available for her. She had no job, had little money, and was sleep deprived and depressed. She told me that when the interview was over, she was going to take the money we pay interview respondents as partial incentives to conduct these interviews and go buy Alice some diapers. At that moment, her entire life was focused on taking care of her baby with very little money. On the positive side, it appeared that having Alice had a powerfully sobering effect on Joy; she quit smoking and drinking and began to think about what her life might look like long term. Nothing in particular changed in her religious outlook, however. Soon after that interview, Joy was put into foster care, though eventually moved back in with her parents.

In the summer of 2008, when I meet and interview Joy again, she seems, at age 21, quite a different person from the teenager I have met twice before. She is enthusiastic on the phone and smiles with genuine happiness when we meet and talk. She is working full-time as a receptionist in a small insurance agency in a nearby town. She is a very happy mom, living in a rented double-wide trailer with her fiancé, Matt, who genuinely cares for her and Alice, she says. Joy and Matt are set to marry in a month and have planned a real honeymoon in the Pocono Mountains. Matt comes home from work every day, and he and Joy eat lunch together. Joy says she is now truly happy with her life.

It is not that everything in the previous few years has gone smoothly. After our second interview, Joy attended the local community college for a year to study nursing, but stopped because she could not manage taking care of Alice while being in school. She also worked for a while in a nursing home but said her coworkers were mean and unfair, so she quit. Joy says her ex-boyfriend, Alice's biological father, has proven worthless: "I don't want to talk to him, he is an alcoholic and always out partying and he'll yell and scream if I talk to him, and he doesn't pay child support or have anything to do with my daughter now. When he had visitation with Alice, he'd drop her off with a friend and go out to the bar drinking." Now, both Joy and Matt are in debt—behind on paying their bills and burdened with a large hospital bill for her maternity ward costs. Two years ago, one of Joy's friends died in a car wreck, which was upsetting. As for education and career, Joy studied to take her state board exam to sell insurance herself and failed the test; nonetheless, she is studying more to take it again, with the help of her boss, who is paying the costs. Joy says she still struggles with self-confidence: "Usually I walk around with my head bowed down, and I'm shy." She also says that she has been diagnosed with bipolar disorder and suffers regular rounds of depression that comes and goes. Unfortunately, she does not have the money to afford the antidepressant medication she should be taking. "I'm supposed to take a medication but right now I'm having to just bear it, because I don't have insurance—I work at an insurance agency but I don't have any myself. Depression hits me every day, but it's simply got to be mind over matter, like, 'if you don't work yourself through it then you're not going to make it.' So I struggle." Matt has some medical and perhaps cognitive problems, too. Joy explains, "He's just a little bit slower, you have to explain things to him, and his memory is bad. So I've told him that I feel depressed, and he'll be like, 'Huh?' He doesn't really get it."

Even so, Matt, who is seven years older than Joy, seems to be a very good influence in Joy's life. "He's just a good old country boy, works hard, and everyone knows him." They met when "he was just hanging out" in town. Joy reports, "We sat down and talked and decided we'd give it a shot, and here we are, been together for over a year now, actually in a relationship, and it's working out really good." They first moved in together—for her, in part to get away from her parents—and decided to marry later. Matt recently took a paternity test and discovered that he was the father of a two-year-old son by a woman he had known prior to becoming Joy's partner and who did not know which of her various sex partners had been the child's father. Matt and Joy have since then been working to get custody of that boy and hope soon to have two children in the house. Meanwhile, one of the reasons Joy had to move out from her parents and in with Matt, she says, was that they were problematic grandparents: "My little girl was getting to the age where she was being mischievous and needed to be disciplined, but Granny and Papa weren't going to. I would try to discipline her, and she'd be screaming. And my stepdad would go get her a cookie, and she'd stop crying. So that wasn't working." Since Joy moved out of her parents' house, however, she says, their relationship has improved. Joy not drinking and doing drugs has helped, and they treat her more like a grown-up now. Joy says she happily calls her mother regularly to talk on the phone.

I learn in this third interview that Joy has had in her life one thing that seems present in the lives of every young person who has struggled successfully—as has Andrea in chapter 6—to overcome major problems and obstacles: at least one stable, loving, mature adult who cares for this young person and will not give up on her or him. In Joy's case, this person has been her foster mother, who has taken her in a few different times over many years. "Put it this way," she explains; "I call her and talk to her probably every day." So, who, I ask, is the most important parent figure in Joy's life?

> Honestly, I'd say my foster mom because she has stronger values and is a stronger person. She doesn't depend on nobody, like my mom depends on my stepdad, and she's straightforward about everything. She's very strong-willed and very opinionated and smart, a role model. I learned who I want to be from my foster mom. If I'm going to mess up, believe me she's going to tell me. She supports me quite a lot. My mom, she don't.

Joy also mentions that she's started informally counseling some 13-year-old girls in her neighborhood, which she enjoys. I ask her to elaborate.

> They show up at my door. We talk about relationships and that I went through a lot of depression and suicidal stuff. One of those girls is having some issues with that, and I really have to work with her. It took a while to get her to open up, and I was like, "Look, I've been through it, I've done it, I can talk to you about it, it's okay." So we talk about everything, school, what's different now at the high school. Oh, I love them to death. I'm like the youngest mama of 13-year-olds already. They nicknamed me Mama Joy, and they come over all the time. Their parents—two of which are drug addicts, by the way—know where they are and know they're safe with me. They just come get them when they're ready and especially now that school is out, the girls'll be there just about every day.

A key part of the change in Joy's life, I learn as our interview unfolds, involves Joy's dedicating her life to God the year before. That happened during an altar call by an out-of-state youth evangelist who came to speak at a Christian teen rally in her high school gym. "It was me and my fiancé and a bunch of my girls, we had three carloads go. He preached God's word to let everybody know that God is there and he knows you and you need to walk in his path." So what happened? I ask.

> Well, the first time I went to the youth rally, it was really, really spiritual. He asked people to come up to the stage to recommit their lives to God, and I went up. I did a recommitment. I came home uplifted and bouncy and it was just, I felt relieved and a lot better. My fiancé also did and the girls I brought actually got saved, three of them did. When we got home, we stayed up all night talking and preaching. And those girls, because they're 13 they thought nobody knows anything, that Christians are boring. They were proved wrong. They were like, "He was awesome!"

I ask Joy if that experience had really changed her or if that was just a one-time event. "No," she said, "that's when I really started focusing more, it really was that powerful. It was really good." So what exactly changed her? I probed.

> When that evangelist came around, it was really, really uplifting. He's a youth evangelist, so very upbeat. Well, basically, when you walked into the gym, you could feel, I guess, like a presence, and you couldn't help but have energy all of a sudden, I mean it was going all through the place. I really do think the Holy Spirit was there. And I didn't expect that. It just happened.

Did it have any lasting effect on the girls? "One of them has stuck with it, and one of them has fallen away. The others, they still go to church every Sunday."

As a result of her spiritual renewal, Joy now attends a Baptist church nearly, but not exactly every, week with her parents, Matt, and Alice. She tries to pray every day and is teaching Alice to pray. She reads the Bible some, which she says is encouraging to her, and wishes she had the time to read more often. Matt reads the Bible more than Joy does, she reports. And now Joy definitely believes not only that God exists but also that he personally cares for her. Looking back, she says, "I know there's been several times that I wouldn't have made it without God—times I overdosed on pills, trying to kill myself, and lived through it. God was like, 'Hey, guess what? You're not dying yet.' So I know that God's there and he's watching out, it's really been proven to me that yes, he's there watching over us every day, whether you want him to be or not." And what about Jesus, I ask, does he fit into any of this? "I believe Jesus died on the cross," Joy replies. "He's there, too, he died for us and gave us life, his own life. He died for all of us so that we wouldn't. He died for our sins." So what then, I inquire, does God actually want from people?

Believe in him and spread the word. You come to God and pray and ask him to forgive you and live in his word, then you'll go to heaven. If you refuse to know that he's there, say you don't believe in him, if you walk in the world, as they say at the church, you're going to go to hell. I believe that. People that pray and ask forgiveness for their sins are saved. They have to be humbled and give their life to the Lord, to pray and talk to God every day. You need to pray every day.

What do Joy's own prayers sound like? "I pray to thank God for the day, I thank him for everything, good or bad. It's like, 'Hey, I'm nothing without you, so I need you when I'm happy and when I'm in need.'" Does Joy have any doubts about her religious faith? Only sometimes when she falls into depression, she explains. "When it hits and I go into my depression, that's when it seems like, you know, nobody cares, nobody's there. But then when I come out of it, it's like, 'Hey, stupid, he is there!'" So what, if anything, I ask, would or could stop Joy from believing in her religious faith? "Nothing," she says. Nothing? I press. "Nothing."

Compared to other people her age, Joy reflects, "I think I'm a lot more mature. They're too busy out partying still, having fun. Me, I've done it—I had a kid, am getting married, and guess what? I don't have time for it, and it's not worth it." She continues, "I still have lots of friends who do weed, crack, meth, all kinds of really bad stuff. I see them doing it and the debt they're getting into and the addiction. I've smoked weed and it just made me sleepy—I don't see the point in it." It helps Joy on this front that her new primary social networks are not big into partying. Matt, for one, has a medical problem that prevents him from drinking any alcohol, so Joy only drinks in moderation whenever she does. At the same time, Joy says her current social networks are not highly religious. "Most of my friends, they don't go to church. I don't know why, I've never asked or invited them, because it's a 30-minute drive and they'd probably say no. But I hadn't never really offered."

Joy says she knows what is true in religion from "the stuff that you learn when you go to church, what you're preached to, and what's in the Bible." Still, as far as Joy thinks, moral right and wrong are "matters of opinion." As for someone who disagrees with her about moral concerns, Joy says, "You can tell them, but me personally, I'd be like, well if that's how you feel, that's how you feel, I'm not going to judge you for saying that." But, I ask, shouldn't people try to persuade each other about what they believe is good and right? "Mm, no, I'd just let them be." When it comes to religious truth, Joy says, along the same lines, "I think that Christianity is the religion that everybody should believe. However, everybody else has their own opinions, and I can't say whether I do believe in another religion or not because I've never studied it, never practiced it. I believe Christianity is true, but whether others are true or not, I'm not sure."

As to her personal spiritual life, Joy reports, "You know, I try to live the Christian life. I'm not like a Christian fanatic or anything like that. I do know that without God I wouldn't have anything that I do today, and I'm very thankful for that." Even so, Joy admits that she is far from perfect: "I cuss a lot [laughs], and I know I shouldn't. And then I guess if we do go out, if I drink, that's a no-no." On second thought, however, Joy is actually not sure whether her church actually teaches that drinking alcohol is sinful. Joy also tells the 13-year-old girls who visit her about her spiritual renewal. "If I had been a stronger Christian when I was those girls' age, I would have been a lot better off as far as making some of the choices that I did." Joy, for instance, now thinks it's better to wait on sex till marriage, although she has a hard time telling that to others because she did not wait. And as to religious faith and her own daughter, Alice, Joy says, "I want her to know and enjoy going to church, and she already loves going to Sunday school and Bible school. Last year she went to three different Bible schools and just had a big old ball! I want her to grow up in church, and I do want to set a good example. But I don't want to force it on her."

Reflecting on the big picture, Joy says she likes where her life is headed: "Everything now is planned out the way I wish it had in the past. I couldn't ask for more with Alice. She's a bundle of joy. We're getting married and have our own place. I have a job opportunity, like I said I'm getting my education to be higher up, so I'm just moving further up than I am now." As for growing in her new faith, Joy explains: "Any Christian out there knows that there's always more to learn, you're never going to stop learning, stop growing. You grow every time you talk and read and learn. I don't think you can ever get enough, I mean I know at the end I don't want there to be a deadline or a finish line, but just keep going and never giving up."

KRISTIN

The contrast between Joy and Kristin when I first met them was stark. Like Joy, Kristin, also 16 years old, encountered early life with real difficulties, including her father's sudden death. When she was a girl living in California, Kristin's parents had separated. One day, when he did not show up for a get-together or respond to phone calls, Kristin, age six, herself found her father in his apartment, dead with a gunshot wound to the head, a suicide. With five young children and little money, however, Kristin's mother did not fall apart. She turned to her conservative evangelical faith to help her family pull their lives together and move forward. They became heavily involved in church, they home-schooled, and they later enrolled in a Christian school where Kristin's mother taught. Kristin's mother chose not to date men, but in due time she married a widower to whom she was introduced by a family member and with whom she had a long-distance courtship. The entire family then moved to the Southwest, which is where Kristin lived when I interviewed her. Kristin impressed me as a happy, healthy, well-grounded, socially involved teenager. She was committed to her personal religious faith, which she clearly understood and allowed to form her daily life.

In 2005, when I interviewed Kristin for a second time, not a lot about her was changed. She was the same person on the same trajectory, just a little further along. High school was coming to an end. Kristin was trying to decide which of the two Christian liberal arts colleges that had admitted her she should attend in the fall. Kristin was still heavily involved in church, youth group, and Bible club. She still volunteered in the community. And she continued to hold conservative theological and social views. Kristin sometimes had conflicts with her parents about typical teenage issues. But overall, Kristin and her family seemed to be thriving.

In 2008, when I catch up with Kristin again, she is working at a Christian camp in the mountains during the summer before her senior year at the West Coast Christian college she attends. Once again, Kristin has not changed dramatically as a person—in her commitments, views, and practices. She is on the same life trajectory she was on five years earlier—she is simply older and more mature. Kristin has enjoyed college, where she majors in education, but has badly missed home, hates the cloudy grey climate where her college is, and dislikes homework. She remains a serious Christian, attending church and Bible study regularly. Kristin is also involved in a traveling college-based praise and drama group that leads worship and performs "inspirational plays" at churches in the region. Kristin prays many times a day, "for wisdom, guidance, discernment in what I'm doing, and for other people." She also tries to read her Bible every day. As for her religious beliefs, they are the same as they were in prior interviews. God is a loving and caring provider and shelter. Jesus is God's one and only Son who came from heaven to live on earth and die for people's sins and rose again to give those who believe in him eternal life. Jesus is the only way to God. "Christianity is the only true thing, so you can be however religious you want, but it's not going to matter if you don't believe in Jesus." At the same time, Kristin confesses that she sometimes struggles with religious doubts. "Like, what if this isn't true? What if I'm just believing a lie that somebody made up about God, that I'm so enthusiastically involved in this ridiculous lie? Those doubts just comes from being human and listening to lies that maybe others have fed me." When she does have doubts, she talks with her mom, teachers, and other Christian friends, who help her out. None of Kristin's doubts, however, come from what she has learned about science; rather, she says, "God uses science to show his glory." She also states that she has personally witnessed other people being healed, which, she reports, "reaffirmed my faith. I was like, wow, God can really do this, it's not just people being wacko—even though there are crazy people like that—this is real!"

Kristin still believes as strongly as ever that all religious and moral truths come from the Bible. "The ultimate standard I think is God's Word, the Bible. Each circumstance that comes I think can be found in there and anything that doesn't line up with the Bible is no good." Even so, Kristin is finding it more difficult to live as a Christian as she gets older. "It gets harder. Some stuff is more confusing and before, when I was in high school, my parents were always there and could monitor everything. But now I do things because I myself do or don't want to, so it's harder." Kristin has struggled in particular with the fact that some of her fellow music and drama troupe members—who publicly lead worship and speak about the Christian life—turn out to party a lot and watch movies that make her uncomfortable. "They were really perverse," she says. "Here we are in a praise band and sometimes we would go to a performance at a church and they'd be hung over from the night before. That was backwards and weird." Kristin is not used to that kind of hypocrisy back home. In fact, it was not until she left home for college, Kristin says, that she realized the true value of her home church. "I never really understood what a church home was until I left and realized *that* was my home!"

Kristin is very close to her parents, especially her mother. "I can talk to my mom about anything and ask for advice, and I know she will be there." She says her parents have "loosened up" and given Kristin and her siblings more freedoms as they've gotten older and gone to college. Kristin also feels more respected by her stepfather, now that he sees she has learned a lot about life and is making wise choices. As for their religious views, "we pretty much agree on everything. We go to church together every Sunday and Wednesday evening, when I'm home, always as a family." More generally, Kristin also believes people have a moral responsibility to help one another. "We're called to love other people and so automatically we should love others because God loves us and other people have loved us. There is no way I'd be at this point in life if other people hadn't helped me, so why not help others?"

After graduating from college, Kristin expects to move back home with her parents in order to get herself more financially stable before someday moving back out on her own. She wants to get married eventually but is not thinking about that much, since she has not even really dated anyone. "I've liked some boys, but they didn't like me back, so no relationships." Meanwhile, she is adamantly opposed to hooking up or sex before marriage. Holding hands and light kissing are okay but nothing beyond that. Eventually, Kristin says, she wants to have a family, own a house, a car, clothes she likes, "the basics." But most important, she says, "I want people to think of me as a person who cares for others, who wants the best for others and not just herself. I know I have a purpose here in life. It's to serve God, spread his love, and serve other people."

Chapter 3 of *Soul Searching* presented two case studies of nonreligious boys, Steve and Raymond. Steve unfortunately declined to participate in the NSYR third wave survey, so I was unable to reinterview him. My sense in exploring his case was that he had issues going on in his life that he did not want to talk about, so refused to participate. Raymond, however, I met up with for a third interview over lunch, in a state neighboring his original home, where he was living with his grandfather.

RAYMOND

This has been a difficult interview to set up. A few months earlier, Raymond readily agreed to do an interview with me and told me to call back when the time drew closer. But when I called again, Raymond was out of town, visiting friends at his old home, and he had no cell phone. After chasing around some different numbers where people thought he might be staying, I finally gave up and waited to hear some word from him through his grandfather. A date and time were eventually set up, indirectly, though his grandfather, who proved very solicitous and cooperative. Even so, on the morning of the interview—to which I have to drive some hours—I am not sure whether Raymond will show. Happily he does, even though he wrote down the wrong meeting time. I am glad the interview has worked out.

In 2003, when I first interviewed Raymond, he was into drugs and alcohol, was in trouble with the law, had dropped out of high school, and had a difficult relationship with his divorced mother, with whom he more or less lived. Raymond's life seemed to be going nowhere. Yet this scrawny kid—an adopted Native American—was unpretentious and likeable. At the time, he was also intrigued by an area evangelical church that he sometimes attended and seemed to want to learn more about God and the Bible. When I interviewed Raymond two years later, his life was not that much more together, although he had had a baby girl with his girlfriend and was thinking about trying to settle down some to help take care of her. Raymond was still into drinking and drugs, including crack cocaine: "I did a little bit more than experiment with it for a couple of months, got pretty bad off, lost a lot of weight, looked like hell." Raymond had also been living with his girlfriend in her parents' house, but just before the interview had gotten into a drunken fistfight with her father so had to move out. Things were tenuous. But Raymond loved his daughter, who he saw about once a month, and wanted to do right by her.

I learn in our third interview that Raymond has not progressed very far in getting his life on track. On the bright side, Raymond has passed his GED exam and has quit smoking marijuana and hard drugs. But Raymond has lived in a number of places, with girlfriends, family, and friends, none of which has been a stable situation. He is also an alcoholic by his own admission (see his Alcoholics Anonymous story in chapter 2) and smokes cigarettes heavily. "I wish I had a little more willpower," he confesses, "Not that I can't, I just wish, willpower. Another thing I need help on is managing my money." Raymond also seems to have a problem managing his anger, having attended some required programs to deal with that difficulty. Raymond attended a government-funded jobs training program but was expelled for punching out another kid who was taunting him, he says, for no apparent reason. "I hope I hurt him," he remarked, "I got kicked out for it." Since then, Raymond has been working short-term manual labor jobs in landscaping, construction, and roofing—about 10 or 15 hours per week. However, he recently slipped two disks in his back from that labor, so he cannot work as much anymore. Having smoked cigarettes for the previous 11 years, Raymond also recently had to go to the emergency room for an inhaler and an overnight stay because he was vomiting blood and having difficulty breathing. The doctors told him he has bronchitis from smoking and gastritis from drinking alcohol. "My stomach lining is coming apart," he says. But Raymond continues to drink and smoke. Raymond now wants to get trained as an automobile technician or a truck driver, and he is actively pursuing joining the National Guard. "One reason I want to join the army," he explains, "is to help me a little more with self-discipline. Plus get more skills, chance of a better job in truck driving. Now that I have my daughter, I have a bit more to live for." Still, the prospect of being blown up in Iraq while driving a fuel truck frightens him, he says.

Raymond is now living with his grandfather, an ex-alcoholic ("He lost my grandma that way") and nominal Mormon, who seems to be doing his best to help Raymond get some order into his life. Grandpa was the force behind the GED completion, for example. As for Raymond's mother, she simply wants him to stop drinking, he says. Raymond does not get along at all with his stepfather, who, he says, "called me a p.o.s. [piece of shit] last time I saw him. Karma, I don't know—one of these days it will come back to him. What comes around goes around, I guess." In turn, Raymond mocks his stepfather, who is Chinese, calling him Buddha: "Yeah, he's a big boy, so I call him Buddha. 'Oh, mighty Buddha,' I say to him." Raymond's biological father, whom he really likes, lives far away, and he sees him only rarely. Raymond says his friends—all of whom he met partying—think he's just "a badass."

Raymond has become less religiously engaged since I first met him. He talks positively about religion but also keeps it at a long arm's distance. When asked if he's attended church since moving to his grandfather's, he replies, "I found one but haven't had a chance to go. I'm kind of shy meeting new people." Raymond had his daughter baptized at his mother's mainline Methodist church a few years ago when she was a baby, and he was baptized then himself. "I don't know, it may sound stupid but I don't really understand exactly what baptism is, a big reason I did it was so my daughter could be baptized, to help her live a good, clean, healthy life, but I don't know." The mother of Raymond's daughter does not go to church. Raymond believes in God. But when asked what God is like, he only says, "I don't really know, none of us really knows, I guess, until we die." Does he have any idea? "He's our father in heaven, cares for everything, every one of us, whether we're good or bad." And what about Jesus? "Son of God, same way as God, I guess." Raymond tries, somewhat successfully, to pray regularly, for God to "watch over" his family and friends. He reads the Bible on occasion—"not as much as I should, haven't read it for a couple of months." Raymond thinks he believes in life after death, in heaven and hell. "I would assume evil people go to hell, I don't know, Satan worshipers and stuff like that, murderers and rapists." Raymond toys with the idea of reincarnation and has some interest in Native American spirituality but does not think that will go anywhere. Religion's influence on his life, he says, is mostly through the Ten Commandments, giving him some moral beliefs. So he believes it is wrong to "use the Lord's name in vain," because "he's our father in heaven, because of him we're here, shouldn't disrespect him." When it comes to morality, to knowing and believing right and wrong, Raymond offers a variety of ideas, including: "Depends on who you are and what you think," "Comes from the inside, a voice inside, I guess," "Do unto others as you would have them do unto you," "What goes around comes around," and "It's for God to judge, not us."

Raymond has had a lot of small exposures to religion but has no consistent religious influence in his life. He and his grandfather never talk about religion.

Nor do his friends very often. "Around here people my age don't really go to church or have anything to say about it, really." Occasionally, he says, when some of his friends are drinking or stoned and "want to sound smart," they'll say "stupid things" like, "Oh, God is such a jerk, always killing people"— and "I'm like, 'What?!'" When Raymond visits his daughter at his old home, he sometimes takes her to church. "People are good there, and the sermons make sense. My daughter likes it, too," he says, laughing, "because she likes the other girls in the nursery." Raymond says he has no doubts about his religious beliefs, such as they are. "It's easy enough, keep praying, asking for guidance." He has never had religious experiences per se, but says, "I think he's letting me know he's there. You get that feeling after you pray. I feel that presence at least, not necessarily that he's talking to you but just letting you know he's there." What does Raymond think of other religions besides Christianity? "I don't know, none of them are necessarily wrong, it's just up to the person to believe or not. Just believing in God, worshiping God, there's no right or wrong. I'd like to believe they're all worshiping the same God." He does, however, definitely think that Islam "is wrong" because it tells believers to kill others. "That's weird, I mean, 'Allah tells us we must kill?' What is that?" Raymond once attended a Mormon church and youth group with a friend for four months, and he liked it, but it had no lasting impact on him. He does not believe in Mormonism because he thinks Mormons insist on paying a tithe to get into heaven. He also thinks Jehovah's Witnesses are ridiculous for giving God the name "Jehovah." Once Raymond caught his sister and her friends having something like a Wiccan séance with candles in a circle around a picture of a dead grandparent, trying to speak to the dead. "Pagan, spooky stuff, witches, tarot cards, like that." He says he flipped out, kicked the candles everywhere, and gave his sister a scar from the hot wax flying around. "I mean Wiccan has something to do with the devil, so that's not good. She never did that again." For a while, one of Raymond's brothers was also into Wiccan, wearing a pendant and dark makeup under his eyes—mostly, Raymond says he found out, because he was being picked on in school by a group of neo-Nazis. "He did it so people wouldn't screw with him, would say he's a badass. So me and my friends went over there and slapped a couple of them [neo-Nazis] around. I asked him if that was why, and he broke down crying and said yeah, that he didn't even understand any of it, but he is still hating other people about being picked on."

Raymond has a serious girlfriend, Kimmie, also native American, whom he met through a friend when he first showed up in his grandfather's town. "She called me up then and was like, 'Hey Cowboy, what ya doing tomorrow? Want to drink a little?' We became a couple about a week after that." Kimmie's parents are divorced, and her mother works as a bartender in a local restaurant Raymond frequents. "She's my drinking buddy. She always has vodka in the kitchen." Kimmie drinks a lot, too. "She loves vodka, can down a fifth of vodka before I'm half done mine." But, he explains, she also has more self-control when it comes to alcohol than he does; she knows when to stop. Kimmie dropped out of high school and does not work, "not yet."

Raymond describes Kimmie as an ex-hippie who is into Satanism and paganism. "I'm trying to get her off it," he says, "She doesn't really wear the pendants and that crap anymore—I actually took her pendant and threw it in the river without telling her. Her being a Satanist bothers me, but I'm not going to let something like that come between us. I don't know, if that is what she likes and want to be, if I have to accept it, if it makes her happy, then I will." Raymond has been reluctant to ask Kimmie to go to church with him. "If she's ready, then she will. I don't want to push it on her. It's her decision, not mine." Kimmie, it turns out late in the discussion, may be pregnant with Raymond's baby. He is not entirely sure. Raymond and Kimmie are talking about getting married. But there are some complications. For one thing, Raymond has to figure out if the army will give him more benefits if he is married when he joins or if he marries later. Another problem, Raymond explains near the end of our interview, as if it is an incidental matter, is that Kimmie may have ovarian cancer. Or maybe cervical cancer or cancer of the uterus. She is being retested in a few days, Raymond thinks. If she does have cancer and is not pregnant, she will have her ovaries or something else removed. If she does have cancer and is pregnant, they will do nothing for now. Raymond does not really seem to know much about the details. Nor, for whatever reason, does he seem particularly worried.

When it comes to sex, Raymond is a bit conflicted. He has definite beliefs about sexual standards, but also admits: "I guess I can't really say anything," because he's been pretty promiscuous himself—he has had sex with four different women in the last year, for example. "Use condoms, of course, that's about all," he says at one point. But he thinks sex should always be in relationships, not hook-ups. "You don't want to mess around, but I can't say that either. I mean, I've met girls and known them for a couple days and then, you know [had sex]. But, I don't know, you should at least know them, I don't think you should just meet them and then half an hour later you're in the sheets, that just seems kind of low." Does his religion teach anything about sex?

> I'm sure God doesn't want you going out and fraternizing with all these women, because that's obviously sinful. You know, go out and have this woman tonight and her sister tomorrow night. I mean, that's no good. It's probably better to wait till you're married. But someone like my girlfriend and I are planning on getting married.

Raymond tells me that he has trust issues with women and sex. Girlfriends have cheated on him, he says, including the mother of his daughter, who, when they were still living together, told Raymond that she had been with another man. "I got all pissed off and stupid and went and cheated on her. That didn't make it any better." Then after they broke up, she told him that she had cheated on him with two other men as well. "That goes back to trust, that's a big one for me, I guess." Raymond then states that he does wish he had behaved differently with sex in the past. "I wish with some of them I would have waited a little longer, known them a little longer. Like, you know them [as friends] and are cool, and then you have sex and it changes the relationship, makes it a little bit more awkward when you see each other. It's different, you see them and expect, I don't know, I would have waited longer." In any case, when it comes to pregnancy, Raymond says he is definitely prolife: "I don't believe in abortion. If you're not going to use protection, don't even have sex. If you start a life, take care of it and nurture it, don't destroy it."

In and through all of Raymond's issues, he has, I think, a winning, unpretentious, almost childlike side. He is excited about taking an "Anyone Can Draw" class at the local community college. He sometimes volunteers to sit with the elderly in a local nursing home and paint, do puzzles, and knit with them. "Makes me feel good," he says. The person he most admires is Brad Pitt, because of his financial contributions to environmental conservancy. Raymond very easily says of his own ideas in a completely un-self-conscious way, "I don't know, that's probably stupid," and then smiles and keeps talking. He likes to hang out at the local park, known as the "Boy's Jungle," where he and his buddies ride bikes over dirt jumps and play on rope swings in the swimming hole.

Looking back on his life, Raymond says, "There are things I would have done differently, not dropping out of school, not getting kicked out of the jobs corps program. But I really can't say I've gotten the short end of the stick because I did it to myself." As for now, he reflects, "I'm not in jail, so that's one thing. Could be going better, could be worse." What about the future? "When my girl's old enough, I'm going to take her to church, when she's old enough to understand it and decide whether she wants to, then that's her choice. I would hope she would at least realize who God is to us. It's up to her whether she goes to church or not, but I hope she would." And what about Raymond himself? "I suppose I'll be the same, probably go to church a little more often. Have a house, work nine-to-five, have weekends off." So what, I ask to close our interview, does Raymond ultimately want to get out of life? "I want to at least have been married for 20 or 30 years, have some grandkids maybe. Retire, of course. Have an old rocking chair, a front porch, and," he says, laughing, "a shotgun." Why a shotgun? I ask. He doesn't know. Just wants one. We say goodbye until next time. I think to my self, I'm not sure Raymond is going to live 20 or 30 years, much less stay married that long. Time will tell.

ALYSSA

Alyssa was first interviewed for the NSYR when she was 15 years old.[2] She lived in a working-class neighborhood in Milwaukee and was the only member of her family attending church. Alyssa's mother died of cancer when Alyssa was six years old, and her father eventually stopped attending the Pentecostal church where they had been going. Alyssa was getting into "drugs and stuff" when her sister directed her into her church's youth group, with which she had a past tie, where Alyssa said she found a second home and support from other teens and adults. She spoke of her youth group leaders at the time, who talked to and helped her a great deal, as her "spiritual mother and father." Alyssa was also attending a Christian school and said her teachers were a big support in her life. Her church even had an "accountability partners" program, which helped people out in life through sharing and praying. Based on what I knew about Alyssa at the time, I concluded in *Soul Searching*: "it appears that a set of important and densely connected social ties, at the center of which stand her youth group leaders, has come in her middle teenage years to provide her with emotional support and relational connections to a serious, committed life of faith."[3]

Alyssa was not reinterviewed in person a second time in the second wave of data collection. But studying her telephone survey answers in retrospect helps to sketch the outlines of a more complicated story of her developing life. Alyssa was indeed into drugs, alcohol, cigarettes, and other "stuff" early on. She had her first sexual intercourse at age 13 and first oral sex at age 14. Both were under the influence of alcohol, she reported in her survey answers, and under pressure from friends and sexual partners. She reported that she felt guilty about things in her life and that religion was both a cause and a relief of this guilt. Her father—who was not attending church and did not talk about religious matters at home—did not know she was involved in these problematic behaviors. Still, she reported that her religious faith was extremely important in her life, that she attended church regularly, that she was a leader in the youth group she attended weekly, and that she had very many adults in church with whom she could talk about issues in life. At the time of a second telephone survey, at age 17, Alyssa was still attending church, but—having earlier reported religious faith as "extremely important" in her life—she now said it was only "somewhat important." She also reported attending youth group somewhat less often and only being a participant, not a leader. Her evaluation of how much she liked her youth group also dropped from a great deal to neutral. Alyssa was at that time getting drunk regularly, smoking pot, and was somewhat involved in delinquent activities, like petty theft, fighting, and drug abuse. She also reported in her second survey that she was very unhappy with her body and physical appearance, only felt somewhat accepted by the people around her for who she really was, and felt guilty very often.

In 2008, three years after her second telephone survey, Alyssa was interviewed in person again. She was 21, unemployed, the unmarried mother of a two-month-old baby girl, and living with her sister and brother-in-law. She said she had spent the previous years partying and "sneaking around everything. I didn't care, I just did what I wanted to do." She had started going to college but dropped out after awhile. Alyssa reports having had sex with 20 different men, 18 of whom she did not have relationships with. She and her partners did not regularly use birth control or protection against sexually transmitted diseases. More recently, Alyssa had a boyfriend whom she met through a friend from work and with whom she partied and had sex. But, she says, they fought all the time over stupid things, so she broke off their relationship. However, even after they broke up, at the end of parties she would not want to hook up with strange guys or to simply go home, so she would go back to her ex-boyfriend's apartment and sleep with him. That is how and when she got pregnant. She considered having an abortion very briefly but decided it would be wrong, she says; "to stop another's life just to fix my own, in the long run that would have hurt me, and a lot of other people if they found out." When she told her father that she was pregnant, he became very upset and kicked her out of the house. So how do they get along now? "Just semiclose. I know he loves me. We're kind of close but not as close. I went from being his little girl, because I'm the youngest of four, to just moving away and having my own life now." Alyssa reports that her father's semiestrangement has been the saddest part of her life in recent years.

Alyssa's story suggests that she has been influenced a lot over the years by peer pressure. One friend in particular, she relates, "hasn't always been a good influence, she's gotten me into a lot of problems when I was younger, drugs and boys and stuff, when I was insecure in who I was." Alyssa says that this friend "was really hurt as a child. She knows who God is and what's right but I don't think she really thinks about it." Her other good friend "doesn't really practice as much" as Alyssa thinks she actually believes. In general, Alyssa observes about people her age: "A lot just don't believe in anything or they might believe in a higher power, but it's not God or Jesus. They don't want to be governed by rules and regulations. The ones who are not religious don't care, they care more about themselves and partying, like selfish ambitions and stuff." Most people these days, Alyssa thinks, are heading toward atheism.

Eighteen months before her last interview, Alyssa had a supernatural experience that she says strengthened her faith. She was at the time feeling that she "actually had something inside of me that was not good. It was kind of like a demonic influence. I felt a lot of oppression. I didn't know where it came from." She prayed a lot and talked with her pastor's wife, and then she "had a vision" that "brought me back to where it came from. It was something that I said when I was really little, the power of my words. Something I said I guess became like a 'stronghold' on my life and gave it room for demonic oppression." In the midst of this experience, she had an actual feeling of God. "I was kind of freaked out at first, but it was a very freeing process. I felt free after it was done, and it was just an eye-opening experience. It increased my faith and gave me a sense that I need to be careful and trust God to protect me and my family." Still, it is clear from the timing of this and subsequent events that this spiritual experience occurred when Alyssa was still partying and sleeping with her boyfriend and others. That experience by itself did not turn her life around and put her back on the straight and narrow.

More generally, it becomes apparent in this interview that Alyssa's life over the years since her last interview has been caught in a struggle between a serious and consistent religious faith versus living however she wants, even though she believes it is wrong. In some ways, that tension seems to parallel the religious orientations of her parents, about which she explains, "My mom was a very strong Christian before she died, and we've all kind of just held on to that, but my dad is not as strong as she was. He believes but doesn't go to church often." So a certain lack of consistency or integrity—understood in Alyssa's own terms—seems to creep into her life. For example, she says she has accounts at both Facebook and MySpace and says about the presentation of herself in them: "My Facebook is more me. My self on MySpace is, um, probably more religious [looking] than I really am." Elsewhere Alyssa says,

> I am not very good at sticking up for myself. I kind of let people run over me. I let people take advantage of me. I'm not good at saying stuff, telling people how I feel. I'm not a very good communicator. I like to keep things inside.

Hearing this, I immediately recall that a friend influenced her toward getting into trouble and a boy and other friends pressured her into having sex at age 13. Later, she remarks specifically about church:

> I'm sort of a different person than everyone else at church. I don't really open up to a lot of people, I like to keep to myself. I mean, I'm friends with everyone there but as getting into my personal life, not really. I feel uncomfortable with that. Before [when I was doing bad stuff] I felt a "fear of man," of people's judgments and of being different. Everybody else there is just the same, and I kinda feel different from them.

Still later in the interview, Alyssa recalls: "Before, the way I was living, every time I would go to church I would feel a lot of conviction, I don't know, very judged. My sin would be in my face when I would go and I would be very uncomfortable because I knew I wasn't living right." These kinds of disconnects and ability to live with dissonance apparently enabled Alyssa to live a double life between church and the party scene. "I always did believe what I do now [about not having sex before marriage], but I just thought, whatever. Whatever I wanted I just went for. I saw the importance of waiting but I kind of just went with how I felt and what I wanted." Still, she was not greatly enjoying her life at that time: "I was feeling guilty, feeling dirty and 'easy,' all of those things. I used to worry about getting a disease, used to get checked up about every six months." Once she had a pregnancy "scare," but it turned out that she had only skipped a period. Another time one of the men she had slept with was rumored to have Chlamydia, so she had to go to her doctor to get treated. In the end, it was getting "caught" pregnant that shocked Alyssa and put an end to her partying. Living with her sister has also helped to bring her faith back, she says, and she is now attending church regularly. She has quit partying and plans not to have sex again until she is married.

> I've learned not to be stupid, to make the right choices. I've made enough mistakes. I wish I would have waited until I was older, not gotten myself into a lot of crap. But I was hard-headed. I should have just listened to people but [I didn't]. I have a lot of regrets.

By the souns of it, however, marriage may not be too far away for Alyssa, as she is dating a man from church who she describes as "a good guy. He's amazing. He really loves my daughter and loves me, doesn't pressure me for anything, is very respectful. He's just a loving man, he's good." Alyssa now reads her Bible and prays every day. She prays for her relationship with her father to be restored and prays "for a man, a good man." God, to Alyssa, is "faithful, forgiving, love, peace, the judge." Jesus is the same. Faith, she says, "puts the fear of God in me, instead of other stuff, which is good. I'm not going to go out and make all the wrong choices again." At this point in her life, however, Alyssa says she values spirituality over religion: "Religion is kind of like bondage to people, just rules and traditions that can actually harm you more than do good. Spirituality is more being in touch with who God is and the Holy Spirit."

Looking back, does Alyssa think her high school youth group was successful in working with her? "Uh, they were successful to a point. I mean, I think [my life choices] had to do with me and what I wanted to go for in the end. I was just not caring and not thinking about it, trying to get it out of my head. They did a good job, though." Alyssa never mentions her previous "spiritual mother and father" during the interview. They seem to have faded in importance. In this interview, she says the biggest spiritual influences on her have been her sister and brother-in-law taking care of her since she became pregnant: "Giving me a place to live. Because they believe, and I live in their house, and that just kind of came back to me." In trying to move forward with her life, Alyssa is looking into training as a nurse's assistant at a local technical school, once her daughter grows a little older and she can get off of state assistance. She has become interested in nursing because that's what her sister does. Alyssa wants to get married:

> Just to have the compatibility and having someone there that knows you inside and out. I want a full life, I guess, family and husband and children, a place to call home, just the normal stuff people want. I'd like to get a degree, be successful, have a career. And I hope my daughter can have everything she needs. Not everything she wants but everything she needs. I definitely want her to have that. I don't want her to ever have to struggle or feel that I'm struggling to support her.

Religiously, Alyssa says that when she is 30 she expects she "will be the same, I'll believe in the same stuff, hopefully get stronger in it. I think I will grow up more, probably be more experienced, smarter."

Chapter 6 in *Soul Searching* focused on the question of Catholic teenagers in the United States, seeking to understand why so many of them were—as the survey findings showed—so relatively indifferent, uninformed, and disengaged when it came to religious faith and spirituality. To help illustrate our analysis in that chapter, we presented three case studies of Catholic teens whose lives embodied what indifferent and permissive Catholic teens can look, feel, and sound like. They did not represent all Catholic teens, only the more typical uninformed and disengaged type. The question now is what do those three cases, now emerging adults, look and sound like, and how do they feel, today?

Have they changed in any ways? What might one learn by checking in with them five years later?

HEATHER

In high school, Heather described herself as "a good kid." She was the oldest of four siblings, whose father was a nonobservant Jew and mother "a pretty strict Catholic." Heather had done "the whole Catholic thing"—mass, CCD,[4] confirmation, and the rest—mostly because her mother wanted her to. "That was what you're supposed to do, what my mom did." Much of it she found boring, however, and she said CCD was painful. She never really understood much about Catholic beliefs or practices but also never made too much of an issue about it. She simply went along and got along until she could decide for herself.

Five years later, when Heather is interviewed again, it is the summer before her senior year of college, and she is working as a waitress and cashier and living with a group of college friends in a rented house in a resort town in New England. "Everyone said I had to do it for one summer. It's fun." Having graduated from high school three years earlier, Heather is completing a degree in education at a Catholic liberal arts college nearby. She has enjoyed college, but has also had a string of difficulties with friends and roommates who have had drug, alcohol, and emotional problems, including being suicidal—lots of drama. All of that, Heather reports, has made her grow up fast. Heather gets along better with both of her parents than she did in high school—even calling her social worker mother for advice on how to help her troubled friends—but is happy to be away from home. "When I graduated, I was itching to get away. I was done. And I have never really missed my parents." Six months before this interview, Heather and one of her best male friends decided that they cared for each other romantically, so they have been dating since then. Heather lost her virginity to a high school boyfriend, with whom she had sex three times, but she did not have sex again for four years, until recently in college with her new boyfriend. She says that she knew that "before me he had slept around quite a bit and so before anything happened with us I made him get tested for STDs [sexually transmitted diseases], and I got tested. And it was all clean, so that was definitely a big worry of mine." Fear of contracting a sexually transmitted disease, Heather says, keeps her from sleeping around as much as she otherwise might. Recently, Heather confessed to her mother over the phone to being sexually active. She felt terribly disappointing to her mother and "felt like a horrible person. But my mother recovered better from the conversation than I did." The hook-up culture at Heather's college seems by her description to be pretty freewheeling. For instance, Heather recalls, with some mirth:

> There have been times when I have been in someone's room or making out with a guy and they've stripped off all their clothes—I've literally never seen someone take off their clothes that fast in my entire

life!—and I was like, "I'm sorry, I think you have the wrong idea. This is not what I was thinking. See you later." Whoops! You're like, "Stop!" And then it's been awkward the next day in the cafeteria because the college is so small.

As far as drinking and smoking pot, Heather says, "I probably went a little crazy freshman year because I was like, oh, my God, I can do everything. Then I got sick a couple of times and toned it down." Now the legal age of 21, Heather and her friends go out to the bar about three times a week. "I still smoke pot now, a lot, if someone has it, I'll smoke. But we don't really know any [suppliers] here and it sketches me out buying it," she confesses, laughing.

Heather still identifies as a Catholic, although her practice of Catholicism has declined a lot since going to college. "I went to chapel the beginning of my freshman year," she recalls, "but then got lazy and stopped going. I didn't know if I even bought everything anymore. It just slowly petered out." One of her religion classes in college especially made her think that her faith "is a lot of crap, it makes no sense." When she voiced her thoughts, her teacher, she remembers, replied, "'Well, you've got to have faith,' and all that jazz." Heather reflects, "I guess I still do believe in God and I pray every now and then and have a little bit of spiritual stuff, but some I don't agree with." On the other hand, Heather took an "alternative religion class" in college, which she really liked. She especially thought that Buddhism, about which she wrote a term paper, was interesting. She also liked her yoga class. "Sometimes they chant, I don't really know what, for me it's just relaxing but I guess for others it's a spiritual thing." But in the end Heather identifies as Catholic. "I do believe in some of it and, I don't know, I'll probably start going to church again. All I would have to do is carve out one hour a week, but there's laziness for a lot of people." Do the sacraments and liturgical rituals mean anything to Heather? "To be honest," she states, "I don't really think about them unless I'm going to church. They're not that important to me. But when I go, I recognize them as important for people who are involved."

So what issues does Heather have with Catholic beliefs?

I guess the whole Trinity thing is a kind of weird concept which I have never really understood. God to me is almost like just someone for you, like a friend per se that you can talk to. I mean for all I know it could be me just talking, just my own thoughts, but for some reason I think it helps. [What about Jesus?] I guess I believe in Jesus, I guess I do, but I don't really think about it that much. To me he was born on Christmas, and that's about the extent of it. I celebrate holidays but don't really have any connection.

What about life after death? "I do believe in heaven and think people go there after they die and are watching out [over the living]. I don't know about the whole hell thing, to the extent of murderers and that kind, I don't think of them in heaven or anywhere else. I guess they just rot." For Heather, what's most valuable in Catholicism are the morals and values, "like treating people equally and that whole deal, being kind to others and loyal and supporting, giving to charity and that kind of stuff. I guess that's the good to get out of it, if anything." Heather does volunteer in a Big Sisters program, which she says she is passionate about. She also seems to have spent a lot of her lifetime trying to help friends around her in trouble. Both of those one might think flow directly from her Catholic upbringing. Still, Heather observes: "I don't think my faith has much of an influence on my life. Most of the kids I hang around with are, like, more not that serious." Then she turns around and says that she went with 15 friends to a recent Ash Wednesday service to receive the imposition of ashes. And when asked about Mary and the saints, she replies, "I guess I would be nothing without them." She also muses that she has a hard time separating what her parents taught her morally from what the church teaches. So the story seems complicated.

How, then, does Catholicism relate to other religions? First of all, Heather explains, "I think now I'd consider myself more spiritual than religious, because I'm not really practicing any religion. Spiritual is just believing in a higher being, but not following a book or organization." Having made that point, Heather continues:

> There is truth in religions. More than one can be right. I feel like it's just whatever suits you. I don't see why there can't be more than one. Catholic say there is only one but I don't see what the big deal is. Institutional religion, I don't really mind it. It's kind of, whatever floats your boat. I mean, who am I to say that what someone is doing is weird or wrong?

Heather wants to get married someday, maybe in her late twenties or early thirties, in order to have "someone you can always rely on and be there and grow up and old with and share, just compatibility." Her boyfriend actually recently asked her to live with him after graduation next spring, but she declined. "I don't know, I feel like, I'm 21. I don't want to be playing house. I still want to have my own space, do my own thing, go where I want to go, that kind of stuff." In fact, Heather recently developed an interest in South Asia and is thinking about joining the Peace Corps or Americorps after college. "I want to go places and do things. I don't think I've done everything I want to do yet, and, not that a husband would hold me back, but it's easier to do things without having to talk to someone else about it." After she "develops a sense of self," she eventually wants to have three children. As for a future lifestyle, "I definitely want to be comfortable. I mean I want to have a house and a car and that stuff—my parents actually just bought a vacation condo, which I think is a nice addition. So I definitely want to be comfortable." As for her larger life goals, Heather says, "I definitely want to have accomplished being happy with myself and having a good knowledge of who I am and what I did and not have any regrets—that's the biggest thing, or if I have regrets, at least learned something from the situation." And what, finally, about Heather's likely religious faith and practice in the future? "I think I'll probably try," she imagines, "if I have kids, to probably bring them to Catholic Church, do what my mom did, and if they want to do that, fine. I think you should give them that, kind of rear them in some religious direction. CCD, baptism, yes, probably do that."

JOHN

(This section contains some profane language and content that could be disturbing.)

I first interviewed John when he was 18 years old. As his sisters were too old for him to grow up with, he was functionally an only child—of divorced parents. He was finishing public high school in an affluent suburb of Hartford, Connecticut. John was a bit heavyset, with blond hair and slightly bulging eyes. He was very much looking forward to heading off to college in a neighboring state. He identified strongly with the Catholic faith of his upbringing, thought well of God, spoke positively about his parish clergy, and defended the church over a recently exposed priest sexual abuse scandal affecting his own diocese and parish. At the same time, John's Catholic faith seemed to influence his own life very little. He badly disrespected his parents, cheated in school, took drugs, drank heavily, was in trouble with the law, and was intent on having sex with as many girls as possible. John had no trouble picking and choosing from Catholicism what he did and did not want to pay attention to. The Catholic Church was good, John said. But discussing his own faith clearly made John very uneasy. At times during the interview I worried that John might be edging toward some kind of emotional breakdown. At the time of a second interview two years later, John was on a very similar track. Other than being suspended for a semester for smoking pot and throwing something at a campus security officer, John said college was going well. John liked his studies and was having fun. He was more heavily into drinking and doing drugs—some were recreational drugs I had never even heard of—and was scoring with women. One of his goals in college, he said, was "to nail as many bitches as possible." He said, in fact, that he was going to use his interview incentive money to buy some cocaine to use to try to get into bed a particular graduate student he'd had his eye on.

By 2008, John, at 23, has grown taller and beefier but is very much the same person, only further along in life. Much of John's life, his interview reveals, revolves around money and sex. John has just graduated from college, with degrees in business and history, and has recently moved to Las Vegas to try to become a semiprofessional gambler and to be within driving distance of California skiing. John aspires to be a high school social studies teacher, but he does not yet have the money to pay the application fee for Las Vegas teaching jobs, so since moving to town he has been substitute teaching on a part-time basis. He is earning enough money to scrape by for the moment. Luckily he has no student loans to pay, as his parents paid for all of his college expenses. John has already received an expensive speeding ticket in Vegas and has had to ask his parents to pay the fine. He has no money to pay for dates, so he is putting women on hold for a month or two. Despite being financially strapped at the moment, however, John says he is having the time of his life doing what unattached young men in America should be doing: going West, living freely, trying his hand at betting, hoping to strike it rich.

While in college, John lived near his grandmother, to whom he was quite close emotionally, and took her to mass every week. She recently died, however, and he moved away, so John has little reason to attend church now. He describes himself as a "C&E Catholic" these days—attending church only on Christmas and Easter. John was never involved in a church youth group, but he did attend CCD as a teen. He knows nothing about the religious faith of his friends, except that some are Jewish. John never talks about religious matters with his mother, who is an irregularly practicing Catholic. Still, he says, "I was born Catholic, [will] stay Catholic. I'm not like an antireligious person," he continues; "I'm just not at a very religious point, you know? But I believe in my religion, I believe it. My life just doesn't center around my religion." John says the sacraments, Mary, the saints, priests, nuns, the pope, all of that is important. His studies of history have also convinced him that Christianity was a major historical force in the "humanization" of the West, in moving civilization away from brutal barbarianism and toward societies where people try to be good and help others. He thinks that is significant. To the questions whether he ever prays, reads the Bible, or believes in life after death, however, John simply answers, "Next question." When pressed on the afterlife, he says, "It's not a real [issue now], maybe when I'm older." So, who then is God to John? "I don't know. It's a good question. Not sure if I'm prepared to answer that, but I believe in Jesus. He was sent down by God." John says he never rebelled against his religion, has stayed the same about faith since he was 13 years old, has no religious doubts, and finds that maintaining his beliefs is easy. "Nothing could stop me, like I told you, I'm not questioning or anything like that." John has never had a supernatural experience, but he says, "I kinda wish I would, that would be cool." When asked if he has interests in any other religions, he replies, "No, I'm not going to switch. You don't do that to your parents, it's not a cool thing to do. You have to go with what your mother is. I'd be pissed off if my kids switched, and that's coming from someone who's not extremely religious." So by what means might John evaluate the truth of different religious claims? "I don't really evaluate it. I have my beliefs, and they're there. And that's about it."

In this interview, John reveals more than he previously has about his troubled relationship with his father, who, he says, has a bad temper and an abusive tongue. He remembers that when his parents divorced, his dad "lost his temper, smashed up the house, stuff like that." John's sisters will not even speak to his dad now, because of "stuff that happened when they were growing up that he's never really taken responsibility for. It's not fun, but." John's dad, who is not religious, now lives in France with a second wife. He came to visit John the previous month, partly because he loves to gamble. John recounts that one night when it was very crowded, the casino without giving them a choice, seated father and son at the same poker table, effectively forcing them to gamble against each other. That angered his dad, and he yelled at John repeatedly during the drive home, calling him a "pig" and a "cunt." So how close or not, then, does John feel to his dad?

> Close enough. We get along and all that. But he doesn't control what he says. When he gets upset he says some really, really bad stuff—like just cursing me out, calling me the C-word and that type of stuff. So that keeps me from feeling a lot closer than I normally would. I mean, it's one thing to be yelled at, it's another thing to be called that by your father.

Later in the interview, when discussing what makes him sad or depressed, John returns to the matter, saying, "Fights with my father, things he said to me, cause I haven't really done anything to provoke it. That's really upset me." John says he feels somewhat closer to his mother than his dad. "We talk a lot. But she usually yells at me, cause I'm not that responsible, can't pay the bills, don't have money, stuff like that." He says he feels bad about letting his mother down by not being responsible.

John does not even pretend to have a basic moral system. "I don't really think about it that much," he says, "I'm not really high on morality or any of that." Asked to clarify, he explains, "Unless you do something really horrible, you know, kill someone, it doesn't really matter, right or wrong. Everything is: do whatever you want. I don't really have moral rules, don't put too much value on right and wrong, it depends on the situation." So, then, would he mind if his roommate was, for example, a car thief? "As long as he doesn't steal my car. Would I encourage it? No. But what people do really doesn't bother me. I don't really care what other people do with their lives as long as they're not stealing from me." Another hypothetical: What if his roommate's girlfriend broke up with him, would it be okay to burn her house down or throw a brick through her windshield for revenge? "Burning down the house is bad enough that it falls into the category of really wrong. But the brick?— depends on how bad it was. Like, if she banged 10 other guys behind his back over five years, then maybe the brick through the windshield would be justified." So would John say that morals are relative? "Everything can be interpreted in different ways." But he adds that terrorists killing people is always wrong. How then does John go about making those kind of moral discriminations? "Everyone's the same," he replies, "I'm just another person." So does John look up to or down on any particular kinds of people? "You know what? Not really." Okay, so what does John think about volunteering for good causes? "Charity is all given to people who aren't gonna do anything with it," he answers, "like giving aid to Africa, all those billions, you're never gonna see a penny back. It's like flushing money down the toilet. It's stupid." How does he feel about America? "I like America. I think it's cool. Good country, I like the West Coast." About politics, John says, "I feel in tune, but not that much. It's not really my thing." John says he's a liberal in general but tends to vote Republican. He cannot stand Hillary Clinton. He'd like to see marijuana legalized and the price of gas lowered. On other policy matters, he does not have opinions. As for a purpose in life, John remarks, "I don't feel lost, but I like the fact that I don't really have any purpose." Any thoughts about materialism and consumerism? "A lot of people's pleasures in life derive from consumerism. Consumerism is good for the economy. No limits in our capitalist society, if you can afford it."

The only real problem John sees with his life at present is that he doesn't have any money. "Apart from wishing I had more money, everything's fine. Being 21, I can do whatever now." When asked what he thinks about the charitable giving of money, he only grunts, "What money?" He does recount, however, that when he went to church with his grandmother he would put a one- or five-dollar bill into the offering plate. John's lack of money has prevented him from smoking pot—which he normally likes to do every day—or doing harder drugs, because he simply cannot afford them. He also has not been drinking of late, he says, "because I don't have any friends here to go out with." Romances are also "on hold, since I don't have a spare cent to do anything. But if I win something big, then I might try to get more friendlier with the neighbors, know what I mean?"

John talks a lot about girls and sex. He says he's had sex with "20 to 30" women, of which he's had relationships with "maybe half a dozen." Of those, three were more serious girlfriends, with whom he had sex "a couple times a day." One was a girl he met in France while visiting his father. One was a girl he hooked up with a lot throughout college and became more serious with during senior year. That ended when she graduated. The third was a 19-year-old friend of a next-door neighbor "party girl" who came over every day to drink. The rest of his sex partners he met during "drunk nights at college, I'd go to a party, meet a girl, that's it. Or maybe not at college, when you're home, call some girl you know from high school." Hooking up was no big deal in college. "It was, you go out, party, try to bring something back. That's college. You start making out, then hopefully you get more, sometimes you do, sometimes not." So no need to be in a relationship? "Nah, you're gonna do it eventually, you know." How many girls has John hooked up with? "Under 50." But, he notes about his new life, "I left my easy, call-whenever-booty-calls back East." No matter. John says he is tired of "immature" girls now anyway and wants "to go online and try to find an older, thirties, 40-year-old woman. I'm gonna tell them I'm 30. I don't know, I just want an older one, a little more mature, have better conversations. Yeah, I like older women." John also does not want a steady girlfriend now, which, he says, involves "a lot of bullshit. I see a lot of my friends and their girlfriends ruin their lives, and that's not gonna happen to me." What does he mean? "I'm someone who marches to the beat of my own drum. I'm not going to waste a significant portion of my life doing what some girl wants me to do. I have never in my life found true love but hopefully when that day comes things will be different." Meanwhile, John elaborates,

Just going out and getting shitty with your friends, that's what I like. And girlfriends don't enjoy that. I like hanging out with my boys and betting on sports we watch and screaming at the TV when they're losing, "Oh, you fucking asshole!" You know? Girls don't really like that [laughs]. They don't really like hanging out, sitting on a couch next to a guy who's screaming at the TV when the quarterback fumbles the snap.

Okay, so does John have any thoughts about sexual morality or rules for being smart about sex? Only this: "If you're a guy, get as much as you can. If you're a girl, don't be a slut—no one likes a chick who's been ran through. Don't screw men into triple digits. There's a different standard for men and women. That's the way the world is, and that's about it." So what about the different standards? "There is a double standard. Go into a crowded bar and most of the guys there are trying to get some. But you don't want your girlfriend to suck five cocks the night before you met her." So are there any useful rules at all? "Nah, there's no rules. It's all bullshit." Still, John says he thinks people should use condoms—"I don't advocate having kids if you can't take care of them"—and views homosexuality as "unnatural." But doesn't the Catholic Church teach anything about sex? "Eh, not really. That's part of it I don't pay much attention to." John mentions something about "gentlemen's clubs" (strip clubs), but states he has never been to one. He has, however, visited prostitutes. "I don't have anything against prostitution. What's wrong with it?" In high school, he tells, he and two friends drove to the next state and visited an Asian massage parlor. "You know, it's a man's world and you're put here. It's the oldest profession, there's no reason not to, if you can afford it. When it's only 30 bucks, that's a lot less money that it would cost to take a girl out to dinner and a movie these days." While visiting his father in France, John and some cousins also made a trip to Amsterdam to visit prostitutes. "It's like 50 bucks. You sit in the café, smoke weed, walk down the street, and say 'All right, I'll take this one, and you take that one.' Like you could pick out a good one that's better looking than the chicks they have in shows in Vegas, for maybe like a quarter of the price." More recently, John and some friends took a trip to Mexico for the same reason.

> It's cool, just you and your boys going across the border. You know, chillin', smokin' weed, drinkin' beers, go fuck hookers, and come back. Well, I didn't have sex with 'em. I just got a blow job. I picked up one for 40. My friends picked out the first ones for 20, you know, a good day, 80 bucks. Wasn't bad. You know, they're just trying to earn a buck the hard way. I have absolutely nothing against prostitution.

John says that he is concerned about sexually transmitted diseases, which is why he always uses a condom. "I mean, I sleep good at night knowing that I haven't been stickin' it raw into nasty bitches."

John definitely wants to get married someday, a little before he turns 30 years old. Why? "American dream, life, kids, house. All that shit, I like that." But first he wants to do "all the shit I'm doing now, in Vegas. You do all that shit before you get married. Maybe move back to Europe for a while."

John says he wants to have "as many kids as I can afford." Is it going to be easy, after all of his previous women, for John to be monogamous? "Yeah, I think so. It's like, you kinda gotta balance everything out, and you can't be running off on your wife with your yoga instructor." But, he adds,

> Some people need more. If your wife gets fat, and she doesn't let you have sex, and you've got money to spare, nothing wrong with ordering a high-class hooker. What's wrong is when you throw it in your wife's face and let her know you have a girl on the side. It's probably better to keep it professional if you need sex with someone other than your wife.

So is that something John can imagine himself doing? "No, hopefully my wife fits the bill and takes—you know, hopefully I don't want that. We'll see." Other than getting married, John wants to go skiing, earn a master's, get certified, become a high school teacher—"I hope to instill into kids that you have to approach things with more of a winner's mentality, get kids more on track"—enjoy his job, coach some school sports teams, buy a big fishing boat, and retire after 30 years of teaching. "Unless," that is, "I win a million here in Vegas." In short, what he wants of life is "I told you, the American Dream, that shit." Finally, what will John be like religiously when he is 30 years old? "Dragging my kids to church, sending them to CCD."

ALANO

At Alano's first interview with NSYR in 2003, he was 16 years old, a pretty good kid who tried in school, appreciated his parents, and loved his girlfriend. Religiously, Alano was a nominal Catholic—his family did not really practice religion. Alano himself did not attend mass but he generally thought religion was a good thing for many people. Alano had a girlfriend, with whom he was having sex, even though he thought ideally it is better to wait for that until marriage. At the time of our first interview, Alano thought he would probably become more religious as he grew older, expecting that he would start attending church more.

By the summer of 2008, Alano was 21, married to his former girlfriend, had a daughter, Junia, and lived in a small home that he built in the backyard of his parents' house. He wears jeans and a tee shirt, stands medium height, is a bit chunky, and sports short hair and a little goatee on his chin. Alano's entire life turns out to revolve around working and taking care of his family. "Just stay above water. Other people my age in college are maybe partying and stuff, but I skipped that stage." Besides work and his family, Alano's only other big activity is playing in an adult baseball league on Sunday mornings. Alano attended two years of college but dropped out because of academic and financial problems. His wife, however, is just about to graduate from a local state university. Alano works on the docks for the shipping industry. He likes his job well enough but wants to return to college someday to become a history teacher. Alano describes himself as a hard worker, responsible, honest, and shy.

Religiously, Alano says he is, "the same as my parents, Catholic—my whole family is basically Catholic. It's a title you have because of your family, but you don't. I grew up Catholic. That's all I have ever known. But not really enough I guess to practice. I really don't participate. My parents don't either." Alano does not attend mass, pray, or read the Bible. So why isn't Alano more involved in his faith? "I'd like it to mean more, but just for one reason or another I don't take the time to get involved. I don't really think about it at all. I have so much other stuff going on." What about his wife and Junia? "If my wife made more of an issue about it, or did it for my daughter, I think we would make more of an effort. Probably should more for Junia. Just hasn't happened, haven't done it." So what about religion and Junia? "At least to expose her to it so if that's something she wants to participate in, giving her an opportunity to like it or participate." All of Alano's friends play on his baseball team, so he guesses that they do not go to church either, although he really doesn't know. More generally, however, Alano admits that religion can be good for people, "For making the right choices, having something to look forward to after you die. For other people it's good if they have a problem with drugs or alcohol. It's a place to help through things." Alano and his wife married at City Hall, not the church.

Alano says that he knows moral right and wrong from "what I feel." He says "It's first instinct. It comes pretty quickly, more or less how I was brought up, parents and grandparents." Of people who disagree with him, for example about the moral responsibility to care for other people, he says, "That's their choice. They don't have to if they don't want to. It's just something I would do." Alano says he was never a big partier and never followed "the crowd." He does what he thinks is right. These days he enjoys a few beers once a month or so. Most everything Alano discusses, however, has to do with caring for his own family. "I have been able to keep a family together, take care of them to the best of my ability, maintain a good relationship with my parents, hopefully keep things going from there. My purpose now is to take care of my family, teach my daughter to be open-minded, let her have a good up-bringing, raise her good. That's it." Alano thinks he is a political liberal. He is concerned that America is losing the separation of church and state. "I thought that's what the country was founded on," he remarks. Alano is concerned that President Bush is a "dictator" who led the country into a wrong war, even that America is losing its democracy. When he votes, it is in favor of gay rights, abortion rights, and similar issues. "It doesn't bother me. Everyone is different." Sex before marriage is also fine for Alano, as long as a couple has "an emotional relationship first," he says. Alano's wife, in fact, was pregnant before they married. Alano does not volunteer for any causes or organizations, nor does he give money charitably, which he thinks is a job "for the more fortunate."

As to the future, Alano would like to have a son. Beyond that, he hopes to be able to provide for his family financially, to have all his bills paid, and maybe someday move into a bigger house. What he most wants to get out of life, he says, is "staying married, just taking care of my family." And what does Alano think he will be like religiously when he is 30 years old? "Honestly, I would like to be more religious, but I don't know if I will be. Probably I'll be about the same."

CONCLUSION

What does this chapter reveal about religious change over time? Of all of the case studies presented in *Soul Searching* and reinterviewed five years later, Joy is the only one whose religious or spiritual life changed significantly during the half decade marking the transition from the teenage years to emerging adulthood. Alyssa's life also changed in the years between interviews, but by age 21 she had come back spiritually to the place she was at age 15—only, in her view, older and wiser and more committed and consistent. The others, we have shown, reflect in their stories much more continuity than change. This observation is largely consistent with what the NSYR and other studies have learned more generally about religious change and stability. The default of most people's lives is to continue being what they have been in the past. This is partly what gives social life the stability it normally exhibits. Significant personal transformation usually requires, first, some kind of new life challenge or problem that exerts pressures on a person to change, and second, the exposure of the person to new potential solutions that he or she can realistically apply to his or her life.[5] In Joy's case, this meeting of problem and solution involved at least three key factors. The first was the challenge of having a baby as a teenager with unhelpful parents. The second was confronting the problems of failed relationships with devious men specifically and of a rudderless, intoxicated life more generally. The third was stumbling on the solution—in the Spirit-charged message of a traveling youth evangelist preaching in a local gymnasium—of the possibility of a spiritually focused, disciplined, and meaningful life for herself, her daughter, and her fiancé. This solution enabled Joy finally to believe that she was the object of divine love and helped to forge stronger bonds between Joy and her parents that were not based on their living together. Joy's insecurity, pain, and depression—which for years she tried to medicate with alcohol and drugs, and a few times to eliminate through suicide—had not been eradicated. But they at least seemed to have been somewhat alleviated by her new faith and outlook on life. Time will tell what is in store over the long run. Sociologically speaking, much of the sustainability of Joy's new life appeared to depend on the faithfulness and devotion of her new husband, Matt. Getting insurance or enough money to be able to afford antidepressant medication, it would seem, would help a great deal as well. But whatever her future holds, Joy's previous life was clearly unsustainable, and her recent religious conversion provided a means to make a new start at a better life. Alyssa's life seems to have followed a similar story, trajectory, and outcome.

The forces that work to stabilize and transform people's lives are to some degree more varied and complicated than what we have presented in this chapter. But some of the basic points of observation remain valid. Most people's lives, including their basic religious lives, even during the teenage and emerging adult years—not merely switching congregations but fundamental religious orientations—reflect a great deal of continuity. Normally, the best predictor of where people are going is where they have come from. Without such continuity, of course, life would be chaos. But in some cases, people's lives really do change. Particular confluences of challenges, problems, alternatives, opportunities, and solutions can give rise to new identities, new commitments, new life strategies, new beliefs, new relationships, and new practices. Sociologically speaking, that is most often how religious and spiritual change happens. Nothing, of course, guarantees that personal transformations during emerging adulthood will be religious in nature. There are many potential alternative life strategies and solutions to people's difficulties. Some people deal with problems by joining the military. Some get divorced. Others end up in prison. Some persist in drinking heavily and taking drugs. Others simply change friends and moderate their behaviors. There are clearly many and complicated possible paths across life. At a general level, however, the important analytical sociological questions concern the structures that maintain religious stability in some people's lives and the combinations of difficulties and resolutions that generate religious or other changes in other people's lives. About those sociologists have much more to learn. But one thing is certain sociologically: operating at the heart of both personal and religious stability and change are the crucial matter of *significant personal relationships*—both those that affirm and bind and those that break down and set loose. Rarely do people's thinking and feeling and behaving change dramatically (or stay the same) without significant social relationships exerting pressures to do so and facilitating these outcomes. Significant personal relationships may not be the heart of religious life itself, but they certainly provide the bones and other muscles within which the heart of religion beats.

Taking a different perspective on these matters, thinking about the cases presented in this chapter in terms of the religious typology developed in chapter 6, this chapter has presented some stable types and some in transition. Joy spent her recent years moving away from being Religiously Disconnected to being a Selective Adherent and is now in the process of shifting toward being a Committed Traditionalist. Kristin, more simply, was raised a Committed Traditionalist and clearly remains one today. Raymond was a Spiritually Open type when first interviewed in 2003 but by 2008 had essentially become Religiously Indifferent. Alyssa shifted in the five years covered in this study from being (it emerged in retrospect) a guilty Selective Adherent to being a weaker Selective Adherent bordering on Religiously Indifferent and then more recently to being a conservative Committed Traditionalist. Heather, John, and Alano, by comparison, are all best categorized as Religiously Indifferent. Again, the default is stability and continuity. As a generalization, only in those cases when people who are facing unworkable problems and motivating challenges meet up with plausible alternatives and attractive opportunities and solutions does significant change, including religious change, happen in people's lives. Otherwise, what has been for and about people in the past is most likely what will be for and about them in the future—even among emerging adults. That is the way of personal and social life generally, and it is borne out by the cases tracked over time and reviewed in this chapter.

Finally, it is necessary to recall that Joy, Kristin, Raymond, Alyssa, Heather, John, and Alano are not typical or representative of all emerging adults in the United States. They are particular cases followed up from a previous book, in which they were presented for the purpose of making specific points in the context of that analysis. Their stories convey a wide range of trajectories and experiences, illustrating how and why certain particular lives both reflect continuity and change over time. One can learn a lot from that for this inquiry, but one must also remember that the majority of emerging adults' lives are usually less dramatic and intense than the lives of most of the seven presented in this chapter—particularly those of Joy, Raymond, Alyssa, and John. As we return, in the following two chapters, to the nationally representative survey data, we will once again be describing the big picture: the experience of more typical emerging adults in the United States.

8

Religious Trajectories from
the Teenage Years
With Kyle Longest

WHAT FACTORS IN ADOLESCENCE influence religious commitments and practices during emerging adulthood? What differences in the lives of teenagers are associated with stronger and weaker religious faith and practice among American 18- to 23-year-olds? Because the NSYR collected data on the same sample of youth over time, we are able to answer those questions here. One unique strength of our longitudinal analysis is not having to depend on (sometimes unreliable) retrospective memories of older respondents surveyed at one point in time about their lives in prior years—we asked our questions of the same people at different times in their developing lives. Another strength of our analysis is the large number of religion variables that were NSYR respondents were asked about in the first wave survey when they were teenagers. With these data, multiple analytic strategies can be used to identify the teenage-era variables that are most strongly associated with religious outcomes measured in the third wave survey during emerging adulthood.

This is the most statistically rich and challenging chapter in this book. But we have written it so that readers with differing levels of statistical aptitude should be able, with a bit of effort, to grasp its main findings and conclusions. One of our central aims here, then, is to identify factors related to the teenage years that correlate statistically with religious differences during the emerging adult years and that we have good theoretical reasons to believe act as causal influences of those differences. Another central goal is to theorize the causal social mechanisms that explain the associations between the identified teenage factors and the emerging adult religion outcomes. We also

211

examine combinations of factors that represent different paths to the same highly religious emerging adult outcome, as well as the main divergent paths that persons take through their religious and spiritual lives from the teenage to the emerging adult years. Finally, we examine the timing of first commitments to God, the question whether higher education corrodes religion, and the possibility that many emerging adults are subjectively but not objectively highly religious. One of the main stories that will unfold in the pages that follow is that the transition from the teenage to the emerging adult years reflects a great deal of religious continuity and stability, but also a significant amount of religious change, most of which works in the direction of religious decline. Many emerging adults continue religiously much as they were as teenagers. Many others become either some or a lot less religious. And a small group becomes more religious.

IDENTIFYING INFLUENTIAL FACTORS

Factors related to teenage religious experience that associate statistically with highly religious lives during emerging adulthood were identified using the following procedure.

Categorizing Religious Strength

The initial task was to determine a good measure of higher and lower religious commitment and practice during emerging adulthood. After exploring a variety of alternative approaches, one excellent measure was chosen that combined information about respondents' frequency of religious service attendance, professed importance of faith in everyday life, and frequency of personal prayer.[1] This measure accounts for both objective public practice of religion (attendance) and more subjective experiential dimensions of religion (importance of faith and personal prayer). All of these are tried and tested measures, in the sociology of religion, of the strength of religious faith and practice. The measure that was chosen also has strong face validity, that is, it uses indicators that most Americans think of as reflecting high levels of religiousness. This measure also enjoys a high internal consistency of measures when treated additively.[2]

Change over Time

The four different levels of religiousness that our categorization produces for both Wave 1 (teenagers) and Wave 3 (emerging adults) respondents are shown in table 8.1. The first row shows that the Lowest, Moderate, and Highest categories share similar numbers of emerging adults, at roughly 22 percent, while the Minimal religious category, which is between the Lowest and Moderate categories, contains the largest percentage of emerging adults, at 32 percent. The second row of table 8.1 shows the same distribution for the respondents when they were surveyed as teenagers in Wave 1. When compared to the first row, we see that the number of respondents in the Highest religious group declined from 34 to 22 percent—a loss of 12 percentage points, which equals

35 percent of the original total (12/34). The Moderate religious group declined between waves from 30 to 23 percent—a loss of 7 percentage points, which represents 23 percent of the original total (7/30). Meanwhile, the Minimal religious group grew 7 percent over these five years. And the Lowest religious group doubled in size, gaining 11 percentage points to grow from 11 percent to 22 percent of the total. This confirms a major finding of chapter 4: the transition from the teenage to the emerging adult years involves in general an impressive amount of stability but also, when it comes to change, a significant decline in religious commitment and practice.

But table 8.1 shows more. The numbers we discussed in the first two rows concern aggregate change, that is, the final distribution at Wave 3 after everyone who moves anywhere, whether up or down, does their moving. But some do become more religious and others less religious between waves. So movement happens in both directions to varying degrees. According to the third and fourth rows in table 8.1, 17–27 percent shifted into higher religious categories between waves; and 34–55 percent moved to lower religious categories. Those who began at one end or the other in Wave 1 had more "room" to move in that direction, so greater percents of them did move elsewhere. Of all the groups, the vast majority of the moderately religious teenagers (Wave 1) exited that category by Wave 3, with 55 percent of them becoming less religious

Table 8.1. Descriptive Statistics Comparing Religious Levels and Change between Survey Waves 1 and 3 (Percents) (N = 2,432) (Weighted)

| | Levels of religiousness | | | |
	Lowest	Minimal	Moderate	Highest
Wave 3— emerging adults	22	32	23	22
Wave 1— teenagers	11	25	30	34
% of wave 1 moving to *more* religious group	27	22	17	N/A
% of wave 1 moving to *less* religious group	N/A	34	55	54
% of wave 1 staying in same type	73	44	29	46
% of wave 1 moving *two or more* categories[a]	8	7	14	25

Source: National Surveys of Youth and Religion, 2002–2003, 2007–2008.
[a]Indicates percentage of lowest that become moderate or highest, minimal that become highest, moderate that become lowest, and highest that become minimal or lowest.

and 17 percent becoming more religious. More than one-half (54 percent) of the Wave 1 Highest religious group became less religious by Wave 3. But, the second to last row shows, fully 73 percent of the Lowest religion group remained in the same category. The final row in table 8.1 shows the percent from each original group that moved the "farthest," that is, two or more categories away. The teenage group that underwent the greatest amount of extreme change was the Highest religion category—one in four high religion teenagers moved to either the Minimal or Lowest religion categories by emerging adulthood. All of the other three groups experienced much lower levels of dramatic religious change, according to this measurement method. Overall, then, we see more than a little flux in levels of religiousness across these five years, and, again, the direction of overall greatest religious change during these five years is downward. Moderately religious teenagers are the most likely to shift to a different level, with well more than half becoming less religious and one in five becoming more religious.

Correlated Factors

The second task was to identify factors from the first survey, conducted when respondents were ages 13 to 17, that correlate with differences in religion during the emerging adult years. Before examining the factors that are related to overall emerging adult religiousness, the relationship between these teenage-era factors and the three component measures—attendance, importance of faith, and prayer—was first investigated. Table 8.2 lists on the left the variables that were investigated, the top of which involve correlations for various single religion measures, and the bottom of which concern different major religious traditions in the United States. Presented in the columns of table 8.2 are the simple correlations (zero-order Pearson's r's) for each variable for the three third wave variables that were used to categorize different levels of emerging adult religion (attendance, importance of faith, and prayer). The closer the correlation is to 1.0, the more highly correlated the two variables are (1.0 is perfectly correlated); and the closer the correlation is to 0, the less correlated they are (0 is absolutely uncorrelated). The variables are listed from generally strongest to weakest in statistical correlation. That means that the higher a variable is on the list, the more strongly it is associated in a simple correlation[3] with the three outcome variables listed at the top. Finally, the interpretation of the strength of correlations generally assigned by sociologists is listed in the far right column.

This simple examination of associations shows that, among first wave (labeled w1) variables, having had highly religious parents, a high importance of faith, frequent personal prayer, a larger number of personal religious experiences, frequent scripture reading, and frequent religious service attendance during the teenage years are most strongly associated with more religious service attendance, greater importance of faith, and more frequent prayer during emerging adulthood. By contrast, having doubts about religious beliefs, other teenagers looking down on one for one's religion, attending a religious high school, having engaged in oral sex, feeling close to their parents, and doing

Table 8.2. Zero-Order Pearson's r Correlations for Three Key Wave 3 Religion
Outcome Variables and Multiple Wave 1 Variables (N = 2,199) [Weighted]

	Religious Service Attendance w3	Importance of Faith w3	Frequency of Praying Alone w3	*Strength of Correlation*
Religious service attendance w3	1.00			
Importance of faith w3	.62	1.00		strong
Frequency of praying alone w3	.57	.69	1.00	strong
Highly religious parents w1	.44	.44	.36	moderately strong
Importance of faith w1	.43	.55	.46	moderately strong
Frequency of praying alone w1	.40	.48	.56	moderately strong
Personal religious experiences w1	.41	.46	.44	moderately strong
Frequency reading scripture w1	.43	.41	.41	moderately strong
Religious service attendance w1	.46	.40	.33	moderately strong
Religious congregation a good place to discuss serious issues w1	.43	.40	.33	moderately strong
Expects to attend similar church when 25 w1	.43	.39	.32	moderately strong
Satisfaction with congregation w1	.41	.39	.31	moderately strong
Frequency of youth group participation w1	.39	.32	.29	moderately strong
Attends Sunday school w1	.39	.33	.29	moderately strong
Satisfaction with youth group w1	.37	.32	.28	moderately strong
Supportive religious adults w1	.34	.35	.31	moderately strong
Believes in divine miracles w1	.33	.36	.37	moderately strong
Number of religious friends w1	.33	.35	.31	moderately strong
Employs religious criteria first in moral decision making w1	.31	.31	.33	moderately strong
Believes in abstaining from sex before marriage w1	.30	.33	.28	moderately strong
Frequently teased about religion w1	.29	.29	.27	moderately strong
Number of extra religious activities w1	.22	.19	.19	weak

Table 8.2. (Continued)

	Religious Service Attendance w3	Importance of Faith w3	Frequency of Praying Alone w3	*Strength of Correlation*
Number of missions trips w1	.17	.15	.13	weak
Close to parents w1	.16	.13	.13	weak
Has engaged in oral sex w1	−.16	−.12	−.14	weak
Attends a religious high school w1	.09	.04[n.s.]	.04[n.s.]	weak
Believes other teens look down on religion w1	.05[n.s.]	.07[n.s.]	.04[n.s.]	weak
Has doubts about religious beliefs w1	.03[n.s.]	.04[n.s.]	.05[n.s.]	weak
Religious Tradition[1]				
Evangelical Protestant w1	.19	.22	.22	weak
Mainline Protestant w1	−.07	−.11	−.07	very weak
Black Protestant w1	.11	.18	.14	weak
Catholic w1	−.09	−.09	−.12	very weak
Jewish w1	−.10	−.09	−.11	very weak
Mormon w1	.16	.09	.10	very weak
Other religion w1	.00[n.s.]	.01[n.s.]	−.02[n.s.]	n.s.
Not religious w1	−.24	−.24	−.20	weak

Source: National Surveys of Youth and Religion, 2002–2003, 2007–2008.
Note: All correlations are significant at p<.01 level, except when labeled [n.s.]. [1]Each religious tradition compared to all of the others combined. Since Pearson's r undervalues correlations for dummy variables, especially if they are skewed, we also ran a polychoric correlation matrix for comparison, the results of which did not substantively alter the findings presented here.

more missions trips are the most weakly correlated factors with the three outcomes. The set of variables in the middle are of intermediate strength. Jumping down to the religious tradition variables, we see that all of them (compared in each case to all of the other traditions combined) are weakly correlated. Being a nonreligious teenager is the strongest (negative) association of this group with higher levels of emerging adult religion—but even those correlations (−.24, −.24, −.20) are weak. It is shown here, then, that some first wave religious factors seem to correlate strongly with emerging adults' religious outcomes, others only moderately strongly, and others weakly or not at all. We use these findings in the analyses that follow.

Identifying Independent Effects

Real human life is more complicated than simple sets of single correlations can represent. Many of these factors, for example, cluster together and interact in people's lives. Some of them are often the causes of others of them, well before the outcome variables even come into play. And the actual stronger effects of some of these may be suppressed by not having accounted for the effects of others. So, one might ask, which of them is more basic or primary than others? Which of the effects of these variables may be driven or produced by the more fundamental influence of other variables? Which remain strongly correlated with the outcomes, even when the possible complicating or overlapping influences of the other variables are removed or "controlled for?" We can partially answer these questions by employing multiple regression techniques that isolate the statistical association of each variable in any statistical model while removing the possible overlapping or suppressing influences of all of the other variables in the same model. In this way, the independent association of each variable is isolated, helping us to identify the independent effects of each, "net of" the possible influences of the others. The statistical output from these procedures is extensive and complex, so we will not present it here in myriad tables.[4] For present purposes, we pull together and summarize the results of these regression analyses in table 8.3.

There, one can see that—when statistical techniques are used to isolate the independent effects of each variable under consideration, in order to minimize possible spuriousness and identify possible suppression effects—five factors measured during the teenage years are consistently very important in associating with emerging adult religion. Perhaps not surprisingly, they are the same as the most strongly correlated variables in table 8.2: frequent personal prayer, highly religious parents during the teenage years, high importance of religious faith in daily life, and frequent doubts and religious experiences. (The actual importance of religious doubts was suppressed in zero-order correlations shown in table 8.2 but, in multivariate analyses, proves to be a significant factor, as does engaging in oral sex.) After them follow factors consistently associated with the outcome in question but of more moderate strength or importance: teenagers believing in miracles, frequently reading scripture, enjoying many supportive, nonparental adults in their religious congregation, engaging in oral sex, and being made fun of for religious faith. Following that are nine variables of moderate strength or importance that are only statistically significant in some but not all analytical models. Finally, three examined variables are shown not to be independently associated with higher religious commitment and practice during emerging adulthood. Thus it is shown that it is possible to use statistical techniques to identify which among many possible life factors from the teenage years are most strongly associated with a more robust religious life during emerging adulthood. The consistently most important of these during the teenage years are frequent personal prayer, having seriously committed parents, engaging religious faith in a way that makes it very important in one's daily life, having few religious doubts, and having many personal religious experiences. Other factors beyond these also matter, in that they also exert independent influences, but not as strongly and consistently as these top five factors.

Thinking a bit more abstractly about these findings, we might make the following sociological observation. In order to sustain high levels of religious commitment and practice during the emerging adult years, five distinct factors seem especially important: first, strong *relational modeling and support* for religious commitment (parental religion); second, genuine *internalization* of

Table 8.3. Summary of Factors Measured during the Teenage Years Associated Significantly with Higher Religiousness during Emerging Adulthood

Teenage period factors	Associations with stronger emerging adult religion
Consistently very important	
Frequent personal prayer	Greater frequency of personal prayer during the teenage years
Strong parental religion	More religiously committed parents (greater religious service attendance and professed importance of faith) during the teenage years
High importance of religious faith	Professed greater importance of religious faith in everyday life during the teenage years
Had few religious doubts	Expressed few or no doubts about religious beliefs during the teenage years
Had religious experiences	Making a commitment as a teenager to God and/ or experiencing a miracle, prayers answered, and/or a "powerful spiritual experience"
Consistently somewhat important	
Believed in divine miracles	Believing in divine miracles during the teenage years
Frequent scripture reading	Reading scripture more frequently during the teenage years
Many supportive religious adults	Enjoying more adults in teenager's religious congregation to whom teenager can turn for support, advice, or help
Sexual chastity	Has not had oral sex or sexual intercourse during the teenage years
Made fun of for religious faith	Has been made fun of by peers for religious faith during the teenage years
Conditionally somewhat important	
Believed sex belongs in marriage	Believing as teenager that people should not have sex until they are married
Religious service attendance	More religious service attendance during the teenage years
Decide morality by religion	Reliance during the teenage years for moral guidance on "what God or scripture says is right" (instead of what makes one feel happy, what helps one to get ahead, or following the advice of a parent, teacher, or other respected adult)
More religious friends	Greater proportion of close teenage friends are religious during the teenage years
Satisfaction with congregation	Combined from (1) reports as teenager that one's religious congregation is a good place to talk about serious issues like family problems, alcohol, or trouble at school; (2) would attend the same congregation if it was totally up to oneself to choose; and (3) does not think other teenagers in one's congregation are hypocrites.
Sunday school attendance	More frequent Sunday school attendance during the teenage years
Liked youth group	Reports liking one's religious youth groups during the teenage years
Teen closeness to parents	Greater relational closeness to parents during the teenage years
Number of religious activities	Greater participation in activities at religious congregation other than regular worship service
Not independently important	
Missions trips	Doing more religious missions trips and service projects during the teenage years
Religious high school	Attended a religious high school during the teenage years
Wanted similar church at age 25	Expects to want to attend a church similar to the one attended during the teenage years

Source: National Surveys of Youth and Religion 2002–2003, 2007–2008.
Note: Factors are ranked in general order of importance within categories on the basis of the magnitude of their standardized regression coefficients for significant variables.

religious significance (importance of faith, religious experiences, no doubts); and third, the *personal practice* of religious faith (prayer). Looking at the second group of variables in table 8.3 (the consistently somewhat important factors) along the same lines, it appears that also important are, first, certain theological *belief commitments* (in miracles), more intensity of *personal practice* of religious faith (scripture reading), another form of *relational modeling and support* (more supportive adults in congregation), and *paying certain costs*[5] for one's religious beliefs (abstaining from sex, being made fun of for faith). We will examine later the effects of combinations of variables for emerging adult religious outcomes, which will enable us to speak more specifically about the most likely necessary conditions and possible patterns of such influential factors. For now it is sufficient to venture the hunch that mixes of different types of influences—such as interpersonal relationships, frequent personal practice, and significant belief commitments—seem important and may work together to shape religious outcomes later in life.

Before moving on, a few words of caution about interpreting these results are in order. First, it would be a mistake to conclude that the factors found to be not independently important or to be only conditionally and somewhat important (those in the bottom half of table 8.3) are useless and irrelevant to the future religious lives of youth. For certain youth, they may very well not be useless and irrelevant but rather crucial and momentous. All the present analysis suggests is that these factors do not associate with significant differences in the outcome for the *statistically average* member of the sample under consideration. So it may very well be, for instance, that for, say, 25 percent of the sample, religious youth group satisfaction is a very important factor shaping their religious and spiritual lives in ways that will matter when they enter emerging adulthood. If that factor has no effect on 75 percent of the sample, then the real difference it does make for the 25 percent could get diluted by the noneffect among the 75 percent. Many teenagers, we know, go to religious youth groups, yet fewer are highly religious as emerging adults. But simply because youth group satisfaction does not produce higher emergent adult religious involvement for most does not mean that youth group was not an important factor for those for whom it was an important influence. The statistics conducted here measure group averages for an entire sample. They are good for telling about the full sample and the populations they represent, but they can miss important effects present in particular subpopulations. Thus, some of these variables may matter a lot for some youth, some for other youth, and none for yet other youth; the present analysis cannot identify those differences. Second, one must remember that the outcome under consideration here concerns levels of religious commitment and practice between the ages of 18 and 23. That time frame is important. But it is not everything. Young people's lives develop and evolve. It may be that by the time the same cohort of youth reaches the ages of, say, 25–31, the causal dynamics operating from the teenage years will have changed. We are not here charting long-term religion, only transitions over the five-year span from the teenage to the early emerging adult years. The factors presented in table 8.3, therefore, are not the final word on youth's lives. But they do show what seems to matter from the teenage years half a decade later during early emerging adulthood.

The Magnitudes of Difference

It is one thing to identify independent variables that statistically significantly associate with an outcome variable. But that itself does not reveal too much that is intuitively comprehensible about the magnitude of the associated differences in question. In order to generate an appreciation for the difference that the most important factors we have identified (the top of table 8.3) make in emerging adult religion outcomes, we turn now to table 8.4. The three numbers presented in the first row are an answer to this question: If the sample is divided into three groups—the top quartile, the bottom quartile, and the middle half of the distribution of respondents, according to their combined scores on the four strongest teenage (Wave 1) factors (i.e., the top group in table 8.3) that are associated with higher levels of emerging adult religion—what percent of each group would be in the Highest emerging adult religion level category at Wave 3? The answer is striking. Fully 84 percent of emerging adults who score in the top quartile of important teenage religion factors in Wave 1 also belongs as emerging adults to the Highest religion category in Wave 3. Only 25 percent of those who score in the middle half ends up in the Highest religion level. And a measly 0.4 percent of those in the Lowest quartile are on the high end of religion as emerging adults. Put differently: a teenager who among his or her peers scored in the top one-quarter of a scale measuring these four factors (parental religion, prayer, importance of faith, scripture reading) stands an 85 percent chance of landing in the Highest category of religion as an emerging adult; but one who scores in the Lowest one-quarter on that scale stands only a minuscule chance (0.4 percent) of landing at the high end of religion when he or she is 18–23 years old. In short, the combination of the teenager's parental religion, importance of faith, prayer, and scripture reading makes an enormous substantive difference in religious outcomes during emerging adulthood.

The second row in table 8.4 answers the same question, only by focusing on the three next most important teenage religion factors (those in the second group down in table 8.3). There we see that 60 percent of emerging adults who as teenagers scored in the top quartile on the three questions—about having supportive nonparent adults in one's religious congregation, having religious experiences, and not doubting religious faith—ended up in the top level of religiousness at Wave 3, as we have defined it in this chapter. By comparison, only 0.8 percent of those who scored in the bottom quartile are the most highly religious as emerging adults.[6] Again, put differently: a teenager who scores in the top quarter of a scale measuring these three questions stands 75 times the chance of landing in the Highest category of religion compared to one who scores in the bottom quarter. These three variables taken alone thus also make a big difference in the probability that a teenager will end up being highly religious as he or she grows into emerging adulthood.[7] The bottom

Table 8.4. Percent of Emerging Adults in the Highest Level of Wave 3 Religiousness by Teenage Years Factors (percents) (N = 2,193) (Weighted)

Teenage years (Wave 1) factors	25th percentile and lower of Wave 1 factor distribution	Middle 50 percent of Wave 1 factor distribution	Greater than 75th percentile of Wave 1 factor distribution
Combined: parental religion + frequency of personal prayer + importance of religious faith + frequency reading scriptures[a]	.4	25	84
Combined: supportive religious adults in congregation + religious experiences + doubts about religious beliefs[a]	.8	—[b]	60
Parental religion	7	24	48
Frequency of personal prayer	8	28	51
Importance of religious faith	7	28	52
Frequency of reading scripture	9	24	54
Supportive religious adults	10	26	40
Religious experiences	7	26	45
No doubts about religious beliefs	16	—[b]	28

Source: National Surveys of Youth and Religion 2002–2003, 2007–2008.
[a]Indicates percent of cases that score in the given percentile group on *all* variables listed who at Wave 3 are at the highest religion level. [b]The doubts in religious beliefs measure is coded dichotomously (having no or few doubts equal to 1), so no middle percentile category exists either in the single variable or in the combined measure relying on it.

half of table 8.4 calculates the same differences for each of the seven variables individually. It is not necessary here to review each one in detail. Suffice it to say that each factor taken by itself also makes a difference of large magnitude in the outcome in question. Scoring as a teenager in the top quartile on any of the first four factors alone, for example, raises the probability of ending up in the Highest level of religion as an emerging adult to around 50 percent. Scoring in the bottom quartile of the same reduces those chances to 7–9 percent. The numbers for the bottom three factors reflect the same kind of difference at a somewhat smaller magnitude, changing the odds of landing in the Highest emerging adult religion category by three or four to one. In brief, with these seven factors alone, we have identified some powerful teenage factors associating with and, we think, causing differences in emerging adult religious commitment and practice.

It is possible to depict the importance of these variables in yet another way, to help solidify understanding of the matter. Figure 8.1 is a graph that shows

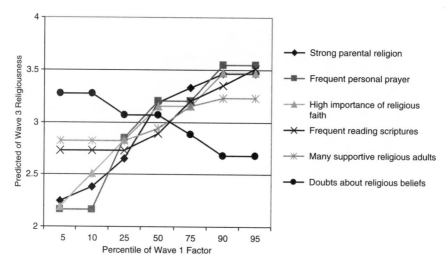

Figure 8.1. Predicted Value of Level of Emerging Adult (Wave 3) Religion as Influenced by Important Wave 1 Factors in Full Ordered Logistic Regression (N = 2,195)

Source: National Surveys of Youth and Religion 2002–2003, 2007–2008.

Note: The Y-axis scores (2–4) are the predicted outcome score in terms of the logit function; the values are calculated by first multiplying each estimated coefficient by its variable's mean, except for the variable of interest, which varies by percentile value; these products are then summed, producing a predicted outcome for that level of the variable of interest, with all other variables set at their mean (this method is similar to the calculation of a predicted value in Ordinary Least Squares (OLS) regression, but the estimation of an ordered logistic regression model transforms the dependent variable into a log odds through the use of a logit function, a transformation that eliminates the direct comparability of these predicted values to the original scale of the dependent variable).

differences in the levels of emerging adult religion at Wave 3 by differences in the top teenage factors identified earlier measured at Wave 1. There we see that the more religious respondents were as teenagers and the fewer doubts they had about their religious faith, as reflected in their higher scores on these six survey questions, the higher their level of religious commitment and practice proved to be in emerging adulthood. The effects are largest for frequency of personal prayer, strong parental religion, and high importance of religious faith in everyday life. But all six variables reflect big differences.

Yet another way to examine religious continuities and differences between the teenage and emerging adult years is to calculate predicted probabilities of teenagers being at one of four levels of religion, from Lowest to Highest commitment and practice, in the Wave 1 survey to ending up as emerging adults in one of four religious groups at the Wave 3 survey, also ranked from Highest to Lowest religious commitment and practice. The more respondents remain in the same group across survey waves, the greater continuity in religion is evident across time—and vice versa. Figure 8.2 shows the results of our calculated predicted probabilities. As a baseline, Wave 1 survey respondents here are divided into four religious groups—the devoted, regular, the sporadic, and the disengaged, as defined by the criteria specified in the table's note. The question then is what are the percent likelihoods that members of each of those four Wave 1 religious groups will end up at Wave 3 in one of our four levels of religiousness during the emerging adult years—Lowest, Minimal, Moderate, and Highest?[8] Figure 8.2 presents the answers. The NSYR respondents who as teenagers in the first wave survey were by this definition religiously devoted (the darkest line with square point markers) have a more than 50 percent chance of ending up in the Highesty religious group and only a 2 percent chance of being in the Lowest religious group, as emerging adults. The same have a 32 percent chance of ending up in the Moderate religious group and a 15 percent chance of being in the Minimal religion group as emerging adults. In short, one can predict the probabilities of a highly religious teenager ending up in different groups by religious commitment as emerging adults. When one does, one finds that they are very likely to end up in one of the two most highly religious groups five years later. Highly religious teenagers are not very likely to become very unreligious five years later.

Looking at the same analysis for teenagers who, by contrast, were religiously disengaged at Wave 1, that is, the least religious (the light line with star

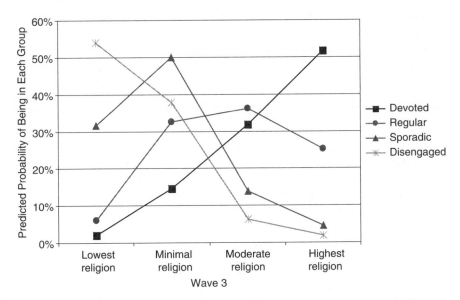

Figure 8.2. Predicted Probabilities of Wave 3 Religiousness by Wave 1 Ideal Types (N = 2,195) (Weighted)

Source: National Surveys of Youth and Religion 2002–2003, 2007–2008.

Note: Probabilities calculated based on the final ordered logistic regression model. All other variables set at their mean. Devoted = attends religious services once a week or more; religion is extremely important; attends youth group more than once a week; prays many times a day; reads the Bible many times a day. Regular = attends religious services once a week or more; religion is very important; attends youth group about once a month; prays many times per week; reads the Bible about once per week. Sporadic = attends religious service a few times per year; religion is not very important; attends youth group almost never; prays less than once per month; reads the Bible less than once per month. Disengaged = never attends religious services; religion is not important at all; not part of a youth group; never prays, never reads the Bible.

point markers), what is apparent? They have a 54 percent likelihood of end-ing up in the Lowest religion level as emerging adults; they have a 38 percent chance of being in the minimally religious group; and they have only 6 and 2 percent chances, respectively, of becoming moderately and highly religious as emerging adults. That is, the group of the least religious teenagers (age 13–17) is also extremely likely to remain in the least religious group of emerg-ing adults (age 18–23). Again, strong tendencies toward continuity in religious commitment and practice are apparent. Finally, the middle two groups—the regulars and sporadics—show a similar pattern. The regulars are most likely to end up in the moderate religious group as emerging adults, and second most likely to end up in the minimal religious group. The sporadic teenagers are most likely to end up among the Minimal group as emerging adults, and second most likely to be among the Lowest group five years later. In sum, even the middle range of teenage religion tends to reproduce itself into the emerging adult years. For both groups, however, any change that does hap-pen moves in the direction of less religion—the second greatest likelihood for regulars is Minimal, not Highest; and the second greatest likelihood for sporadics is Lowest, not Moderate. More generally, according to this analy-sis, it is quite unlikely that the most religious teenagers will end up among the least religious emerging adults—if they shift "downward," most do not shift too far. Likewise, the least religious teenagers are also highly unlikely to become among the most religious emerging adults—the vast majority remain at the low level of religion they occupied before or in a position "nearby." In short, teenage religion measured at Wave 1 strongly predicts emerging adult religion measured at Wave 3. At least across this five-year time span, the forces of religious continuity are stronger than the forces of change. Most youth tend as emerging adults to remain generally the kind of religious people they were as teenagers. In the midst of this continuity, we do observe a stronger "downwardly"-shifting tendency among many youth when it comes to reli-gion. But what we clearly do not observe are random outcomes in which the religious orientations of teenagers are "thrown into the air" during the transi-tion to emerging adulthood and then land in quite unpredictable places.[9]

COMBINATIONS OF CAUSAL FACTORS

Our analysis so far has focused on identifying variables that appear to exert independent effects on religion outcomes and on theorizing the causal mecha-nisms explaining how and why they do so. But everyone knows that many causal processes in this world do not work as isolated independent effects. Often *combinations* of causes are required to produce certain outcomes.[10] For example, in North Carolina, neither torrential rain nor high winds will by themselves independently topple a lot of big trees. Both when it rains with-out wind and when the wind blows without rain, most of the trees remain standing. However, the combination of torrential rain and high winds—with hurricanes—does in fact bring down a lot of trees. Massive rainfall is required to soften the soil and so loosen the grip of the tree roots in what normally holds them fast, and the swift movement of air mass in the form of wind is required to force the trees over. Such combinational or conjunctural causal patterns of a variety of factors are often commonly needed to produce assortments of other kinds of outcomes in life. For present purposes, the question is what combinations of factors actually can and do lead to particular religious outcomes in the lives of emerging adults? Are there particular *configurations* of multiple variables that produce high religious commitment and practice among emerging adults? Are different emerging adult religious experiences and conditions the result of identifiable combinations of other factors operating earlier in their lives? We will explore answers to these questions using the statistical method known as QCA, which identifies the combinations of variables that together are more likely than not to produce outcomes of interest.[11]

Figure 8.3 shows the basic results of our QCA analysis of conjunctions of teenage-era factors that most likely lead to the Highest level of emerging adult religion five years later. The outcome measure here is, again, based on high levels of religious service attendance, high professed importance of faith, and frequent personal prayer. The Highest level of religion identified here, based on those three variables, represents 21 percent of the emerging adult population.[12] That outcome is represented by the oval shape on the far right. In boxes to the left of that, strung together by plus signs, are the combinations of teenage-era factors that together tend to produce the Highest emerging adult religion. All of these factors represent the same most-important variables shown at the top of table 8.3. In all but one case, the factors represent the high end (e.g., higher religiousness) of the measure. In one case, however, which is shown with darker shading, the necessary factor represents the low end of the measure (low parental religiousness). Our QCA analysis reveals six different patterns of combinations of four factors that reflect six different paths that teenagers who are most likely to become highly religious emerging adults might take.[13] These six configurations are not the only combination of factors that produces the most highly religious emerging adults—small percentages of lots of other combinations of factors also join the most religious group. These six configurations are simply the combinations of factors that do so at a rate higher than 50 percent—that is, more often than not. Here, then, is what the first path reveals: one of the six most likely ways that teenagers grow up to be highly religious emerging adults is by experiencing the combination of the four factors shown here. These are teenagers who had highly religious parents, for whom religious faith was exceptionally important in their lives, who had had many religious experiences,[14] *and* who prayed and read scripture frequently. Fully 68 percent of youth whose lives embodied the combination of those four factors ended up as highly religious emerging adults five years later.

Path 2 shows a very similar configuration of factors leading to high emerging adult religion, except that in this combination, teenagers having many religious experiences is replaced with their having no doubts about their religious beliefs. Path 3 looks very much like the second path, except that frequent prayer and scripture reading is replaced with having no doubts about one's religious beliefs. The first three paths, then, all require teenagers to have had

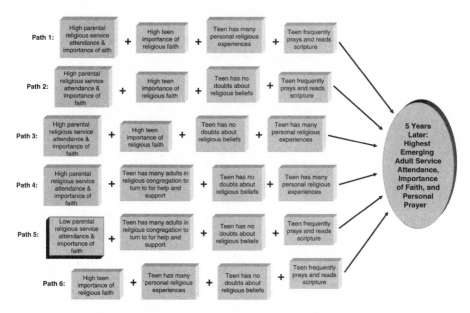

Figure 8.3. Qualitative Comparative Analysis Showing Sufficient Combinations of Teenage-era Causal Factors Most Likely Producing Highest Emerging Adult Religious Practice

Source: National Surveys of Youth and Religion 2002–2003, 2007–2008.

Note: "Many religious experiences" means teen has (1) committed life to God, (2) had prayers answered, (3) has experienced a miracle, *and* (4) has had a moving spiritual experience.

highly religious parents and to have said that their religious faith was exceptionally important in their lives. Then, combinations of two other among three possible factors—having many religious experiences, praying and reading scripture frequently, and having no doubts about religious beliefs—are also necessary to more than likely land the teenagers in the high emerging adult religion category. A fourth path begins to add complexity. In Path 4, for teenagers to join the religiously Highest 21 percent of emerging adults requires them to have had highly religious parents, many nonparental adults in their religious congregations to whom they could turn for help and support,[15] no doubts about their religious beliefs, *and* many personal religious experiences. Compared to the common conditions in the previous three cases, supportive nonparental adults in religious congregations can "substitute" in Path 4 for very high importance of religious faith. Still, a combination of a minimum of four total factors remains necessary for teens to avoid most likely ending up outside of the most highly religious group of emerging adults. Youth in Paths 2, 3, and 4 joined the most highly religious emerging adult group after five years at rates of 70, 68, and 67 percent, respectively.

Path 5 introduces a further wrinkle into our analysis. Here we have teenagers more likely than not becoming among the most highly religious emerging adults *without* having parents who were highly religious, unlike those in all four of the previous configurations. What is necessary for that to happen under that condition, however, is for these teenagers to have the presence of many nonparental adults in their religious congregations to whom they could turn for help and support *and* to possess no doubts about their religious beliefs *and* to be engaging in frequent prayer and scripture reading. In other words, teenagers whose parents are not highly religious may nevertheless be able to become highly religious emerging adults, but in order to overcome that parental "deficit," they must have supportive religious nonparental adults in their lives, harbor no doubts about their faith, and pray and read scripture a lot. Finally, Path 6 reveals a configuration of factors more likely than not to lead to high-end emerging adult religion that does not include either parental or nonparental social ties to religion. In this case, teenagers may become among the most highly religious emerging adults "on their own." But they need to be "superreligious"—believing that faith is exceptionally important in their lives, having many personal religious experiences, having no doubts about their faith, *and* frequently praying and reading scripture. (Furthermore, an ancillary analysis revealed that such teenagers had parents who were in fact quite highly religious, at a level just below the threshold required to count as the most highly religious parents in this QCA investigation—meaning that they did not actually have entirely no or few relational ties to religious faith.) Sixty-four percent of Path 5 and 77 percent of Path 6 youth ended up in the most highly religious emerging adult group after five years.

Sorting through these alternative teenage pathways to becoming most highly religious emerging adults can get complicated. But even the findings we have examined so far reveal some important insights. First, no single factor can produce high levels of emerging adult religiousness. Instead, multiple combinations of factors working together are necessary to more likely than not produce that outcome. When teenagers' lives reflect only one strong factor, their chances of becoming highly religious emerging adults are lower than average. Second, echoing a theme discussed earlier, every most-likely path to highly religious emerging adulthood must include combinations of *distinctly different kinds* of causal factors, almost always including groupings of relational, personal-subjective, and devotional-practice factors. In almost all cases, necessary among these variables are strong, personal relationships with adults who bond teenagers to faith communities (either parents or supportive nonparents), strong expressions of subjective teen personal faith commitment and experience (high importance of faith, few doubts, many religious experiences), *and* high frequencies of religious practice (prayer, scripture reading). In five of the six configurations, teenagers' having no religious doubts is a necessary condition for strong emerging adult religion. In four of the six configurations, four different factors—high parental religiousness, high importance of faith, having many religious experiences, and frequently praying and reading scripture—are all necessary conditions. In these mixtures of influences, adult relational ties to faith, both parental and nonparental, are clearly very important. The only combination of factors in which high parental religiousness or supportive nonparental adult ties are not necessary (Path 6) involves a fourfold combination of other religious factors indicating a kind of "superspiritual" religious teenager. In sum, the paths from the teenage years that more often than not lead to highly religious emerging adulthood almost inevitably involve strong relational ties to religion *and* a faith that is personally embraced very strongly *and*, typically, regular personal devotional religious practices. Not single influences but rather combinations of different kinds of factors are what shape lives toward achieving this outcome. A third observation already mentioned but worth underscoring here is that certain factors can "substitute" for other similar ones. For example, we have shown that the religious lives of parents are normally very important in shaping the religious outcomes of their growing children. But our QCA analysis here has also shown that in some circumstances, supportive nonparental adults with whom teenagers have real relationships in religious organizational contexts can provide the necessary social bonding to and support in religious faith and practice to "replace" the normally crucial role of highly religious parents when that is absent (Path 5). For that situation to work, however, teenagers also need to hold no doubts about their faith *and* frequently practice personal religious devotions (prayer, scripture reading). If any of those are missing, and if the teenagers are not "superspiritual" youth (Path 6), then highly religious parents simply must be in the picture for teenagers to be more than 50 percent likely to end up highly religious as emerging adults. Likewise, teenagers with some doubts about their religious faith can become among the most highly religious emerging adults (Path 1). But to do so, in addition to having highly religious parents, they need to counter those doubts by having many personal religious experiences and frequently praying and reading scripture.

Altogether, the six pathways presented in figure 8.3 account for the specific combinations of factors by which 34 percent of all highly religious emerging adults become highly religious. And of all of the teenagers who traveled one or another of these six pathways, 68 percent ended up five years later belonging to the relatively small highly religious emerging adult group. That means, on the one hand, that we have here identified the complex combinations of factors that are the most likely to produce the Highest level of religion among emerging adults. On the other hand, it also means that there are many other ways to become a highly religious emerging adult. Every other combination of factors examined here—and there are many—tends more likely to produce emerging adults who are not highly religious. That is in part due to the fact that most emerging adults are not highly religious—by our measure in this analysis, 79 percent are not. Still, *some* youth whose lives reflect the many other possible combinations of these variables, improbably, do in fact end up highly religious as emerging adults. It is not likely, but when added altogether, the small number of improbable pathways ends up accounting for the majority of highly religious emerging adults.[16] However, despite that fact, when we step back and examine the actual probabilities of U.S. teenagers ending up as highly religious during the ages 18–23, there are only six combinations of these the most important factors that are more likely than not to produce that outcome: the six pathways described in figure 8.3. Every other combination of factors makes it more likely that a teen will not become a highly religious emerging adult, even if some in those other combinations some teens improbably do.

WHAT CAUSES DECLINE FROM HIGH TEENAGE RELIGIOUSNESS TO LOW?

We continue to develop our analysis by focusing next on the causes of religious decline from the teenage to the emerging adult years, using the QCA method. Our purpose is to identify combinations of factors that differentiate highly religious teenagers who over five years experienced religious decline from those who remained highly religious. What conjunctures of factors made the difference? To answer that question, we narrow our sample down to those first wave teenagers who scored in the two highest religious categories, the Highest and Moderate groups, essentially the most religious half of the overall sample.[17] We then use QCA to examine combinations of factors that led some but not others of these teenagers to decline from the highest two to either of the lowest two levels of religion as emerging adults—that is, to the religiously bottom half of the sample—Minimal and Lowest. Here we focus on the possible influences of the same six factors that have already proven themselves important in such matters: the religiousness of parents, the number of supportive nonparental adults in one's religious congregation, the importance of faith, the frequency of prayer and scripture reading, doubts about religious faith, and multiple religious experiences.[18] The question, again, is what combinations of these factors tend to lead more highly religious teenagers to shift over five years down into one of the two lowest religious groups as emerging adults—compared to those from the same higher-end starting point who remained in the two highest religion groups as emerging adults? Figure 8.4 presents the findings of our QCA analysis answering this question.

According to our analysis, for youth who as teenagers were among the more highly religious to slip down as emerging adults into the lowest two categories of religion takes combinations of factors that together reflect lower parental religiousness, lower personal importance of religion, and combinations of doubts about faith, less frequent personal devotion, and fewer religious experiences. In figure 8.4, we see three distinct possible paths that more often than not lead the more highly religious teenagers into not very religious emerging adult lives. In all three of the configurations of factors, we see as necessary conditions having parents who are not among the most religious *and* expressing lower levels of the importance of one's faith. In all three configurations, we also see combinations of two of either greater doubts about faith, less frequent personal prayer and scripture reading, and fewer personal religious experiences. In Path 1, it takes the combination of these factors plus having fewer supportive nonparental adults in one's religious congregation to lead to lower levels of emerging adult religion. Path 2 shows that the combination of somewhat lower parental religiosity and personal importance of faith, fewer personal religious experiences, and some doubts about religious faith is

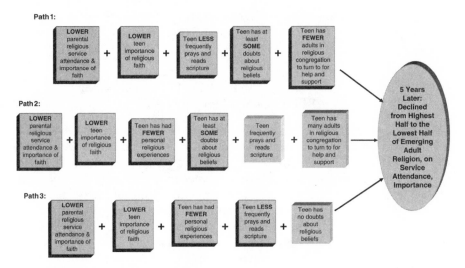

Figure 8.4. Qualitative Comparative Analysis Showing Sufficient Combinations of Causal Factors Most Likely Shifting the More Highly Religious Teenagers into the Least Religious Emerging Adult Religious Groups within Five Years

Source: National Surveys of Youth and Religion 2002–2003, 2007–2008.

Note: "Many religious experiences" means teen has (1) committed life to God, (2) had prayers answered, (3) has experienced a miracle, *and* (4) has had a moving spiritual experience.

enough to neutralize and overwhelm the fact that these highly religious teenagers also prayed and read scripture very frequently and had many supportive nonparental adults in their religious congregations. Similarly, Path 3 reveals that the combination of somewhat lower parental religiosity and personal importance of faith, fewer personal religious experiences, and less frequent prayer and scripture reading are sufficient to counteract and overpower the fact that these highly religious teenagers also said they had no doubts about their religious faith.

Altogether, 60 percent of teens who experienced one of these three combinations of factors ended up as emerging adults in the low religion categories.[19] And 56 percent of all of those higher religion teenagers who did end up as emerging adults in a low religion category got there by following one of these three paths. All of these six variables, in other words, appear in various combinations to be important influences on the outcome. Thus, even for youth who are as teenagers quite highly religious, the lack of the strongest parental and nonparental ties to religious faith combined with holding a religious faith that is not extremely important to one's life and/or praying and reading scripture less frequently and/or having fewer personal religious experiences and/or harboring some doubts about religious faith puts those highly religious teenagers at "risk" of becoming low religion emerging adults five years later. When present, in other words, the same factors that combine to make "life recipes" for sustaining high religious faith and practice into the emerging adult years are also those that, when absent, combine to make recipes for declining religion over the same years. Again, stated at a more abstract theoretical level, what clearly matters in the teenager's situation, for shaping the religious outcomes under consideration, is relational ties with religious adults—with both parents and others in one's religious congregation—importance of one's faith, and other combinations of one's religious practices, experiences, and assurance. These factors operating in opposite directions either reinforce or let disintegrate even relatively high religious commitments and practices held during the teenage years as youth move into emerging adulthood.

THEORIZING OPERATIVE SOCIAL CAUSAL MECHANISMS

Next we step back from our empirical analysis and reflect theoretically on the operating social causal mechanisms that give rise to the observed associations between the significant factors we have identified thus far and our emerging adult religion outcome. Many social scientists are content simply to use multiple regression analyses to find statistically significant independent variables, and then to fudge the basic causal questions with ambiguous phrases about those variables "leading to" or "predicting" dependent variables. As we have already mentioned, that is not good enough. Social science worth the name must seek to identify real social mechanisms that cause and therefore explain facts and events of interest. The challenge, however, is that causal forces, despite being fully real, are often not directly observable. So strict empiricism will never be able to complete the job. One has to, instead, adopt a realist perspective and work backward from one's observed empirical associations, which themselves never establish causation, through the conceptual labor of theoretical analysis as informed by one's personal understanding of how the world and social relations work, in order to try to understand the real causal forces and mechanisms at work in any situation or process in question.[20] We have in this chapter already identified a number of measured variables that seem to correlate significantly with differences in observed levels of emerging adult religion. Therefore, the *causal* question, now, is if these factors not only correlate with but actually cause those outcomes, then exactly why and how do they do so? What social mechanisms are at work to causally produce those different results? Here we attempt to spell out some answers to those questions.[21] At this stage of our scientific understanding, we do not yet possess the data needed to validate all of the causal mechanisms we may believe are operative. More research will be needed to sort through possible alternative causal explanations and to connect them to established understandings in fields such as social psychology. But to encourage further study in that direction, the following pages offer what we think are the most plausible theoretical accounts.

We will begin with the influence of *strong parental religion* during the teenage years. Why and how does that function through specific social causal mechanisms to produce stronger emerging adult religion?[22] The possibilities are multiple.[23] One obvious possibility is simple *religious socialization*—that teenagers with seriously religious parents are more likely than those without such parents to have been trained in their lives to think, feel, believe, and act as serious religious believers, and that that training "sticks" with them even when they leave home and enter emerging adulthood. Emerging adults who grew up with seriously religious parents are through socialization more likely (1) to have internalized their parents' religious worldview, (2) to possess the practical religious know-how needed to live more highly religious lives, and (3) to embody the identity orientations and behavioral tendencies toward continuing to practice what they have been taught religiously. In this case, religious socialization operates in much the same way as gender, social class, ethnic, and political socialization. Parents (and other agents of socialization) more or less effectively transmit to children and youth certain outlooks, meanings, values, and practices about different domains of life in the form of ideas believed, knowledge and skills acquired, and habits and lifestyles formed. At the heart of this social causal mechanism stands the elementary process of *teaching*—both formal and informal, verbal and nonverbal, oral and behavioral, intentional and unconscious, through both instruction and role modeling. We believe that one of the main mechanisms by which empirically observed strong parental religion produces strong emerging adult religion in offspring is through the teaching involved in socialization. We think of this socialization as the "positive" side of the dynamic. But we also believe it is only part of the story.

A second social causal mechanism that we think connects strong parental religion to strong emerging adult religion is the more "negative" one of *the avoidance of relationship breakdown*. Most parents and children enjoy relationships—however imperfect—that they value and want to sustain. Parents and children in highly religious families, in fact, as we will show in the next chapter, enjoy even closer and happier relationships than those of the national average. In most parent-child associations, in other words, both or all parties involved usually have a great deal invested in the relationships and normally desire to protect and not lose their investments. While good relationships often involve a certain amount of change, growth, development, and even tension, most close relationships also face limits in their capacity to handle disagreements and conflict. People who are trying to maintain ongoing relationships—particularly intimate ones—therefore usually work to preserve their shared perspectives, values, priorities, commitments, and acceptable behaviors, in order not to offend, disturb, or alienate the other party. When one person significantly violates what is important to the other, the relationship is likely to be threatened. People who are greatly invested in particular relationships are therefore typically averse to making choices or taking actions that they believe will jeopardize them. They have strong incentives to do what it takes instead to maintain good relations. When it comes to parents, children, and religion, when religious faith and practice are particularly important to parents, it is usually the case that they want it to also be important in the lives of their children. When their children accept, embrace, and practice that religious faith, therefore, the relationship tends to be affirmed and sustained. When their children neglect or reject that religious faith, the relationship tends to be threatened. Children of seriously religious parents who are generally invested in avoiding relational breakdown therefore have an incentive not to disregard the religious faith and practice that they (usually accurately) believe their parents want them to continue. It is in their interest to be seriously religious and against their interest to threaten the relationship by disdaining religion. Unless some other overriding factor comes into play, therefore, the consequence of not believing and of living as a nonreligious person is too costly to accept. So we think that in part in this way, too, religious commitment and practice is reproduced from one generation to the next.

We cannot go farther without acknowledging a few obvious points. First, neither of these two causal social causal mechanisms—religious socialization or relationship breakdown avoidance—operates with absolute, controlling influence. Children are active agents in their own socialization and can and sometimes do modify or reject what their parents teach them. Children also sometimes actively look for ways not to affirm but to disturb their parents and trouble their relationships. And some seriously religious yet more laissez-faire parents let their children know that they do not need to believe and practice as their parents do in order to maintain a good relationship with them. In such cases, these two causal social causal mechanisms will likely not operate as they normally do. We must always bear in mind that in human social life a great many different social causal mechanisms work in complex ways together, against each other, and with indifference to each other to produce different and sometimes similar outcomes. We are not here trying to postulate a universal "covering law" of social life. Our purpose is simply to begin conceptually to describe and understand some of the real—even though not necessarily directly observable—social causal mechanisms that help to explain our empirical observations. We believe that strong parental religion is linked to higher emerging adult religion through at least the two social causal mechanisms, one positive and one negative, of religious socialization and the avoidance of relational breakdown.

A second factor associated with stronger emerging adult religion is the teenager *having more adults in a religious congregation to whom he or she can turn for support, advice, and help.* One social causal mechanism that we think helps create this statistical association is a *heightened enjoyment of religious congregational participation.* People generally tend to enjoy groups more the more they personally know other people involved in them. In most ongoing social situations, being a stranger is less rewarding than being recognized and known by others involved, particularly others with higher status. The more relationships in their religious congregations that teenagers enjoy with nonparental adults whose social statuses are superior to their own, the more likely they will be to experience involvement in their congregations as enjoyable and rewarding. They stand a greater chance of actually looking forward to going to, rather than simply getting through, religious services. They are more likely to be drawn into more of the religious activities of the congregation. They are also more likely to shift their involvements in their religious congregations closer to the center instead of out on the periphery of their social lives overall. Some may even wish, once they are older, to reproduce the positive experiences they had as teenagers with other teenagers younger than them. All of this has the effect of establishing for teenagers an active life in a religious congregation as a valued priority to maintain even into emerging adulthood.

Besides this mechanism, we think two others are involved that are similar to those operating with the strong parental religion factor. The first is *religious socialization*. The more nonparental adults teenagers have in their religious congregations to whom they are personally tied, the more teachers and role models they have, coming from different social positions, to train them in the right believing and living of their faith. The second mechanism is *avoidance of relational breakdown*. Assume that teenagers value the relationships they have with the supportive adults in their religious congregations, and that those relationships are not terminated at the end of the teenage years. We should then expect emerging adults to have an investment in maintaining relationships with these other people who presumably have personally cared about them. Since these relationships were forged in religious contexts, emerging adults dramatically reducing their religious commitment and participation could threaten to damage those relationships, to disappoint the others involved. Thus, emerging adults having histories of positive social ties to supportive nonparental adults in their teenage religious congregations will for these reasons increase the chances that they will remain religiously committed and practicing five years later.

A third key factor associated with stronger emerging adult religion is intense teenage devotional practice in the form of frequent *personal prayer* and *reading of scripture*. Why and how do these religious practices or what about them cause stronger emerging adult religion? What mechanisms give rise to this significant association? Since these factors—prayer and scripture reading—appear usually to exert *independent* effects on the emerging adult religion outcome, after controlling for the effects of high importance of faith in life, we do not presume that they are simply behavioral markers for a more basic, driving commitment to religion. They may be this as well. But they also appear to be related to mechanisms exercising their own causal powers somehow. What are those powers and by what mechanisms do they operate? Again, numerous possibilities come to mind. One possibility is simply *religious belief and desire reinforcement*, the idea that praying and reading scripture cognitively and emotionally fortify the moral belief that being a committed and active person of faith is the right thing to do in life. The assumption here, which we think is fair, is that people's actions are driven in part by their beliefs and desires. Some people's belief that religious commitment and practice are good and their desire to achieve that good thus motivate them to be committed to practicing their faith as their lives develop. We suppose here that acts of regular personal prayer and scripture reading are generally self-affirming and reinforcing, insofar as they help reinforce the believer's relationship with God, strength of personal faith, and understanding of and benefit from the practices themselves. This self-propagating dynamic then combines with processes of *habituation*, in which routines and habitual practices become established and so are easier to continue than to break. As a result of their reinforced beliefs and desires concerning religious devotion, emerging adults who as teenagers engaged in frequent and regular personal prayer and reading of scripture prove more likely than those who did not to continue on as more highly committed believers, more capable of resisting countervailing forces and mechanisms that would reduce their religious commitments and practices.

Another relevant mechanism is the tendency toward *conserving accumulated "religious capital."*[24] The idea of religious practices generally, sociologically speaking, is that, like practicing at most things more broadly (e.g., a musical instrument, sports, speaking a foreign language), they train the one practicing to move closer toward excellence in exercising or expressing the skill, activity, or way of life in question. By practicing religion—through, for instance, prayer and scripture reading—one enhances one's ability to be a good believer, through greater familiarity and engagement with and knowledge about the religious faith. And as with most other things, generally, the more one practices religion, the more rewarding it becomes. So the more one prays, the more one has an opportunity, for instance, to see prayers answered or to be comforted by praying. The more one reads scripture, the more one is likely to understand scripture, the more the faith itself becomes meaningful, the more opportunities one has to find passages that are helpful and applicable to one's life, and the more one understands what the faith calls one to and why it does so. In other words, the more one practices religion, generally the more capacity one builds up to benefit in various ways from belonging to and living out the faith. Some social scientists call this increased capacity and enjoyment "religious capital." An associated idea in this line of thought is that most people seek to avoid squandering accumulated religious capital and, rather, attempt to conserve, protect, and capitalize on it. If so, then young persons who as teenager have invested themselves in the practices of frequent personal prayer and scripture reading will have as a result accumulated a quantity of religious capital that promises ongoing "payoffs" in the form of a better informed, observed, performed, and therefore more fulfilling life of faith. To drop or dramatically discount that life of faith would mean to fail to use that accumulated religious capital, to waste it, to squander the investment that helped accumulate it in the first place. Most people prefer to benefit from rather than to waste the various forms of capital that they have gained through effort, all else being equal. So emerging adults who, through committed religious practices during their teenage years, have accumulated such religious capital will be more likely than those with less of it to capitalize on it by continuing strongly in the faith in which that capital is able to realize payoff. Put differently, people who have not seriously practiced their faith in prior years simply have less to lose, in the way of religious capital, if they drop out of the faith than do those who have seriously practiced it. And so those who as teenagers prayed and read scripture a lot are more likely to tend to stick with the serious practice of their faith when they are older.

A third social causal mechanism related sociologically to personal prayer and scripture reading that we think helps to explain higher levels of emerging adult religion is the *drive for identity continuity*. Religious practices not only work to accumulate religious capital. They also help to define, establish, and confirm religious identities. Persons who pray regularly become as a result known both to themselves and to others as more faithful religious persons than those who does not. The same is true about frequent scripture reading. People are not simply preoccupied with increasing their rewards and benefits but are perhaps more fundamentally concerned with knowing, confirming, and protecting their own and others' sense of who they *are*, that is, their personal and social identities. The assumption here is that people have a strong interest in conserving their senses of self, of sustaining the continuity of their identities over time and space. Of course, sometimes people's identities do change. But such change must be limited in extent if one is to maintain a healthy human existence. The transition from the teenage to the emerging adult years is certainly one of identity development, but, contrary to common misperceptions, it is not usually one of massive identity transformation.[25] Most emerging adults—however much they may yearn to alter their surrounding environments in some ways—generally continue being essentially the same persons they have been in the past. So emerging adults who as teenagers, in part through their religious practices, established personal and social identities for themselves as people of serious religious faith will be more likely than those who were only moderately religious to continue forms of life, or contexts in which meanings occur, that will sustain that serious religious identity. Having become a serious religious person in part through these practices, and having the interest in sustaining a continuity of identity that most people have, such a person will, other things being roughly equal, tend later in life to remain that kind of serious religious person. Again, this is not an iron law, simply a tendency.

Yet another key factor associated with stronger emerging adult religion is *high teenage importance of religious faith*. Emerging adults who as teenagers reported higher importance of faith in everyday life proved more likely to remain most highly religious as 18- to 23-year-olds. What social causal mechanisms are at work producing this effect? We think some of those already discussed do so. One is again *religious belief and desire reinforcement*. Part of being someone for whom religious faith is highly important in everyday life itself involves embracing sets of particular beliefs and desires—about what is real, good, right, true, and worthy—that themselves commend the continuing investment in that religious faith. Generally, something being important in life is simultaneously constituted by, generates, and fortifies beliefs and desires that help to sustain its importance. Other forces and events can of course intervene to erode that importance. Then again, matters of such importance have powerful ways of resisting such challenges. Thus cognitive and emotional forces operate to sustain the high importance of faith into the emerging adult years.

Another, related mechanism involved in high importance of faith is the *drive for identity continuity*. When people understand themselves to be the kind of selves for whom faith is highly important, the basic human interest in sustaining a continuously coherent identity will—all else being equal—tend to motivate them to remain highly religious into future years. The same is true when other people believe someone to be defined by a certain strong identity, in that there are social goods gained by sustaining that identity and potential costs paid by altering it—for instance, the good of being perceived by others as being stable, reliable, and consistent versus the costs paid for potentially being seen as unpredictable, undependable, and changeable. The more frequently people change themselves, the less seriously others take any given self that such a person presents. Thus, if one is at one time a serious religious believer for whom faith is extremely important in one's life and then subsequently drops that religious aspect of one's identity, one then has some explaining to do in order to maintain a credible sense of reliable self to others. It certainly can be done, and many youth end up doing it. But within a larger constellation of factors at work, this can serve as an influence sustaining faith. This connects to the third social causal mechanism likely linking high teenage importance of faith and stronger emerging adult religion: *avoidance of relationship breakdown*. We know that teenagers for whom religious faith is highly important in their daily lives are much more likely than teens for whom faith it is not so important to enjoy social relationships with others who are also highly religious—parents, siblings, relatives, friends, and other adults in their religious congregations. For them to drop their highly religious way of life in their transition to emerging adulthood would probably cause damage to what are likely highly valued relationships. So there is a relational incentive to sustain and a disincentive to lose serious religious faith and practice.

The social causal mechanisms at work in two other key factors remain to be theorized. The first is teenagers *having no doubts about their religious beliefs*. The causal mechanism at work here concerns elementary cognitive belief commitment. Most American religions, especially as they are typically practiced by the most faithful, involve, among other things, adherence to sacred belief systems that specify the nature of reality and how humans ought to live within that reality. Commitment to the serious embrace and practice of faith thus normally requires accepting and trusting the rightness of those descriptive and normative religious beliefs. The more a believer questions or doubts them, the more susceptible over time he or she is to revising, discounting, or abandoning his or her associated religious faith and practice. By contrast, the faith of the believer who encounters fewer doubts about his or her religion is more likely to remain intact and maintained. Therefore, teenagers reporting that they have no doubts about their religious beliefs indicates possible negative and positive causal mechanisms at work. Negatively, it suggests that mental structures and life experiences are shielding them from cognitive and existential forces that could potentially undermine their religion. Positively, it indicates that their existing cognitive religious belief systems are formed in such a way as to be robust and resilient enough to withstand threats to faith. Such negative and positive mental operations achieving this kind of intellectual and existential security are important cognitive mechanisms helping to sustain strong religious faith and practice over time.

The final key factor leading to higher emerging adult religion is teenagers *having many religious experiences*. Here this means having specifically committed their lives to God, having had definite answers to prayers, having experienced at least one miracle, *and* having one or more moving spiritual experiences. By what mechanisms might these teenage religious experiences propel youth over five years into the group of most religious emerging adults? Many of those already described would seem relevant to this factor. Such religious experiences should, in normal circumstances, reinforce religious cognitive belief commitments and desires. In a culture that puts such a high premium on the reliability and validity of individual subjective experience as American culture does, simply having personally had an answer to prayer, witnessed a divine miracle, or encountered an emotionally moving spiritual experience will tend to confirm and validate the larger religious faith associated with those experiences. They should help to make the religion more "real" and therefore personally reliable and important to believers. Such experiences are also often integral parts of religious socialization processes, as new or young members of religious communities come not simply to cognitively understand religious ideas but also to experience and personalize their faith for themselves. Furthermore, these religious experiences may in some cases heighten the enjoyment of participating in religious communities in which such experiences are normative. For many, they may enhance a sense of belonging and sharing in religious groups. Such religious experiences also tend to increase believers' religious capital: their stocks of religious knowledge, familiarity, skills, and other learned resources that increase proficiency in understanding and practicing the faith. This in turn normally makes religious believers more invested in their faiths and so in continuing to sustain them. And all of this should work toward the formation of particular religious identities, which believers over time will tend to want to conserve, because of the drive for identity continuity. Any and all of these, we expect, will work causally toward producing stronger rather than weaker religious faith and practice into the future.

Readers studying table 8.3 may ask by what mechanisms some of the other factors listed there—particularly around certain beliefs—causally produce high religion effects. Two other mechanisms on which this chapter has not focused may be worth mentioning. One other factor we found to be associated with a higher level of religious commitment and practice during emerging adulthood is *having believed in divine miracles* as a teenager. What actual social causal mechanism could link this to stronger emerging adult religion? One answer, we think, is *cognitive resistance to modern secular assumptions*. Believing in the historical reality and possible contemporary actuality of divine miracles in the context of contemporary U.S. adolescent culture is a form of strong resistance to the authority claims of modern secular presuppositions and culture. It is an act of engagement in "cognitive deviance." This act effectively relativizes the authority of metaphysically naturalistic science by placing limits on its capacity to explain all events within the terms of its worldview—thus rejecting scientism. And this act expresses faith in a powerful God actively at work in the world—thus rejecting deism. In addition, this act is usually based on a more conservative hermeneutical reading of scripture—thus rejecting a liberal "demythologizing" of the scriptural text when it fails to conform to a modern secular perspective. All of this, of course, relates to the process of *religious belief and desire reinforcement* discussed earlier. By taking a cognitive stand on miracles during the teenage years, youth who do so solidify a certain intellectual and affective structure that is more likely to resist the authority claims of secular modernity than those who did not. We thus take believing in miracles as a teenager to be both a substantively significant faith-defending position itself, as well as an indicator of a kind of larger cognitive position that prioritizes religious authority claims and is prepared to live with dissonance arising from the conflict of these claims with competing authority claims of secular modernity. Teenagers who have established such a cognitive position should therefore be theoretically more likely to remain seriously committed persons of faith as they move into emerging adulthood—and, the evidence suggests, they actually do so.

Another perhaps more enigmatic factor we will address here that associates with stronger emerging adult religion is teenagers *believing that people should not have sex until they are married*. We think there are two social causal mechanisms that link this belief to the outcome of stronger emerging adult religion. First is one described earlier: *cognitive resistance to modern secular culture*. Believing in the rightness of waiting to have sex until marriage is, in the context of contemporary U.S. youth culture, another form of strong resistance to the authority claims of the modern secular, religiously liberal, or even indecisively religious outlook. The widespread norm, instead, is for youth to start having sex when they want to or when they feel "ready" for it. For most young Americans, the idea of waiting to have sex until one is 26 or 29 or 32—whenever one expects to get married—is foolish, perhaps even literally impossible. To think otherwise, therefore, is to take a distinctive stand by rejecting some of the key assumptions, values, or priorities of what such teens typically view as the dominant culture. As described earlier, this helps to establish for such believers a larger, cognitively deviant mental-affective structure. And that kind of traditional and religiously grounded outlook, prepared to resist the forces of secular modernity, tends—compared to the alternative—to propel youth to continue their lives with a strong religious faith and practice into emerging adulthood.

Second, we think another causal mechanism is also operative here that is more specifically linked to the issue of the timing of sex: the tendency toward *increased cognitive-emotional dissonance with serious religious identity and practice that teenage and emerging adult sexual activity generate*. Most youth know that most religions teach sexual restraint, self-discipline, and often even abstinence until marriage. When such religious youth begin to engage in sex themselves, many of them feel increasingly uncomfortable attending religious services, praying, and hanging out with other highly religious people. One of the major means youth rely on to relieve such discomfort is minimizing the religious aspect of their lives. For many youth, therefore, initiating sexual activity is a significant turning point in pulling away from religion, in part because of the mental and emotional dissonance that willfully having sex on an ongoing basis causes in the religious contexts of their lives, even when nobody religious knows they are having sex. Of course, simply believing that sex properly belongs in marriage relationships does not guarantee that those who believe that will remain virgins until marriage. Still, believing that sex should be saved for marriage does in fact noticeably delay the start of sexual activity for some, reduces the intensity and length of sexual activity for others, and helps to encourage yet others to indeed remain virgins. In these cases, the cognitive-emotional dissonance about being religious generated by being sexually active is greatly reduced, so there is one fewer force pushing these youth away from religion. In other words, not believing in saving sex for marriage is associated for youth with becoming sexually active sooner and with greater intensity, and that, in turn, tends to produce discomfort with religion and often a move away from religious commitments and involvements. By contrast, believing in saving sex for marriage is positively associated with behaviors (abstinence or delayed and reduced sex) that tend not to trigger the same cognitive-emotional dissonance about religious matters, which generates fewer forces pushing emerging adults away from religion.[26] In the end, it is through these mechanisms, we think, that those who believe in sexual abstinence before marriage turn out to be religiously stronger as emerging adults.

We have here theorized what we think are the actual causal dynamics involved in what appear to be the seven most important teenage-year factors associated with strong emerging adult religion. Table 8.5 summarizes the main mechanisms behind the variables primarily analyzed in this chapter. In each case, it is not simply a particular score on a survey measure itself that produces the outcome. Rather, "below the surface" of the observations, complex sets of social causal mechanisms—usually not directly observable—are operating, according to the real nature of the things in question, to generate the observed result. The explanation comes not simply by establishing statistical significance between variables. Explanation comes rather by identifying the social causal mechanisms that link the cause to the effect, that explain how and why the latter is produced by the former. In this way, we can deepen our understanding of the hows and whys of the fact that certain independent variables statistically associate with certain dependent variables. Social scientific efforts to understand the religious lives of American youth can greatly benefit by developing this kind of causally realist approach and so enhancing, through shared disciplined methods, knowledge about the nature, the triggers, the dynamics of, and the contextual conditions affecting such social causal mechanisms. Clearly, more empirical research and theorizing focused directly on these mechanisms are needed to validate or revise our treatment of them here. We may not have gotten all the mechanisms right. What we have offered in the preceding pages is one step toward a needed and much better development: a mechanisms-focused research program.

Table 8.5. Summary of Theoretical Mechanisms Leading to Higher Religiosity in Young Adulthood

Theoretical mechanism	Description	Significant variables supporting operation
Socialization	Values, behaviors, and beliefs are transmitted from important others to youth through formal teaching and informal modeling.	Strong parental religion Supportive religious adults
Avoidance of relationship breakdown	Youth act in ways toward shared agreement to maintain valued relationships.	Strong parental religion Supportive religious adults High importance of religious faith
Enjoyment of participation rewarding continuation	Intrinsically rewarding activities are more likely to be continued to be pursued and have its associated messages internalized.	Supportive religious adults Having many religious experiences
Belief and desire reinforcement	Cognitively and emotionally solidifying and fortifying one's beliefs about what is true, good, and right in life.	Frequently praying Frequently reading scripture High importance of religious faith Having many religious experiences
Habituation	Meaningful behaviors that become routine and practiced are more likely to be continued into the future.	Frequently praying Frequently reading scripture
Conserving accumulated religious capital	Investment in activities and communities accrues potential benefits, which discontinuing participation in would eliminate.	Frequently praying Frequently reading scripture Supportive religious adults
Drive for identity continuity	Desire to maintain one's sense of who one is and presentation of that self to others.	Frequently praying Frequently reading scripture High importance of religious faith Having many religious experiences
Cognitive belief commitment	Embracing a belief system that explains lived reality and provides direction for one's life.	Having no doubts about religious beliefs

MULTIPLE CHANGE TRAJECTORY SLOPES

Another way to understand the kind of religious trajectories teenagers take as they enter emerging adulthood is to identify the most important distinct courses of religious faith and practice that different clusters of them traverse across those years. To do this, we employ a statistical technique known as growth mixture modeling, which requires multiwave data like those we are analyzing here. Calculating trajectories in this way essentially involves identifying the major types of paths for some outcome that clusters of respondents undergo together as they age. The religious outcome variable we analyze here is very similar to the one examined earlier, except that it combines measures of emerging adult religious service attendance, importance of faith, and frequency of personal prayer into a single scale, as is required by the growth mixture modeling technique. The question is what groups of teenagers reflect religious stability or change at various levels over time, as they become emerging adults? Because religious trajectories might differ for younger and older teenagers as they mature, we have split our analysis into two groups, 13- to 15-year-olds and 16- and 17-year olds. Figure 8.4 displays the results of our growth mixture modeling analysis for the younger group.[27]

Figure 8.5 identifies six different groups reflecting quite distinct religious trajectories across a five-year time span, beginning at age 13–15. On the left side of the figure, at the top, are shown the most highly religious and stable

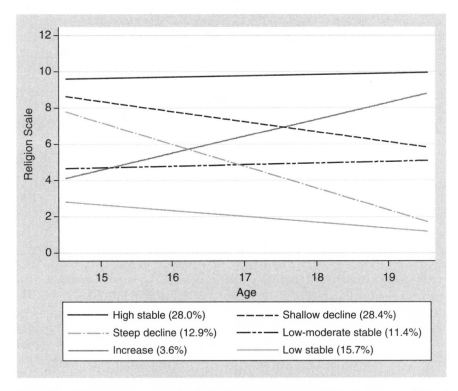

Figure 8.5. Growth Curves Tracking the Six Most Important Distinct Trajectories of Religious Change among Teenagers 13–15 Years Old in 2002

Source: National Surveys of Youth and Religion, 2002–2003, 2005, 2007–2008.

Note: Religious change here is based on a composite measure of frequency of attendance at religious services, reported importance of faith in daily life, and frequency of personal prayer.

group, representing 28 percent of the total, which over five years maintains relatively high scores (nearly 10 out of 12) on this scale. Below them is another group of about 28 percent who began relatively high but declined somewhat over time (shallow decline). Just below them is another group of almost 13 percent who began relatively high (scoring about 8 out of 12) but dropped much more steeply five years later, down to nearly 2 out of 12 (steep decline). The next trajectory line down represents the low- to moderate-stability group (composed of about 11 percent), whose members started out fairly weakly religious and remained so over five years. Just below that line is a small group (3.6 percent) that counters the overall stable and downward trends evident in the other five groups by starting off second to lowest in religious terms (scoring about 4 out of 12) yet increasing to more than 8 out of 12 five years later. This is the only group of the six, and a small one at that, that dramatically grew in religiousness. Finally, at the very bottom, we observe a low-stability group of about 16 percent who as early teenagers were low on religion and five years later were still low, in fact slightly lower.

Standing back and looking at all of the trend lines together, we observe four important points. First, adolescents reflect a great deal of variance on religiousness over time—some are highly religious, some are quite unreligious, and many are in between. Second, religious practice between the early teenage and early emerging adult years shows a substantial amount of stability over time. The three clusters reflecting minimal change—the high stable, low to moderate stable, and low stable groups—represent about 55 percent of the total sample. Third, when noticeable change does happen over the five-year period represented in this figure, most of it (more than 40 percent of the total) consists of religious decline. Only a very small group, of 3.6 percent, experiences a significant increase in religiousness. Fourth and finally, many teenagers' religious "starting points" matter for their subsequent religious experience over time. Those who over five years sustained the relatively highest levels of religiousness began at the highest level of all the groups. Those who experienced modest declines in religiousness began at somewhat lower levels than they did. And those who underwent the greatest loss of religiousness over these five years began at even lower levels than they did. Of the groups who began on the lower end of this religion scale (between 2 and 5 out of 12 at the start), the vast majority remained at low to moderate stable or declined somewhat. Only a small proportion increased in religiousness. Put differently, the religious lives of younger teenagers transitioning into the early emerging adult years do not over this time period spin out into a confused, random jumble. Rather, the vast majority either remains essentially what it was religiously five years earlier or declines more or less from its earlier levels of religiousness.

Figure 8.6 presents the growth mixture modeling findings for the older cohort, those who were 16 and 17 years old in the first wave survey. The story here is similar to that portrayed in the figure 8.5. At the top, about 23 percent remain religiously high and stable over these five years (maintaining a score of about 10 out of 12). More than one in four (27 percent) show a modest decline from a relatively high baseline. Nearly 1 in 10, below them, experience a steep decline. A low to moderate stable group and a low stable group then each represents about 17 percent of the total—both of which experience very modest decline. And, again, a small group of older teenagers (6.9 percent) counter the dominant trends with a rise over the five-year transition into emerging adulthood. This is a modestly sized cluster, yet comparatively is nearly twice the size of the group of 13- to 15-year-olds in the figure 8.5 whose religiousness increased. There thus appears to be something about developing life after age 20, some kind of life-experience or maturity factor, compared to life before age 20, that slightly increases the chances of becoming more religious over a five-year time frame. Surveying all of the trends in figure 8.6, however, we see that their overall significance is very similar to that of figure 8.5. Most obvious are large differences among new emerging adults' levels of religiousness, a large amount of stability over time as they mature, decline as the major form of change when change does happen, and a modest countertrend of increased religiousness among only a small cluster of young emerging adults.

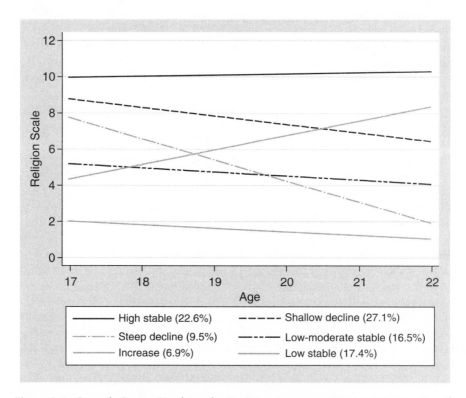

Figure 8.6. Growth Curves Tracking the Six Most Important Distinct Trajectories of Religious Change among Teenagers 16 and 17 Years Old in 2002

Source: National Surveys of Youth and Religion, 2002–2003; 2005; 2007–2008.

Note: Religious change here is based on a composite measure of frequency of attendance at religious services, reported importance of faith in daily life, and frequency of personal prayer.

Each of the six distinct religious trajectory groups, for both age cohorts analyzed here, comprises a variety of types of religious traditions and racial groups and both men and women. But certain trajectory groups tend especially to consist of particular types of youth. Additional analyses (not shown here) reveal that the high stable group, for instance, tends disproportionately to include conservative Protestants, black Protestants, African Americans, and females. The shallow decline group contains a somewhat larger than average number of conservative Protestants, mainline Protestants, black Protestants, Catholics, and females. The steep religious decline group comprises somewhat higher percentages of mainline Protestants, Catholics, and whites. The low to moderate stable group contains slightly disproportionate numbers of Catholic and Jewish youth. By comparison, the small group experiencing an increase in religiousness comprises a greatly disproportionate number of teenagers who were not religious at the Wave 1 baseline, African Americans, Hispanics, and women. Finally, the stably low religion group tends especially to consist of Jewish, nonreligious, white, and male youth. All of that is consistent with the statistics and changes we observed in chapter 4. In sum, the chances that any teenager will follow one or another of the six different religious trajectories shown here, on which most teenagers tend to track, are influenced somewhat, though not powerfully, by their religious tradition, race, and sex.

Even more important in determining placement in these trajectories, however, are other factors that this chapter has already identified as the most crucial in shaping the religious outcomes of young people's lives. The high stable religious group, for example, contains a much higher percentage of youth whose parents attend religious services frequently, report high importance of faith, and pray very often for their children. The same group is also more likely to have reported in their first survey that they had many nonparental adults in their religious congregations with whom they enjoyed talking and that adults in their congregations are generally very easy to talk with and get to know. The same group also contains higher percents of those who as teens prayed and read scripture more frequently, definitely believed in miracles, and believed in waiting until marriage to have sex. All of the other groups score noticeably lower on all of those measures. For instance, for the younger age cohort, 70 percent of the high stable religious group had parents who attended religious services weekly or more often, compared to 39 percent of the steep decline group and 11 percent of the low stable group. Similarly, 71 percent of the high stable group had parents who reported that their faith was extremely important in their lives, compared to 36 percent of the steep decline group and 16 percent of the low stable group. And while 77 percent of the high stable group had parents who prayed for them daily or more often (a new variable we introduce here to make this specific point), only 47 percent of the steep decline group and 39 percent of the low stable group had the same. Among the same younger cohort, 47 percent of the high stable group said that the adults in their religious congregations as teenagers were very easy to talk to and get to know (another new variable), compared to 30 percent of the steep decline and 29 percent of the low stable groups. That is, some of the exact

same teenage-era factors that we found earlier in this chapter as foreshadow-
ing greater emerging adult religious commitment and practice (listed in table
8.3) also significantly influence the chances of persons moving along one or
another of religious trajectories examined in this section. Thus, the transition
from teenage to emerging adult religion examined again from yet a different angle reveals the same essential, consistent story. Parents matter a great
deal, other religious adults in teenagers' lives can *also* be quite important, and
teenagers' personal faith commitments and practices matter *as well* in shaping
religion during the emerging adult years.

THE TIMING OF FIRST COMMITMENTS TO GOD

We have shown that youth committing to live their lives for God is one important religious experience that is among the most important factors in leading
teenagers into the highest levels of emerging adult religion. Another way to
explore trajectories from earlier life periods to the religious and spiritual lives
of emerging adults, therefore, is to examine changes in their commitments to
live their lives for God over time. How many American teenagers and emerging adults commit their lives to God and at what ages do they do it? All three
waves of the NSYR survey asked respondents whether they had committed
to live for God at different points in their lives.[28] Analyzing the data from all
three surveys reveals the following.

First, 31 percent of respondents reported never committing their lives to
God at any of the three times they were asked. By the time the third wave the
survey was completed, in other words, nearly one-third of them had never
committed to live their lives for God. And on the basis of what we will now
show, one can expect that few of them probably ever will. These are the more
hard-core nonreligious youth who have little in their backgrounds to suggest
that in the future they will become more religious. That 31 percent figure,
however, of course means that the other 69 percent of the sample did, at least
one of the three times they were asked, at some point in their lives committed
themselves to living for God. Because respondents were asked this question
in three different surveys over their developing lives, we can pinpoint more
specifically when in their lives they made those commitments.[29] Figure 8.6
shows what the data reveal. On the darker bar on the far left are the 31 percent who in none of the three surveys had committed to live their lives for
God. The remaining 69 percent of those who had at some time in their lives
committed to God are then broken into three age groups according to their
first-time commitment.[30] We estimate that the largest of these groups, 58.8
percent of the total sample (85 percent of the ever-committing group), made
their first commitment to live their lives for God before the age of 14.[31] Most
of these probably committed to God during their childhood years, although
we cannot pinpoint the exact years of commitments with these data. By comparison, 5.3 percent (7.7 percent of the ever-committed group) appear to
have made a first commitment to live their lives for God during the teenage
years 14–17. And 4.9 percent of the sample of 18- to 23-year-olds (7 percent

of the ever-committed group) reported committing their lives to God after the age of 18.[32]

The vast majority, then, of those youth—85 percent—who have by the age of 18–23 ever committed to live their lives for God appear to have made their first commitments before age 14. Most first religious commitments thus appear to be made during childhood and the preteen or very early teen years, whether or not these commitments are reaffirmed in later years.[33] A total of 10 percent of the full sample of youth (15 percent of all those who had committed to God), then, did make their first commitment to God after the age of 13. About half of those each did so during the teenage years and the emerging adult years. The latter numbers are not insignificant, but neither are they large. In short, neither the teenage nor the emerging adult years (at least as we have measured them so far) are the ages at which most youth who commit to live their lives to God do so. Most, rather, appear to first commit to God during their childhood or preteen years. (For additional tables showing the timing and distribution in religious traditions of first and subsequent religious commitments, see figures A.4–6.) These findings complement and reinforce one of the larger stories of this book: that the religious commitments and orientations of most people appear to be set early in life and very likely follow

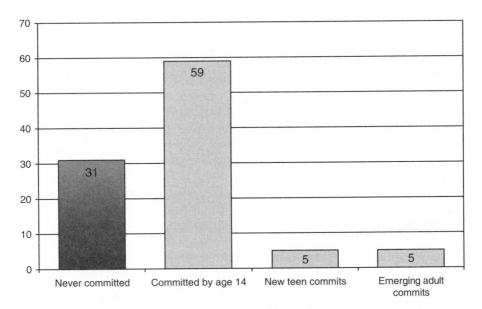

Figure 8.7. Percentage of Total Respondents on Timing of Committing to Live Life for God (N = 3,132)

Source: National Surveys of Youth and Religion 2002–2003, 2004–2005, 2007–2008.

Note: "By 14" is the percentage of respondents who reported having ever committed their lives to God at the Wave 1 survey, when asked "Have you ever committed your life to God?" which, because there was no growth across age groups in the percentage of respondents who had committed their lives to God at Wave 1, we assume to have happened before the age of 14—see note 31.

a consistent trajectory from that early formation through the adolescent and into the emerging adult years. Some young people do make dramatic shifts into lower and higher religious commitments and practices later in life that would not be expected from their early life experience and formation. But they are a minority. Most are set early in life to follow one religious trajectory or another—mostly, we showed earlier, formed by the religious lives of their parents and by social connections to their congregations and embraced in personal religious beliefs and practices—which they tend to follow as they grow into emerging adulthood. When it comes to first commitments to God, it is not that experiences and changes during the teenage and emerging adult years do not matter religiously for youth—they do, especially for some. It is instead simply that what matters for most *even more* is what happens religiously *before* the teenage years, which powerfully conditions most of everything that happens thereafter.[34]

DOES COLLEGE CORRODE RELIGIOUS FAITH?

Next, we address a question that interests many people about emerging adult religion: Does going to college cause the religious and spiritual lives of 18- to 23-year-olds to weaken or decline? The idea that higher education is corrosive to religious faith and practice is widely believed, and an older body of sociological research substantiates it.[35] The explanations for this religion-undermining effect of higher education are many. For example, it has been thought that students learn new ideas in college that cause religious doubts and sometimes apostasy. High-school-era relational social networks that once provided students with religious "plausibility structures" have also been said to erode with the transition to college, making it harder for students to maintain their religious faiths and practices. In addition, religious parents, who may have encouraged or required religious practice of their children during high school, exert less oversight and control over their college-age children. Finally, significant numbers of college students engage in partying, drinking, drug consumption, and sexual behaviors that are proscribed by many religions, which has been said to provoke cognitive dissonance that is often relieved by those students decreasing their ties to religion. Such ideas are so well established in the popular and, sometimes, academic imagination, in fact, that researchers for a while began to neglect the question, simply continuing to assume that college tends to corrode religious faith and practice.

However, something very interesting emerged when scholars took a second look at the question more recently. They found that the religiously undermining effect of higher education on recent generation of youth has disappeared. Most of the older research was conducted on baby boomers, for whom college did indeed seem to tend to corrode religious faith and practice. But many studies more recently have shown that the conventional wisdom about baby boomers does not apply to today's youth. Higher education no longer seems to diminish the religion of emerging adults. One recent study, for instance, using some of the best longitudinal data available, has shown that it is not those who attend college but in fact those who do *not* attend college who are the most likely to experience declines in religious service attendance, self-reported importance of religion, and religious affiliation.[36] Another showed that among recently surveyed college students, 2.7 times more report that their religious beliefs have strengthened during their college experience than say their beliefs weakened.[37] Yet another investigation suggests that emerging adults' religiousness does not vary with educational achievement.[38] Another study specifically focused on Catholic college students draws the same conclusion.[39] Yet another sophisticated investigation has found no secularizing effect of college on the latest college graduates and concludes that the data suggest that "secularization as a result of college attendance may be waning.... The overarching trend seems to be that educational attainment may have been related to some forms of religious decline in the past, however this is less the case for recent college graduates."[40]

If all of this is true—and it certainly seems to be—then this change represents a major shift in the role of higher education in American religion. According to one metaanalysis of the relevant literature, that clearly perceptible change appears to have begun in the 1990s.[41] But what caused it? Multiple, interactive factors seem to have worked together to produce this historic transformation.[42] One factor seems to be a growing influence of campus-based religious and parachurch groups that provide alternative plausibility structures for sustaining religious faith and practice in college.[43] Another is that colleges and universities themselves seem to be changing their attitudes and programs in ways that are more supportive of the religious and spiritual interests of their students.[44] Yet another part of the explanation may be an apparently growing number of committed evangelical and Catholic faculty who are teaching in secular American colleges and universities, providing role models to religious students of ways to combine higher learning and religious faith.[45] Another factor is the growth of religious colleges and universities that train their believing students to integrate faith and learning and to go on to influence the larger society and culture.[46] Still another causal influence could, ironically, be the major long-term decline in American college students' interest in answering questions about the meaning of life—which the dominant worldview of higher education over much of the twentieth century would have replied to with largely secularist answers—and the concomitant long-term increase in college students' interest in becoming financially very well off, which to many students is a religiously neutral matter.[47] Also relevant is the influence of postmodern relativism in the academy, especially in the 1990s, which undercut the authority of positivism, epistemological foundationalism, and scientism, all of which historically have tended strongly to marginalize and disparage religion.[48] More broadly, adolescents today are generally quite conventional, and specifically so with regard to religion—less rebellious, for instance, than they were during the baby boom generation—and so are generally content to continue in the faith traditions in which they were raised, however much that faith may or many not mean to them.[49] And at a very general level, American culture and perhaps Western culture seems to have shifted from a secular to a

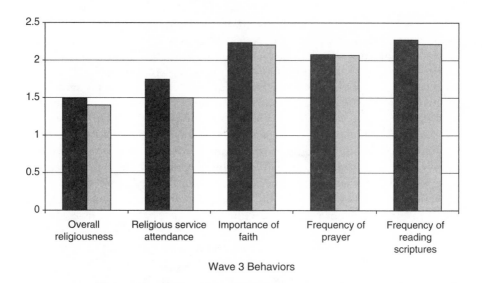

Figure 8.8. Average (Mean) Levels of Wave 3 Religiousness by Current College Attendance (N = 2,423)

Source: National Survey of Youth and Religion 2007–2008.

Note: Overall religiousness is a categorical combination of religious service attendance, important of faith, and frequency of prayer. Variable ranges: religiousness (0–3); service attendance, importance of religion, frequency of prayer (0–4); frequency of reading the Bible (1–7). Only the difference for religious service attendance is statistically significant using a t-test at the *p <.05 level.

postsecular era in which secularist assumptions are no longer simply taken for granted but are rather on the table for questioning, and religion is increasingly considered a legitimate subject of discussion—a cultural shift that has likely much affected contemporary youth.[50] Through the influence of these and other factors, American higher education seems to have become an environment and experience that is less corrosive than it was in the past of college students' religiousness. Indeed, some researchers conclude from their fieldwork on religion at college campuses that at least certain campuses have actually become "a breeding ground for vital religious practice and teaching."[51]

Our findings, based on NSYR data, about the influence of college on the religious faith of emerging adults confirm those of recent studies. While the transition from the teenage to the emerging adult years does entail an overall decline in religious involvement, as we have shown, attending college per se is not an experience that particularly contributes to that decline. For instance, consider the findings presented in figure 8.7, which compares religious measures for emerging adults currently in college with those not currently in college. We see there are very little differences in overall religiousness, service attendance, professed importance of faith, and frequency of prayer and reading scripture. In every case, emerging adults currently in college are slightly more religious than those who are not in college, although only the differences in overall religiousness and service attendance are statistically significant. In short, if anything, it is *not* attending college that is associated with lower levels of religious practice, though those differences are slight. This is confirmed by the fact, revealed in ancillary analyses (not shown), that more highly religious youth did not select into college in the first place and then decline in religiousness to the levels shown in figure 8.8, which would have indicated a secularizing effect of higher education. Furthermore, our analysis of religious differences between emerging adults who have *ever* attended college (not simply *currently* enrolled) versus those who have not reveals identical findings—those who ever attended college are slightly more religious but not often statistically significantly so.

In short, for contemporary emerging adults, going to college does not increase the "risk" of religious decline or apostasy as it did in the not-too-distant past. Some evidence now even suggests that it may actually *decrease* that risk, compared to not attending college.[52]

THE MYTH OF INTERNAL-WITHOUT-EXTERNAL RELIGION

Finally, before concluding, we engage one last analysis to dispel another common myth about religious change in emerging adulthood. Doing so will help to clear the ground of some unhelpful misperceptions, toward a more accurate understanding of the religious and spiritual lives of emerging adults. It will also help to bolster the validity of the composite measure of strong emerging adult religion that we are using in this chapter—which combines religious service attendance, importance of faith, and personal prayer into one indicator. We are speaking here about what we call the "internal-without-external religion" myth. That is the widespread belief that, as teenagers grow into emerging adults, they tend to drop out of public, external expressions of faith—like religious service attendance and other religious group participation—but that their religious faith nevertheless remains highly valued and vital in their private, subjective, internal lives, as might be expressed in a high importance of faith or high frequency of personal prayer. The subjects of such a belief, in short, do not participate much in religious congregations or do much else socially that looks religious, but for them religious faith nonetheless is greatly valued and practiced in private. Such a view is commonly assumed in both the popular imagination and in some scholarly works.[53] The idea is that many young people remain stable in being quite highly religious subjectively or privately, on the interior. They simply allow their outward, public, social expression of religious faith to recede during these years.[54] The implication is often that what "really" matters about religion—interior personal commitment—is in fact well established and secured during the emerging adult years, that it is only the external "trappings" of religious practice that decline during this life phase. Many of them, it is presumed, will in due time—with marriage and children—bring their levels of external religious participation back up to match their allegedly higher levels of continuously sustained internal religious commitment and importance.[55]

Whether emerging adults do or do not increase their levels of external religious participation as they grow older is not our intention here to determine.
What we can say here, however, is that little evidence supports the idea that
emerging adults who decline in regular external religious practice nonetheless
retain over time high levels of subjectively important, privately committed,
internal religious faith. Quite the contrary is indicated by our analysis. The
emerging adults who do sustain strong subjective religion in their lives, it turns
out, are those who also maintain strong external expressions of faith, including religious service attendance. Most emerging adults, by contrast, who significantly reduce their external religious participation also substantially reduce
their subjective, private, internal religious concerns. Such conclusions became
evident to us as we constructed this chapter's main outcome variable, which
required matching levels of religious service attendance, importance of faith,
and personal prayer for each survey respondent in every possible combination.
What we noticed while doing so was that—as shown in figure 8.9—less than
7 percent of the entire emerging adult sample reflects *low* levels of religious
service attendance (external) *along with high levels* of importance of faith and
prayer (internal). By comparison, nearly 40 percent of the sample shows either
consistently high or consistently low levels of these forms of religious expression across all three variables.[56] Furthermore, viewed from the other side, it

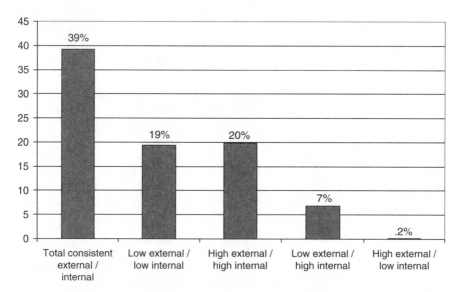

Figure 8.9. Percentage of Emerging Adults Reporting Combinations of High and/or
Low External and Internal Religious Expressions (Percents) (N = 2,438)

Source: National Surveys of Youth and Religion 2007–2008.

Note: External is measured by frequency of attendance at religious services; internal is measured with reported
importance of religion in daily life and frequency of personal prayer. All variables on 0 (never/not important at
all) to 4 (more than once a week/extremely important/many times a day) scale. Low is defined as <= 1; high is
defined as >= 3. Respondents scoring 2 (moderate) on any measure are not included in percents, which is why
percents do not add to 100.

also turns out that it is extremely rare for emerging adults attending religious services (external) at high levels to not also simultaneously display high levels of internal religious commitment—less than *1 percent* of the sample could be classified into this high external/low internal category.

Let us examine this matter from a different angle. According to NSYR findings presented in figure 8.10, which compares changes in levels of religion between the first and third survey waves, only 7 percent of emerging adults who as teenagers were high on all three of the measures for service attendance, importance of faith, and personal prayer shifted to being high on the latter two (internal) but shifted to low levels of service attendance (external) five years later.[57] Respondents were much more likely to either remain highly religious on all counts or to drop down to low religion levels on all. It simply happens quite infrequently that emerging adults sustain high internal but simultaneously fall to low external religious concerns and practices. It is true that external forms of religion tend among emerging adults to drop at more substantial rates than internal forms. But as a reliable broad generalization, for most emerging adults, religious life appears to be an all-or-nothing proposition. Only small percentages of emerging adults maintain highly inconsistent levels of religious expression between the internal and external dimensions of

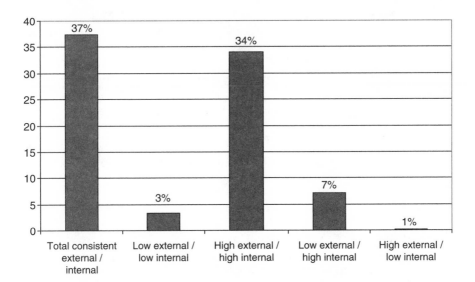

Figure 8.10. Percentage of Emerging Adults Who Were High External and High Internal Religion at Wave 1 Reporting High versus Low External and/or Internal Religious Expression at Wave 3 (N = 880)

Source: National Surveys of Youth and Religion 2002–2003, 2007–2008.

Note: External is measured by frequency of attendance at religious services; internal is measured with reported importance of religion in daily life and frequency of personal prayer. All variables on 0 (never/not important at all) to 4 (more than once a week/extremely important/many times a day) scale. Respondents considered high external and internal at Wave 1 if they score 3 or 4 on attendance, importance, and prayer. Low in Wave 3 is defined as <= 1; high is defined as >= 3. Respondents scoring 2 (moderate) on any measure are not included in percents, which is why percents do not add to 100.

their religious lives. For most, when subjective, private, internal religious life is strong, so also is their external, public expression of and participation in religion. Conversely, when external religion is weak, in most cases so is their subjective, private, internal religion. Therefore, certain people interested in seeing strong religious and spiritual lives among emerging adults and who wish to take comfort in the hope that religion remains subjectively robust for them even when they have dramatically reduced participating in more objective, public expressions of faith are not, we see, supported in that hope by the empirical evidence. For most emerging adults, strong religion comes in fairly coherent packages—they basically either have it internally and externally or they do not in either. Strong religion on the inside, when it exists, is, for the majority, accompanied by strong religion on the outside.

CONCLUSION

Standing back and reviewing this chapter's findings about religious trajectories from the teenage to the emerging adult years, what has been revealed? First, it is apparent that among a host of possibly significant factors operative during the teenage years, certain ones powerfully shape emerging adult outcomes, others are significant but not as consistent or potent, and yet others exert little to no influence on outcomes. Frequent teenage personal prayer, for instance, is more influential than having a lot of religious friends, and both are more important than going on missions or service trips. Likewise, having highly religious parents matters more than attending Sunday school, but both of those are more significant than attending a religious high school. Sorting out details about the relative influence of these various factors advances substantive knowledge of religious transitions during these years. Second, it is apparent that the most influential of these shaping factors are not only technically significant statistically but make differences of sizeable magnitudes in substantive outcomes. Among these are personal prayer, parental religious commitment, importance of faith, religious doubts, and personal religious experiences. The variance observed in emerging adult religious outcomes related to these most crucial factors is very large. They really do seem to make important differences. Third, it is apparent that in the transition from the teenage to the emerging adult years, the religious lives of youth in the process are not thrown up into the air to land in a random jumble. To the contrary, where youth end up religiously as emerging adults is highly governed by the nature of their religious upbringings, commitments, and experiences in earlier years. Most lives during this transition into emerging adulthood, in other words, reflect a great amount of continuity with the past. Emerging adulthood does, of course, involve many transitions, but many of them do not radically alter religious lives; and in most cases whatever religious change there is does not outweigh the continuity. In other words, the religious lives of youth during this period reflect a lot more stability and consistency than many seem to have previously realized, compared to the amount of change and upheaval that has so often been assumed.

Fourth, we have seen that the important factors shaping emerging adult outcomes noted above tend *not* to operate in isolation with sufficient independent effects on outcomes but rather conglomerate in various combinations to exert their strongest effects. In order to understand who in the transition from the teenage to the emerging adult years ends up among the most highly religious at the end of five years, it is therefore necessary to study not only independent effects of individual variables but also different configurations of factors that most likely lead to the same outcome. General factors that seem consistently to be at work are strong relational ties to religious faith, embrace of and commitment to religious faith, and the frequent practice of religious devotion. Combinations of these factors are also most important in determining who among the most highly religious teenagers will remain highly religious as emerging adults and who will shift down to the less religious half of emerging adults. Causal thinking, in other words, needs to consider not only isolated influences but also conjunctural or combinational causation. Fifth, this chapter has also shown that researchers can and ought to move beyond simply identifying statistical associations between correlated variables and toward actually theorizing the real causal social mechanisms at work "beneath" and giving rise to those associations, as well as they can be understood. Researchers need to move beyond the simple fact *that* certain factors are statistically correlated toward much fuller understandings of *why* and *how* they are correlated. This chapter has taken steps in that direction, although more mechanisms-focused research and theorizing is clearly needed to improve social scientific understanding of these matters. Sixth, this chapter has shown that entire age cohorts of youth can be disaggregated into distinct trajectories of religious stability, decline, and growth. Descriptive summary statistics about group aggregates often cover over the fact that different subgroups are actually doing very different things. Using growth mixture modeling, we showed that about half of today's emerging adults have sustained religiously stable lives over five years, at distinctly high, medium, and low levels; that most of the balance has declined religiously, either moderately or sharply, during the same time; and that a small group (about 3 to 6 percent) has significantly increased in religious faith and practice since the teenage years. That is important to know. Analytical methods that combine those different types into single groups and report undifferentiated summary statistics about them fail to reveal some of the most important differences among divergent subgroups. There are in fact dominant trends well worth knowing. But divergent tendencies and countertrends exist that also need to be seen and understood.

Seventh, this chapter has shown that of the approximately 70 percent of youth who at some time or other before mid–emerging adulthood commit to live their lives for God, the vast majority appear to do so early in life, apparently before the age of 14. Some make first commitments to God during their teenage years and others as emerging adults, but these are the minority. Most make their first commitments to God as children or during the preteen or very early teen years. Again, many religious trajectories followed in the course of life's development seem to be formed early on in life. Furthermore,

eighth, this chapter has shown that going to college no longer seems to corrode the religious faith and practice of students as it did in decades past. New
evidence is accumulating, including findings shown in this chapter, that for
various reasons, since the 1990s, higher education has not been undermining
the religion of students as it did for prior generations. Given the importance of
higher education in forming American society, class structure, and culture, this
change will likely have significant implications for the future of religion in the
United States. Finally, ninth, this chapter has shown that internal, subjective
religion and external, public religion tend strongly to go together in coherent packages. The NSYR's findings indicate that the common idea that many
emerging adults remain subjectively highly committed to religious faith even
though their outward religious practices significantly contract is false, a myth.
When the public practice of religion declines among emerging adults, for the
vast majority, their internal, subjective interest in faith does as well. Religion,
it would seem, tends to be lived in fairly consistent bundles of expression and
engagement.

To summarize most briefly, religious outcomes in emerging adulthood are
not random happenstances about which all bets are off after age 18. Instead,
they often flow quite predictably from formative religious influences that
shape persons' lives in earlier years. The transition into emerging adulthood
is clearly accompanied by a significant amount of religious decline among
many. But even that decline is quite predictable, using information about the
set of the most important factors that lead to decline. Furthermore, the lives
of many teenagers who are transitioning into the emerging adult years reflect
a lot more religious stability and continuity than is commonly realized. Everything simply does not change. The past continues to shape the future. This is
important to know, because it means that religious commitments, practices,
and investments made during childhood and the teenage years, by parents and
others in families and religious communities, matter—they make a difference.
Appreciating the stabilities and continuities that usually override unpredictable changes also reinforces the basic sociological insight that people's lives
are profoundly formed by the social networks and institutions that socialize
them, that the relational and social structures that compose and order life are
not easily changed or inexplicably made irrelevant. Again, who people are is
very much a product of where they are socially located, of what social and
relational forces have formed their lives. And who people are usually does not
randomly and unaccountably change over time. What people have been in the
past is generally the best indicator of why they are what they are in the present
and what they will likely be in the future. That is a fact that needs to condition
the understanding of emerging adult religion.

9

Religious Faith and Emerging
Adult Life Outcomes

D OES RELIGIOUS FAITH AND PRACTICE make any difference in the
lives of contemporary emerging adults? Are more highly religious emerging adults visibly different in how they live their lives from their less religious
peers? In short, does religion even *matter* when it comes to practical outcomes
in the lives of 18- to 23-year-olds today? Or do most emerging adults end up
living pretty much the same regardless of their religious identities and commitments? This chapter addresses those questions and brings to bear solid
data from the NSYR to respond to them. The short answer to these questions
that our analyses of the data yield is yes; religion definitely makes a significant
difference in the lives of emerging adults in many ways—but it does so only
among certain types and generally only at the highest end of religious faith
and practice. The following pages unpack and explain this idea.

MAJOR RELIGIOUS TRADITIONS REVEAL FEW DIFFERENCES

We began our analysis of these questions by examining possible differences
in emerging adult life outcomes across major American religious traditions
as measured by the state-of-the-art categorization system used by sociologists
today.[1] This is a congregation- and denomination-based method of religious
categorization, not one that relies on doctrinal beliefs or self-identification. By
this method, emerging adults are categorized into one or another of the major
traditions according to the specific denomination of the particular religious
congregation they attend or are most closely associated with. These traditions,

again, are conservative Protestant, mainline Protestant, black Protestant, Catholic, LDS, Jewish, other religion, and not religious. These are the same religious tradition categories used in the analyses of chapter 4, except grouped to reflect emerging adults' religious affiliations at the Wave 3 survey. We then examined whether emerging adults' belonging to one or another of those religious traditions made any difference in average percents calculated on a variety of survey measures concerning life outcomes. These included the areas of relationships with parents, education, employment, debt, participation in social activities, sexual behaviors, cohabitation, pregnancy, drugs, alcohol and tobacco use, pornography viewing, financial giving, volunteering and community service, informal helping behaviors, physical health, subjective well-being, gratitude, guilt feelings, purpose, life satisfaction, locus of control, mass consumerism, and more.

It turned out that this approach to the analysis revealed relatively few and only small religious differences in such life outcomes, when religion was measured as different major religious traditions. In short, being in one or another of these religious traditions generally did not greatly increase or decrease the probabilities of being different from others in other traditions on this variety of life outcomes. Very often conservative Protestants, for example, were not terribly different from mainline Protestants or Catholics or the nonreligious. In many cases, LDS emerging adults exhibited somewhat fewer risk behaviors, and Jewish teenagers exhibited somewhat more risk behaviors. But most of those differences were minor. The emerging adults in most of those religious traditions simply do not look that much different from nonreligious emerging adults. That is because each of these traditions embraces both a wide range of levels of personal religious belief, commitment, and practice and a wide range of attitudes and behaviors concerning the life outcomes in question. Therefore, emerging adults simply being conservative Protestant or Catholic or in some other category in this method per se does not make them especially different with regard to the life outcomes under consideration. For the sake of economy of space and focus of interest in this chapter, we therefore do not present the tables showing all of those minor differences here.[2]

The fact that we did not find large and significant differences in life outcomes across those religious traditions does not, however, mean that religion makes no difference in the life results of emerging adults. It only means that these differences are not well sorted by using major religious traditions as categories. We can and do, in fact, observe major differences in emerging adult life outcomes when we instead focus not on differences of religious tradition but on differences in religious commitment and practices. Again, because each religious tradition comprises a wide range of internal variance regarding commitment to religious practices, differences in outcomes are not evident when using the standard religious tradition categorization method. However, when we use a method directly distinguishing different types and levels of religious commitment and practice, we see real differences in life outcomes among emerging adults. We will show these next.

PERSONAL RELIGIOUS COMMITMENT REVEALS
SIGNIFICANT DIFFERENCES

Here, following the same method used in chapter 7 of *Soul Searching*, we sort respondents into four different religious types. The goal is to devise a measure of religious difference that pulls the various dimensions of religiosity together into meaningful categories. In order to be as clear and crisp as possible in our presentation of findings and in a way that reflects common understandings of religious types of people, we have again created four types of religious and nonreligious emerging adults to compare across to look for possible differences in their life outcomes. These categories have been created around common cultural understandings of specific religious types of people. To fit into any of the categories, the respondents have to reflect a number of specific characteristics that qualify them for that category. All of those who do fit those characteristics then belong together in that religious type, and those who don't do not. Specifically, we have created and defined for analysis these four categories:

The Devoted (5% of Emerging Adults)

Attend religious services weekly or more often
Faith is very or extremely important in everyday life
Feel very or extremely close to God
Pray a few times a week or more often
Read scripture once or twice a month or more often[3]

The Regular (14.3% of Emerging Adults)

Attend religious services two to three times a month or weekly
Faith ranges from very to not very important in everyday life
Closeness to God, prayer, and scripture reading are variable but less religious than these criteria for the Devoted

The Sporadic (17.9% of Emerging Adults)

Attend religious services a few times a year to monthly
Faith ranges from somewhat to not very important in everyday life
Closeness to God, prayer, and scripture reading are variable

The Disengaged (25.5% of Emerging Adults)

Never attend religious services, or do so only a few or many times a year and identify as "not religious"
Faith is somewhat, not very, or not important in everyday life
Feel only somewhat close to God or less close
Pray one to two times a month or less often
Read scripture one to two times a month or less often

Sixty-three percent of U.S. emerging adults fit one of these four ideal-type categories. A bit more than 37 percent do not fit cleanly into one of these four and so are categorized as "mixed." Some of them might, for example, satisfy four of the features defining a "Devoted" emerging adult but not the fifth, so closely approximate the type categorized but do not perfectly fit the type, so are not included. All of those who do fit are included in the categories. The following analyses will not focus on those who do not fit cleanly into one of the categories. This means that not all emerging adults are included in the analyses represented in tables 9.1–16. There are nevertheless three important advantages of using this ideal-type approach. First, the types we use to compare them reflect the concrete way many ordinary Americans normally think about categories of religious people—extra-devoted believers, regular church-goers, sporadic participants, and so on—much more so than any abstract, numerical "scale of religiosity" we might construct from multiple survey variables. Second, we can more clearly identify any differences that exist between the 63 percent of emerging adults who do fit these quintessentially distinct kinds of religious and nonreligious types, without having the comparisons and differences clouded by more ambiguous cases. Third, by combining the multiple dimensions of religiosity into a single set of type comparisons, instead of examining each dimension separately, we can keep the number of tables of findings in this chapter to a reasonable limit.[4] (To examine the distribution of major religious traditions and demographics in relation to these types, see tables A.3 and A.4.)

Many of the outcomes we will examine here are also known to sometimes be affected by age, gender, race, family structure, parents' education, and so on. And the religious types used in this chapter's analyses also reflect significant, though not major, differences among emerging adults on some of those demographic variables. In order to remove the possible effects of those related variables influencing the outcomes indirectly through the religious types, we also use, when testing for statistically significant differences between the religious types on outcome measures, multivariate regression analyses to control for eight key demographic variables: emerging adult age, sex, race, region of residence, parental education, parental marital status, individual income, and parental assistance with expenses. Thus, some of the observed percentage differences between Devoted and Disengaged emerging adults, for instance, may be due to the fact that the former comprises more females than the latter. But having used appropriate regression techniques to control for gender and the seven other related variables, we can be confident that differences across the religious types are statistically significant even when the effects of these demographic variables are removed. This reduces worries that the observed differences across the religious types are really being produced by nonreligious factors and so making the religion association spurious. The reference category for all comparisons is the Disengaged emerging adult group. Numbers for the Devoted, the Regular, and the Sporadic that are statistically significantly different from those of the Disengaged are marked in bold. Numbers reported not in bold are not statistically significantly different from those of the Disengaged. When numbers in the tables are in bold, therefore, because we have controlled for eight other most likely possible confounding factors, what appear to be differences across religious types can thus confidently be understood as real differences in fact.

Relationships with Parents

Table 9.1 begins our analysis of religion and life outcomes by examining emerging adults' relationships with their parents. The first thing we see there is that religion makes no difference in the probability of emerging adults still being in contact with their mothers and fathers. The vast majority of all types remain in contact with both of their parents. Nevertheless, the rest of the table reveals statistically significant differences between the Devoted and the Disengaged when it comes to the quality of relationships with parents. The Devoted emerging adults are more likely to feel close to, get along well with, talk about personal subjects with, and feel well understood by their mothers than are the Disengaged emerging adults.[5] The same is true about emerging adults' relationships with their fathers, except for getting along well with fathers, where we see no significant differences. By comparison, neither the Regular nor the Sporadic are significantly different from the Disengaged. The Devoted alone across these types, as a group, tend to have a better quality of relationships with their parents. In some cases, the differences are rather modest, but in others they are more substantial. Altogether, however, the consistent story of table 9.1 is that the Devoted have noticeably better relationships with both their mothers and fathers than do the Disengaged. There are

Table 9.1. Quality of Parental Relationships of Emerging Adults by Religious Types, Ages 18–23 (Percents)

	U.S.	Religious type			
		Devoted	Regulars	Sporadic	Disengaged
Still in contact with mother	98	98	98	99	98
Still in contact with father	94	96	94	94	94
Feels extremely or very close to mother	76	**88**	75	71	71
Gets along extremely or very well with mother	74	**83**	72	70	71
Talks to mother about personal subjects very often	26	**35**	22	21	20
Feels mother understands one very much	46	**60**	43	45	36
Feels extremely or very close to father	56	**64**	54	54	49
Gets along extremely or very well with father	64	68	61	64	60
Talks to father about personal subjects very often	9	**12**	10	5	6
Feels father understands one very much	33	**41**	27	31	26
Parental breakups					
None	58	**76**	65	61	51
2+ times	15	**11**	13	15	16

Source: National Survey of Youth and Religion, 2007–2008.
Note: Percentages are rounded to the nearest whole number. Differences that are statistically significant at the 0.05 level from the Disengaged category after controlling for seven control variables (age, sex, race, region of residence, parental education, individual income, and parental assistance with expenses) are in bold.

likely many reasons for this. However, one of the specific mechanisms linking religion and quality of parental relationships for emerging adults may be differences in the number of parental breakups that emerging adults have personally encountered, reported at the bottom of table 9.1. There we see across that the more highly religious emerging adults are, the less likely they are to have experienced during their lives any parental breakup and, for those who have, multiple parental breakups—both of which tend to reduce the overall quality of parental relationships. The Devoted, for instance, are 25 percent less likely to have endured a parental breakup than the Disengaged.[6] This factor probably helps to explain some, though not all, of the difference observed in this table.

Giving and Volunteering

Table 9.2 examines giving and volunteering behaviors among emerging adults. Here see some very large differences between religious types appear. Both the Devoted and the Regular are significantly more likely than the Disengaged to have given more than $50 to an organization or cause in the previous year—with the percent of the Devoted being *three times* larger (75 versus 25 percent) than that of the Disengaged. All religious types were also much more likely

Table 9.2. Giving and Volunteering Behavior of Emerging Adults by Religious Type, Ages 18–23 (Percents)

	U.S.	Religious type			
		Devoted	Regular	Sporadic	Disengaged
Gave more than $50 to organization or causes in last year	34	**75**	**40**	26	25
Volunteered for community service that was not required	40	**67**	**49**	43	30
Frequency of volunteer activities in past year					
10 or more times	12	**26**	10	**14**	9
1–2 times	13	8	18	14	12
Helped homeless or needy informally, not through an organization					
A lot	12	**19**	11	7	7
A little or none	55	**44**	60	66	69
Proportion of five closest friends who volunteer for community service					
None	51	**20**	49	50	58
Less than half	31	**38**	36	35	29
Half or more	18	**42**	15	14	13

Source: National Survey of Youth and Religion, 2007–2008.
Note: Percentages are rounded to the nearest whole number. Differences that are statistically significant at the 0.05 level from the Disengaged category after controlling for seven control variables (age, sex, race, region of residence, parental education, individual income, and parental assistance with expenses) are in bold.

than the Disengaged to have volunteered for community service that was not required by a school program or legal sentence. The percentage of the Devoted is more than twice that of the Disengaged (67 versus 30 percent). The higher end types also more often helped homeless or needy people informally, not through an organization, during the previous year than did the Disengaged. Again, there are likely numerous causes of these differences. But the bottom set of numbers in table 9.2 suggest one of them: that more highly religious emerging adults tend to have close friends who also volunteer and do community service. Whereas nearly 60 percent of the Disengaged have closest friends none of whom volunteer for community service, only 20 percent of the Devoted have the same. And while 42 percent of the Devoted have half or more of their friends who volunteer, only 13 percent of the Disengaged have the same. The most religious emerging adults thus are more likely volunteer for community service, in part, because they have strong friendship networks that encourage it.

Organized Activities and Social Networking Websites

Table 9.3 examines emerging adult participation in organized group activities and in social networking websites. There we see religious differences in the number of organized activities in which emerging adults are involved. The Devoted, for example, are involved in an average of 2.4 activities, the Disengaged only 1.2. Part of this difference is due to more religious emerging adults participating in activities sponsored by religious organizations. Even so, the more religious types at every level still participate in an average absolute number of more activities not sponsored by religious organizations than do the Disengaged. In short, religious emerging adults participate in more

Table 9.3. Organized Activity Involvement and Online Social Networking of Emerging Adults by Religious Type, Ages 18–23 (Percents)

	U.S.	Religious type			
		Devoted	Regulars	Sporadic	Disengaged
Total number of organized activities involved with	1.6	**2.4**	**1.8**	**1.8**	1.2
Number of organized activities sponsored by a religious organization (not including worship or youth group)	0.3	**1.1**	**0.4**	**0.1**	0
Number of organized activities not sponsored by a religious organization	1.2	**1.3**	**1.4**	**1.6**	1.2
Member of a social networking website	76	**69**	81	83	77
Visits a social networking website once a day or more (members of websites only)	53	**46**	54	57	58

Source: National Survey of Youth and Religion, 2007–2008.
Note: Percentages are rounded to the nearest whole number. Differences that are statistically significant at the 0.05 level from the Disengaged category after controlling for seven control variables (age, sex, race, region of residence, parental education, individual income, and parental assistance with expenses) are in bold.

religious and nonreligious activities than do the religiously Disengaged. The religious differences work in the opposite direction when it comes in participating in social networking Internet websites, like MySpace and Facebook. The Devoted are significantly less likely, while the Sporadic are more likely, than the Disengaged to be members of such websites. And among those who are members, the Devoted are also less likely than the other groups to visit their websites daily or more often. In short, the most religious emerging adults are the most likely to participate in face-to-face organized activities and the least likely to participate in social networking websites.

Moral Beliefs

The NSYR third wave survey also asked respondents about their moral beliefs and concerns, the results of which are reported in table 9.4. We see, first, that higher levels of religiousness are associated with greater resistance to the idea that it is okay to break moral rules if doing so works to one's advantage and one can get away with it. Only 4 percent of the Devoted agreed with that statement, compared to nearly one-quarter of the Disengaged. Religion is also significantly associated with belief in moral relativism, with nearly four times the number of the Disengaged than the Devoted (63 versus 16 percent), for instance, agreeing that morals are relative, that there are no definite rights and wrongs for everybody. Similarly, the more religious emerging adults are significantly more likely than the Disengaged to personally care about equality between different racial groups and about the needs of the elderly and the poor—with differences of 22, 24, and 30 percentage points between the religiously Devoted and the Disengaged. In various ways, then, differences in

Table 9.4. Moral Orientation of Emerging Adults by Religious Type, Ages 18–23 (Percents)

	U.S.	Religious type			
		Devoted	Regulars	Sporadic	Disengaged
Believes it is okay to break moral rules if it works to one's advantage and one can get away with it	16	**4**	**10**	17	22
Believes that morals are relative, that there are no definite rights and wrongs for everybody	47	**16**	**40**	**52**	63
Personally cares very much about equality between different racial groups	46	**65**	49	40	43
Personally cares very much about the needs of the elderly	53	**68**	**54**	40	44
Personally cares very much about the needs of poor people in the United States	51	**71**	**50**	37	41

Source: National Survey of Youth and Religion, 2007–2008.
Note: Percentages are rounded to the nearest whole number. Differences that are statistically significant at the 0.05 level from the Disengaged category after controlling for seven control variables (age, sex, race, region of residence, parental education, individual income, and parental assistance with expenses) are in bold.

religious commitment among emerging adults distinguish disparities in moral beliefs and concerns.

Risk Behaviors

Table 9.5 presents findings on differences in risk behaviors among emerging adults along religious lines. The Devoted and the Regular are much less likely to drink alcohol regularly and much less likely to binge-drink. More than four times the proportion of the Disengaged than the Devoted drink alcohol weekly or more often, for example. And more than eight times the proportion of the same groups binge-drank alcohol three or more times during the two weeks prior to the survey. Nine out of ten of the Devoted never binge drink alcohol, compared to only 41 percent of the Disengaged. More religious emerging adults are also less likely to be surrounded by friends who drink a lot of alcohol or do drugs—with a 33.5 percent difference between the religiously Devoted and the Disengaged. Likewise, the most religious are also much less likely to smoke cigarettes and marijuana. The vast majority of the Devoted never smoke either, whereas significant minorities of the Sporadic and the Disengaged smoke both weekly or more often. Furthermore, while 26–28 percent

Table 9.5. Risk Behavior of Emerging Adults by Religious Type, Ages 18–23 (Percents)

	U.S.	Religious type			
		Devoted	Regulars	Sporadic	Disengaged
Drinks alcohol					
Weekly or more	35	**11**	**28**	48	48
A few times a year or never	37	**75**	**43**	21	22
Frequency of alcohol binge-drinking					
Three or more times in the last 2 weeks	17	**3**	**12**	24	25
Never	53	**90**	**58**	39	41
Percent of five closest friends who do drugs or drink a lot of alcohol	40	**16**	**33**	47	50
Smokes cigarettes					
Weekly or more	24	**1**	**20**	27	28
Never	67	**90**	**73**	62	61
Smokes marijuana					
Weekly or more	12	**0**	**5**	15	18
Never	70	**98**	**77**	65	58
Has been in a serious fight more than once in the last two years	26	**12**	27	28	26
Likes to take risks	72	**64**	73	79	74

Source: National Survey of Youth and Religion, 2007–2008.
Note: Percentages are rounded to the nearest whole number. Differences that are statistically significant at the 0.05 level from the Disengaged category after controlling for seven control variables (age, sex, race, region of residence, parental education, individual income, and parental assistance with expenses) are in bold.

of emerging adults in the other types had been in more than one serious fight during the previous two years, only 12 percent of the Devoted had. Only on the survey question asking respondents whether they like to take risks or not do we find no significant patterns of differences across the groups.

Physical Health and Subjective Well-Being

How does all of this translate into measures of health and subjective well-being? Table 9.6 shows that the more religious emerging adults are generally healthier, happy with their bodies, and thoughtful about the meaning of life than the least religious. The Devoted, for example, rate 21 percent higher on a self-rated scale of physical health than do the Disengaged. The Devoted are also 11 percent higher on normal body weight as measured by objective scales of Body Mass Index relying on calculations of body height and weight, as well as lower on being overweight and obese, though not statistically significantly so on the latter two. Greater religious commitment and practice are also statistically significantly associated with feeling happier about one's own body and physical appearance. More than twice the proportion of religiously Disengaged emerging adults compared to the Devoted are either somewhat or very unhappy about their bodies. Likewise, the more

Table 9.6. Health and Subjective Well-being of Emerging Adults by Religious Type, Ages 18–23 (Percents)

	U.S.	Religious type			
		Devoted	Regulars	Sporadic	Disengaged
Physical health is excellent or very good	63	**79**	64	62	58
BMI categories					
Normal	56	**66**	56	59	55
Overweight	27	22	24	29	28
Obese	13	10	16	9	13
Feelings about own body and physical appearance					
Very or somewhat happy	73	**82**	74	72	65
Very or somewhat unhappy	18	**11**	16	17	23
Thinks about and plans for the future					
Very or fairly often	82	**86**	82	81	78
Rarely or never	4	**2**	3	3	5
Thinks about the meaning of life					
Very or fairly often	44	**63**	45	32	32
Rarely or never	24	**10**	24	31	33

Source: National Survey of Youth and Religion, 2007–2008.
Note: Percentages are rounded to the nearest whole number. Differences that are statistically significant at the 0.05 level from the Disengaged category after controlling for seven control variables (age, sex, race, region of residence, parental education, individual income, and parental assistance with expenses) are in bold.

religious emerging adults here both more often think about and plan for the future and more often think about the meaning of life than the least religious emerging adults (although the clear differences are only statistically significant for the latter measure).

Mental Health and Social Bonding

The NSYR third wave survey also asked emerging adults questions about their mental health and bonding in social relationships. Table 9.7 shows that stronger religion among emerging adults is positively associated in nearly linear progression with both rarely or never feeling sad or depressed and rarely or never feeling that life is meaningless. In addition, the more religious emerging adults are more likely to report feeling loved and accepted by others for who they are, not feeling alone and misunderstood by others, and never feeling invisible to other people. These differences are not enormous, but they are noticeable and significant. At the same time, questions about the frequency of feeling guilty in life and having experienced a traumatic event in the previous two years reflect no patterns of religious differences. At the very least, this reveals that the observed differences in emerging adults feeling sad or depressed, social isolation, and meaningless in life are not due to differences in experiencing the shock of traumatic events, since just as many of the Devoted as the Disengaged had suffered traumatic events.

Table 9.7. Mental Health and Bonding in Social Relationships of Emerging Adults by Religious Type, Ages 18–23 (Percents)

	U.S.	Religious type			
		Devoted	Regulars	Sporadic	Disengaged
Rarely or never feels sad or depressed	63	**71**	**69**	**66**	61
How often life feels meaningless					
Very or fairly often	6	**2**	**4**	**4**	8
Rarely or never	80	**88**	**85**	**83**	74
Feels loved and accepted a lot	73	**82**	**76**	**76**	69
Never feels alone and misunderstood	42	**51**	**46**	**43**	35
Never feels invisible	69	**73**	66	**72**	66
How often feels guilty about things in life					
Very or fairly often	21	20	24	**14**	18
Rarely or never	41	37	39	**49**	44
Has experienced a traumatic event in the last 2 years	48	49	**44**	44	49

Source: National Survey of Youth and Religion, 2007–2008.
Note: Percentages are rounded to the nearest whole number. Differences that are statistically significant at the 0.05 level from the Disengaged category after controlling for seven control variables (age, sex, race, region of residence, parental education, individual income, and parental assistance with expenses) are in bold.

Purpose and Gratitude

Tables 9.8–11 examine religious differences in four different important life outcomes using concepts and measures that are well established in social science research: sense of purpose, gratitude, locus of control, and life satisfaction.[7] In keeping with the pattern of results observed so far, the most religious emerging adults generally score higher on these four life outcome measures. Table 9.8, for instance, shows that the religious emerging adult is significantly less likely than the Disengaged to say that life often lacks clear goals or directions, that he or she does not have a good sense of what he or she wants to accomplish, and that he or she is someone who wanders aimlessly through life. All of those separate differences are statistically significant, as are the scores of the three measures when combined together into one scale of purpose. The

Table 9.8. Sense of Purpose of Emerging Adults by Religious Type, Ages 18–23 (Percents)

	U.S.	Religious type			
		Devoted	Regulars	Sporadic	Disengaged
Life often seems to lack clear goals or directions	25	**15**	**24**	**19**	27
Does not have a good sense of what one wants to accomplish	21	**9**	**17**	**18**	25
Not someone who wanders aimlessly through life	82	**93**	**83**	**88**	80
Average purpose scale score	11.4	**12.5**	**11.5**	**11.7**	11.2

Source: National Survey of Youth and Religion, 2007–2008.
Note: Percentages are rounded to the nearest whole number. Differences that are statistically significant at the 0.05 level from the Disengaged category after controlling for seven control variables (age, sex, race, region of residence, parental education, individual income, and parental assistance with expenses) are in bold.

Table 9.9. Feelings of Gratitude of Emerging Adults by Religious Type, Ages 18–23 (Percents)

	U.S.	Religious type			
		Devoted	Regulars	Sporadic	Disengaged
Long amounts of time go by before feeling grateful to something or someone	41	**28**	**38**	42	46
Does not see much to be grateful for in the world	5	**2**	**2**	5	7
Has so much in life to be thankful for	98	**100**	99	99	97
Average gratitude scale score	12.0	**13.0**	**12.2**	**12.0**	11.7

Source: National Survey of Youth and Religion, 2007–2008.
Note: Percentages are rounded to the nearest whole number. Differences that are statistically significant at the 0.05 level from the Disengaged category after controlling for seven control variables (age, sex, race, region of residence, parental education, individual income, and parental assistance with expenses) are in bold.

most religious, in other words, appear to have the most purpose in life, while the least have the least purpose. The same pattern is evident in table 9.9, which examines differences in feelings of gratitude. By margins of difference that are statistically and sometimes substantively significant, the Devoted tend to feel gratitude more frequently, see more in the world to be grateful for, and think they have much in life for which to feel thankful. They therefore, again, score significantly higher in scores on the combined gratitude scale.

Locus of Control and Life Satisfaction

Table 9.10 reveals fewer significant differences across religious groups in measures of locus of control, that is in feeling generally capable of exerting influence in life and so personally contributing to the determination of events. Only on one question, about feeling helpless in dealing with life's problems, do the more religious stand out with greater locus of control. On three other questions, religious emerging adults are either marginally different or not different at all. Still, when the questions are combined into individual average scores on a single locus-of-control scale, these accumulated marginal difference add up to a small but statistically significant difference between the Devoted and the Disengaged, the former of whom exhibit higher overall locus of control. Table 9.11 reveals stronger differences between religious emerging adults and the religiously Disengaged on measures of overall life satisfaction. In short, the more religious emerging adults are, the more likely they are to report that their lives are close to ideal, that the conditions of their lives are excellent, that they feel satisfied with their personal lives, and that they have gotten the important things in life. Again, the observed differences are not enormous, but they are generally sizeable and significant. Differences in

Table 9.10. Locus of Control of Emerging Adults by Religious Type, Ages 18–23 (Percents)

	U.S.	Religious type		
		Devoted	Regulars	Sporadic	Disengaged
Feels one has little control over things that happen	27	26	24	22	25
Feels there is no way to solve some personal problems	27	19	29	27	25
Feels there is little one can do to change many of the important things in life	23	17	22	21	22
Often feels helpless when dealing with problems of life	23	**12**	20	19	24
Average locus of control scale score	14.8	15.7	14.8	15.0	14.8

Source: National Survey of Youth and Religion, 2007–2008.
Note: Percentages are rounded to the nearest whole number. Differences that are statistically significant at the 0.05 level from the Disengaged category after controlling for seven control variables (age, sex, race, region of residence, parental education, individual income, and parental assistance with expenses) are in bold.

Table 9.11. Life Satisfaction of Emerging Adults by Religious
Type, Ages 18–23 (Percents)

	U.S.	Religious type			
		Devoted	Regulars	Sporadic	Disengaged
Feels that life is close to ideal	69	**86**	72	72	63
Feels that the conditions of life are excellent	74	**88**	76	77	70
Feels satisfied with personal life	87	**94**	88	90	85
Have gotten the important things in life	70	**82**	74	70	65
Average life satisfaction scale score	14.6	**16.0**	14.7	14.7	14.1

Source: National Survey of Youth and Religion, 2007–2008.
Note: Percentages are rounded to the nearest whole number. Differences that are statistically significant at the 0.05 level from the Disengaged category after controlling for seven control variables (age, sex, race, region of residence, parental education, individual income, and parental assistance with expenses) are in bold.

scores on the single life-satisfaction scale are also significant. In these four tables, then, we see fairly consistent and meaningful differences among emerging adults in their experiences of purpose, gratitude, personal control, and satisfaction in life that are associated with religious differences. The more religiously committed and practicing the emerging adults are, the more purpose, gratefulness, control, and satisfaction with life they feel.

Education, Employment, Debt, and Mass Consumerism

Table 9.12 looks at four indicators of education, employment, and debt among emerging adults. On two of the four measures, the Devoted are significantly different from the Disengaged—they are more likely to have completed some college or more education, and they are less likely to be unemployed. Among emerging adults not enrolled in school, however, we observe no differences between types in average number of hours worked. Nor do we see differences on credit card debt, either in the average dollars owed or in dollars owed as a percentage of personal income. In both cases, the differences between the two highest religious categories and the Disengaged are substantial but not statistically significant after taking into account possible related effects of the eight other control variables. Religion thus seems to make a difference in educational attainment and employment but not in hours worked and credit card debt.

Table 9.13 focuses on emerging adults' attitudes toward mass consumerism. Fewer of the Devoted and the Regular than of the Disengaged say they would be happier if they could afford to buy more things. Furthermore, fewer of the Devoted than of the Disengaged say they admire people who own expensive homes, cars, and clothes. Likewise, fewer of the same group report that the things they own say a lot about how well they are doing in life. The fourth measure, however, on shopping and buying giving a lot of pleasure, does not reveal the same pattern of answers. Again, the Devoted emerging adults score statistically significantly lower on the combined mass consumerism scale than do the Disengaged.

Table 9.12. Education, Employment, and Debt of Emerging Adults by Religious Type, Ages 18–23 (Percents)

	U.S.	Religious type			
		Devoted	Regulars	Sporadic	Disengaged
Highest level of education completed some college or more	66	**80**	65	73	68
Unemployed	13	**5**	12	12	14
Average work hours (among those not enrolled in school)	30	31	31	31	30
Credit card debt					
In average (mean) dollars	1,244	1,007	885	1,331	1,417
As percentage of personal income	17.3	12.3	8.8	26.3	20.3

Source: National Survey of Youth and Religion, 2007–2008.
Note: Percentages are rounded to the nearest whole number. Differences that are statistically significant at the 0.05 level from the Disengaged category after controlling for seven control variables (age, sex, race, region of residence, parental education, individual income, and parental assistance with expenses) are in bold.

Table 9.13. Attitudes about Consumerism of Emerging Adults by Religious Type, Ages 18–23 (Percents)

	U.S.	Religious type			
		Devoted	Regulars	Sporadic	Disengaged
Would be happier if could afford to buy more things	54	**30**	**51**	59	56
Admires people who own expensive homes, cars, and clothes	37	**22**	34	40	38
Feels that things owned say a lot about how well one is doing in life	47	**30**	50	43	45
Shopping and buying things gives a lot of pleasure	65	59	**68**	67	60
Average consumerism scale score	12.1	**10.6**	12.1	12.2	12.0

Source: National Survey of Youth and Religion, 2007–2008.
Note: Percentages are rounded to the nearest whole number. Differences that are statistically significant at the 0.05 level from the Disengaged category after controlling for seven control variables (age, sex, race, region of residence, parental education, individual income, and parental assistance with expenses) are in bold.

Pornography, Physical Involvements, and Cohabitation

Finally, Tables 9.14–16 examine various sexual outcomes in the lives of emerging adults. Table 9.14 begins with a question about the frequency of pornography viewing in the previous year. The Devoted and the Regular are noticeably less likely than the Disengaged to have viewed pornography more than five times and more likely never to have viewed pornography. (These results are statistically significant even after controlling for the sex and gender of the respondents in each group.) The Devoted and the Regular are also significantly less likely than the Disengaged to ever have willingly touched

Table 9.14. Sexual Activities of Emerging Adults by Religious
Type, Ages 18–23 (Percents)

	U.S.	Religious type			
		Devoted	Regulars	Sporadic	Disengaged
Frequency of viewing pornography in the last year					
More than five times	16	**6**	**13**	18	21
Never	50	**80**	**57**	43	41
Ever willingly touched private area of another person or been touched by another person in private area under clothes (only those never married)	85	**56**	**82**	89	89
Median number of people ever been physically involved with, more than holding hands and light kissing (only those never married)	3	**1**	3	4	4
Number of nights in the past 4 weeks spent overnight with a significant other (only those never married)					
None	56	**80**	**63**	47	50
1–8	29	**17**	**28**	36	30
9–20	9	**1**	**6**	12	12
21–28	6	**1**	**3**	5	8
Ever cohabited	27	**7**	**18**	**24**	31
Will likely marry person currently in a romantic relationship with (only those currently in a romantic relationship)	85	**97**	85	85	79
Has a lot or very many regrets over sexually intimate experiences (only those never married and physically involved)	10	**42**	**12**	5	4

Source: National Survey of Youth and Religion, 2007–2008.
Note: Percentages are rounded to the nearest whole number. Differences that are statistically significant at the 0.05 level from the Disengaged category after controlling for seven control variables (age, sex, race, region of residence, parental education, individual income, and parental assistance with expenses) are in bold.

the private areas of another person or been touched by another person in their private areas under their clothes, by differences of 33 and 17 percent, respectively. Fully 44 percent of Devoted report having never touched another or been touched by another under their clothes in private areas—a relatively remarkably high proportion, compared to the national average of 15 percent for the same status and 11 percent for the Disengaged. Furthermore, the types of emerging adults differ in the average number of people with whom they have ever been physically involved beyond the level of holding hands and light kissing, from one at the highest end of religion to four at the lowest end. When it comes to the number of nights spent overnight with a significant other in the previous four weeks, among the never-married the Devoted and the Regular are noticeably different in less frequently sleeping over with partners. Four out of five of the Devoted never had, compared to half of the Disengaged; only 1 percent of the Devoted had more than 21 times, compared to 8 percent of the Disengaged. Similar differences are observed on the matter of cohabitation outside of marriage. More than four times the proportion of the Disengaged have ever cohabited in their lives than the Devoted (31 versus 7 percent). Moreover, among those who are in romantic relationships, significantly higher proportions of the Devoted than other types expect to marry the person with whom they are currently in a relationship, and so presumably are in more committed relationships. At the same time, more highly religious emerging adults who are unmarried and have been physically involved are much more likely to express significant regrets over their sexually intimate experiences.

Oral Sex

Table 9.15 focuses on oral sex behaviors among emerging adults. There we see that the more religious never-married emerging adults, particularly the Devoted, are much less likely than the less religious never-married to have ever had oral sex (for example, 34 percent of the Devoted compared to 82 percent of the Disengaged). Of those who have had oral sex, the more religious were also somewhat older when they first had oral sex. Furthermore, the more

Table 9.15. Oral Sex Behavior of Emerging Adults by Religious Type, Never Married Ages 18–23

	U.S.	Religious type			
		Devoted	Regulars	Sporadic	Disengaged
Have had oral sex	71	**34**	**64**	79	82
Mean age of first oral sex (if has had oral sex)	16.2	**16.8**	**16.3**	16.1	16.0
Median number of oral sex partners (if has had oral sex)	3	**1**	**2**	3	3
Percent of oral sex partners in casual relationship (if has had oral sex)	30	**26**	**25**	36	36
Frequency of oral sex (if has had oral sex)					
Once	4	**10**	4	3	2
A few or several times	46	**56**	57	43	39
Many times	51	**34**	38	53	59
Recentness of oral sex (if has had oral sex)					
Last month	54	**29**	**52**	60	58
More than 1 year ago	9	**44**	7	6	8
Used protection against STDs during oral sex (if has had oral sex)?					
Every time	14	**19**	**17**	12	12
Never	52	**67**	**47**	56	55

Source: National Survey of Youth and Religion, 2007–2008.
Note: Percentages are rounded to the nearest whole number. Differences that are statistically significant at the 0.05 level from the Disengaged category after controlling for seven control variables (age, sex, race, region of residence, parental education, individual income, and parental assistance with expenses) are in bold.

religious emerging adults who have had oral sex have had on average fewer oral sex partners than the less religious (a median of one partner for the Devoted compared to three for the Sporadic and the Disengaged). And of those emerging adults who have had oral sex, the more religious are somewhat less likely to have been in only a casual relationship with their oral sex partners than were the less religious—at roughly one-quarter versus more than one-third, respectively. As for the amount of oral sex, for those emerging adults who have engaged in oral sex, the more religious are more likely to have had oral sex only once or a few times and less likely to have had oral sex many times than the less religious. In addition, among those who have ever had oral sex, the Devoted are much less likely than the other groups to have had oral sex within the previous month and much more likely to have had oral sex most recently more than one year ago. Finally, the Devoted are in simple percentages somewhat more likely than both the national average and the less religious to have used protection against sexually transmitted diseases both every time and never—although neither percent difference is statistically significant in a multivariate regression model.[8] To summarize the overall findings of table 9.15, then, high levels of religious commitment and practice among emerging adults are associated with less engagement in oral sex and, for those who have had oral sex, somewhat delayed age at first oral sex, fewer oral sex partners, less frequent and recent oral sex, and less oral sex in causal relationships. In brief, greater religiousness decreases oral sex behaviors.

Sexual Intercourse

Finally, table 9.16 presents findings on religious differences in sexual intercourse among never-married emerging adults. The findings are similar to those of table 9.15 on oral sex. Far fewer of the most religious never-married emerging adults have had sexual intercourse than have their least religious counterparts—compare 35 percent of the Devoted with 82 percent of the Disengaged. The more religious never-married who have had sexual intercourse also somewhat delayed their age at first sex on average; have had significantly fewer sexual partners on average; and have been significantly less likely to have had sexual intercourse in casual relationships. They are also significantly more likely to have had sexual intercourse only once, less likely to have had sex many times, less likely to have had sex during the month prior to completing the survey, and more likely to have had their most recent sex more than one year before. Still, only the never-married Regular are significantly more likely than the Disengaged to have used condoms to protect against sexually transmitted diseases. The Devoted never-married females are the most likely, at 93 percent, to have never been pregnant, just as the Devoted never-married males are the least likely to have gotten someone pregnant. Finally, the Devoted females are the least likely of all of the religious types, at 1 percent, to have ended a pregnancy with an abortion—although those differences are not statistically significant in a multivariate regression model. In summary, greater religious commitment and practice tends to significantly reduce sexual intercourse and pregnancy among never-married American emerging adults.

Table 9.16. Sexual Intercourse Behavior of Emerging Adults by Religious Type, Never Married Ages 18–23 (Percents)

	U.S.	Religious type			
		Devoted	Regulars	Sporadic	Disengaged
Has had sexual intercourse	73	**35**	**67**	77	82
Mean age of first sexual intercourse (if has had sex)	16.2	**17.0**	**16.4**	16.3	16.3
Median number of sex partners (if has had sex)	3	**2**	3	4	4
Percent of sexual partners in "casual" relationship (if has had sex)	36	27	29	39	39
Number of times respondent has had sexual intercourse (if has had sex)					
Once	2	**17**	**4**	1	1
A few or several times	32	**38**	**43**	28	26
Many times	64	**39**	**54**	70	71
Recentness of last sexual intercourse (if has had sex)					
Last month	66	**41**	**61**	73	69
More than 1 year ago	6	**30**	6	4	5
Used condom to protect against STDs during most recent sexual intercourse (if has had sex)	63	67	**74**	64	60
Has been pregnant (never married females)					
Never	80	**93**	84	79	85
Once	13	**4**	9	13	10
More than once	6	3	7	8	5
Has impregnated someone (never married males)	12	**4**	12	12	9
Has had an abortion (all females)	3	1	3	5	2

Source: National Survey of Youth and Religion, 2007–2008.
Note: Percentages are rounded to the nearest whole number. Differences that are statistically significant at the 0.05 level from the Disengaged category after controlling for seven control variables (age, sex, race, region of residence, parental education, individual income, and parental assistance with expenses) are in bold.

CONCLUSION

We began this brief chapter with the question whether religious emerging adults in the United States are different from nonreligious ones. Does religion make any difference in the lives of emerging adults in America? The answer we have discovered is most definitely yes, highly religious emerging adults are different on a host of outcome measures from less religious emerging adults. *Soul Searching* found consistent, sizeable, and significant religious differences in many of the same life outcome measures among American teenagers.[9] We have shown in this chapter that those differences, particularly between the most and the least religious youth, continue on into emerging adulthood. The significant association between high-end religious commitment and practice and higher scores on most multiple measures of positive life outcomes continues to be evident among 18- to 23-year-olds. We should not overstate the magnitude of these differences. In most cases they are not enormous. Sometimes they are substantial, other times only modest. To keep the picture as complicated as the reality, one needs to remember that there are in fact many nonreligious emerging adults who are enjoying very positive outcomes in their lives, as well as highly religious ones who are greatly struggling. Nevertheless, big-picture analyses show that the overall tendency of stronger emerging adult religion to associate with particular patterns of life outcomes is real, quite consistent, and significant.

Different readers will of course evaluate the meaning of these variations in life outcome differently, depending on their own particular values and visions for what a good life looks like. Most will agree that recurrently being depressed, feeling distant from parents, frequently risking contracting sexually transmitted diseases, and feeling dissatisfied with life in general are not good emerging adult life outcomes. Many will also agree that higher educational achievement, more financial giving and volunteering, caring about the poor and elderly, and normal body weight are also good outcomes. But fewer will agree about the value or merits of social networking websites, moral relativism, heavy alcohol consumption, mass consumerism, uncommitted sex, and cohabitation. Our purpose here is not to decide such questions. Our more modest purpose is simply to show that—however varyingly some of these life outcomes may be evaluated—differences in religious commitment among emerging adults are significantly associated with disparities in life outcomes that are of interest to many people. Religion still matters in ways that make a difference in a variety of relationships, attitudes, experiences, and behaviors, even among 18- to 23-year-olds, and especially among the most highly religious.

Many of the specific cases of emerging adults we have presented well illustrate the life outcome differences that this chapter has captured in quantitative terms. When it comes to the categories used in this chapter, Brad (from chapter 1), for instance, is a Sporadic. June (from chapter 1) is a Disengaged, and Amanda (also chapter 1) is a Devoted. Many of the findings presented in the tables here—when it comes to family relationships, giving and volunteering, organizational activities, moral orientations, risk behaviors, subjective well-being, life satisfaction, consumerism, and sexual attitudes and behaviors—play out quite clearly in their lives as one would expect. Andrea (chapter 6), whose life was in trouble during her teenage years when she was a Disengaged, has recently turned her life around in a way that involves becoming a Regular. The lives of Andy and Ruth (chapter 6)—both Disengaged—also embody many of this chapter's findings about religion and life outcomes for emerging adults. The cases of Joy, Kristin, Raymond, Alyssa, Heather, John, and Alano (chapter 7), who as teenagers were described at some length in *Soul Searching* and who were since interviewed again five years later, show once more that the older adolescents who are more religiously committed and involved are also generally doing what most people consider to be better in life, while those who are most distant from religion reflect less optimal kinds of life outcomes. The associations are not perfect, of course, but they are real and evident in the lives of specific emerging adults.

Finally, the question remains whether religion is a mere statistical correlate or actually a real cause of varying life outcomes among emerging adults. Are the differences we have observed simply spurious statistical associations or the results of actual causal effects of religious beliefs, commitments, and practices on life outcomes? Not all sociologists agree on these matters. But the weight of evidence very strongly suggests that definite causal religious effects are at work producing the outcome differences we have observed here. We can begin by recognizing that the causal relationships between religion and many of the outcome variables examined here may be reciprocal. For example, we have every reason to believe that the higher religious commitment of the most religious emerging adults causally reduces the amount of alcohol they consume and sex in which they engage. But we also have reason to believe that the more sexually active emerging adults become and the more they party with alcohol, the more they will also pull back on their religious investments.[10] The causal mechanisms can and often do work in both directions. Even so, in these complicated causal processes, religion still can and does exert causal forces on outcomes. Reciprocal effects operating in both directions do not eliminate religious effects operating in one of those directions.

Furthermore, the analyses that tested for statistically significant differences here controlled for the possible effects on the outcomes in question of emerging adults' age, sex, race, region of residence, parental education, parental marital status, individual income, and parental assistance with expenses. The fact that we still find many significant differences across religious types means that the religious effects are not spurious as a result of the influence of any of those eight most relevant variables. If there is some other factor, besides religion, that is really causing the observed differences in life outcomes, which breaks the apparent causal association between religion and outcomes, then it must be something other than one of those eight variables. And it remains unclear what that other factor or factors might be. Until someone identifies the mystery variable or variables that eliminate our religion/life outcomes statistical association—something that nobody has yet done when it comes to youth and emerging adults—we have very good reasons to believe that religion is itself one significant cause helping to produce those life outcome differences.

This is true especially in light of the fact that scholars have already identified and confirmed many specific causal mechanisms by which religious faith and practice operate to shape life outcomes. As *Soul Searching* describes nine distinct causal mechanisms by which religion can influence adolescent life outcomes, in an in-depth section that explores the question of religious causal influences, we need not discuss this matter at length here.[11] Religion provides teenagers with moral directives, confirming spiritual experiences, role models, community and leadership skills, coping skills, cultural capital, social capital, greater network closure in relationships, and intercommunity links—all of which, solid social scientific reasoning indicates, can be expected to enhance their life experiences. Most of the same mechanisms apply equally well in the lives of emerging adults. So there is little mystery about how and why religion could and does causally influence the life outcomes of 18- to 23-year-olds—in fact, we have a reasonably solid understanding of how such causal processes actually work. Of course, there are complicated selection effects, reciprocal causes, and indirect causal influences at work here.[12] But none of that negates the idea that religious causal effects are also real, that a number of identifiable mechanisms operating through religious faith and practice shape the life outcomes of emerging adults. It is, and they do. Religion therefore matters and makes a significant difference in the life experiences, beliefs, and behaviors of American 18- to 23-year-olds.

10

Making Some Sense of It All

THIS CONCLUDING CHAPTER CONTAINS both summaries of what we have presented in this book as well as some of our own broader interpretations of our findings. In coming to the end of such an investigation, one has to remember the limits to the comprehension that is possible. There is no one summary perspective or integrated interpretation, much less set of identifiable social laws, by which emerging adult religion in America can be understood. Rather, a variety of trends, tendencies, conditions, casual mechanisms, and forces are involved that deserve attention. This conclusion will attempt to highlight and comment on some of the more important of these. But not every finding in this book will be reiterated, not every loose end tied up, and not every interpretive idea will necessarily fit into one, single, larger framework of understanding. What follow are merely some of what we think are the more important final points worth highlighting in closing.

TAKING SERIOUSLY A NEW LIFE PHASE

The starting point for our entire inquiry was taking seriously the new phase of young American life that has developed over the last four decades, known as emerging adulthood. Emerging adulthood is not simply an extension of teenage life, which normally remains highly dependent on parents and structured by high school. Nor is it the beginning of fully settled adulthood, as marked by marriage, children, career jobs, and home ownership. Rather, emerging adulthood embodies its own distinctive characteristics, tendencies, and experiences.

279

Many of these have implications for religious faith and spiritual life. This new phase of life is the product of a variety of social and technological changes, including the expansion of higher education, delays in the average age of marriage, transformations in the American and global economy, the growing readiness of many parents to extend material support to their children well after they leave home, and the development and easy access to a variety of affordable and relatively safe birth control technologies. As a result of these complicated social transformations, the transition from the teenage years to fully achieved adulthood has stretched out into an extended stage that is often amorphous, unstructured, and convoluted, lasting upward of 12 or more years. During this time frame, emerging adults experience a freedom that is historically unparalleled, a life structure that is often at most only loosely governed by older adult authorities. This enables emerging adults for many years to explore, experiment, discover, succeed or fail, move on, and try again. For many, this age is also marked not only by a lot of fun and growth but also by a great deal of transience, confusion, anxiety, self-obsession, melodrama, conflict, stress, disappointment, and sometimes emotional damage and bodily harm. It is a phase in life that needs to be taken seriously for American religion to be fully understood.

The emerging adult years often entail repeated life disruptions, transitions, and distractions—which poses challenges for sustaining religious commitments, investments, and practices. These years involve complex processes of incorporating new relationships and experiences into ongoing, developing lives, while sustaining and renegotiating old relationships with parents, siblings, friends, former adult mentors, and others. Religious faith, community involvement, and personal practices all are sorted out one way or another in this larger process of struggling to balance differentiation, consolidation, and integration of relations, identities, goals, and resources. Often an uncomfortable unevenness typifies this period, as emerging adults pursue lives with one foot in what seems like helpless dependence and another in what feels like complete autonomy and total responsibility. Most of them are at pains to keep open as many options as possible, to honor all forms of social and cultural diversity without judgment or even evaluation, and as quickly as possible to get on the road to autonomous self-sufficiency. Little of that encourages them to put down roots within particular religious communities that engage in committed faith practices. And that reluctance is reinforced by the postponement of family formation and childbearing, both of which tend to encourage religious investment. What is good and bad also seem to most emerging adults to be self-evident—it seems that no particular history or people or heritage or revelation or tradition are needed to navigate moral choices. And during the years before settling down for good, very many emerging adults believe that they are supposed to devote themselves to hanging out, partying, and perhaps drinking, doing drugs, and hooking up. Little in that encourages strong religious faith and practice.

At the same time, most emerging adults maintain ongoing relationships with their parents and other appreciated adult influences, which most of them seem truly to value. And some of these older adults continue to encourage emerging adults in their religious and spiritual lives. Other emerging adults who have already survived serious life difficulties and breakdowns are working on getting their lives together, and many of them find religion to be a helpful resource in undertaking that challenging task. Further, a certain number of emerging adults have by family background simply always been, continue to be, and likely always will be very religious—whatever the challenges of emerging adult life. This historically new phase of life, then, involves a variety of forces, tendencies, and influences that shape religious outcomes. To adequately understand the religious and spiritual lives of emerging adults requires not simply collecting data on a certain age group, but more fully understanding the cultural and institutional contexts that emerging adults are in part generating and that in turn powerfully form their lives. Among these are mass-consumer capitalism, youth-targeted advertising, economic transformations, new career imperatives and strategies, mass education, revolutionary communications technologies, the proliferation of media programming, moral pluralism, and continuing waves of the sexual revolution. Religion, in short, must always be understood, if it is to be understood well, in the broader social, cultural, and economic contexts that shape it, help explain it, and give it meaning.

Part of gaining such an understanding is placing religion into age-comparative and historical perspective. Emerging adult religion, we have shown, is not typical of adults of all age groups in the United States. Younger adults in America tend to be significantly less religious in a variety of ways than older adults. Emerging adults are, on most sociological measures, clearly the least religious adults in the United States today. Catholic and mainline Protestant emerging adults tend especially to be less religious than evangelical Protestants and black Protestants. However, according to available evidence, emerging adults in America since 1972 have generally not become less religious, at least as measured by the variety of sociological survey questions examined in chapter 3. Most emerging adults have since 1972 either remained stable in their levels of religiousness or have actually increased somewhat. The significant exception to that rule is frequent church attendance by Catholic and mainline Protestant emerging adults, which has dropped noticeably in past decades. Thus, we see little evidence here of massive secularization among America's emerging adults in the last quarter century, at least the kind that survey questions are able to detect. At the same time, we must remember that the development of the new life phase of emerging adulthood was already in full swing by the 1970s. Our analysis does not involve data for ages 18 to 23 before the advent of emerging adult culture, so any possible religious changes associated with the development of emerging adulthood are not captured here. In short, emerging adults are as a whole less religious than are older adults and than they themselves were when they were teenagers; but today's emerging adults do not appear to be dramatically less religious than former generations of emerging adults have been, at lest going back to the early 1970s.

RELIGIOUS CONTINUITY AND CHANGE IN INDIVIDUAL LIVES

Our study has established with new precision the extent and location of continuity and change in the religious lives of youth transitioning from the teenage
into the emerging adult years. Popular conceptions of the matter typically
suppose that this life course transition is marked simply by a massive overall
decline in religious faith and practice. Some studies of emerging adults suggest
that a major rupture during this transition breaks any observable connection
between teenage religion and emerging adult religious faith and practice—
such that one cannot anticipate the character of the latter by knowing features
of the former. Others have even referred to the religious lives of young adults
as a "black hole."[1] We find that these views and images point to certain elements of truth, but in the end we think they are overstated. We agree—to
keep the metaphor going—in a very general sense that certain social and cultural forces at work during emerging adulthood, elucidated in the foregoing
chapters, exert influences something like the powerful gravitational field of a
black hole, which seems almost inexorably to pull everything that comes close
enough to it into its consuming darkness. But we have also learned that those
forces are not so strong that they always engulf all of the visible "light" of
religion among youth simply because their lives have passed the demographic
"event horizon" from the teenage years into emerging adulthood. Nor do
our findings support the idea that the coming of emerging adulthood entails
an overall, massive decline in religion. Nor again have we discovered a dis-
orienting rupture between the teenage and emerging adult years breaking all
continuities between them, so that emerging adults end up with inexplicably
random religious outcomes as a result.

What we have found instead is the following. A little more than half of
emerging adults remain quite stable in their levels of religious commitment
and practice or lack thereof. That stability is found at the highest, moderate, and lowest levels of religiousness. A certain portion of highly religious
teenagers remains highly religious as emerging adults, as do significant groups
of moderately religious and not very religious teenagers. The primary conclusion about emerging adult religion, therefore, is not one of change but of
continuity. More often than not, what's past is prologue.[2] The next largest
group of emerging adults does reflect change in religious lives over the five
years studied here. These tend to come from the somewhat less than highest
ranks of teenage religiousness and represent nearly 40 percent of all emerging adults. Some of these cases decline modestly in religiousness, while others
decline more sharply. Yet even in these cases, identifiable factors from their
teenage lives enable us to differentiate them from those who remained highly
religious in emerging adulthood. In other words, while there is less continuity
in their *levels* of religiousness over time, there still *is* continuity in the kind of
characteristic factors in their lives that lead to their collective religious decline.
Religious outcomes are simply not so random that sociologists with the right
tools cannot make sense of why and for whom they tend to occur. Finally,
small minorities of emerging adults counter the dominant trends by increasing

in religious faith and practice. These cases typically come from the lower end of teenage religiousness and grow over the five years examined here into much more highly religious emerging adults. These are the few new converts, the nominally religious making new commitments to God later in life, and those whose difficult nonreligious experiences have led them, like Joy and Andrea, to search for answers in new religious commitments.

Emerging adulthood tends both to raise the stakes on and remove social support for being seriously religious. As a result, many youth do pull back from, or entirely out of, religious faith and practice during their transitions out of the teenage years. For the most part, those who keep believing and practicing religion with serious devotion during the emerging adult years are those who were the most invested in religion to begin with, plus a very small group of newly religious emerging adults. But, it is worth noting, these more seriously committed emerging adults do in fact exist, and not simply as a struggling remnant. More than a few do buck the trends of religious decline and indifference. And another minority even more clearly bucks those trends by growing dramatically in their seriousness about religious faith and practice. So the myth of overall religious decline among emerging adults must be dispelled. At the same time, there is no denying that some emerging adults undergo a waning of their religious belief and practice during this life phase. Numerically, these outweigh those who are becoming more religious, so aggregate descriptive statistics sum to an overall noticeable decline in emerging adult religiousness. But that is an artifact of proportions in the simple calculating process of addition, subtraction, and no-change cases, which tends to mask underlying and more interesting facts. Those facts are that most emerging adults tend not to change religiously, many tend to decline, and a few tend to increase religiously. Distinguishing these different trajectories and their causes is much more revealing than simply pondering aggregate percentage sums.

THE POWER OF SOCIALIZATION

One of the most pervasive and powerful myths about children is that as they enter adolescence, their parents increasingly cease to matter in their lives. Adolescence is commonly—but mistakenly—assumed to be a phase during which parents become irrelevant, replaced instead by the influences of their peers, the media, and the children's own independent personalities and desires. In the course of the NSYR research, for example, we have repeatedly been told by parents things like "Ever since my daughter turned 13, she doesn't listen to me anymore." All too often, it seems, those parents then take such messages as opportunities to "check out" from a series of concerns or responsibilities about their children, which they tell themselves they no longer can influence anyway. This dynamic often seems to involve a mixture of not wanting to inappropriately control or meddle in their growing teenagers' lives, fear of being "uncool" by remaining too involved with them, a readiness to cooperate in not "embarrassing" their children by being part of groups involving their friends, and a sense of relief in being able to convince themselves that the job of parenting is finished, however successfully or unsuccessfully. So when teen-agers send signals to "Get out of my life," many parents seem all too ready to comply, even if with mixed emotions.[3] In short, most Americans have swallowed hook, line, and sinker the "Parents of teenagers are irrelevant" myth. So allegedly autonomous people ritualistically play out this myth in their own lives as a self-fulfilling prophecy, as if their fates as parents and children are predestined by divine oracle. Oddly, this withdrawal of parental influence on adolescents seems most especially evident when it comes to religious commitments and practices. Many parents remain at least somewhat concerned to continue to exert some control over things like their children's sports prospects, educational futures, and choice of marriage partners. But when it comes to religion, many parents seem keen not to "impose" anything or to "shove religion down their throats." Very often, as a result, many adolescents are thrown back on themselves and left floating in a directionless murk to figure out completely on their own some of life's most basic questions concerning reality, truth, goodness, value, morality, and identity. Thus, in the name of individual autonomy—informed here by a cultural myth that is sociologically erroneous—the usually most crucial players in teenagers' lives disengage from them precisely when they most need conversation partners to help sort through these weighty matters.

There is, of course, a germ of truth in the "Parents of teenagers are irrelevant" myth that makes it plausible. Adolescents and parents indeed are normally continually renegotiating the terms of their relationships. Teenagers do tend to become more independent from their parents over time. Teenagers can become quite absorbed into groups of peers. And adolescents often do go through phases and have characteristic situations where they do act like they want their parents to "butt out." But none of that actually means that parents have become irrelevant, that their influence is vanishing, that they no longer matter. Such teenage developments simply do not mean for parents that it is time to check out, that their children no longer need or often even want them to appropriately act like responsible parents who continue to invest in and talk with them about matters of importance. Most adolescents in fact still very badly want the loving input and engagement of their parents—more, in fact, than most parents ever realize.[4] They simply want that input and engagement on renegotiated grounds that take seriously their growing maturity and desired independence. All too often, however, parents misinterpret their teenager's signals about renegotiated relationships as simple demands to be entirely left alone and, for whatever reasons, they readily comply. So just at the time when teenagers most need engaged parents to help them work out a whole series of big questions about what they believe, think, value, feel, are committed to, and want to be and become, in many cases, their parents are withdrawing from them. Thus does American individualism leave its youth to themselves, thrown back on their own devices, often lacking the cognitive and emotional tools and concerned conversation partners needed to intelligently sort out life's big issues, including those about which religion makes claims.

What the best empirical evidence shows about the matter, however, is that even as the formation of faith and life play out in the lives of 18- to 23-year-olds, when it comes to religion, parents are in fact *hugely* important. Of the many teenage-era factors that our study investigated as possible influences on emerging adult religious outcomes, one of *the* most powerful factors was the religious lives of their parents—how often they attended religious services, how important religious faith was in their own lives, and so on. Those parental factors are always significantly related to outcomes in every statistical model, no matter how many other variables are also introduced into the equations. By contrast, it is well worth noting, the direct religious influence of *peers* during the teenage years—which common stereotypes say becomes all-important among teenagers—proved to have a significantly weaker and more qualified influence on emerging adult religious outcomes than parents. Parental influences, in short, trump peer influences. In addition, we know sociologically that the other very important teenage-era factors powerfully shaping emerging adult religious outcomes—frequency of prayer and scripture readings, having religious experiences, harboring few religious doubts, and believing in miracles—are normally also most powerfully formed by the influence of parents' beliefs and examples in these matters. In the long run, then, who and what parents were and are for their children when it comes to religious faith and practice are much more likely to "stick" with them, even into emerging adulthood, than who and what their teenage friends were.

Furthermore, it is not only parents who matter in forming the religion of emerging adults. Other nonparental adults in the lives of youth are often also important and, in certain circumstances, can actually "substitute" for parents as formative influences in the lives of youth. These may be other family members, such as grandparents or aunts and uncles. They may be congregational youth ministers or pastors. They may simply be other adult members of religious congregations who have reached out to youth and built meaningful personal relationships with them. Whatever the case may be, the empirical evidence tells us that it does in fact matter for emerging adult religious outcomes whether or not youth have had nonparental adults in their religious congregations to whom they could turn for help and support. It matters whether or not teenagers have belonged to congregations offering youth groups that they actually liked and wanted to be part of. It matters whether or not teenagers have participated in adult-taught religious education classes, such as Sunday school. Adult engagement with, role modeling for, and formation of youth simply matters a great deal for how they turn out after they leave the teenage years.[5] So, stated negatively, when adults who have bought into the common myths and stereotypes as a result disengage from the lives of teenagers who are on the road to emerging adulthood, these teenagers are forced to travel that road either alone or only with peers and, more likely than not, end up less religiously committed and practicing as emerging adults.

We see, then, that much about emerging adults' religious outcomes is explained by the elementary sociological principles of socialization. New members of any society are always inducted into the group by elder members who form them in different ways to become active participants of various sorts. This is done through role modeling, teaching, taking-things-for-granted, sanctioning, training, practicing, and other means of inculcating and internalizing basic categories, assumptions, symbols, habits, beliefs, values, desires, norms, and practices. This is simply how most youth learn religion and everything else. And this provides the framework within which youth sort out over time how much religion matters to them, what, if anything, it means to them, and to what degree they will continue to practice religion or not. Thus, whether adults—particularly parents—know it or not and like it or not, they are in fact always socializing youth about religion. The question is never *whether* adults are engaged in religious socialization, but only *how* and with what effect they are doing so. The form, content, and intensity of religious socialization are therefore crucial in shaping the later religious outcomes of those being socialized. And since most of broader American society is not in the business of direct religious socialization, this task inevitably falls almost entirely to two main social entities. First are individual family households, where parents predictably do the primary socializing. Second are individual religious congregations, where other adults can exert socializing influences on youth. If nothing else, what the findings of this book clearly show is that for better or worse, these are the two crucial contexts of youth religious formation in the United States. If formation in faith does not happen there, it will—with rare exceptions—not happen anywhere.

THE DOMINANT OUTLOOK ON RELIGION

Not all emerging adults think about religion in the same way, but there definitely is a dominant outlook when it comes to religion. Most emerging adults are okay with talking about religion as a topic, although they are largely indifferent to it—religion is just not that important to most of them. So for the most part, they do not end up talking much about religion in their lives. To whatever extent they do talk about it, most of them think that most religions share the same core principles, which they generally believe are good. But the particularities of any given religion are peripheral trappings that can be more or less ignored. The best thing about religion is that it helps people to be good, to make good choices, to behave well. For this reason, it can be a good thing for children to be raised in a religious congregation, since they need to be taught the basics of morality. At the same time, once youth learn what it means to be good, there is no real need to continue being involved in a religious congregation. The time comes to "graduate" and move on. Some emerging adults do of course continue to be part of congregations, but few name them as important places of social belonging. Furthermore, among emerging adults, religious beliefs do not seem to be important, action-driving commitments, but rather mental assents to ideas that have few obvious consequences. What actually do have the power and authority to drive life instead are the feelings and inclinations of the emerging adults themselves. They as individuals can determine what is right, worthy, and important. So they themselves can pick and choose from religion to take or leave what they want. At the same time, the personal outlooks of most emerging adults are highly qualified—sometimes even paralyzed—by their awareness of the relativity of their own cultural and social locations. The latter tend to undercut any confidence they might have in the possibility of holding true beliefs, rendering valid judgments, making worthy commitments. In any case, when it comes to authorities about knowledge, most emerging adults put a lot more weight on the empirical evidence, proof, and verified facts of science than on the claims of religious traditions, which, they believe, ultimately require "blind faith" to embrace. Even so, for the moral good that it can promote, most of mainstream religion in America is probably okay. It depends on the individual case, of course, but most religious leaders are probably well-meaning and are likely fairly harmless, not that it actually matters that much to most emerging adults. In any event, religion should always in the end remain a personal matter, something an individual may or may not choose to get into because it is meaningful to him or her. But when religion starts to become a primarily social or institutional concern, it tends to become rigid and inauthentic, which, needless to say, are bad. Finally, and overarching all of these assumptions and outlooks, most emerging adults are stuck at the place of thinking that nobody ultimately really knows what is true or right or good. It is all so relative and impossible to know in a pluralistic world with so many competing claims. Best, then, they suppose, to remain tentative, to keep options open, to not get too committed, to push dealing with religious matters off to some future date when through marriage and parenting it becomes more practically important. In the meanwhile, emerging adults have self-sufficiency to achieve, materially secure lifestyles to secure, and fun to be enjoyed.

THE CULTURAL TRIUMPH OF LIBERAL PROTESTANTISM

It is old news by now that mainline-liberal Protestant denominations in the United States are suffering major declines in membership and social prestige. Sociologists have for decades been documenting a hemorrhaging of members from mainline Protestant churches. And the religious and political ascendancy of American evangelicalism since the 1970s has drawn the spotlight away from the once mainstream religious presence of the more liberal Protestant churches. What was once mainline is now regularly dubbed the "sideline" and the "old-line." These are not the glory days of mainline-liberal Protestantism in America. Yet many observers are so focused on membership statistics and apparent political influences that they miss an important fact: that liberal Protestantism's organizational decline has been accompanied by and is in part arguably the consequence of the fact that liberal Protestantism has won a decisive, larger cultural victory. In this idea, we follow the argument of the University of Massachusetts sociologist of religion N. Jay Demerath, in a perceptive but we think underappreciated journal article he published in 1995 entitled "Cultural Victory and Organizational Defeat in the Paradoxical Decline of Liberal Protestantism."[6] Demerath's argument is fairly simple. "Far from representing failure," he says, "the decline of Liberal Protestantism may actually stem from its success. It may be the painful structural consequences of [its] wider cultural triumph....Liberal Protestants have lost structurally at the micro level precisely because they won culturally at the macro level." What Demerath means by this is that liberal Protestantism's core values— individualism, pluralism, emancipation, tolerance, free critical inquiry, and the authority of human experience—have come to so permeate broader American culture that its own churches as organizations have difficulty surviving. One reason for this development is that these very liberal values have a tendency to undermine organizational vitality. The strongest organizations are generally not built on individualism, diversity, autonomy, and criticism. Furthermore, having won the larger battle to shape mainstream culture, it becomes difficult to sustain a strong rationale for maintaining distinctively liberal church organizations to continue to promote those now omnipresent values. Liberal Protestantism increasingly seems redundant to the taken-for-granted mainstream that it has helped to create. Why organize to promote what is already hegemonic?

Evidence supporting Demerath's thesis was abundant in the NSYR interviews with emerging adults. Their dominant discourse about religion, faith, and God—as prefigured in chapter 2 and developed in chapters 5 and 7—often clearly reflected the basic cultural values and sometime speech modes of liberal Protestantism. Individual autonomy, unbounded tolerance, freedom from authorities, the affirmation of pluralism, the centrality of human self-consciousness, the practical value of moral religion, epistemological skepticism, and an instinctive aversion to anything "dogmatic" or committed to particulars were routinely taken for granted by respondents. So, assuming they had not already become irreligious "cultural despisers of religion"— whom the liberal Protestant Friedrich Schleiermacher was keen to win over with apology[7]—most Catholic and Jewish emerging adults, for example, talked very much like classical liberal Protestants. Many evangelical Protestant and black Protestant emerging adults even talked like liberal Protestants. And very many mainline Protestant emerging adults simply could not care enough to talk about religion in any specific terms, but those who did in fact usually talked like classical liberal Protestants. In short, many emerging adults would be quite comfortable with the kind of liberal faith described by the Yale theologian H. Richard Niebuhr in 1937 as being about "a God without wrath [who] brought men without sin into a kingdom without judgment through the ministrations of a Christ without a Cross."[8] They simply would have no idea about the genealogy of their taken-for-granted ideas, that is, from where historically they came. On more than a few occasions, in fact, while listening to emerging adults explain their views of religion, it struck us that they might just as well be paraphrasing passages from classical liberal Protestant theologians, of whom they have no doubt actually never heard, from the nineteenth and early twentieth centuries. The likes of Adolf von Harnack, Albrecht Ritschl, Wilhelm Hermann, and Harry Emerson Fosdick would be proud. People, it is clear, need not study liberal Protestant theology to be well inducted into its worldview, since it has simply become part of the cultural air that many Americans now breathe.

The one crucial thing emerging adults plainly do *not* share with the classic liberal Protestant outlook, however, is its characteristic humanistic optimism about historical progress and the growth of the kingdom of God through cultural development and political reform. This would make no sense to emerging adults today. They are, as we have shown, highly optimistic about their own personal futures. But they are dubious about the future of society, politics, and the world beyond their individual lives. They do not see God working immanently in the movement of history. They doubt that historical Progress is real, not that they think about it much. Few feel compelled to get involved in public life, whether for religious or other reasons. And among emerging adults, liberal Protestantism's social gospel is out of gas. That liberal movement, which historically called Christians to face urban blight and industrial exploitation by asking the question "What would Jesus do?"[9] has already, for this generation, been co-opted and tamed by the brief evangelical youth fad of wearing "WWJD?" bracelets. The civic and political worlds are simply much too confusing and discouraging to emerging adults today for them to have much hope for rising above hopelessness and distraction. In any case, working, studying for classes, chatting and texting with friends, keeping up with social networking websites, and hanging out at parties keeps emerging adults too busy to worry much about public life and the common good. In this sense, among emerging adults, the individualistic humanism and personal moralism of liberal Protestantism have overrun and eradicated its historical emphasis on social and political responsibility for reform and betterment. So the liberal Protestantism that has culturally diffused in youth culture is a rather selective version of that larger tradition.

Even so, liberal Protestants have more to be happy about than it seems they often realize. The obvious breakdown of liberal Protestantism at one level in fact signals a larger triumph in performance on a much more important stage. And evangelical Protestants, if we are correct here, should have much more to worry about than their apparent recent successes, measured in church membership numbers and recent political attention, might lead them and other observers to assume. That is because a historical nemesis of evangelicalism, liberal Protestantism, can afford to be losing its organizational battles now precisely because long ago it effectively won the bigger, more important struggle over culture. Liberal Protestantism's last word may be more diffuse in cultural discourse, but no less influential as a result. And ideas and values that are the most invisible are precisely also those that, as a result, are the most powerful. Therefore, if we wish to understand the religious and spiritual lives of contemporary American emerging adults, we must not lose sight of the power liberal Protestantism still exerts among the majority of them through its cultural formation of the dominant, taken-for-granted terms of discourse, valuation, and outlook, in ways and with influence about which most emerging adults have no idea.

CULTURAL MUTATIONS OF EVANGELICAL PROTESTANTISM

Liberal Protestantism is not the only big religious tradition that has formed the contemporary emerging adult world. The evangelical Protestant tradition has also laid down some of the tracks on which run important trains of contemporary emerging adult thoughts about religion. We begin to clue into the significant background influence of evangelical religious culture more broadly when, for example, we hear a committed American Muslim girl speaking glowingly about her "personal relationship with God."[10] Something curious is going on there. But evangelical influences run much deeper and wider than simply the diffusion of particular bits of evangelical popular lingo. Many emerging adult attitudes about religion represent no more than somewhat mutated versions of core, historical evangelical theological themes. For example, it is the centuries-old, central evangelical insistence on the ultimate consequence of each individual's salvation in standing alone before a holy God that emerging adults are resonating when they articulate their radically individualistic view of religious faith and practice. Each individual stands alone in matters of faith, ultimately unaffected by and not accountable to any other human. All that is needed is to decenter the holy God part of the scenario, and what is left is the autonomous individual. Emerging adults carry this individualism to new and—from evangelicalism's point of view—misguided levels and directions.[11] But the places where today's emerging adults have taken that individualism in religion basically continues the cultural trajectory launched by Martin Luther five centuries ago and propelled along the way by the subsequent development of evangelical individualism, through revivalism, evangelism, and pietism. The same is true of emerging adults' antiinstitutional view of religion. When emerging adults say that religion is really a personal affair that is sullied by the restrictions and artificialities of social institutions, including religious institutions, they are echoing the strong antiinstitutional bias that has characterized American evangelicalism since the revolutionary era.[12] Against Roman Catholicism, which emphasizes the church as a visible social institution carrying on the "deposit of faith" as a historical tradition, American Protestantism has insisted on a view of the church as essentially a local voluntary organization guided solely by divine revelation in the Bible, which is accessible to all individual believers, and uncorrupted by (unbiblical) human "traditions." Evangelical doctrines of the church thus strongly tend to code institutions themselves as ultimately superfluous to what *really* matters, and human traditions as suspect, if not dangerous, to the true faith. The dominant emerging adult view of religious congregations and traditions that respondents repeatedly expressed in the interviews is in fact only a few steps down the line from the most traditional or "biblical" evangelical theologies of the church.

Furthermore, the strong individualistic subjectivism in the emerging adult religious outlook—that "truth" should be decided by "what seems right" to individuals, based on their personal experience and feelings—also has deep cultural-structural roots in American evangelicalism. Again, the center of

American evangelicalism has long resisted formal confessional and episcopal traditions as representations and carriers of theological truth. Rather, only the Bible—*sola scriptura*—tells the truth. And the Bible, evangelicalism has taught, is not only infallible but also clear in its teachings, so that each individual can read it and know and understand its truth.[13] Few evangelicals know that, originally, it was in fact liberal Protestant activists in the late eighteenth and early nineteenth centuries who insisted most absolutely that any ordinary person could sit down with the Bible and understand all of its teachings. These liberal activists used that argument to challenge the dominant, "orthodox" Calvinism of their day, which they believed taught unbiblical and increasingly unfashionable doctrines, such as divine predestination to heaven and hell.[14] Evangelicals themselves, however, quickly picked up and took over this every-layperson-can-understand-the-Bible belief in order to promote democratized Bible study in the young democracy, in which people were being encouraged to "pull themselves up by their own bootstraps." It thus became the sacred right and responsibility of all individuals to read the Bible and understand it for themselves. Right theology no longer needed to be preached by the seminary-educated pastor. All persons could simply read, understand, decide, and know the biblical truth for themselves. Naturally, within evangelicalism, final authority was and is supposed to reside in the Bible, not the reader. But as it turned out, in the American evangelical experience, different well-intentioned readers ended up saying that the Bible taught many different things, which produced massive denominational fragmentation. In the course of events, the nation also ended up fighting a horrifically bloody civil war in part because it could not agree on what the Bible taught about slavery.[15] Thus, having democratized to every individual the full authority to know religious truth for themselves, yet having failed thereby to produce anything like an agreement about what the Bible actually teaches, evangelical biblicism set up powerful religious cultural structures that, it so happens, govern many non-evangelical (and evangelical) emerging adults today. Young Americans' assurance that the Bible, or any other alleged authority, contains the truth by which to live has, compared to evangelical convictions, been severely weakened. And in the intervening years, for complicated reasons, final authority has decisively shifted from the Bible to the individual reader. But most emerging adults' basic assumption that it is the right and responsibility of each individual to decide religious truth for himself or herself—based on his or her own "reading" of relevant matters—is in fact simply one cultural mutation away from historic evangelical orthodoxy.

Finally, contemporary emerging adults' positive valuation of religion primarily because of the practical benefits it bestows on individual lives in the form of moral behaviors also has cultural roots in American evangelicalism. Mark Noll, among others, has clearly described the key emphasis in historical American evangelicalism on the centrality of practical activism.[16] Evangelicalism was never essentially a religion of contemplation, mysticism, or careful intellectual scholarship. Rather, it was about the gospel leading to personal transformation and—especially after the Second Great Awakening—moral reform activism.

Evangelicals (and liberals, in a different way) have long believed that faith does and must have real consequences, that it should make an observable difference in the person and in the world. Once a soul has secured its way to heaven through personal conversion, it must then devote itself to sanctification and self-reform. Often, the methods (think *Method*ism) and purposes of this have been very pragmatic—to end alcoholism, gambling, sexual immorality, and other forms of "worldliness" that threaten personal and family well-being. Further, to the extent that evangelicals have historically more or less believed America to be something like a special nation chosen by God, salvation ought also to have consequences for the betterment of the nation.[17] The conversionism central to evangelical revivals, evangelistic crusades, and altar calls is not simply about conveying new ideas, but is also about visceral repentance from sin, dramatically changing lives, and giving believers "new hearts" so they can live upright lives to the glory of God.[18] Such a version of the gospel, which emphasized practical, personal results of religious conversion and subsequent sanctified activity in holiness, turns out to have been set up to slip, and has in fact very easily slipped, into a popular mentality about religion that presumes that the sum total purpose and value of religion per se are simply the practical benefits it affords believers. Religious faith becomes good *if* and *because* it makes people do better, if it helps them live more moral lives. That itself has become religion's very raison d'être, its legitimating purpose and value, for which it may be appreciated. Along the way, God can get lost in the shuffle. Of course, historical evangelicalism was not purposely intended to promote such an outcome. But that, with a bit of cultural mutation, is what the internal structure of evangelical religious culture has facilitated. Thus, while evangelical readers may be among the most concerned about some of the religious trends described in this book, they would be myopic not to see that some very particular features of historical evangelicalism have themselves deeply structured many of the religious cultural categories and mentalities that today's emerging adults are using to make sense of their world.

SOVEREIGN INDIVIDUALS LACKING CONVICTION OR DIRECTION

One of the important larger conditions that it is necessary to grasp in order to understand emerging adult life is (what in our view is) the contemporary cultural crisis of knowledge and value. Emerging adults have been raised in a world involving certain outlooks and assumptions that they have clearly absorbed and that they in turn largely affirm and reinforce. Stated in philosophical terms, their world has undergone a significant epistemic and axiological breakdown. It is difficult if not impossible in this world that has come to be to actually know anything objectively real or true that can be rationally maintained in a way that might require people actually to change their minds or lives. Emerging adults know quite well how they personally were raised in their families, and they know fairly well how they generally "feel" about things. But they are also aware that all knowledge and value are historically conditioned and culturally relative. And they have not, in our view, been equipped with the intellectual and moral tools to know what to do with that fact. So most simply choose to believe and live by whatever subjectively feels "right" to them, and to try not to seriously assess, much less criticize, anything else that anyone else has chosen to believe, feel, or do. Whether or not they use these words to say it, for most emerging adults, in the end, it's all relative. One thought or opinion isn't more defensible than any other. One way of life cannot claim to be better than others. Some moral beliefs may personally *feel* right, but no moral belief can rationally claim to be really true, because that implies criticizing or discounting other moral beliefs. And that would be rude, presumptuous, intolerant, and unfeeling. This is what we mean when we use the terms *crisis* and *breakdown*.

Such a condition arguably encourages the true virtues of humility and openness to difference—precious commodities, we think, that are all too scarce in the world today. But when life's push comes to shove for emerging adults, such a condition also thwarts many of them from ever being able to decide what they believe is really true, right, and good. Thus, their commonly unsettled lifestyles are often accompanied by a troubling uncertainty about basic knowledge and values. Very many emerging adults simply don't know how to think about things, what is right, or what is deserving for them to devote their lives to. On such matters, they are very often simply paralyzed, wishing they could be more definite, wanting to move forward, but simply not knowing how they might possibly know anything worthy of conviction and dedication. Instead, very many emerging adults exist in a state of basic indecision, confusion, and fuzziness. The world they have inherited, as best as they can make sense of it, has told them that real knowledge is impossible and genuine values are illusions. Behind this, we think, are in part the powerful influences of various intellectual and cultural movements that have saturated the institutional worlds in which most emerging adults have grown up. One of those is academia's wave of deconstructive postmodernism, which has sought to reduce all knowledge and value claims to arbitrary exertions of power and control.[19] Another is the glut and fragmentation of information on the Internet and elsewhere, which lacks authorized gatekeepers to judge, evaluate, and rank the merits or value of its excess of data. Yet another is the diffuse influence of anthropological and sociological teachings on social constructionism and cultural relativism, which undercut any sense of objective standards for evaluating self and others. Still another influence comes from various multicultural movements, particularly as taught in schools—many of which we think have real value but which also, in their less thoughtful modes, often degenerate into mere assertions that all differences of any type must simply be accepted without reflection, dialogue, or assessment.

Whatever the relative worth of these various movements and trends, their intended and unintended effects have clearly powerfully shaped emerging adults today. In some ways, this has been for the good, we think. But in other ways, the effects have been confusing and debilitating. Emerging adults struggle earnestly to establish themselves as autonomous and sovereign individuals.

But the crises of knowledge and value that have so powerfully formed their lives leaves them lacking in conviction or direction to even know what to do with their prized sovereignty. Emerging adults are determined to be free. But they do not know what is worth doing with their freedom. They work very hard to stand on their own two feet. But they do not really know where they ought to go and why, once they are standing. They lack larger visions of what is true and real and good, in both the private and the public realms. And so, it seems to us, a small set of predefined default imperatives quickly rush in to fill that normative and moral vacuum. One of those is mass consumerism's slavish obsession with private material comfort and possessions, the achieving of which nearly every emerging adultviews as a key purpose in life. Other imperatives, in the meantime, may be the amusements of alcohol and drug intoxication and the temporary thrills of hook-up sex. Yet even in the early emerging adult years, signs were evident to us that many already find these culturally given, default purposes, amusements, and thrills unsatisfying, if not outright wounding. Many know there must be something more, and they want it. Many are uncomfortable with their inability to make truth statements and moral claims without killing them with the death of a thousand qualifications. But they do not know what to do about that, given the crisis of truth and values that has destabilized their culture. And so they simply carry on as best they can, as sovereign, autonomous, empowered individuals who lack a reliable basis for any particular conviction or direction by which to guide their lives.

A DIVERSITY OF TYPES AND TRAJECTORIES

Much of this chapter's summary has focused on generalizations that apply to the majority of today's emerging adults. Such generalizations are important and can be illuminating. However, even as we process findings about the central tendencies observable among emerging adults, we must also remember that emerging adult religion comprises considerable diversity. About 15 percent of emerging adults are what we call Committed Traditionalists, who embrace a strong religious faith, whose beliefs they can reasonably well articulate and which they actively practice. About 30 percent are what we label Selective Adherents, who believe and perform certain aspects of their religious traditions but neglect and ignore others. Something like 25 percent are Religiously Indifferent, who neither care to practice religion nor oppose it. About 15 percent are Spiritually Open—not personally very committed to a religious faith but nonetheless receptive to and at least mildly interested in some spiritual or religious matters. Another 5 percent are Religiously Disconnected, who have little to no exposure or connection to religious people, ideas, or organizations. And a final 10 percent is positively Irreligious, holding skeptical attitudes about and making critical arguments against religion generally, rejecting the idea of personal faith. Much of what we have offered as generalizations that pertain to the majority of emerging adults may apply differently or sometimes may not apply at all to different religious groups in this typology. Below the level of valid generalizations, in other words, many nuances, qualifications, exceptions, and counternarratives of various sorts remain that are well worth taking into account. Every valid study of emerging adult religion must therefore balance the lumping and the splitting, the general and the particular, the dominant and the alternative, the similar and the diverse. Taking either side too far produces a distorted view. We hope especially that this typology of six emerging adult religious categories presented in chapter 6, along with both the "less typical" cultural themes presented in chapters 2 and 4 and the multiple change trajectory slopes using growth mixture modeling plotted in chapter 8, help to balance some of the larger generalizations also offered in this book.

ARE EMERGING ADULTS INTERESTED IN "SPIRITUALITY?"

A quite common belief about emerging adults nowadays is that they are very interested in matters spiritual. Surveys of emerging adults, particularly by educational researchers of those enrolled in colleges and universities, repeatedly report high levels among them of interest in "spirituality." All of this seems to connect to the phrase, commonly heard in the media, about young people today being "spiritual but not religious" or being "spiritual seekers." And various popular books report that youth today are keen on spiritual matters but hate churches and traditional religion. We do think, on the basis of the NSYR findings, that there is some basis in fact for these claims and ideas. But we think that these claims are often exaggerated and misunderstood. In our study, we found that roughly 15 percent of emerging adults are what we called Spiritually Open. We definitely did see a somewhat greater readiness, especially among some of those teenagers who had previously been not very religious, to consider the idea that spiritual, supernatural, or divine things may be real and worth learning about. And there is definitely a larger segment among emerging adults than among teenagers that feels alienated from religious faith and organized religion. But we think the recognition of these facts needs to be tempered and put into context by realistic proportions and perspectives, as follows.

First, a solid majority of emerging adults simply are not that interested in matters religious or spiritual. They are either Selective Adherents who do what they want religiously and otherwise do not pay it much mind; or they are Religiously Indifferent, simply not really caring one way or the other; or they are Religiously Disconnected, simply lacking the social and institutional ties to religion to know or care that much about it in the first place. Think, for example, of Brad, Andy, and June. Beyond them, the Irreligious are not interested in "spirituality," other than to criticize it. Remember Ruth. Thus, it is primarily among the Committed Traditionalists and the Spiritually Open that genuine interest in spiritual matters is to be found. However, for most of the Committed Traditionalists, "spirituality" is not some free-floating experience of individualistic interiority and self-exploration—rather, it concerns specific practices, meanings, and experiences that are fairly closely tied to traditional religious faiths. Think of Amanda and Joy. Furthermore, among most of the Spiritually Open, "spirituality" is not the "holy grail–like" object of sustained, high-priority, personal quests to realize divine enlightenment or ultimate meaning. Most are in fact nothing more than simply *open*. They are not *actively* seeking, not taking a lot of initiative in pursuit of the spiritual. Someday it might come, but in the meantime they are not going after it as a project in life. They think about spiritual matters sometimes. They are happy to talk about spirituality in the right contexts. They have a lot of questions and uncertainties. And they are willing to entertain the possibility that reality consists of more than energy and matter, that the universe is not finally random and purposeless, that there could be more to reality than meets the eye. Beyond that, the seeking is often minimal. In this sense, Andrea is an example of a Spiritually Open emerging adult who is more actively seeking than are most. Therefore, while there is definitely some interest and openness to spiritual matters among today's emerging adults, it is not as pervasive and intense as some accounts say it is.

We suspect that one of the reasons some survey research reports higher levels of interest in spirituality among emerging adults than we found is this: the surveys themselves are constructed in a way that leaves the language of "spirituality" as the only way for respondents to register any kind of religious or nonatheistic interest. Thus, all respondents—from the most rigidly fundamentalist to the most nominal of Catholics or mainline Protestants to the most confused, nonatheistic, nonreligious emerging adult—get funneled as a matter of methodological procedure into the category of "is interested in spirituality," when in fact the reality is much more complex than that. And the more "spirituality" is discussed in the media with some fascination, the fewer emerging adults sitting with survey bubble sheets in hand will report that they are not interested in spirituality. Increasingly, to say such a thing seems to mean that one has no interest in one's own subjective, interior life. Meanwhile, there is no real cost to reporting on a survey that one cares about spiritual things. In this way, we suspect, emerging adult interest in spirituality may often be overestimated by survey research. Another analogous way to distort the actual extent of spiritual seeking or of a warm embrace of spirituality coupled with the angry rejection of organized or traditional religion is to conduct interviews with nonrepresentative samples of emerging adults whose speech validates the kind of interpretive story one wants to tell about religion. In our observation, these tend to take one of two typical forms. First are books and articles by authors who are themselves alienated from mainstream religion and wish to promote a "spiritual but not religious" agenda. Second are publications by pastoral and ecclesial reformers within mainstream religion—usually younger evangelical Protestants—who want to make the case that traditional churches are failing to reach young people today and so need to be dramatically transformed in a postmodern or some other allegedly promising way.

Again, there are elements of truth in both claims. Some people are "spiritual but not religious," and many traditional churches are often not effectively "reaching" young people today. Our point is not that those claims are entirely bogus. Our point is that what is true in them is often blown far out of proportion, misrepresenting the true extent and intensity of such attitudes about religion and spirituality among American emerging adults today. It is important, then, that we distinguish between the findings of good social science, the reports of methodologically limited survey research, and the claims of cultural and religious activists who are pushing their own agendas. All may be legitimate in their own ways. But they are not the same things. And their conclusions ought not to be consumed by readers and hearers with equal naïveté. So yes, some emerging adults, including students in college, are interested in spirituality. But for a good number of them, that simply means doing traditional religion. And for another chunk of them, that means they simply do not want to say that they are positively *not* interested in spirituality. Yet others may say whatever about matters spiritual but in fact are simply too distracted by other affairs to care very much. Only for quite a small minority of emerging adults are spiritual seeking and practicing lives that are spiritual-but-not-religious on the priority list—certainly more than among teenagers, but not all that much more.

POSITIVE LIFE OUTCOMES, NONETHELESS

Whatever else we might observe about emerging adulthood, religious continuity and change, influences of socialization, and the transformation of American religious culture, one other finding of this book merits underscoring before closing. That is that emerging adult religion—whatever its depth, character, and substance—correlates significantly with, and we think actually often acts as a causal influence producing, what most consider to be more positive outcomes in life for emerging adults. Whether we focus on relationships with parents, giving and volunteering, participation in organized activities, substance abuse, risky behaviors, moral compassion, physical health, bodily self-image, mental and emotional well-being, locus of control, life satisfaction, life purpose, feeling gratitude, educational achievement, resistance to consumerism, pornography use, or potentially problematic sexual activity, the more religious emerging adults are consistently doing better on these measures than the least religious emerging adults. These differences hold up even after controlling statistically for the possible influence of the seven variables of age, sex, race, region of residence, parental education, individual income, and parental assistance with expenses. We found no major or consistent differences between life outcomes and major religious traditions. Differences had to do not with belonging to one or another religious category—such as evangelical Protestant or Catholic or black Protestant—but rather with level of personal importance of faith and practice, in the forms of religious service attendance and prayer. Although the differences are sometimes only statistically significant for the most religiously devoted emerging adults, the overall patterns of difference clearly tend to work in linear fashion with progressively higher levels of religiousness. Thus, even among emerging adults, it is not the case that religion does not matter for forming the shapes of their lives. It does. Emerging adults who are more religious are living developing lives that undeniably look, feel, and produce results that are quantifiably different from those of the least religious emerging adults. And we have many good reasons to believe that religious faith and practice are at least partly the cause of those differences. Religion thus makes important differences in areas of life that matter to nearly everyone and have consequences for collective well-being and social and financial costs for society as a whole. Far from having dwindled into irrelevance, religion still matters and makes a positive difference in the lives of America's emerging adults.

CONCLUSION

Religion shapes society and culture. And social institutions and culture shape religion. Individual persons are powerfully formed by the traditions, cultures, and institutions in which they are raised and live their lives. Yet all people make ongoing choices and commitments and engage in practices that also affect the character and outcomes of their own lives and collectively sustain and shape the larger social world. In these ways, the continual exercise of social structurally shaped human agency gives rise to and sustains the same and other social and cultural structures, even while those social and cultural structures continue to form human persons precisely through their developing exercise of their own agency. All of this is very evident in the lives of emerging adults, including if not especially in their religious and spiritual lives. Notwithstanding their devotion to the ideas of personal freedom, autonomy, and self-direction, the lives of emerging adults are in fact profoundly formed and governed by the social and cultural structures of the world into which they are growing. At the same time, many of the same social and cultural structures are sustained and perpetuated only because millions of emerging adults and others involved in their lives have internalized and, through their ongoing thoughts, feelings, and behaviors, maintain them. No particular life is entirely determined by the social and cultural structures that it encounters and reproduces. But every emerging adult's life also in different ways clearly embodies and reflects the qualities and influences of the social and cultural structures in and by which it is lived. Swept along by powerful cultural and institutional currents, emerging adults sometimes even think, feel, and behave in ways that they do not understand or maybe even really want. That is the power of social life in and on individual persons. Emerging adulthood involves a host of particular social and cultural features and experiences that are characteristic of its newly existent phase in American life. And the religious and spiritual interests, assumptions, beliefs, experiences, values, and practices of emerging adults are always and in many ways powerfully formed by those social and cultural features and experiences.

Therefore, if emerging adults want in fact to pursue lives that are genuinely free and self-directed in ways that are worthy of their commitment and devotion, they will have to come to terms with many of the larger social and cultural forces to which their lives are now subject that do not obviously serve that end. They will have to exercise understanding and agency in ways that do not simply reproduce but rather challenge some of the more problematic aspects of emerging adult culture and life. And if communities of other adults who care about youth wish to nurture emerging adult lives of purpose, meaning, and character—instead of confusion, drifting, and shallowness—they will need to do better jobs of seriously engaging youth from early on and not cut them adrift as they move through the teenage years. More broadly, if anyone in the future is ever to know what is really good, right, and true, the challenges of the crises of knowledge and value that beset American culture today, described earlier, must be addressed, in order to learn more justifiably sure-footed ways to understand reality and the moral good. Lacking that, American culture has little to pass on to American youth with which they can navigate life beyond their experiences of their own subjective desires and feelings—on which alone it is not possible to build good lives. Finally, if traditions and communities of religious faith want better to foster ways that more of their own emerging adults can engage in lives of serious religious faith and practice, they, too, will have to come to terms with the social, cultural, and institutional structures and forces that govern emerging adulthood and shape religion and spirituality during this phase of life. It will not be enough simply to purify one's theological ideas or to ramp up new programs supposedly "relevant" to young people. The larger challenges to engage here are immense, and, complicating matters, certain religious traditions themselves—particularly liberal and evangelical Protestantism, as described above—are implicated in the structured character of emerging adulthood.

Yet, as noted, nothing is determined or static. Society, culture, and institutions are always evolving. Exactly where American culture and society, emerging adulthood itself, and religious communities and traditions in particular actually end up going in the future will in some measure be shaped by the beliefs, desires, commitments, decisions, and actions of emerging adults and those who care about their lives. Our purpose in writing this book has been to shed light on many crucial facts, issues, problems, challenges, and opportunities related to the religious, spiritual, and, more generally, personal and social lives of emerging adults in America. What comes next has yet to be written by the very people who have been the subject of this study.

Appendix A. Additional Tables and Figures

Table A.1. Summary of the Influence of Variables on Religiosity at Wave 3 for Five Model Specifications (N = 2,195) (Weighted)

	Wave 3 Religiosity					
	No LDV	LDV	From mod/ high to min/low	From min/low to mod/ high	From mod/min/ low to mod/high[a]	Percent significant[c]
Frequency of prayer	A	A	—	—	—	100
Religiosity of parents	A	A	A	A	A	100
Importance of teen faith	A	A	—	—	—	100
Few religious doubts	A	A	A	N	A	80
Religious experiences	A	A	B	A	A	90
Believes in divine miracles	A	A	B	A	A	90
Frequent scripture reading	A	A	A	N	N	60
Supportive religious adults	A	A	A	N	N	60
Has had oral sex or intercourse	A	A	A	N	N	60
Made fun of for religion	B	B	B	N	B	40
Believes in sex in marriage	B	B	A	N	N	40
Religious service attendance	B	B	—	—	—	50
Decide Morality by religion	B	B	A	N	N	40
Number of religious friends	B	B	B	N	N	30
Satisfied with congregation	B	N	N	N	A	30

(*continued*)

Table A.1 (Continued)

	Wave 3 Religiosity					
	No LDV	LDV	From mod/ high to min/low	From min/low to mod/ high	From mod/min/ low to mod/high[a]	Percent significant[c]
Sunday school attendance	B	B	B	N	N	30
Likes youth group	B	N	N	B	N	20
Parent-teen closeness	B	N	B	N	N	20
Number religious activities	B	N	B	N	N	20
Number mission trips	B	N	N	N	N	10
Enrolled in religious school	N	N	N	N	B	10
Wants similar church at 25	B	N	N	N	N	10
Parent income	B	N	N	N	N	10
Parent education	N	N	N	N	N	0
age	N	N	N	N	N	0
Race (White = reference)						
Black	A	A	A	A	A	100
Hispanic	B	N	N	A	A	50
Other	N	N	N	N	B	10
Female	B	N	N	A	N	30
Two-parent biological family	B	B	A	N	N	40
Enrolled in college (Wave 3)	B	N	N	N	N	10
N	2,193	2,193	1,393	800	1,471	

Source: National Study of Youth and Religion, 2002–2003, 2007–2008.

Note: A = significant in all models, including final; B = significant only in reduced block model; N = never Significant; — = not included in given model specification. The first two models are ordered logistic regressions. The final three models are logistic regressions and represent "initiation" models, meaning only respondents who were not in the outcome at Wave 1 were included in the analysis.

[a]The Moderate group was only counted if they moved into the Highest group, while the Lowest and Minimal counted if they moved into either the Moderate or Highest.

[b]Term is significant only in Final model and is in opposite direction from expected; not included in percent calculation.

[c]Percent calculated using A = 1; B = .5; N = 0.

Table A.2. Summary of Rankings of the Influence of Variables on Religiosity at Wave 3 for Five Model Specifications (N = 2,195) (Weighted)

	Wave 3 religiosity					
	No LDV	LDV	From Mod/ High to Min/Low	From Min/ Low to Mod/ High	From Mod/ Min/Low to Mod/ High[a]	Average Rank
Frequency of prayer	1	1	—	—	—	1.0
Religiosity of parents	2	2	2	1	1	1.6
Importance of teen faith	3	3	—	—	—	3.0
Few religious doubts	5	5	4	N/S	3	4.5
Religious experiences	6	6	14	2	2	6.0
Believes in divine miracles	8	8	13	3	4	7.2
Frequent scripture reading	4	4	1	N/S	N/S	4.0
Supportive religious adults	7	7	3	N/S	N/S	5.6
Has had oral sex or intercourse	9	9	5	N/S	N/S	6.6
Made fun of for religion	10	11	7	N/S	5	7.4
Believes in sex in marriage	21	14	12	N/S	N/S	11.6
Religious service attendance	11	10	—	—	—	11.5
Decide morality by religion	14	12	6	N/S	N/S	8.6
Number of religious friends	17	15	9	N/S	N/S	10.4
Satisfied with congregation	12	N/S	N/S	N/S	N/S	10.6
Sunday school attendance	16	N/S	10	N/S	N/S	10.6
Likes youth group	20	N/S	N/S	4	N/S	12.0
Parent-teen closeness	19	N/S	11	N/S	N/S	11.4
Number religious activities	13	N/S	8	N/S	N/S	9.6
Number mission trips	18	N/S	N/S	N/S	N/S	11.8
Enrolled in religious school	N/S	N/S	N/S	N/S	N/S	N/S
Wants similar church at 25	15	N/S	N/S	N/S	N/S	11.0
N	2,193	2,193	1,393	800	1,471	

Source: National Study of Youth and Religion, 2002–2003, 2007–2008.
Note: The first two models are ordered logistic regressions. The final three models are logistic regressions and represent "initiation" models, meaning only respondents who were not in the outcome at Wave 1 were included in the analysis. Rankings are derived from standardized coefficients. Rank is determined first within terms significant in final model, and then within variables only significant in block models. N/S = term never significant in any model (assigned highest rank value in model + 1 for average calculation).

[a]The Moderate group was only counted if they moved into the Highest group, while the Lowest and Minimal counted if they moved into either the moderate or highest.

[b]Term is significant only in Final model and is in opposite direction from expected.

Table A.3. Religious Ideal Type by Religious Tradition, Ages 18–23

Religious Tradition	Religious ideal type					
	Devoted	Regular	Sporadic	Disengaged	Mixed	Total
Conservative Protestant	52	39	25	7	34	28
	15	19	16	6	43	100
Mainline Protestant	9	14	18	6	10	11
	7	18	30	14	31	100
Black Protestant	5	7	7	2	12	7
	6	13	16	8	56	100
Roman Catholic	4	28	39	11	16	19
	2	19	36	15	28	100
Jewish	1	0	2	2	0	1
	7	4	40	36	14	100
LDS	21	3	1	1	2	3
	56	15	4	5	19	100
Nonreligious	0	1	1	69	17	24
	0	1	1	74	25	100
Other Religion	5	2	3	1	3	3
	15	10	23	11	40	100
Independent	3	5	4	2	6	4
	5	16	18	10	52	100
Total	100	100	100	100	100	100
	8	13	18	26	35	100

Source: National Survey of Youth and Religion, 2007–2008.
Note: Shaded portions of the table indicate row percentage totals; unshaded portions indicate column percentage totals. Percentages are rounded to the nearest whole number and may not add to 100.

Table A.4. Demographic Traits of Religious Ideal Types of U.S. Emerging Adults, Ages 18–23 (Percents)

	U.S.	Religious ideal type			
		Devoted	Regulars	Sporadic	Disengaged
Age					
18	18	13	26	15	17
19	20	20	23	22	22
20	21	23	20	26	18
21	21	27	17	20	22
22	17	15	12	14	19
23	2	2	1	2	3
Female	52	61	49	52	43
Race					
White	68	72	67	70	79
Black	15	13	13	13	5
Hispanic	11	12	15	12	9
Other	5	3	4	5	5

Source: National Survey of Youth and Religion, 2007–2008.
Note: Percentages are rounded to the nearest whole number.

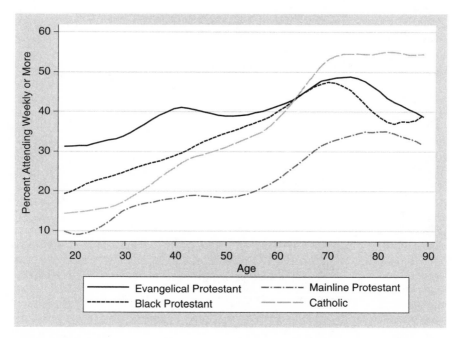

Figure A.1. Percent Attending Religious Service Weekly or More by Religious Tradition and Age

Source: GSS 1990–2006.

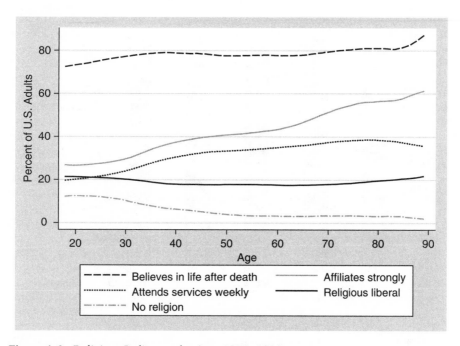

Figure A.2. Religious Indicators by Age, 1972–1980

Source: GSS 1972–1980.

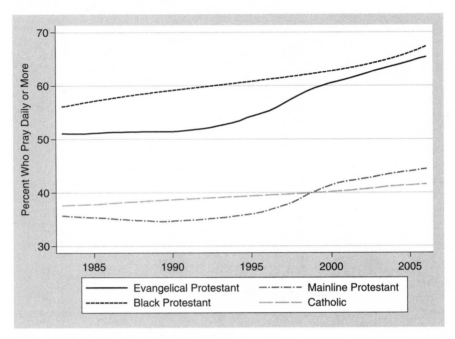

Figure A.3. Percent of 18- to 25-year-olds Praying Daily or More by Religious Tradition, 1983–2006

Source: GSS 1983–2006.

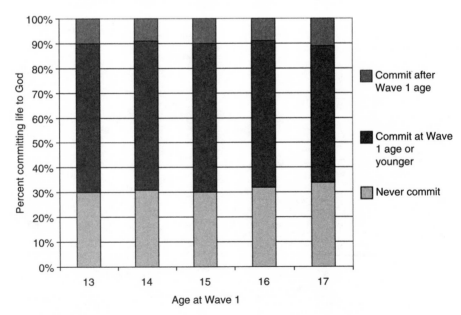

Figure A.4. Percentage of Commitments within Each Wave 1 Age Group (N = 3,132)

Source: National Study of Youth and Religion 2002–2003, 2004–2005, 2007–2008.

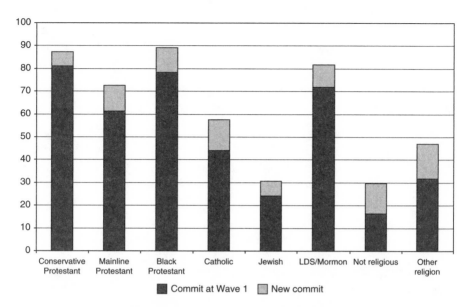

Figure A.5. Percent of each Major Religious Tradition Affiliation who Commit Life to God (N = 3,132)

Source: National Study of Youth and Religion, 2002–2003, 2007–2008.

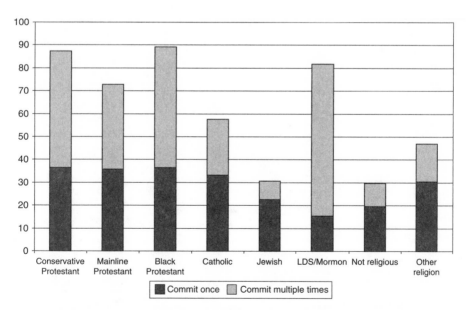

Figure A.6. Percent of Each Major Religious Tradition Affiliation Who Commit Life to God (N = 3,132)

Source: National Study of Youth and Religion, 2002–2003, 2007–2008.

Appendix B. Research Methodology

This appendix describes the methods used to collect the survey and interview data analyzed in this book.

TELEPHONE SURVEY METHODOLOGY
AND SAMPLE STATISTICS

In conducting the third wave NSYR wave survey, every attempt was made to reinterview all English-speaking Wave 1 youth survey respondents. At the time of the third survey, respondents were between the ages of 18 and 23. The survey was conducted from September 24, 2007 through April 21, 2008, using a computer-assisted telephone interviewing (CATI) system programmed using Blaise software. The Howard W. Odum Institute for Research in Social Sciences at the University of North Carolina at Chapel Hill (Odum Institute) was hired to field the Wave 3 survey. Telephone calls were spread out over varying days and times, including nights and weekends. Every effort was made to recontact and resurvey all original NSYR respondents (whether they completed the Wave 2 telephone survey or not), including those out of the country, in the military, and on religious missions. There were more difficulties in contacting and completing the survey with respondents who were in the military during Wave 3 because some of them were serving on active duty and were unable to be reached; even their families were often unaware of their specific locations and did not have any knowledge of phone numbers or addresses where they could be reached. The Wave 3 survey instrument replicated many of the questions asked in Waves 1 and 2, with some changes made to better capture the respondents' lives as they grew older. For example, there were fewer questions on parental monitoring and more on post–high school educational aspirations.

The Odum Institute conducted a pretest with 60 respondents, some of whom had been pretests in previous waves and some who were newly recruited using a targeted-age sample (18–23 years) obtained from Survey Sampling International (SSI). The pretest cases were recruited by the survey interviewers to give them practice on the phone. Before conducting the pretest surveys, the interviewers, who were hired by the Odum Institute, participated in a four-day project-specific training session led by the call center director, supervisors, and the NSYR project staff. Many of the survey interviewers had previous experience working for the NSYR or had worked as interviewers on other projects at the Odum Institute. All NSYR survey interviewers were required to take part in Human Subjects Research Certification verifying that they understood the importance of participant's confidentiality and the rights of research participants. As in Wave 2, survey interviewers were routinely monitored remotely by both Odum Institute supervisors and the NSYR staff. As in previous waves, prior to beginning the telephone survey, each respondent's verbal consent was obtained. As all respondents were over the age of 18 at the time of the third wave survey, parental consent was no longer required. In Wave 3, respondent identity was confirmed using name, date of birth, and the name of the city and state where the respondent had completed the first wave survey.

In between Waves 2 and 3, NSYR project staff maintained all in-between survey respondent tracking efforts. Going into the Wave 3 telephone survey, the project staff had viable respondent addresses for over 92 percent of the original survey respondents and viable phone numbers for almost 80 percent. Some of the phone numbers that were valid at the start of the survey had been changed or disconnected during the period of time the survey was being fielded. In Wave 3, the Odum Institute was contracted to conduct during-survey respondent tracking so that when new phone numbers were identified they could immediately be transferred to the call center to be attempted and verified. Their tracking efforts included calling and tracing all contact numbers available for each "lost" respondent, using all available public records to search for new respondent phone numbers, and contracting with an outside vendor, LexisNexis. Names of lost respondents, along with available contact information, were sent to and returned from LexisNexis in batches. When new phone numbers were identified, they were first entered into the NSYR master contact database, and then the new phone numbers were tried in the call center. During the survey, all contact with respondents was carefully documented and recorded in the NSYR contact database. This detailed record keeping is critical so that in future waves it is known what has been tried and worked (or not worked) previously for keeping in touch with respondents.

Some new respondent-tracing challenges were encountered in Wave 3. More of the respondents than in previous waves were using cell phones exclusively, having moved away from their family homes, and most had not set up land phone lines. Cell phone numbers are largely unpublished, so it proved somewhat difficult for the staff to come up with ways to try to reach these respondents. This meant that staff relied heavily on the mailing addresses that were known to be correct and on getting messages to the respondents through their family members and contacts. Another challenge was persuading respondents to call back in to the call center. It is very common for young adults of this age range to screen their cell phone calls. It was quite rare for a respondent to answer on the first call. Also a challenge was trying to get the respondents to do the interview when they did finally answer their phones. There seemed to be a tendency among the respondents to procrastinate and put off doing the survey for as long as they could. It was not that they did not want to do the survey, just that they sometimes did not want to do it right at the moment they were called. Many repeatedly scheduled and reschedule the survey, right up until the date the survey fielding was finishing.

Of the total 3,328 original respondents (the 3,364 original sample minus those found to be date-of-birth outliers in Wave 2; and those who were discovered to have passed away before the fielding of the Wave 3 survey) who in Wave 3 all attempts were made to resurvey, 36 were found to be ineligible to participate (10 on active military duty overseas; 1 incapable; 11 institutionalized; 5 having a language barrier; 9 deceased). The following are the Wave 3 survey rates: (1) W3 OVERALL RETENTION RATE—Of the remaining eligible 3,282 Wave 1 respondents, 2,532 participated in the Wave 3 survey (including 13 partial cases [cases were only counted as partials if they had completed up through the first religion section of the survey]), for a Wave 3 completion rate of 77.1 percent; (2) W2/W3 RETENTION RATE—Of the respondents who completed the Wave 2 survey, 86.3 percent completed the Wave 3 survey; (3) W1/W2/W3 RETENTION RATE—Of the original eligible respondents, 68.4 percent completed both the Wave 2 and the Wave 3 surveys (note that 274 respondents who did not complete the W2 survey did complete the W3 survey) (4) W1/W3 COMBINED RESPONSE RATE—43.9 percent (calculated by multiplying the W1 and W3 response rates); (5) W3 ATTRITION RATE—Of the total original eligible respondents, 22.9 percent did not complete the Wave 3 survey; (6) W3 REFUSAL RATE—Of the total original eligible respondents, 6 percent refused to participate in the Wave 3 survey; (7) W3 CONTACT RATE—Of the total original eligible respondents, 87.7 percent were successfully contacted (whether they completed the survey or not).

On key demographic variables, only very minor differences were found between Wave 1 and Wave 3 responders and even smaller differences between the Wave 2 and Wave 3 responders (see tables B.1 and B.2). Key behavioral variables, such as never drink alcohol, never use marijuana, and regular smoking of cigarettes again reveal very minor differences between W1 and W3 responders and even smaller differences between W2 and W3 responders (see tables B.3 and B.4). Similar to what was found in Wave 2, when analyses are run comparing Wave 3 responders to nonresponders, we see that nonresponders are slightly more likely to never attend religious services. This finding is consistent with other social science research. Longitudinal weights were calculated for use when analyzing data from Wave 3 with *either* Wave 1 or Wave 2 of the NSYR survey data (excluding data from the Jewish oversample). To develop the new raw weight, a simple correction factor was applied within each region-income stratum (defined by the four census regions and five income levels at Wave 1) to adjust the weight for each individual. This accounts for the change in the distribution of the respondents of the NSYR by census regions and income groups resulting from Wave 3 sample attrition.

METHODOLOGICAL DESIGN AND PROCEDURES FOR THE NSYR WAVE 3 PERSONAL INTERVIEWS

The third wave of in-person interviews for the NSYR involved in-depth personal interviews with 230 of the third wave telephone survey respondents. The purpose of the interviews was to provide extended follow-up discussion about teens' religious, spiritual, family, and social lives. The questionnaire included much of what was used in Waves 1 and 2, with the addition of several new topics of interest. Interviews were conducted almost exclusively in person and were digitally recorded. They lasted an average of approximately 135 minutes, and ranged from 40 to 272 minutes long. Respondents were offered a $75–$100 cash incentive to complete the interviews. The in-person interviews were conducted between May and September 2008, begun approximately one month after the official close-out of the Wave 3 telephone survey. Of the interview subjects, 151 were selected from the 267 teens who had given in-person interviews in Wave 1, and an additional 79 interviews were conducted with survey respondents who had never completed an in-person interview for the study. New in-person interview sample subjects were selected in order to refresh the sample and to check through the comparison of their answers with those of prior interviewees for the possible "contamination" or "training" of interview answers as a result of prior interviewees' experiences of completing prior interviews. We did not detect significant differences between the two types of sample. To be eligible for the Wave 3 in-person interview, a subject was required to have participated in the NSYR's Wave 3 telephone survey.

Our sampling strategy for the 151 original in-person interview respondents was to replicate the Wave 1 sample, which represented a range of demographic and religious characteristics and took into account region, residential location (urban/suburban/rural), age, sex, race, household income, religion, and school type. The new in-person interview respondents were chosen by combinations of geographic region, religious type, race/ethnicity, and sex to balance out the original sample. The researchers clustered the respondents with whom they were still in contact into geographic areas for ease of travel in interviewing. The time lapse between a respondent completing the Wave 3 telephone survey and completing a personal interview ranged from 1 to 12 months. The age range of the respondents when they completed the Wave 3 personal interviews was between 18 and 23, with a mean age of 20.5.

Twelve interviewers conducted interviews in 35 states in all geographic regions (West, South, Northeast, and Midwest) of the United States; each interviewer conducted between 6 and 31 interviews. Five of the interviewers had conducted personal interviews for the NSYR in either Wave 1 or Wave 2, and respondents were matched with their Wave 1 or Wave 2 interviewers as much as possible. Before the fielding of the in-person interviews, six of the new interviewers took a semester-long course, taught by the principle investigator, on personal interviewing techniques and project-specific NSYR interview details. All new interviewers participated in a day-long training meeting, held by the NSYR project manager and the principle investigator. The training covered the logistics of the interview process, procedural requirements, Institutional Review Board (i.e., Human Subjects) concerns, protection of human participants, safety and liability concerns, and keys to NSYR interview success. In addition to that training, all interviewers were required to obtain Human Participants Training Certification.

The 12 project interviewers were assigned to sets of specific geographic locations around the United States. Each interviewer was provided with groups of contact sheets for teens in their assigned geographic areas. The contact sheets included respondent name, respondent nickname (if known), parent name, address, phone number, respondent birth date, respondent gender, respondent race, household income, religious affiliation, and religious denomination or tradition. The contact sheet also included space to note any changes to the contact information provided (new phone number, additional email address, etc.) and provided a call record. Interviewers recorded each household contact, noting the date, time, with whom they spoke, and the content of each contact. In additional to the original sample, as the project progressed through the interviews, the priorities shifted somewhat according to what types of respondent interviews were still needed. In this way, the researchers attempted to match the demographics of the original Wave 2 in-person interview sample as much as possible.

In addition to the demographic information on the contact sheet, interviewers were also asked to review the transcripts of the previous in-person interviews. If an interviewer had not conducted the previous personal interviews with his or her respondents, the transcripts provided background information about that respondent to help facilitate a smooth interview. Using a standard call script provided by the NSYR, interviewers made contact with potential interviewee households. Interviewers identified themselves as researchers with the "National Youth Study." The full name of the research project was not used in order to avoid introducing any response bias by identifying religion as a key focus of the study. It was often helpful for interviewers to explain their connection with the project, for example, graduate student, coinvestigator, and so on. However, since much of the interview was about religion and the researchers did not want to bias the respondents' answers, interviewers were instructed to avoid divulging revealing information about their own personal beliefs and commitments (of which there was considerable diversity on the interviewing team).

Interviewers were required to obtain verbal consent to conduct the interview from the respondent. If respondents seemed hesitant about participating, an additional script provided more information about the project and offered the phone number of the principal investigator, whom they could call with questions or concerns. In addition, interviewers offered to mail written information about the project to hesitant respondents and then call back in a few days. When a respondent seemed reluctant to participate or was hesitant about the time commitment, an additional incentive was offered. However, in cases when respondents refused to participate even after being offered additional information, interviewers made no further attempts to convert those who refused. On receiving verbal consent from the respondent and scheduling an interview time, interviewers mailed packets of information to households. The packet contained a cover letter from the principle investigator, multiple copies of respondent written consent forms, and an appointment letter, including a portrait photo of the interviewer. Interviewees were required to bring the copies of the written signed consent form with them to their interviews. Interviewers also called the respondents at least one week prior to the interview and again the day before the interview to confirm that the respondents were still planning to participate.

Interviews were conducted in public settings that nevertheless provided confidentiality for the respondent. The ideal location for these interviews was in study rooms at local libraries. However, when these were not available, interviews were also conducted in restaurants, coffee shops, mall food courts, and outdoor settings. Interviewers were given guidelines for how to present themselves during the interviews as well as appropriate attire to be worn in order to ensure consistency in the presentation of interviewers across the interviews. Specifically, interviewers did not attempt to "relate" to respondents by dressing down or dressing in a more "trendy" fashion. Interviewers presented themselves as professional researchers with a sincere interest in young people's lives. At the close of the interview, respondents were given the cash incentive for their participation and in appreciation of their time and effort. The final sample of interviews included 230 complete interviews selected from the respondents who had completed the Wave 3 telephone survey. Of these, 151 were sampled from the original Wave 1 personal interview respondents and 79 were new in-person interview subjects. Out of the 116 original Wave 1 interview cases who were not reinterviewed, 14 were purposely never contacted, and an additional 29 could not be contacted because they had recently relocated. Fifty-nine could not be interviewed in person because they had failed to complete the Wave 3 phone survey, and 9 interviews failed for reasons such as scheduling problems and emergencies. Five original Wave 1 respondents who were eligible to conduct an interview refused to participate in the Wave 3 interview. Table B.5 provides the demographics of all 230 interviews in Wave 3. With the exception of age, the table reflects the demographic information that was collected at the time of the Wave 1 telephone survey. The age listed is the age of the teen at the time of the Wave 3 personal interview.

Table B.1. Comparison of W1 Respondents, W2 Respondents, W3 Respondents, and W3 Nonrespondents on Key Demographic Characteristics (Unweighted)

Wave 1:	W1 Respondents	W2 Respondents	W3 Respondents	W3 Nonrespondents[b]
Census region				
Northeast	15	15	15	15
Midwest	23	24	25	17
South	42	41	41	45
West	20	20	19	23
Gender				
Male	51	50	49	56
Female	49	50	51	44
Age				
13	19	19	19	18
14	20	20	20	18
15	21	22	22	20
16	20	20	20	20
17	20	19	19	25
Race/ethnicity				
White	65	69	69	55
Black	17	16	16	22
Hispanic	12	10	10	17
Asian/Pacific Islander/ American Indian/ mixed/other	5	5	5	6
Missing	1	1	1	1
Family Structure[c]				
Lives with two biological/ adoptive parents	51	56	55	38
Income				
Less than $10K	3	3	3	6
$10K–20K	7	6	6	10
$20K–30K	12	11	11	17
$30K–40K	13	12	12	17
$40K–50K	13	14	14	12
$50K–60K	11	11	11	9
$60K–70K	7	8	8	6
$70K–80K	6	7	7	3
$80K–90K	5	6	6	3
$90K–100K	4	4	4	3
More than $100K	11	12	13	7
Missing	6	6	6	6
N[a]	3,259	2,530	2,458	782

Note: Numbers represent percents. Percents may not add to 100 due to rounding.

[a]N does not include the Jewish oversample cases (N = 80 for Wave 1; N = 74 for Wave 2; N = 78 for Wave 3). N also does not include "ineligibles" (N = 31).

[b]Nonrespondents do not include deceased or "ineligibles." At Wave 3, N = 782 or 24 percent of the original 3,259 respondents.

[c]Family structure contains some missing data. The appropriate N by wave is Wave 1 = 3,227; Wave 2 = 2,510; Wave 3 = 2,433.

Table B.2. Comparison of W1 Respondents, W2 Respondents, W3 Respondents, and W3 Nonrespondents on Key Demographic Characteristics (Weighted)

Wave 1:	W1 Respondents	W2 Respondents	W3 Respondents
Census region			
Northeast	17	17	17
Midwest	22	23	22
South	37	36	37
West	24	24	24
Gender			
Male	51	49	48
Female	49	51	52
Age			
13	18	19	18
14	20	20	20
15	21	21	21
16	21	21	21
17	20	19	19
Race/ethnicity			
White	66	69	68
Black	16	14	15
Hispanic	12	10	11
Asian/Pacific Islander/ American Indian/ mixed/other	5	6	5
Missing	1	1	1
Family structure[a]			
Lives with two biological/adoptive parents	55	59	57
Income			
Less than $10K	5	3	4
$10K–20K	9	8	10
$20K–30K	9	8	9
$30K–40K	10	9	10
$40K–50K	10	10	10
$50K–60K	8	8	8
$60K–70K	9	10	8
$70K–80K	7	8	7
$80K–90K	5	6	5
$90K–100K	4	5	4
More than $100K	18	18	17
Missing	6	6	6
N[b]	3,259	2,530	2,458

Note: Numbers represent percents. Percents may not add to 100 due to rounding. Wave-specific weights used.

[a]N does not include the Jewish oversample cases (N = 74 for Wave 2; N = 78 for Wave 3). Total Wave 2 N = 2,604; total Wave 3 N = 2,532.

[b]Family structure contains some missing data. The appropriate N by wave is Wave 1 = 3,227; Wave 2 = 2,510; Wave 3 = 2,433.

Table B.3. Comparison of W1 Respondents, W2 Respondents, W3 Respondents, and W3 Nonrespondents on Key Lifestyle Characteristics (Unweighted)

Wave 1:	W1 Respondents	W2 Respondents	W3 Respondents	W3 Nonrespondents[a]
Never drinks alcohol	62	62	62	61
Never used marijuana	74	77	76	67
Smokes cigarettes regularly	8	7	7	11
Nights per week eats dinner with one parent (*mean*)[b]	5	5	5	7
School type attending				
Public	87	87	86	87
Private religious	7	7	8	4
Private secular	2	2	2	2
Home-schooled	2	2	2	2
Other	2	2	2	4
Missing	0	0	0	1
Attends religious services weekly or more often	39	41	42	29
Never attends religious services	18	17	17	24
N[c]	3,259	2,530	2,458	786

Note: Numbers represent percents. Percents may not add to 100 due to rounding.

[a]N does not include the Jewish oversample cases (N = 74 for Wave 2; N = 78 for Wave 3). Total Wave 2 N = 2,604; total Wave 3 N = 2,532.

[b]Nonrespondents do not include deceased or "ineligibles." At Wave 3, N = 782 or 24 percent of the original 3,259 respondents.

[c]Of nonmissing data.

Table B.4. Comparison of W1 Respondents, W2 Respondents, W3 Respondents, and W3 Nonrespondents on Key Lifestyle Characteristics (Weighted)

Wave 1:	W1 Respondents	W2 Respondents	W3 Respondents
Never drinks alcohol	63	63	63
Never used marijuana	75	78	78
Smokes cigarettes regularly	7	6	7
Nights per week eats dinner with one parent (*mean*)[a]	5	5	5
School type attending			
Public	87	87	87
Private religious	7	8	8
Private secular	2	2	2
Home schooled	2	2	2
Other	2	1	1
Missing	0	0	0
Attends religious services weekly or more	41	43	43
Never attends religious services	18	17	17
N[b]	3,260	2,530	2,454

Note: Numbers represent percents. Percents may not add to 100 due to rounding. Wave-specific weights used.

[a]N does not include the Jewish oversample cases (N = 74 for Wave 2; N = 78 for Wave 3). Total Wave 2 N = 2,604; total Wave 3 N = 2,532.

[b]Of nonmissing data.

Table B.5. NSYR Wave 3 Personal Interview Demographics

Gender	N	Region	N
Female	114	Midwest	77
Male	116	Northeast	28
		South	68
Age	**N**	West	57
18	23		
19	50	**Religion***	**N**
20	52	Protestant	109
21	36	*Adventist*	1
22	49	*Assemblies of God*	2
23	19	*Baptist*	44
24	1	*Bible Church*	1
		Brethren	1
Race	**N**	*Christian or just Christian*	18
White	149	*Church of Christ*	2
Hispanic	25	*Church of the Nazarene*	2
Black	33	*Congregationalist*	1
Asian	8	*Episcopalian*	1
Native American	4	*Evangelical*	1
Other	11	*Lutheran*	8
		Methodist	11
HH income	**N**	*Nondenominational*	6
Less than $10K	5	*Pentecostal*	3
$10K–$20K	13	*Presbyterian*	7
$21K–$30K	25	Catholic	35
$31K–$40K	12	Mormon	14
$41K–$50K	36	Jewish	16
$51K–$60K	22	Buddhist	2
$61K–$70K	24	Muslim/Islamic	3
$71K–$80K	19	Jehovah's Witness	1
$81K–$90K	13	Hindu	1
$91K–$100K	11	Eastern Orthodox	2
More than $100K	40	Unitarian Universalist	1
Don't know/refused	10	Native American	1
		Other	3
		Don't know	5
		Not religious	37

* Where respondent attended in Wave 1.

Notes

INTRODUCTION

1. To avoid confusion, we will use the first person plural—*we, us, our*—throughout to refer to this book's coauthors, except in certain parts that, we will note, will be recounted by Christian Smith (and in which we will use the first person—*I, me, my,* etc.).

2. The meaning of this term is explained later. Here we wish to say that our use of the word "emerging" is not intended to have any connection to the movement currently afoot among certain generally younger Christians in the United States known as the "emerging church," "emergent church," about which this book takes no particular position.

3. For detailed information about the research methodology used in the first wave of NSYR, see Christian Smith and Melinda Lundquist Denton, *Methodological Design and Procedures for the National Survey of Youth and Religion (NSYR)* (Chapel Hill, NC: National Study of Youth and Religion, 2003); Christian Smith, with Melinda Lundquist Denton, *Soul Searching: The Religious and Spiritual Lives of American Teenagers* (New York: Oxford University Press, 2005), 272–310.

4. Smith with Denton, *Soul Searching.*

5. For detailed information about the research methodology used in the second wave of the NSYR, see Christian Smith, Lisa Pearce, and Melinda Lundquist Denton, *Methodological Design and Procedures for the National Study of Youth and Religion (NSYR) Longitudinal Telephone Survey (Waves 1 & 2)* (Chapel Hill, NC: National Study of Youth and Religion, 2006).

6. See Christian Smith, Lisa Pearce, and Melinda Lundquist Denton, *National Study of Youth and Religion Telephone Survey Codebook Introduction and Methods (Waves 1, 2 & 3)* (Chapel Hill, NC: National Study of Youth and Religion, 2008).

7. Additional information about empirical data that this book analyzes and inter-
prets, which serve as the basis of its findings and story, is as follows (and described in
further depth in appendix B). The data come, as noted, from a nationally representative telephone survey of 2,532 18- to 23-year-old Americans and in-depth personal
interviews conducted with a subsample of 230 of those survey respondents living in
37 states around the United States (all states but Alaska, Hawaii, Tennessee, Arkansas,
Iowa, Oklahoma, Kansas, Nebraska, South Dakota, North Dakota, Wyoming, Colorado, and Montana). (In addition, chapter 2 presents findings from analyses of data
from the GSS, years 1972 to 2006.) Of these 230 interview respondents, 158 had been
interviewed before in prior waves of the study, and 71 were interviewed for the first
time in this third wave. The new interviewees were introduced in order to refresh the
sample and to check through the comparison of their answers with those of prior interviewees for the possible "contamination" or "training" of their interview answers as a
result of their experience of completing prior interviews (the interviews in fact did not
suggest that this happened). All participants in this sample were originally recruited
to take part in a nationally representative, random-digit-dial telephone survey first
conducted in 2002 and 2003. Those participants were at that time randomly sampled
and shown by subsequent analyses to closely represent all American youth of that age
group (see Smith and Denton, *Methodological Design and Procedures*). Between survey waves, NSYR researchers made every reasonable effort to remain in contact with
first wave respondents and to track down apparently "lost cases." Those efforts met
with success. The retention, or response, rate of first wave participants in this third
wave study is 77.1 percent—very high for a study of this age population tracked over
this number of years. The third wave cooperation rate of respondents contacted was a
high 87.7 percent. The refusal rate for the third wave survey was a low 6 percent. In
short, the large majority of those who completed the first wave survey also completed
(the second wave survey and) the third wave survey, and a very large percentage of
those we contacted agreed to participate. The vast majority of the first wave survey
who are not represented in the third wave study were cases that were "lost" between
surveys, due mostly to their moving and not sending new contact information to the
study tracking supervisors, with the result that they were not able to track these first
wave participants down.

Actually, however, more important than the calculated third wave refusal, cooperation, and response (attrition) rates is of whether any possible nonresponse bias
is present in the third wave NSYR data. The issue here is whether those first wave
respondents who did not complete the third wave survey (i.e., nonresponders) are
significantly different from those who did complete it. If they were different, then
the third wave data would be biased in the direction of characteristics of those who
were disproportionately likely to have completed the survey. If, for example, white or
southern or wealthy youth were more likely to complete the third wave survey, then
that survey's data would be biased toward answers that would be more likely to be
given by whites or southerners or wealthy youth for questions on which their answers
would tend to differ. Fortunately, the third wave survey data contain no detectable
nonresponse biases—as a result of many factors, including the rigorous contact and
tracking methods employed by the NSYR, the generally positive experience enjoyed
by respondents of previous NSYR survey waves (as reported to NSYR researchers
by many survey and interview respondents), the professional skills of the research
survey calling center staff who conducted the surveys (the second and third waves of
the NSYR survey were conducted by the Odum Call Center of the Howard W. Odum
Institute for Research in Social Science at the University of North Carolina at Chapel

Hill, under the gifted leadership of Teresa Edwards, Michelle Temple, Thu-Mai Christian, and Terri Clark), and a reasonable incentive to participate (third wave survey
respondents were paid $45 to complete the 52-minute, on average, telephone survey).
As with the first wave of NSYR data, minor original disproportions have been statistically corrected by applying a weight variable that adjusts for slight sample differences
in region and income. But analyses of the weighted third wave NSYR data, comparing
them to known population characteristics represented in Census and other highly reliable datasets, show that the third wave NSYR survey data can be taken to be statistically representative of all American 18- to 23-year-olds who are not in prison, serving
in the military, or otherwise institutionalized (see tables B.1–B.4); according to the U.S.
Census Bureau's American Community Survey, 1.59 percent of the total U.S. population who were between the ages of 18 and 24 in 2007 were incarcerated that year:
specifically, 475,900 U.S. citizens between the ages of 18 and 24 were held in state or
federal prisons or in local jails in 2007; see William Sabol and Heather Couture, *Prison
Inmates at Midyear 2007: Bureau of Justice Statistics Bulletin,* U.S. Department of Justice, June 2007, table 9, p. 7. According to the Department of Defense Manpower Data
Center 2006 report, 2.7 percent of the same 18- to 24-year-old population: specifically, 145,774 U.S. citizens between the ages of 18 and 24 were serving active military
duty in that year; see U.S. Department of Defense, Defense Manpower Data Center,
Population Representation in the Military Services 2006 (Washington, DC: Department of Defense, 2006). Furthermore—although stratified quota sampling were used
to select the third wave interview respondents—the subsample of survey respondents
with whom the 230 in-depth, personal interviews were conducted in 2008 proved to
be essentially representative of the proportions found in the general population on a set
of key demographic variables (see table B.5). That means, in short, that the statistical
and interview evidence presented in this book can be assumed with high confidence to
accurately represent the entire U.S. emerging adult population about which it intends
to speak. Stated even more simply, we can be very confident on social scientific grounds
that the evidence on which this book is based is solid and valid for authorizing the kind
of findings and conclusions that we present in this book. Methodologically, the data
are sound.

   For another longitudinal study of religion over the life course, see Michele Dillon
and Paul Wink, *In the Course of a Lifetime: Tracing Religious Belief, Practice, and
Change* (Berkeley: University of California Press, 2007).

   8. Many major extant scholarly works on emerging adulthood pay relatively little
sustained attention to the religious and spiritual lives of emerging adults: for example,
Richard Settersten, Frank Furstenberg, and Rubén Rumbaut, eds., *On the Frontiers
of Adulthood* (Chicago: University of Chicago Press, 2005); Jeffrey Arnett and Jen-
nifer Tanner, eds., *Emerging Adults in America: Coming of Age in the Twenty-first
Century* (Washington, DC: American Psychological Association, 2005); Jeffrey Arnett,
Adolescence and Emerging Adulthood: A Cultural Approach (Upper Saddle River, NJ:
Pearson, 2007). One major work on difficulties and solutions during emerging adult-
hood for socially vulnerable populations appears to make no mention of religion at all:
D. Wayne Osgood, E. Michael Foster, Constance Flanagan, and Gretchen Ruth, *On
Your Own without a Net: The Transition to Adulthood for Vulnerable Populations*
(Chicago: University of Chicago Press, 2005).

   9. We will also suggest later that some of the findings provide a corrective to some
alarmist and (we think) inaccurate views on these matters by some authors who stress
the deep-seated alienation of most emerging adults from mainstream American religion, particularly Christianity, including, for instance, David Kinnaman and Gabe

Lyons, *UnChristian: What a New Generation Thinks about Christianity...and Why It Matters* (Grand Rapids, MI: Baker Books, 2007), and Dan Kimball, *They Like Jesus but Not the Church: Insights from Emerging Generations* (Grand Rapids, MI: Zondervan, 2007).

10. This study benefits from and builds on a number of other very good, prior research projects on the religion of American youth—including Robert Wuthnow, *After the Baby Boomers: How Twenty- and Thirty-somethings Are Shaping the Future of American Religion* (Princeton, NJ: Princeton University Press, 2007); Tim Clydesdale, *The First Year Out: Understanding American Teens after High School* (Chicago: University of Chicago Press, 2007); Richard Flory and Donald Miller, *Finding Faith: The Spiritual Quest of the Post-boomer Generation* (New Brunswick, NJ: Rutgers University Press, 2007); for a view from the British context, see Sara Savage, Sylvia Collins-Mayo, Bob Mayo, and Graham Cray, *Making Sense of Generation Y: The World View of 15- to 25-Year-Olds* (London: Church House, 2006); and from an Australian context, see Michael Mason, Ruth Webber, and Andrew Singleton, *The Spirit of Generation Y: Young People's Spirituality in a Changing Australia* (Mulgrave, Victoria, Australia: John Garratt, 2008). But this book is also unique in certain important ways. The combination of first, the national scope of its research; second, its mixing of survey and interview methods for data gathering; and third, the longitudinal nature of the data collection, which has tracked and studied the same respondents over time in order to follow developmental changes in their lives, together make this study distinctive. Some prior studies of emerging adults offer depth and insight of analysis but are not based on nationally representative samples and so leave one unsure about to whom their findings can actually be generalized. Other previous studies are based on solid, nationally representative survey data but lack in-depth interviews to help contextualize and interpret the meaning of their numbers. That, we think, is a drawback. Still other previous studies nicely combine both survey and interview data but are limited to cross-sectional evidence—data collected at only one point in time—restricting their ability to speak to the ways characteristics, influences, and outcomes may change developmentally over time. All of these prior studies are valuable in different ways. But this book's contribution to the conversation combines many strengths that together make it distinctive—a study we hope will greatly enhance readers' knowledge and understanding of the issue in question. For other related studies, see Search Institute, *With Their Own Voices: A Global Exploration of How Today's Young People Experience and Think about Spiritual Development* (Minneapolis: Search Institute Center for Spiritual Development in Childhood and Adolescence, 2008).

11. This and the following three paragraphs are revised versions of part of a book review, Christian Smith, "Getting a Life: The Challenge of Emerging Adulthood," *Books and Culture*, November–December 2007, 10–13.

12. Jeffrey Arnett, "Emerging Adulthood: Understanding the New Way of Coming of Age," in Arnett and Tanner, *Emerging Adults in America*, 5.

13. Note that some of the statistics about emerging adulthood today are not historically unique. For example, young Americans in the nineteenth and very early twentieth centuries, when society was more rural and agricultural, also married later in life than they did in the 1950s. But changes in the larger culture and social order in late twentieth-century America make the experience of emerging adulthood today very different from the young adulthood of a century ago. Today's unprecedented freedom and mobility, available lifestyle options, and greater influence of secular culture make the years between 18 and 30 less orderly and in various ways more risky for most.

14. Robert Schoeni and Karen Ross, "Material Assistance from Families during the Transition to Adulthood," in Settersten et al., *On the Frontiers of Adulthood*, 396–416.

15. Jeffrey Arnett, *Emerging Adulthood: The Winding Road from the Late Teens through the Twenties* (New York: Oxford University Press, 2004).

16. The NSYR is continuing work toward a fourth wave of data collection in the future, which, if all goes well, will produce empirical data-based answers to the question about the religious and spiritual lives of 24- to 29-year-olds—time will tell.

CHAPTER 1

1. Chapter 2 explains the complex meanings of the phrase "hooking-up."

2. In chapter 6, we lay out a typology of six major categories of emerging adults' orientations to religion and spirituality. Among the typology's categories, Brad is a clear instance of what we call a Selective Adherent. He is religious but picks and chooses what he wants to believe and practice. The Selective Adherent type represents about 30 percent of the emerging adult population. By comparison, June belongs to the religious type we call the Religiously Disconnected. The structures of her life and experience have simply exposed her to almost no religion, and so she knows or cares about religion very little. On the interviews, we estimate that the Religiously Disconnected represent no more than 5 percent of American emerging adults. Finally, Amanda is what we call a Committed Traditionalist. This type of emerging adult has a strong religious faith that matters to him or her a lot—usually of a traditional or conservative sort. Committed Traditionalists know what they believe, are committed to living consistent and faithful lives, and so practice their faith fairly regularly. They comprise about 15 percent of the U.S. emerging adult population. In addition to these three types, our typology categorizes other emerging adults as Spiritually Open, Religiously Indifferent, and Irreligious. We will have more to say about them in chapter 6.

CHAPTER 2

1. Ron Rindfuss, "The Young Adult Years: Diversity, Structural Change, and Fertility," *Demography* 28(4) (1991): 493–512.

2. See Jeffrey Arnett, "Learning to Stand Alone: The Contemporary Transition to Adulthood in Cultural and Historical Context," *Human Development* 41 (1996): 295–315.

3. This is not a repeated case of others cited in this book, of romantic partners having sex with best girlfriends and boyfriends; each reference in this book is a unique case. Although survey and interview data do not provide systematic data on the subject, our impression from the interviews is that romantic partners sleeping with best friends is not a very rare occurrence among emerging adults.

4. In these pages, we sometimes refer to emerging adults not having the "ability" to see, think, or do certain things. By this we do *not* mean that individual emerging adults are somehow entirely personally responsible for their abilities and inabilities. As a sociologist, one is highly aware of the many ways that social institutions and structures powerfully shape all persons' lives—including the lives of emerging adults— in ways it seems that they themselves often cannot see. What follows here in the text should be read in the light of this basic sociological insight: that emerging adults, while clearly exercising personal agency in the formation of their own lives, also always do so in the context of powerful social institutions and structures that profoundly shape

their cultural assumptions, categories, beliefs, desires, opportunities, choices, tendencies, behaviors, and practices. The emerging adult world is not an isolated subculture or counterculture. It is firmly embedded in the larger American society and reflects, like a mirror, the character of American institutions and culture more broadly. So if emerging adults are unable to see, think, or do certain things, as we say at times in what follows, it is our understanding that this is largely because the larger mainstream adult world into which they have been socialized has failed to equip them otherwise.

5. Alasdair MacIntyre, *After Virtue: A Study in Moral Theory* (Notre Dame, IN: Notre Dame University Press, 1984).

6. See, for example, G. E. Moore, *Principia Ethica* (1903) (Mineola, NY: Dover, 2004); Richard Rorty, *Consequences of Pragmatism* (Minneapolis: University of Minnesota Press, 1982); Richard Rorty, *Objectivity, Relativism, and Truth* (Cambridge: Cambridge University Press, 1990).

7. See Kathleen Bogle, 2008, *Hooking Up: Sex, Dating, and Relationships on Campus* (New York: New York University Press); Donna Freitas, *Sex and the Soul: Juggling Sexuality, Spirituality, Romance, and Religion on America's College Campuses* (New York: Oxford University Press, 2008); Norval Glen and Elizabeth Marquardt, *Hooking Up, Hanging Out, and Hoping for Mr. Right: College Women on Dating and Mating Today* (New York: Institute for American Values, 2001); Laura Sessions Stepp, *Unhooked: How Young Women Pursue Sex, Delay Love, and Lose at Both* (New York: Riverhead Books, 2007); Michael Kimmel, *Guyland: The Perilous World Where Boys Become Men* (New York: HarperCollins, 2008), 169–241; Kylie Harrell, "Recreational Hookups, or Emotional Hang-Ups?" *Durham (NC) Herald-Sun*, August 17, 2008, F1–F3; also see Anonymous, M.D., *Unprotected: A Campus Psychiatrist Reveals How Political Correctness in Her Profession Endangers Every Student* (New York: Sentinel, 2006).

8. See, for example, Elizabeth Thompson and Ugo Collela, "Cohabitation and Marital Stability: Quality or Commitment?" *Journal of Marriage and the Family* 54 (1992): 259–68; Lee Lillard, Michael Brien, and Linda Waite, "Pre-marital Cohabitation and Subsequent Marital Dissolution: Is It Self-Selection?" *Demography* 32 (1995): 437–58; in addition, cohabiting relationships are more likely than marital ones to involve higher levels of violent conflicts, general unhappiness, sexual happiness, sexual infidelity, and wealth accumulation—see Linda Waite and Maggie Gallagher, *The Case for Marriage: Why Married People are Happier, Healthier, and Better Off Financially* (New York: Broadway Books, 2000).

9. Note the connection between this and Clydesdale's notion of "managed gratification"; Tim Clydesdale, *The First Year Out: Understanding American Teens after High School* (Chicago: University of Chicago Press, 2007), 105.

10. See Joseph Heath and Andrew Potter, *Nation of Rebels: Why Counterculture Became Consumer Culture* (New York: HarperBusiness, 2004).

11. See Peggy Giordano, "Relationships in Adolescence," *Annual Review of Sociology* 29 (2003): 257–81.

12. For example, Robert Bellah, Richard Madsen, William Sullivan, and Ann Swidler, *Habits of the Heart: Individualism and Commitment in American Life* (Berkeley: University of California Press, 1985); Robert Putnam, *Bowling Alone: The Collapse and Revival of American Community* (New York: Simon and Shuster, 2000); Richard Sennett, *The Fall of Public Man* (New York: Knopf, 1977).

13. We are indebted to Terri Clark, NSYR's project manager, who conducted numerous third wave personal interviews, for her keen insight into and some of the language used here to describe this theme of absorption into interpersonal relationships through

communications gadgets, at the expense of participation in public life. See Eugene Halton, *The Great Brain Suck* (Chicago: University of Chicago Press, 2008); David Mindich, *Tuned Out: Why Americans under 40 Don't Follow the News* (New York: Oxford University Press, 2005); Mark Bauerlein, *The Dumbest Generation: How the Digital Age Stupefies Young Americans and Jeopardizes Our Future* (New York: Tarcher, 2008). As this relates to religion, see two popular accounts: Christian Piatt and Amy Piatt, *MySpace to Sacred Space: God for a New Generation* (St. Louis: Chalice Press, 2007); Mike Hayes, *Googling God: The Religious Landscape of People in Their Twenties and Thirties* (New York: Paulist Press, 2007).

14. Getting married tends to associate positively with religious involvement.

15. Roger Stump, "Regional Migration and Religious Commitment in the United States," *Journal for the Scientific Study of Religion* 23 (1984): 292–303; Robert Wuthnow and Kevin Christiano, "The Effects of Residential Migration on Church Attendance in the United States," in *The Religious Dimension: New Directions in Quantitative Research*, ed. Robert Wuthnow (New York: Academic Press, 1979), 257–74. The one exception is moving to the American South—see Christian Smith, "Devotion in Dixie and Beyond: A Test of the 'Shibley Thesis' on the Effects of Regional Origin and Migration on Individual Religiosity," *Journal for the Scientific Study of Religion* 37(3) (1998): 494–506.

16. See Jeremy Freese, 2004 "Risk Preferences and Gender Differences in Religiousness: Evidence from the World Values Survey," *Review of Religious Research* 46(1) (2004): 88–91; Alan Miller and John Hoffmann, "Risk and Religion: An Explanation of Gender Differences in Religiosity," *Journal for the Scientific Study of Religion* 34(1) (1995): 63–75; Alan Miller and Rodney Stark, "Gender and Religiousness: Can Socialization Explanations Be Saved?" *American Journal of Sociology* 107(6) (2002): 1399–1423.

17. Throughout this book, we will recurrently mention the social "causal mechanisms" that we think are producing the religious and spiritual expressions and outcomes that we empirically observe among emerging adults. "Mechanism" is a somewhat infelicitous term, insofar as it suggests life operating in a mechanistic universe of the sort envisioned by the seventeenth-century Newtonian worldview. It is generally understood today that neither the natural world in large measure nor certainly human social life operate in a mechanistic way. Still, life does happen as it does in part through various sorts of causal dynamics—both natural and social—producing certain characteristic outcomes. And the term many social scientists use to talk about these causal dynamics these days is "causal mechanism." See, for example, Peter Hedström and Richard Swedberg, eds., *Social Mechanisms: An Analytical Approach to Social Theory* (Cambridge: Cambridge University Press, 1998); Philip Gorski, "Social 'Mechanisms' and Comparative-historical Sociology: A Critical Realist Proposal," in *The Frontiers of Sociology*, ed. Björn Wittrock and Peter Hedström (Leiden: Brill, 2009); Douglas Porpora, "Recovering Causality: Realist Methods in Sociology," in *Realismo Sociologico*, ed. Andrea Maccarini, Emmanuele Morandi, and Ricardo Prandini (Milan: Marietti, 2008), 225–258; Jose Lopez and Garry Potter, eds., *After Postmodernism: An Introduction to Critical Realism* (New York: Continuum, 2005); Andrew Bennett, "The Mother of All 'Isms': Organizing Political Science around Causal Mechanisms," in *Revitalizing Causality: Realism about Causality in Philosophy and Social Science*, ed. Ruth Groff (New York: Routledge, 2008), 205–19; Douglas Porpora, "Sociology's Causal Confusion," in Groff, *Revitalizing Causality*, 195–204; Doug McAdam, Sidney Tarrow, and Charles Tilly, *Dynamics of Contention* (Cambridge: Cambridge University Press, 2001). Robert Merton mentions social mechanisms in "The Self-fulfilling

Prophecy," in Merton, *Social Theory and Social Structure* (Glencoe, IL: Free Press, 1957), 43–44. Since we do not currently have a better term to offer, we will in this book use the term "causal mechanism" and the language generally associated with it to describe the social dynamics that causally produce changes in social life. Readers should keep in mind throughout the subtle but important difference between a mecha*nism* operating in a nonmechanistic universe versus the image of life as fundamentally mecha*nistic*. We endorse the former and reject the latter.

By way of a bit of background, many sociological studies, particularly quantitative ones—typically influenced by the philosophy of positivist empiricism—have been largely content with isolating statistically significant correlations between empirically measured variables. Higher incomes, it might be observed, for instance, are significantly associated with lower levels of voluntary financial giving (this empirical association is, in fact, true; see Christian Smith and Michael Emerson with Patricia Snell, *Passing the Plate: Why American Christians Do not Give Away More Money* (New York: Oxford University Press, 2008). But from our perspective—which is influenced by the philosophy of social science known as critical realism (see the citations that follow)—and that of a growing number of other scholars, identifying regular associations between empirical events is not enough. Instead, it is necessary to identify and understand the causal mechanisms that operate—by virtue, we believe, of the natural causal powers inherent in the entities and agents involved in characteristic situations—to causally produce the observed events, patterns, or outcomes. Stated differently, the central goal of (social) science is not to observe and count what things correlate with other things. "If Y, then (probably) X" is not adequate. Natural and social science's real, central goal is to understand *what* exists in reality and *how* and *why* parts of reality recurrently operate the way they do through causal forces to produce certain kinds of results. So what really matters in chemistry, for example, is not knowing that two particular substances always combine to make, say, a toxic gas. What matters, rather, is knowing and understanding the underlying structure of chemical elements, modeling their molecular compositions, identifying the general laws that govern the relation and interaction of different aspects of elements, and therefore being able to explain how and why all of the elements in the periodic table interact in various combinations under diverse conditions to produce different recurrent outcomes. That is what makes chemistry *science* and not merely accumulated observational information about regular occurrences.

While human social life operates quite differently in many ways from the natural world—by virtue of the personal agency, self-reflexivity, and human capacities for intentionality and not-entirely-determined purposive decision-making, among other factors—the social scientific study of human social life rightly shares with the natural sciences the basic purpose and logic that are the same in all scientific disciplines: to know and describe social reality as it really is, as accurately as possible, and to understand the underlying capacities, structures, and causal mechanisms that give rise to the world that the scientist observes empirically. This is how as a social scientist one *explains* social life—not merely by correlating statistically significant variables in a positivist empiricist manner ("If Y, then [probably] X") but rather by identifying, as critical realists, specific underlying social causal mechanisms that are responsible for producing the facts and events one observes and experiences. Of course, in addition to explaining social life, one also wants to produce meaningful interpretations of it—but one renders these interpretations not simply in order to tell others about the meanings that actions have for actors but also to help *explain* why actors act in the ways they do. Interpretation and explanation are thus inseparable in social science. Therefore, in this book we will recurrently identify—as the dynamics producing characteristics and features of emergent adult religious and spiritual life that we have observed—specific causal mechanisms. We trust that our discussions of them will help the reader better understand the hows and whys of the matters in question.

For more on critical realism, see Roy Bhaskar, *A Realist Concept of Science* (London: Verso, 1997); Roy Bhaskar, *Critical Realism* (New York: Routledge, 1998); Christian Smith, *What Is a Person?* (Chicago: University of Chicago Press, 2010); Andrew Collier, *Critical Realism: An Introduction to Roy Bhaskar's Philosophy* (London: Verso, 1994); Mats Ekström et al., *Explaining Society: Critical Realism in the Social Sciences* (New York: Routledge, 2002); Andrew Sayer, *Realism and Social Science* (New York: Sage, 2000); Andrew Sayer, *Method in Social Science: A Realist Approach* (New York: Routledge, 1992); Margaret Archer, *Realist Social Theory: The Morphogenetic Approach* (Cambridge: Cambridge University Press, 1995); Margaret Archer et al., eds., *Critical Realism: Essential Readings* (New York: Routledge, 1998); Justin Cruickshank, *Realism and Sociology: Anti-foundationalism, Ontology, and Social Research* (New York: Routledge, 2002); Gorski, "Social 'Mechanisms' and Comparative-historical Sociology"; Lopez and Potter, *After Postmodernism*; Margaret Archer, *Being Human: The Problem of Agency* (Cambridge: Cambridge University Press, 2000); David Harvey, "Agency and Community: A Critical Realist Perspective," *Journal for the Theory of Social Behavior* 32(2) (2002): 163–94; George Steinmetz, "Critical Realism and Historical Sociology," *Comparative Studies in Society and History* 40(1) (1998): 170–86; Peter Manicas, *A Realist Philosophy of Social Science* (Cambridge: Cambridge University Press, 2006); Stephen Kemp and John Holmwood, "Realism, Regularity, and Social Explanation," *Journal for the Theory of Social Behavior* 33(2) (2003): 165–87; Douglas Porpora, *The Concept of Social Structure* (New York: Greenwood Press, 1987), and "Four Concepts of Social Structure," *Journal for the Theory of Social Behavior* 19(2) (1989): 195–211; Sam Porter, "Critical Realist Ethnography," in *Qualitative Research in Action*, ed. Tim May (London: Sage, 2002), 53–72; Douglas Porpora, "Social Structure: The Future of a Concept," in *Structure, Culture, and History: Recent Issues in Social Theory*, ed. Sing Chew and J. David Knottnerus (London: Rowman and Littlefield, 2002), 43–59, "Cultural Rules and Material Relations," *Sociological Theory* 11(2) (993): 212–29, "Recovering Causality," and "Sociology's Causal Confusion"; Mats Ekström, "Causal Explanation of Social Action: The Contribution of Max Weber and of Critical Realism to a Generative View of Causal Explanation in Social Science," *Acta Sociologica* 35 (1992): 107–22; David Harvey, "Agency and Community: A Critical Realist Paradigm," *Journal for the Theory of Social Behavior* 32(2) (2002): 163–94; William Outhwaite, *New Philosophies of Social Science: Realism, Hermeneutics, and Critical Theory* (New York: St. Martin's Press, 1987); Peter Manicas, *A History and Philosophy of the Social Sciences* (Hoboken, NJ: Wiley, 1989).

18. The other possibility, of course, is to forego complete identity differentiation by remaining closely tied to the family-of-origin identity and network.

19. Ross Stolzenberg, M. Blair-Loy, and Linda J. Waite, "Religious Participation in Early Adulthood: Age and Family Life Cycle Effects on Church Membership," *American Sociological Review* 60 (1995): 84–103.

20. Evelyn Lehrer, "Religion as a Determinant of Economic and Demographic Behavior in the United States," *Population and Development Review* 30(4) (2004): 707–26, and "The Role of Religion in Union Formation: An Economic Perspective," *Population Research and Policy Review* 23 (2004): 161–85; Stolzenberg et al., "Religious Participation in Early Adulthood."

CHAPTER 3

1. James Allan David, Tom W. Smith, and Peter V. Marsden, *General Social Surveys, 1972–2006: Cumulative Codebook* / Principal Investigator, James A. Davis; Director and Co-Principal Investigator, Tom W. Smith; Co-Principal Investigator, Peter V. Marsden. Chicago: National Opinion Research Center, 2007. 2,552 pp., 28 cm. (National Data Program for the Social Sciences Series, no. 18).

2. The frequency of prayer answer categories were several times a day, once a day, several times a week, once a week, less than once a week, and never.

3. The exact wording of the religious service attendance question is "How often do you attend religious services? 1. More than once a week; 2. Every week; 4. Nearly every week; 5. Two to three times a month; 6. Once a month; 7. Several times a year; 8. Less than once a year; or 9. Never."

4. The exact wording of the Bible belief question is "Which of these statements comes closest to describing your feelings about the Bible? 1. The Bible is the actual word of God and is to be taken literally, word for word; 2. The Bible is the inspired word of God but not everything in it should be taken literally, word for word; 3. The Bible is an ancient book of fables, legends, history; and moral precepts recorded by men."

5. From our sociologists' perspective, being religiously liberal is not equated here with being less religious per se. Religious believers adhering to American liberal theological and denominational traditions must be sociologically understood as doing religion and being religious in diverse, tradition-specific—which does not necessarily mean more problematic or weaker—ways than more moderate and conservative adherents in American religion. Each religious tradition needs to be measured or evaluated sociologically against its own standards and expectations and not those of different traditions. It is therefore difficult to identify one or more sociological metric or metrics that can neutrally be applied in order to directly compare the "religious strength" or "vitality" of different religious traditions, even within the one larger faith tradition of Christianity, as if even in their substantive differences they were thoroughly commensurate in sociological evaluation. Nevertheless, in American religious culture broadly, liberal religion is commonly associated and empirically positively correlated with less frequent average religious service attendance and lower levels of authority of historical religious traditions for determining the beliefs and practices of individual adherents. In addition, the NSYR interviews with contemporary emerging adults show that by religiously "liberal" they themselves commonly mean lower levels of religious commitment, institutional involvement, private and public religious practices, and conformity to religious teachings. With the proviso noted here, therefore, we use the concept of liberal religion as one among a set of many sociological religion measures to try to map religious differences between recent Americans of different age groups and emerging adults at different points during the last quarter century.

6. Brian Steensland, Jerry Park, Mark Regnerus, Lynn Robinson, W. Bradford Wilcox, and Robert Woodberry "The Measure of American Religion: Toward Improving the State of the Art," *Social Forces* 79 (2000): 291–318.

7. The confidence intervals concern the size of the range around the mean average percent sample estimate in which the population estimate is expected to fall with a 95 percent degree of confidence, giving the probability that the range produced by the method employed to estimate mean averages includes the true value of the parameter; by providing a range of values that are likely to contain the population parameter of interest, confidence intervals tell us about the precision of the statistical mean estimates we have computed and so give us an estimate of the amount of possible error involved

in the data. The confidence intervals for each age group here (and each religious group later) vary by group at each point of measurement. Space does not allow us to report specific confidence intervals for each measure at each point, but we can report that the 95 percent confidence intervals for GSS religious tradition findings are as follows. First, religious tradition by *age* (calculated ages 18–65 for GSS 1990–2006) in "plus or minus" minimums and maximums in percents for religious service attendance are evangelical Protestant (2.62–4.98), mainline Protestant (2.51–4.42), black Protestant (2.75–5.54), Catholic (2.03–4.94); for strength of affiliation, evangelical Protestant (2.24–4.15), mainline Protestant (2.37–4.54), black Protestant (3.76–7.33), Catholic (2.32–5.05); for Bible is inspired or literal, evangelical Protestant (1.16–2.24), mainline Protestant (2.02–3.71), black Protestant (2.67–5.33), Catholic (1.83–3.8); for prays daily, evangelical Protestant (2.88–5.66), mainline Protestant (4.36–9.74), black Protestant (3.88–8.15), Catholic (2.83–5.11); for belief in life after death, evangelical Protestant (1.46–2.58), mainline Protestant (2.32–5.95), black Protestant (3.61–6.88), Catholic (1.94–3.92). Second, for religious tradition by *time period* (ages 18–25 for 1972–2006), for religious service attendance, evangelical Protestant (2.48–3.51), mainline Protestant (2.47–5.17), black Protestant (3.69–6.34), Catholic (2.44–5.65); for strength of affiliation, evangelical Protestant (3.36–6.13), mainline Protestant (3.95–8.17), black Protestant (5.27–8.47), Catholic (3.16–6.50); Bible is inspired or literal, evangelical Protestant (2.06–4.23), mainline Protestant (5.38–10.38), black Protestant (5.19–7.70), Catholic (2.70–4.71); prays daily, evangelical Protestant (5.05–9.43), mainline Protestant (7.30–14.80), black Protestant (7.89–14.84), Catholic (5.15–10.62); belief in life after death, evangelical Protestant (3.18–7.32), mainline Protestant (3.81–8.98), black Protestant (6.81–11.77), Catholic (2.55–3.99).

8. For typical use of the label emerging adult, see J. J. Arnett, "Emerging Adulthood: A Theory of Development from the Late Teens through the Twenties," *American Psychologist* 55(5) (2000), 469–480.

9. Again, see note 5 for this study's approach to the use of "liberal" religion as a particular measure of religiousness in America's broader religious culture.

10. Robert Putnam, *Bowling Alone: The Collapse and Revival of American Community* (New York: Simon and Schuster, 2000), 36, 119, 249. Engagement in these activities tends to decline in the later decades of life after middle age.

11. The prayer frequency and Bible beliefs questions were not asked by the GSS before the early 1980s.

12. Results are available on request from Christian Smith.

13. Evident indicates that significant religious declines among young adults in the United States occurred in the 1950s and 1960s—before the time period this chapter's data measure. See David Moberg and Dean Hoge, "Catholic College Students' Religious and Moral Attitudes, 1961–1982: Effects of the Sixties and Seventies," *Review of Religious Research* 28(2) (1986): 104–17; Dean Hoge, Jann Hoge, and Janet Wittenberg, "The Return of the Fifties: Trends in College Students' Values between 1952 and 1984," *Sociological Forum* 2(3) (1987): 500–519.

14. Bruce Schulman, *The Seventies: The Great Shift in American Culture, Society, and Politics* (Cambridge, MA: Da Capo Press, 2002); Philip Jenkins, *Decade of Nightmares: The End of the Sixties and the Making of Eighties America* (New York: Oxford University Press, 2006); Barbara Epstein, *Political Protest and Cultural Revolution* (Berkeley; University of California Press, 1993).

15. Stephen Toulmin, *Cosmopolis: The Hidden Agenda of Modernity* (Chicago: University of Chicago Press, 1990); Jürgen Habermas, *The Philosophical Discourse of Modernity* (Cambridge, MA: MIT Press, 1990).

16. Particularly in the humanities, the arts, and various sectors of publishing, broadcasting, social science, and mainline religion.

17. Lynn Schofield Clark, *From Angels to Aliens: Teenagers, the Media, and the Supernatural* (New York: Oxford University Press, 2005), and *Religion, Media, and the Marketplace* (New Brunswick, NJ: Rutgers University Press, 2007); Stewart Hoover, *Religion in the Media Age* (New York: Routledge, 2006).

18. Jennifer Lindholm, "The 'Interior' Lives of American College Students: Preliminary Findings from a National Study," in *Passing on the Faith: Transforming Traditions for the Next Generation of Jews, Christians, and Muslims,* ed. James Heft (New York: Fordham University Press, 2006), 75–102; Michael Lindsay, *Faith in the Halls of Power: How Evangelicals Joined the American Elite* (New York: Oxford University Press, 2008); Kathleen Mahoney and John Schmalzbauer, "Religion: A Comeback on Campus," *Liberal Education* 87(4) (2001): 36–41; John Schmalzbauer and Kathleen Mahoney, "American Scholars Return to Studying Religion," *Contexts* (winter 2008): 16–21; Conrad Cherry, Betty DeBerg, and Amanda Porterfield, *Religion on Campus* (Chapel Hill: University of North Carolina Press, 2001); Thomas Bartless, "Most Freshmen Say Religion Guides Them," *Chronicle of Higher Education* 51(33) (2005): A1, A40; Mark Taylor, "The Devoted Student," *New York Times*, December 21, 2006, A39.

19. Jonathan Hill, "Religious Involvement during the Transition to Adulthood" (Ph.D. diss., University of Notre Dame, 2008); Ross Stolzenberg, Mary Blair-Loy, and Linda Waite, "Religious Participation in Early Adulthood: Age and Family Life Cycle Effects on Church Membership," *American Sociological Review* 60 (1995): 84–103.

CHAPTER 4

1. Because LDS youth going on "missions" during this age is so common and because living overseas can reduce the probability of completing a national survey, the NSYR data on LDS youth, in theory, might potentially have suffered some nonresponse biases in the sample resulting in an underestimation of religiousness, since those on missions are likely to be among the most highly religious LDS youth. Focused analyses of the LDS Wave 3 survey completions, however, revealed no tendency to undercount LDS emerging adults on mission. The NSYR staff made monumental efforts, in fact, to gain permission to complete surveys with LDS youth on missions—with which LDS authorities were generally very cooperative. As a result, 80 percent of the LDS respondents who were identified as being on a mission completed the Wave 3 survey. Furthermore, few of the LDS respondents who could not be contacted to complete the survey are likely to have been on missions, since it was common for other contacts (relatives and friends) with whom the NSYR spoke in its efforts to try to track its missing survey respondents to report that fact. We are therefore confident that the NSYR Wave 3 data do not involve systematic nonresponse biases for LDS youth on mission trips.

2. The difference is calculated between third wave respondents and first wave respondents who completed the third wave, not the entire first wave sample.

3. To be sure, Native American faiths lost 50 percent and Muslims lost 33 percent of their original affiliation totals, but the numbers of respondents in these religious categories in the sample are too small to place too much weight on the validity of these findings.

4. Brian Steensland, Jerry Park, Mark D. Regnerus, Lynn Robinson, W. Brad Wilcox, and Robert Woodberry, "The Measure of American Religion: Toward Improving the State of the Art," *Social Forces* 79 (2000): 291–318.

5. The 2.9 percent lower number of nonreligious emerging adults in table 4.2 compared to table 4.1 suggests that a small number of self-identified nonreligious emerging adults continue to attend services at some religious congregation and so are categorized as religious in table 4.2. The other possibility is that most of the indeterminate cases here are, as we suspect, actually nonreligious.

6. Baptist here does not represent one denomination but many by that name, among which the Southern Baptist Convention (SBC) is the largest. In the first wave NSYR data, 7.45 percent of teens' parents were SBC; in Wave 3, 5.48 percent of emerging adults were SBC—reflecting an estimated decline of 1.97 percent.

7. Measured as proportions of original percents changed, charismatic, Christian and Missionary Alliance, and independent and nondenominational churches appear to have gained the most; while Congregationalist, Nazarene, and independent evangelical churches seem to have lost the most. Readers are advised here, however, that the total numbers of respondents in cases of smaller denominations are smaller than what researchers generally consider most reliable to work with, so findings concerning them have to be interpreted with caution.

8. Christian Smith, with Melinda Lundquist Denton, *Soul Searching: the Religious and Spiritual Lives of American Teenagers* (New York: Oxford University Press, 2005).

9. Finally, 17 percent were indeterminate religions as emerging adults in the last survey.

10. The simple Pearson's r correlation on the two variables measuring similarity to mother and to father is .67; the gamma .7625.

11. See Christian Smith, ed., *The Secular Revolution* (Berkeley: University of California Press, 2003).

CHAPTER 5

1. Here parallels exist between not talking about religion and not talking about politics. Both have inherited reputations as divisive subjects. Yet most emerging adults can discuss both quite civilly, nonetheless, if and when they want to. And yet both are topics that are in fact rarely discussed by emerging adults among friends. Lack of knowledge about both religion and politics, and perhaps vague feelings of guilt for not knowing or caring more about them, make some people uneasy and so avoid discussing these topics.

2. We think this finding and some others in this chapter provide an important corrective to more alarmist and (we think) lopsided views of the matter by some authors who, sometimes based on mere personal life experiences and impressions, stress a deep-seated alienation of most emerging adults from mainstream American religion, particularly Christianity. See, for instance, David Kinnaman and Gabe Lyons, *UnChristian: What a New Generation Thinks about Christianity....and Why It Matters* (Grand Rapids, MI: Baker Books, 2007); Dan Kimball, *They Like Jesus but Not the Church: Insights from Emerging Generations* (Grand Rapids, MI: Zondervan, 2007).

CHAPTER 6

1. John Murray Cuddihy, *No Offense: Civil Religion and Protestant Taste* (New York: Seabury, 1979); Terry Eagleton, *The Idea of Culture* (London: Blackwell, 2000), 64–65.

2. Percentage differences estimated here and in the following paragraphs are based on the categorization of all 230 interview respondents with adjustments to correct for the oversampling of certain religious traditions.

3. All three interviews are recounted here by Smith.

CHAPTER 7

1. Despite best efforts, we were unable to locate one *Soul Searching* case, "Antwan," originally described in the section "Hope and Prayer in the City," in Christian Smith, with Melinda Lundquist Denton, *Soul Searching: The Religious and Spiritual Lives of American Teenagers* (New York: Oxford University Press, 2005), 251–57; he could not be located—apparently because of the transience often associated with lower socioeconomic situations.

2. Alyssa appears in *Soul Searching*, Chapter 3, in the subsection entitled "Religious on Their Own," 114–15.

3. Smith with Denton, *Soul Searching,* 114–15.

4. That is, Confraternity of Christian Doctrine classes often taught to Catholic teenagers.

5. See, for example, Lewis Rambo, *Understanding Religious Conversion* (New Haven, CT: Yale University Press, 1995); John Lofland and Rodney Stark, "Becoming a World-Saver," *American Sociological Review* 30 (1965): 863–74.

CHAPTER 8

1. We used three measures from the third wave survey to create a single measure of religiosity: attendance at religious services, importance of faith, and frequency of prayer. For attendance, all respondents were asked "Do you attend religious services more than once or twice a year, not counting weddings, baptisms, and funerals?" Respondents who answered yes to this question were then asked "About how often do you usually attend religious services there?" which offered the response options of a few times a year, many times a year, once a month, two to three times a month, once a week, and more than once a week. Respondents who said they did not attend religious services were set to "never" on the measure of religious service attendance. Regarding importance of faith, respondents were asked "How important or unimportant is religious faith in shaping how you live your daily life?" which offered these response options: not at all important, not very important, somewhat important, very important, and extremely important. Finally, respondents were asked "How often, if ever, do you pray by yourself alone?" which had these response options: never, less than once a month, one to two times a month, about once a week, a few times a week, about once a day, and many times a day. Before combining these measures into one index, they had to be coded onto similar scales in order to weight their contribution to the resulting index equally. Because importance has five response options, attendance and prayer were recoded from their original seven categories to five (0–4). For attendance, respondents who said "many times per year" and "about once a month" were coded into the same category, and respondents who reported attending "once a week" and "more than once a week" were coded into one category. Similarly for prayer, respondents who reported praying "one to two times a month" and "about once a week" were collapsed into one category, and respondents who claimed to pray "a few times a week" and "about once a day" were placed into one category. These decisions were made on the basis of the substantive similarity of these answer categories. These

categorizations also maintain a relatively even distribution of cases across categories on these measures.

A simple way to combine these variables would have been to take individuals' additive or average score across all three. This method, however, does not accurately distinguish between qualitative differences in respondents' overall levels of religiosity. For example, a respondent who attended two to three times per month, said religion was very important, and prayed many times per week would have the exact same average sum as someone who only attended a few times per year but thought religion was extremely important and prayed many times per day (i.e., they would both have summative scores of 9, or averages of 3). Yet these two cases are seemingly quite different in terms of their overall expression of religion. To avoid this purely quantitative combination, a single measure was created that was based on informed decisions reflecting specific combinations of the three variables. The resulting index separates respondents into four categories: Lowest, Minimal, Moderate, and Highest levels of religiosity. We began by categorizing all of the "consistent" cases. All respondents reporting to be in the two lowest categories on all three variables (that is, all 0's and 1's out of 0–4) were put into the Lowest category, and respondents reporting to be in the top two categories on all three variables (that is, all 3's and 4's out of 0–4) were put in the Highest category. Next, respondents belonging to the two middle-lower categories (scoring 1 and 2 on all measures [except for all 1's]) were put into the Minimal group, and respondents scoring only in the two middle-higher categories (all 2's and 3's [except all 2's or all 3's]) were put into the Moderate group. The next step in the categorization placed respondents who were "inconsistent" on only one measure. Respondents who were in the lowest category on two out of three variables, with the third measure not being in the highest category (that is, who reported two 0's with the third measure not being higher than 3) were put in the Lowest group. Respondents reporting being in the middle category on two measures, with the third measure being in the lowest category (two 2's with the third measure being a 0) were placed into the Minimal group, two 3's and a 1 in the Moderate group; and two measures in the highest category and the third in the middle category (two 4's and one 2) in the Highest group. This fairly straightforward categorization classified 70 percent of cases that had no missing data on the three component measures. The remaining 30 percent of cases were all in slightly ambiguous configurations (e.g., 2 on attendance, 4 on importance, and 1 on prayer). The majority of these combinations, in our studied judgment, however, fell into one or another of the middle two categories of the overall religiosity index (i.e., they were not representative of the Highest or Lowest levels of religiosity). Therefore, to distinguish between and categorize the remaining cases, the sum of the three scores was used, with cases scoring a total between 3 and 6 being placed in the Minimal group, and cases scoring between 7 and 9 in the Moderate group. Using the sum of the scores to make these classifications avoids the previous criticism of such a method, because it was done for a qualitatively limited group. For these remaining cases, the sum of their scores provided the best distinction. The Minimal and Moderate groups have significantly more combinations included in their coding, but the majority of these combinations are the aforementioned "inconsistent" configurations, which are experienced by many fewer respondents than the more consistent combinations. By employing this more qualitatively informed method to combine these measures and examining the actual combination of the three measures, we believe we are able to reflect more accurately the real-world lives of these cases than by simply using a mathematical formula. We are able to distinguish different levels of religiosity based on their overall meaning and typical experience of combinations of these three variables.

2. Cronbach's alpha is .83.

3. That is, not controlling through more complex regression techniques for the possible effects of other related variables.

4. These tables are available, however, at www.nd.edu/~csmith22/tables.html. Note that we ran a series of ordered logit and binary logistic regressions on five analytical configurations of the dependent variable, using blocks of independent variables and demographic controls, to assess the strength of the independent correlates of emerging adult religion. These five unique models were constructed (1) using a lagged dependent variable, (2) not using a lagged dependent variable, and (3–5) examining movement from low to high and high to low levels of religiosity modeled three different ways across survey waves (see tables A.1 and A.2).

5. From some religious perspectives, paying such costs is a kind of *investment*.

6. Because the doubts about religious beliefs variable is coded dichotomously (having no or few doubts equal to 1), no middle percentile category exists either in the single variable or in the combined measures relying on it.

7. We were not able to calculate the percents for all seven variables combined, since only 26 cases in the entire sample scored in the top quartile in a measure including all seven factors considered in table 8.4.

8. The latter four categories are as defined by note 1 above.

9. This finding qualifies the tentative conclusion of Jeffrey Arnett about emerging adult religion, that "the most interesting and surprising feature of emerging adults' religious beliefs is how little relationship there is between the religious training they received throughout childhood and the religious beliefs they hold at the time they reach emerging adulthood.... In statistical analyses [of interview subjects' answers], there was *no* relationship between exposure to religious training in childhood and *any* aspect of their religious beliefs as emerging adults.... This is a different pattern than is found in adolescence [which reflects greater continuity].... Evidently something changes between adolescence and emerging adulthood that dissolves the link between the religious beliefs of parents and the beliefs of their children.... How could it be that childhood religious training makes no difference in the kinds of religious beliefs and practices people have by the time they reach emerging adulthood? It doesn't seem to make sense.... It all comes to naught in emerging adulthood? Yet that seems to be the truth of it, surprising as that may be"; *Emerging Adulthood: The Winding Road from the Late Teens through the Twenties* (New York: Oxford University Press, 2004), 174–75. We are not, however, able to sort out whether this difference stems from Arnett's lack of nationally representative interview data or from the NSYR's lack of data on 25- to 29-year-olds. It could in theory be that these findings will change dramatically as the NSYR's sample ages over the next five years, though we do not anticipate that to be the case.

10. Charles Ragin, *Fuzzy-set Social Science* (Chicago: University Chicago Press, 2000).

11. Charles Ragin, "Introduction to Qualitative Comparative Analysis," in *The Comparative Political Economy of the Welfare State,* ed. Thomas Janoski and Alexander Hicks (Cambridge: Cambridge University Press, 1994), 299–319; Charles Ragin, "Using Qualitative Comparative Analysis to Study Configurations," in *Computer-Aided Qualitative Data Analysis,* ed. Udo Kelle (London: Sage, 1995), 177–19.

12. Our QCA analysis here works with unweighted numbers, which explains the difference between the 21 percent here and the 22 percent of the same group reported in table 8.1.

13. Two additional paths emerged from the analysis but together explain no more than a handful of cases and are not theoretically interesting and so are not worth covering here.

14. That is, the teenager has (1) committed life to God, (2) had prayers answered, (3) has experienced a miracle, *and* (4) has had a moving spiritual experience.

15. Interview data suggest that some of these nonparental adults are other family members, such as grandparents, aunts, and uncles.

16. By setting aside our primary interest in pathways that more often than not lead to a highly religious outcome and focusing instead on the fewest number of pathways that lead to the greatest percentage of the outcome, we can narrow down to three configurations that do not in fact lead to the outcome at high rates but, because they represent common combinations, nevertheless account for 69 percent of the most highly religious emerging adult group. Those pathways are (1) high importance of teen faith + nonparental religious adult support + holding no doubts about religious beliefs + having many personal religious experiences; (2) high importance of teen faith + high parental religiosity + nonparental religious adult support + having many personal religious experiences; and (3) high importance of teen faith + frequent prayer and scripture reading + holding no doubts about religious beliefs + having many personal religious experiences. Again, 69 percent of all of the most highly religious emerging adults got there through one of these three pathways. Once again, we see the importance of relational ties to faith, personal religious experiences, high importance of faith in daily life, and lack of religious doubts. To be clear, however, unlike the paths presented in the text earlier, these three pathways do not represent configurations producing greater than 50 percent chances of joining the group of highly religious emerging adults—only 43 percent of all emerging adults represented by these three configurations are among the most highly religious. That is, 57 percent of the teenagers in one of the configurations did *not* end up in the highly religious group in young adulthood.

17. Again, this is based on scoring in greater than the top half of answers to questions about religious service attendance, importance of faith, and frequency of personal prayer, as determined by the method described in note 1.

18. Using importance of faith and frequency of prayer (part of the devotion variable) could potentially be problematic in this particular analysis because these measures are used to define the current analytic subsample (i.e., they are used to help determine the "moderate" and "highest" religious teens). Therefore, we ran a similar analysis without these variables. We find that the primary conclusions presented here are upheld. Not having highly religious parents combined with low personal religious devotion (in the sensitivity analysis measured by frequency of reading scriptures only) and low support from other religious adults consistently leads to highly religious teens becoming either completely disengaged or minimally religious as young adults.

19. Compared to 39 percent of the Highest/Moderate group at Wave 1 who dropped down to either the Minimal or Lowest category by Wave 3.

20. See, for example, Philip Gorski, "Social 'Mechanisms' and Comparative-historical Sociology: A Critical Realist Proposal," in *The Frontiers of Sociology*, ed. Björn Wittrock and Peter Hedström (Leiden: Brill, 2009); Douglas Porpora, "Recovering Causality: Realist Methods in Sociology," in *Realismo Sociologico*, ed. Andrea Maccarini, Emmanuele Morandi, and Ricardo Prandini (Milan: Marietti, 2008), 225–258); "Sociology's Causal Confusion," in Groff, *Revitalizing Causality*, 195–204; Jose Lopez and Garry Potter, eds., *After Postmodernism: An Introduction to Critical Realism* (New York: Continuum, 2005); Andrew Bennett, "The Mother of All 'Isms': Organizing Political Science around Causal Mechanisms," in *Revitalizing Causality: Realism about Causality in Philosophy and Social Science*, ed. Ruth Groff (New York: Routledge, 2008), 205–19; Doug McAdam, Sidney Tarrow, and Charles Tilly, *Dynamics of Contention* (Cambridge: Cambridge University Press,

2001). Robert Merton mentions social mechanisms in "The Self-fulfilling Prophecy," in Merton, *Social Theory and Social Structure* (Glencoe, IL: Free Press, 1957), 43–44).

21. We are not claiming that these mechanisms work universally the same for all religions everywhere at every point in time. Our philosophy of social science is much more attuned to the importance of scope conditions and context than that. Our more modest claim here simply has to do with American religion, the dominant portion of which is Christianity, Mormonism, and Judaism.

22. In addition, as we will show in the next chapter, strong religion tends to enhance the quality of youth-parent relationships, in what we believe is a reciprocal causal relation.

23. One possibility we do not address is that variable human interest in religion is in part a genetically coded trait, an attitudinal and behavioral disposition that is embedded in the genetic features of people's bodies, and so passed on naturally from parents to offspring; see, for instance, Matt Bradshaw and Christopher Ellison, "Do Genetic Factors Influence Religious Life? Findings from a Behavior Genetic Analysis of Twin Siblings," *Journal for the Scientific Study of Religion* 47(4) (2008): 529–44. We do not address that here, however, primarily because if some religiosity is genetically inherited, then genetic factors would "wash out" of analyses of religious transitions over time that control for the Wave 1 baseline, since we are comparing the same people, with the same genetic material, over time. More generally with possible genetic explanations, the relevant causal mechanism would not be social but biological, but as sociologists we are interested in understanding *social* causal mechanisms that we assume to be irreducible to biological or genetic processes.

24. See Laurence Iannaccone, "Religious Practice: A Human Capital Approach," *Journal for the Scientific Study of Religion* 29(3) (1990): 297–314.

25. Tim Clydesdale, *The First Year Out: Understanding American Teens after High School* (Chicago: University of Chicago Press, 2007).

26. See Donna Frietas, *Sex and the Soul: Juggling Sexuality, Spirituality, Romance, and Religion on America's College Campuses* (New York: Oxford University Press, 2008).

27. All models were estimated using an unconditional growth mixture model (GMM) in the software program Mplus (Linda K. Muthén and Bengt O. Muthén, *Mplus User's Guide*, 5th ed. [Los Angeles: Muthén and Muthén, 2007]). The GMM combines latent class analysis with growth curve analysis (Tony Jung and K. A. S. Wickrama, "An Introduction to Latent Class Growth Analysis and Growth Mixture Modeling," *Social and Personality Psychology Compass* 2 [2008]: 302–17; Bengt O. Muthén, "Latent Variable Analysis: Growth Mixture Modeling and Related Techniques for Longitudinal Data," in *Handbook of Quantitative Methodology for the Social Sciences,* ed. David Kaplan [Newbury Park, CA: Sage, 2004], 345–68). Unlike standard growth curve analysis, which makes the assumption that individual trajectories deviate from one grand trajectory, GMM assumes that individuals deviate from multiple normative trajectories; or alternatively, that we are sampling from distinct subpopulations that have qualitatively different growth patterns. These different classes of trajectories are a latent function of the data, so no a priori assumptions concerning how individuals change religiously are necessary. We used various goodness-of-fit indices to determine the optimal number of growth patterns for each table. The percents are calculated as population estimates based on posterior probabilities.

28. Wave 1 asked "Have you ever made a personal commitment to live your life for God? (Yes/No)." Waves 2 and 3 asked "In the last two years have you made a personal commitment to live your life for God? (Yes/No)." The difference between the "ever" and the "last two years" questions makes assigning ages somewhat challenging but possible. Readers should be aware that the very meaning of the phrase "commitment to live your life for God" could change significantly between childhood, the preteen years, adolescence, and early adulthood—that is, this question may not be measuring the same event or experience over time. Furthermore, the possible impact on a person's life of committing to live for God could vary tremendously, depending on the stage of developing life at which such a commitment was made. The researchers chose to employ this "commitment to live your life for God" phrasing—rather than, say, "born again" or "religious conversion" language—in order to avoid religious-tradition-specific lingo as much as possible, so as to maximize question validity across as many religious traditions as possible.

29. At least, for those who completed all three surveys. A smaller number completed only the first survey, and a much smaller number completed the first and second but not the third or the first and third but not the second. We are able to adjust our estimates in what follows by taking into account the different denominators in each survey number.

30. Some of these reported committing to God only once and others more than once.

31. Our assigning this number as representing "before the age of 14" is based on a logical inference about the structure of the first wave survey findings on committing to live for God between the ages of 13 and 17, which showed no increase in the percent of teenagers committing to God between the ages of 13 and 17—that is, cross-sectional first wave survey data showed that no more 17-year-olds than 13-year-olds had ever committed their lives to God. This flat percent across all of these teenage years that reported having ever committed their lives for God can most reasonably be interpreted as indicating that those commitments had taken place before age 14—since, if any of these first wave respondents were committing their lives to God during these teenage years, we would see a resulting increase in first commitments across those years, a growth from age 13 to 17.

32. The reader should remember that this figure does not represent the percent of all possible commits between the ages of 18 and 23, since most of the sample had not yet aged through to the completed age of 23. Because the median age of our third wave survey sample is 20.5, one might best think of this percent as representing commitments for 18- to 20.5-year-olds. Note also that the figures for the teenage and emerging adult first commits are calculated from imputed ages spread in probabilities over two years prior to the survey, since the second and third wave survey asked about commitments in the prior two years.

33. Multivariate regression analysis of who committed to God ever, earlier, and later in life revealed few interesting findings.

34. The findings here generally comport with those of Edwin Starbuck's classic study *The Psychology of Religion* (New York: Scribner's, 1900) 28–44, which emphasized adolescent religious conversions, though we place the preponderance of religious commitments at somewhat earlier ages than does Starbuck. As a related aside, one study of American former Catholics showed that the ages at which they "stopped thinking of themselves as Catholic" are spread out across a wide range of years, with only 36 percent of Catholic defections happening between the ages of 18 and 29; see Center for Applied Research in the Apostolate, "The Impact of Religious Switching

and Secularization on the Estimated Size of the United States Adult Catholic Population," *Review of Religious Research* 49(1) (2008): 457–60.

35. See, for instance, Kirk Hadaway and Wade Clark Roof, "Apostasy in American Churches: Evidence from National Survey Data," in *Falling from the Faith: Causes and Consequences of Religious Apostasy*, ed. David Bromley (Beverley Hills, CA: Sage, 1988), 29–46; David Caplovitz and Fred Sherrow, *The Religious Drop-Outs: Apostasy among College Graduates* (Beverly Hills, CA: Sage, 1977); Darren Sherkat, "Counterculture or Continuity? Competing Influences on Baby Boomers' Religious Orientations and Participation," *Social Forces* 76 (1998): 1087–1115; Richard Funk and Fern Willits, "College Attendance and Attitude Change: A Panel Study, 1970–81," *Sociology of Education* 60 (1987): 224–31; Robert Wuthnow, *The Restructuring of American Religion* (Princeton, NJ: Princeton University Press, 1988). Dean Hoge, Jann Hoge, and Janet Wittenberg, "The Return of the Fifties: Trends in College Students' Values between 1952 and 1984," *Sociological Forum* 2(3) (1987): 500–519.

36. Jeremy Uecker, Mark Regnerus, and Margaret Vaaler, "Losing My Religion: The Social Sources of Religious Decline in Early Adulthood," *Social Forces* 85(4) (2007): 1–26.

37. Jenny Lee, "Religion and College Attendance: Change among Students," *Review of Higher Education* 25 (2002): 369–84.

38. Jeffrey Arnett and Lene Jensen, "A Congregation of One: Individualized Religious Beliefs among Emerging Adults," *Journal of Adolescent Research* 17 (2002): 451–67.

39. Michele Dillon, "The Persistence of Religious Identity among College Catholics," *Journal for the Scientific Study of Religion* 35 (1996): 165–70.

40. Jonathan Hill, "Religious Involvement during the Transition to Adulthood" (Ph.D. diss., University of Notre Dame, 2008). Also see Phil Schwadel, "The Effects of Education on Americans' Religious Practices, Beliefs, and Affiliations," paper presented at the annual conference of the Society for the Scientific Study of Religion, Tampa, Florida, November 2, 2007; Phil Schwadel, "The Declining Impact of Education on American Apostasy, 1973 to 2006," unpublished paper, University of Nebraska at Lincoln.

41. Ernest Pascarella and Patrick Terenzini, *How College Affects Students: A Third Decade of Research* (Hoboken, NJ: Jossey-Bass, 2005).

42. Uecker et al., "Losing My Religion"; Hill, "Religious Involvement during the Transition to Adulthood."

43. Conrad Cherry, Betty DeBerg, and Amanda Porterfield, *Religion on Campus* (Chapel Hill: University of North Carolina Press, 2001); Alyssa Bryant, "Evangelicals on Campus: An Exploration of Culture, Faith, and College Life," *Religion and Education* 32 (2005): 1–30; Paul Bramadat, *The Church on the World's Turf: An Evangelical Christian Group at a Secular University* (New York: Oxford University Press, 2000); T. W. Cawthon and C. Jones, "A Description of Tradition and contemporary Campus Ministries," *College Student Affairs Journal* 23(2) (2004): 158–72; Rebecca Kim, *God's New Whiz Kids? Korean American Evangelicals on Campus* (New York: New York University Press, 2006). Neil Swidey, "God on the Quad," *Boston Globe Magazine*, November 30, 2003, 14–17.

44. See Arthur Chickering, Jon Dalton, and Liesa Stamm, *Encouraging Authenticity and Spirituality in Higher Education* (Hoboken, NJ: Jossey-Bass, 2006); Alexander Astin, "Why Spirituality Deserves a Place in Liberal Education," *Liberal Education* 90

(2004): 34–41; Robert Nash, *Religious Pluralism in the Academy* (New York: Peter Lang, 2001).

45. See, for example, J. Budziszewski, *How to Stay Christian in College* (Colorado Springs: TH1NK Books, 2004). See Kathleen Mahoney and John Schmalzbauer, "Religion: A Comeback on Campus," *Liberal Education* 87(4) (2001): 36–41; John Schmalzbauer, *People of Faith: Religious Conviction in American Journalism and Higher Education* (Ithaca, NY: Cornell University Press, 2003). Michael Lindsay, *Faith in the Halls of Power: How Evangelicals Joined the American Elite* (New York: Oxford University Press, 2008); John Schmalzbauer and Kathleen Mahoney, "American Scholars Return to Studying Religion," *Contexts* (Winter 2008): 16–21.

46. Naomi Schaefer Riley, *God on the Quad: How Religious Colleges and the Missionary Generation Are Changing America* (New York: St. Martin's Press, 2004).

47. Alexander Astin, "The Changing American College Student: Thirty-year Trends, 1966–1996," *Review of Higher Education* 21 (1998): 115–35.

48. See Peter Sacks, *Generation X Goes to College: An Eye-opening Account of Teaching in Postmodern America* (Chicago: Open Court, 1999); Anthony Smith and Frank Webster, *The Postmodern University? Contested Visions of Higher Education in Society* (Maidenhead, Berkshire, England: Open University Press, 1997); Roger Mourad, *Postmodern Philosophical Critique and the Pursuit of Knowledge in Higher Education* (Westport, CT: Bergin and Garvey, 1997).

49. Christian Smith, with Melinda Lundquist Denton, *Soul Searching: The Religious and Spiritual Lives of American Teenagers* (New York: Oxford University Press, 2005); also see Thomas Bartless, "Most Freshmen Say Religion Guides Them," *Chronicle of Higher Education* 51(33) (2005): A1, A40.

50. Charles Taylor, *A Secular Age* (Cambridge: Harvard University Press, 2007). Joseph Ratzinger and Jürgen Habermas, *The Dialectics of Secularization: On Reason and Religion* (Fort Collins, CO: Ignatius Press, 2007). Highly notable is the 2004 conversion of one of the twentieth century's most influential atheist philosophers, Antony Flew, to a definite belief in God—see Antony Flew, with Roy Abraham Varghese, *There Is a God: How the World's Most Notorious Atheist Changed His Mind* (New York: HarperCollins, 2007).

51. Cherry et al., *Religion on Campus*, 295. Also see Mark Taylor, "The Devoted Student," *New York Times*, December 21, 2006, A39.

52. Uecker et al., "Losing My Religion."

53. For example, Ernest Pascarella and Patrick Ternzini, *How College Affects Students: A Third Decade of Research* (Hoboken, NJ: Jossey-Bass, 2005).

54. This is another variant of the "believing-without-belonging" image that in a different context the sociologist Grace Davie has hypothesized characterizes many British Christians; *Religion in Britain since 1945: Believing without Belonging* (Oxford: Wiley-Blackwell, 1994).

55. See Ross Stolzenberg, Mary Blair-Loy, and Linda Waite, "Religious Participation in Early Adulthood: Age and Family Life Cycle Effects on Church Membership, *American Sociological Review* 60 (1995): 84–103.

56. Figure 8.9 excludes the "moderate" answer category of 2; analyses that included 2 as "low," however, revealed the exact same pattern of distributions.

57. Figure 8.10 also excludes the moderate answer category of 2; analyses that included 2 as "low," however, revealed the exact same pattern of distributions.

CHAPTER 9

1. Brian Steensland, Jerry Park, Mark Regnerus, Lynn Robinson, W. Bradford Wilcox, and Robert Woodberry, "The Measure of American Religion: Toward Improving the State of the Art," *Social Forces* 79 (2000): 291–318.

2. These tables are available for view, however, at www.nd.edu/~csmith22/tables.html.

3. One change from the analysis used in *Soul Searching* has been made here, reflecting differences in culturally age-appropriate religious expression between teenagers and emerging adults: being currently involved in a religious youth or other group has been removed as a screen for any of these ideal-type categories. Since we are not comparing changes in these ideal-type categories between waves, that alteration does not complicate the present analysis.

4. The pattern of findings we see hereafter does hold when the individual religion variables composing the types used in this chapter are used independently in this way—these findings are not an artifact of the particular construction of the types. We do recognize that these types are somewhat Christian-centric, particularly leaning toward some Protestant ideals. There is simply no way to construct a religion-neutral, one-size-fits-all ideal-type system. This categorization, however, ought not to exaggerate differences between types, since highly religious emerging adults in non-Protestant and non-Christian traditions who were screened into less religious categories because of the criteria used would normally have the effect of *reducing*, not increasing, differences between the category types.

5. This relationship, probably like many examined in this chapter, is often probably causally reciprocal—that is, religion affects relationships, and relationships also in turn affect religion.

6. The causal direction here—it is worth noting—likely works both ways: higher religiosity decreases marital breakups, and marital breakups decrease religious commitment and participation.

7. For some of the pertinent literature on the survey measures and scales used by the NSYR, see Carol Ryff, "Psychological Well-being in Adult Life," *Current Directions in Psychological Science* 4 (1995): 99–104; Carol Ryff and Corey Keyes, "The Structure of Psychological Well-being Revisited," *Journal of Personality and Social Psychology* 69 (1995): 719–27; Carol Ryff, "Happiness Is Everything, or Is It? Explorations on the Meaning of Psychological Well-Being," *Journal of Personality and Social Psychology* 57 (1989): 1069–81; James Charles Crumbaugh, "Cross-validation of Purpose in Life Test Based on Frankl's Concepts," *Journal of Individual Psychology* 24 (1968): 74–81; James Charles Crumbaugh and Leonard T. Maholick, "An Experimental Study in Existentialism: The Psychometric Approach to Frankl's Concept of Noogenic Neurosis," *Journal of Clinical Psychology* 20 (1964): 589–96; Sheryl Zika and Kerry Chamberlain, "On the Relation between Meaning in Life and Psychological Well-Being," *British Journal of Psychology* 83 (1992): 133–45; Jared Kass, Richard Friedman, Jane Leserman, Margaret Caudill, Patricia Zuttermeister, and Herbert Benson, "An Inventory of Positive Psychological Attitudes with Potential Relevance to Health Outcomes: Validation and Preliminary Testing," *Behavioral Medicine* 17 (1991): 121–29; Ed Diener, Robert Emmons, Randy Larsen, and Sharon Griffin, "The Satisfaction with Life Scale," *Journal of Personality Assessment* 49(1) (1985): 71–75; William Pavot and Ed Diener, "Review of the Satisfaction with Life Scale," *Psychological Assessment* 5(2) (1993): 164–72; Marsha Richins and Scott Dawson, "A Consumer Values Orientation for Materialism and Its Measurement: Scale Development and Validation," *Journal of Consumer Research* 19 (1992): 303–16; Marvin Goldberg, Gerald Gorn, Laura Peracchio, and

Gary Bamossy, "Understanding Materialism among Youth," *Journal of Consumer Psychology* 13(3) (2003): 278–88; Robert Emmons and Michael McCullough, eds., *The Psychology of Gratitude* (New York: Oxford University Press, 2004); Michael McCullough, Robert Emmons, and Jo-Ann Tsang, "The Grateful Disposition: A Conceptual and Empirical Topography," *Journal of Personality and Social Psychology* 82 (2002): 112–27; Robert Emmons and Charles Shelton, "Gratitude and the Science of Positive Psychology," in *Handbook of Positive Psychology*, ed. Charles Richard Snyder and Shane J. Lopez (New York: Oxford University Press, 2002), 459–71.

8. This suggests that a segment of Devoted emerging adults exists that consists of persons who are particularly concerned and careful when they do have oral sex, which they engage in a more intentional and prepared way than some of their less religious peers do, perhaps in order not to be "caught" by being discovered to have been infected with a disease. In theory, it should also be easier to use protection "every time" when the absolute number of times is fewer. By comparison, another, different segment of the Devoted that likely believes that oral sex is morally wrong yet nevertheless has had oral sex appears not to have planned or prepared for oral sex, indeed was perhaps was swept into it more spontaneously in "the heat of the moment," and so never used protection against sexually transmitted diseases. If so, for the former, the moral wrongness of oral sex was countered with particular care in committing the sin; for the latter, the moral wrongness was countered by having never planned for it in the first place and so not being guilty of premeditated sin. In any case, we do observe among the Devoted a modest polarization toward either always or never using protection during oral sex.

9. More generally, see Mark D. Regnerus, "Religion and Positive Adolescent Outcomes: A Review of Research and Theory," *Review of Religious Research* 44 (2003): 394–413.

10. See, for example, Jeremy Uecker, Mark Regnerus, and Margaret Vaaler, "Losing My Religion: The Social Sources of Religious Decline in Early Adulthood," *Social Forces* 85(4) (2007): 1–26; Alyssa Bryant, Jeung Yun Choi, and Maiko Yasuno, "Understanding the Religious and Spiritual Dimensions of Students' Lives in the First Year of College," *Journal of College Student Development* 44 (2003): 723–45; Brent Benda and Nancy Toombs, "Religion and Drug Use among Inmates at Boot Camp," *Journal of Offender Rehabilitation* 35 (2002): 161–83; Mark Regnerus and Jeremy Uecker, "Finding Faith, Losing Faith: The Prevalence and Context of Religious Transformations during Adolescence," *Review of Religious Research* 47 (2006): 217–37.

11. Christian Smith, "Theorizing Religious Effects among American Adolescents," *Journal for the Scientific Study of Religion* 42(1) (2003): 17–30, "Religious Participation and Network Closure among American Adolescents," research note, *Journal for the Scientific Study of Religion* 42(2) (2003): 259–67, "Research Note: Religious Participation and Parental Moral Expectations and Supervision of American Youth," *Review of Religious Research* 44(4) (2003): 414–24, "Why Christianity Works: An Emotions-focused Phenomenological Account," *Sociology of Religion* 68(2) (2007): 165–78, and "Why 'Why Christianity Works' Works," *Sociology of Religion* 69(4) (2008): 473–88.

12. See, for example, Mark Regnerus and Christian Smith, "Selection Effects and Social Desirability Bias in Studies of Religious Influences," *Review of Religious Research* 47(1) (2005): 23–50; Mark Regnerus, Christian Smith, and Brad Smith, "Social Context in the Development of Adolescent Religiosity," *Applied Developmental Science* 8 (2004): 27–38.

CHAPTER 10

1. Tobin Belzer, Richard Flory, and Nadia Roumani, "Illuminating the Black Hole: Successful Programs for Young Adults in Four Religious Traditions," paper presented at conference entitled "Faith, Fear, and Indifference: Constructing Religious Identity in the Next Generation," University of Southern California, Los Angeles, October 11, 2004; Jack Miles, "Closing the Gap on Believers," community brief, *Jewish Journal*, November 4, 2004, www.jewishjournal.com/community_briefs/article/closing_the_gap_on_believers_20041105/.

2. William Shakespeare, *The Tempest*, act 2, scene 1, lines 253–54, Antonio speaking.

3. They should be alerted to the greater complexities of the matter, however, by the fact that the actual message is usually more like "Get out of my life, but first could you drive me and Cheryl to the mall?" as per Anthony Wolf, *Get Out of My Life, but First Could You Drive Me and Cheryl to the Mall?—A Parent's Guide to the New Teenager* (New York: Farrar, Straus, and Giroux, 2002).

4. In the Wave 1 interviews with 13- to 17-year-olds, at the end of the early section of questions about family relationships, respondents were asked this question: "If there was one thing that you could change about your family, what would it be?" One of the most common, if not *the* most common, among the variety of answers that teenagers offered was that they wished they were closer to their parents. They wanted to know their parents better, to hear more stories about their parents' pasts, to spend more time together and get along better. When then asked why they were not as close to their parents as they wished they were, they said they did not know, they didn't know how to do that, that their parents were busy, and they simply did not know how to make that happen. This was only one piece of a larger body of evidence that drove home to us the fact that very many adolescents not only objectively need strong connections to mature adults in their lives, but they actually themselves semiconsciously *want* those connections. However, give the culture's controlling stereotypes and myths about teenagers being "from another planet," and so on, and given the pervasive structural disconnection of adolescents from adult lives and schedules, teenagers simply have a hard time asking for that connection or knowing how to make it happen.

5. Also see Sharon Daloz Parks, *Big Questions, Worthy Dreams: Mentoring Young Adults in Their Search for Meaning, Purpose, and Faith* (San Francisco: Jossey-Bass, 2000).

6. N. Jay Demerath, "Cultural Victory and Organizational Defeat in the Paradoxical Decline of Liberal Protestantism," *Journal for the Scientific Study of Religion* 34(4) (1995): 458–69; quotations that follow are from 459–60, 463. Also see John Murray Cuddihy, *No Offense: Civil Religion and Protestant Taste* (New York: Seabury, 1978).

7. Friedrich Schleiermacher, *On Religion: Speeches to Its Cultural Despisers* (1893; repr., Whitefish, MN: Kessinger, 2008).

8. H. Richard Niebuhr, 1937, *The Kingdom of God in America* (New York: Harper, 1937), 193.

9. Charles Sheldon, *In His Steps: What Would Jesus Do?* (London: Simpkin, Marshall, Hamilton, Kent, 1897).

10. For a similar argument about unintended evangelical influences on the rise of supernatural interests in the general media, see Lynn Schofield Clark, *From Angels to Aliens: Teenagers, the Media, and the Supernatural* (New York: Oxford University Press, 2003).

11. Dennis Hollinger, *Individualism and Social Ethics: An Evangelical Syncretism* (Lanham, MD: University Press of America, 1983); Michael O. Emerson and Christian Smith, *Divided by Faith: Evangelical Religion and the Problem of Race in America* (New York: Oxford University Press, 2000); more generally, see Phillip Hammond, *Religion and Personal Autonomy* (Columbia: University of South Carolina Press, 1992).

12. Nathan Hatch, *The Democratization of American Christianity* (New Haven, CT: Yale University Press, 1991).

13. This reflects the Reformation doctrine of the "perspicuity" of scripture.

14. Nathan Hatch, "*Sola Scriptura* and *Novus Ordo Seclorum*," in *The Bible in America: Essays in Cultural History* ed. Nathan O. Hatch and Mark A. Noll (New York: Oxford University Press, 1982), 59–78.

15. Willard Swartley, *Slavery, Sabbath, War, and Women: Case Issues in Biblical Interpretation* (Scottdale, PA: Herald Press, 1983); Mark Noll, *The Civil War as a Theological Crisis* (Chapel Hill: University of North Carolina Press, 2006).

16. Mark Noll, *The Scandal of the Evangelical Mind* (Grand Rapids, MI: Eerdmans, 1995).

17. Michael Young, *Bearing Witness against Sin: The Evangelical Birth of the American Social Movement*, (Chicago: University of Chicago Press, 2007).

18. David Harrington Watt, *A Transforming Faith: Explorations of Twentieth-century American Evangelicalism* (New Brunswick, NJ: Rutgers University Press, 1991).

19. See Peter Sacks, *Generation X Goes to College; An Eye-opening Account of Teaching in Postmodern America* (Chicago: Open Court, 1996).

Index